Operating Systems
A Systematic View

THIRD EDITION

William S. Davis

Miami University
Oxford, Ohio

ADDISON-WESLEY PUBLISHING COMPANY

Reading, Massachusetts   Menlo Park, California
Don Mills, Ontario   Workingham, England   Amsterdam
Sydney   Singapore   Tokyo   Madrid   Bogotá
Santiago   San Juan

Sponsoring Editor: *David B. Jackson*

Managing Editor: *Karen Guardino*

Production Supervisor: *Mary Coffey*

Text Design and Illustrations: *To The Point*

Cover Design: *Marshall Henrichs*

Library of Congress Cataloging-in-Publication Data

Davis, William S., 1943–
  Operating systems.

  Includes index.
  1. Operating systems (Computers)   I. Title.
QA76.76.063D38   1987   005.4'3   86-10898
ISBN 0-201-11185-3

Materials in Appendix D reprinted by permission from IBM System Control Statements DOS/VSE (GC33-5376), and materials in Appendix E (including illustrations) from IBM OS/VS JCL References (GC28-0618) by International Business Machines Corporation.

ABCDEFGHIJK-DO-89876

P R E F A C E

Change is perhaps the only constant in the computer field. The first edition of *Operating Systems: A Systematic View* was published in 1977. Six years later, a second edition updated the technology and added some new material. This third edition will bear a 1987 copyright, following the second edition by only four years. It's a major revision, with virtually all chapters rewritten and considerable new material added. The rate of change continues to accelerate. Perhaps that's why so many people find the computer such a fascinating field of study.

Although time-sharing and minicomputers did exist, batch processing was the accepted mode of computer access in the 1970s, and the first edition reflected that standard. Today, given microcomputers, intelligent workstations, and networks, modern programmers and users have come to expect interactive access. That change is more than superficial. Indeed, we no longer look at computers in quite the same way; our viewpoint has shifted. Thus, a major revision was necessary.

Early in 1986, as plans for a third edition began to crystallize, Addison-Wesley undertook a comprehensive survey of the operating systems course as taught in colleges, community colleges, and universities across the nation. The results of that survey were invaluable in shaping the new edition; if you were one of the several thousand instructors polled, I thank you again for your cooperation and your input.

In spite of substantial changes, *Operating Systems: A Systematic View* remains an *applied* introduction to operating system concepts. This is *not* a theoretical text. The intent of the first two editions was to show *why* operating systems are needed and *what*, at a functional macro level, they do. This third edition retains those objectives, along with the pace, level, and writing style of the first two. It also retains such pedagogical features as chapter overviews, summaries, key word lists, and exercises. As before, the numerous illustrations closely follow the flow of the text and visually elaborate the concepts. New to this edition is a glossary of key words.

The book looks at operating systems from an application programmer's point of view, and assumes little or no mathematics beyond high school algebra. The only prerequisites are a reasonable understanding of basic computer concepts and some programming experience in at least one compiler language. Part I, Chapters 2 through 4, reviews essential concepts; you should understand this material before moving on. Those students who need a brief review of number systems should read Appendix A.

Part II (Chapters 5 and 6) overviews key operating system concepts. In earlier editions, this section took an historical perspective. These two chapters have been almost completely rewritten, with Chapter 5 describing single-user, microcomputer operating systems, and Chapter 6 introducing multiple-user systems, multiprogramming, and time-sharing. Later in the text, when you begin reading about the internals of several different operating systems, you'll encounter considerable detail, and it's easy to "miss the forest for the trees." The intent of this second part is to give you a map of an operating system's key functions.

Users and programmers communicate with an operating system through a job control or command language, the subject of Part III. Chapter 7 discusses the general functions of any command or job control language. MS-DOS (or PC-DOS) commands are introduced in Chapter 8, while Chapter 9 discusses UNIX commands; both are presented in tutorial form. Although the operating system is no longer fully supported by IBM, our survey indicated that many second edition users of this text wanted coverage of DOS/VSE, so its job control language is the subject of Chapter 10. Chapters 11 and 12 introduce IBM's OS/JCL. Chapter 13 discusses libraries and the linkage editor in general terms, and illustrates key concepts with OS/JCL examples. Appendixes B, C, D, and E summarize, respectively, MS-DOS, UNIX, DOS/VSE, and OS job control or command languages and serve as a useful reference.

Part IV moves inside the operating system. MS-DOS, the most popular microcomputer operating system, is covered in Chapter 14. Segmentation, paging, and virtual memory are essential concepts in many current operating systems, and thus are introduced in Chapter 15. UNIX, the subject of Chapter 16, incorporates ideas that have influenced the design of many modern operating systems. An operating system is a function of its environment. To illustrate this idea, IBM System/370 principles of operating are introduced in Chapter 17, and then two operating systems designed to run in that environment, DOS/VSE (Chapter 18) and OS/VS1/VS2 (Chapter 19), are discussed.

The computer field is incredibly dynamic. Part V is intended to convey a sense of that dynamism. Modern large-scale operating systems are introduced in Chapter 20, with an emphasis on VM. The ongoing merger of computing and communication technologies is the subject of Chapter 21, with an emphasis on networks and network operating systems. The book ends with an overview of data base management systems (Chapter 22).

Finally, two new supplement packages have been developed for this edition. The instructor's guide has been expanded both in size and in content, and includes numerous transparency masters. The new student guide is designed to help the student identify, isolate, and relate important concepts.

Although the changes are substantial, the book is still aimed at those whose orientation is using (rather than designing) computers. Professional programmers, systems analysts, and technical managers should also find the applied orientation valuable. I'm excited about this new edition, and I sincerely hope it fills your needs.

Acknowledgments

Broadly based surveys, such as the operating system course survey conducted by Addison-Wesley, are useful in identifying trends and general requirements, but they do little to ensure technical accuracy or depth of coverage. Consequently, as the manuscript for the third edition of *Operating Systems: A Systematic View* was being written, Mr. David Jackson, the sponsoring editor, set in motion a substantial review process. I would like to thank the the following reviewers for their contributions:

Gary Baney, *Judson College*
Karen L. Broughton, *Scott Community College*
Thomas R. Cikoski, *Madonna College*
Donald B. Distler, Jr., *Belleville Area College*
Sallyann Z. Hansen, *Mercer County Community College*
Gary Heisler, *Lansing Community College*
Karl Hunt, *Dalton Junior College*
Dennis Kafura, *Virginia Polytechnical Institute and State University*
Robert L. Sedlmeyer, *Indiana University-Purdue University at Ft. Wayne*
Norman J. Smith, *Purdue University Calumet*
Michael Trombetta, *Queensborough Community College*
Douglas A. Troy, *Miami University, Oxford, Ohio*
Sandy Tush, *Tulsa Junior College*
Jack H. Weir, *Rock Valley College*
Ann L. Wilson, *Southwest Missouri State University*

Most were very positive. Some identified errors or oversights; to those reviewers we are particularly grateful. All were useful. Additionally, I would like to acknowledge the efforts of Mary Coffey (the production supervisor), Joyce Snow (who copyedited the manuscript and prepared the glossary), Janet Bemis (who designed the text), and Maureen Fox (who created the illustrations).

WSD
Oxford, Ohio

CONTENTS

APPENDIXES

CHAPTER

1

Introduction and Overview

KEY IDEAS

What is an operating system?
Why study operating systems?
An overview of the text

What Is an Operating System?

A computer fresh off the assembly line, with no software in place, can do absolutely nothing. It cannot accept characters from the keyboard or display characters on a screen. It cannot even *load*, much less execute an application program. Faced with the raw "iron," even experienced programmers find it difficult to accomplish much, and nontechnical users are completely lost. Pure hardware presents a most unfriendly interface. Thus, people rarely communicate directly with the hardware. Instead, users and application programmers deal with the hardware through a system program called the **operating system** (Fig. 1.1).

Providing an easy-to-use hardware interface is the operating system's most obvious function, but that's not all it does. A computer's basic resources are hardware, software, and data. A modern operating system, particularly on a large machine, manages these resources (Fig. 1.2).

Fig. 1.1   The operating system serves as an interface between the application software and the hardware.

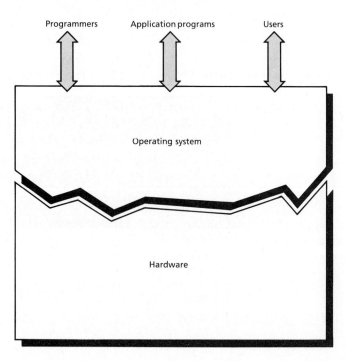

Fig. 1.2   On many large computer systems, the operating system is a
resource manager, allocating hardware, software, and data.

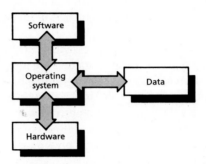

Why Study Operating Systems?

For a few students, the need to study operating systems is obvious. Future
system programmers must learn how to design or modify one. Systems
analysts, managers, and consultants may be asked to select or recommend
one. Not all computer professionals become system programmers, however,
and selecting an operating system is at best an occasional task. Most computer people deal with applications. Why should *they* learn about operating
systems?

One reason is simple curiosity: most professionals like to know something about all aspects of their field, and computer professionals are no
exception. Second, understanding how an operating system works can provide valuable insight into the design of any large, computer-based system. A
third reason is derived from the operating system's resource management
role. Because it coordinates hardware, software, and data, studying its functions gives the student a unique opportunity to pull together a variety of
topics covered piecemeal in other courses.

The key argument, however, is that the operating system is the application programmer's primary interface with the computer. Thus the programmer, to be effective, must understand at least the basics of the operating
system. This book is designed to provide just such an understanding.

An Overview of the Text

The material supports a first course in operating systems. It emphasizes the
application of this specialized software to a real-world environment; this is
not a theoretical text. The book takes a systematic, top-down approach.
First, those operating system features the application programmer is most
likely to encounter—compilers, a job control or command language, access

methods, linkage editors, and loaders—are explained. Gradually, layer by layer, operating systems are analyzed in more and more detail until, finally, we reach the actual hardware/software interface.

The book is divided into five parts. Part I, Chapters 2 through 4, covers basic hardware, software, and data concepts. These are the resources managed by an operating system. For many students, this material will be review.

Part II overviews the essential functions performed by modern operating systems. Chapter 5 focuses on the single-user systems common on personal computers. Building on that base, Chapter 6 introduces multiprogramming and time-sharing.

Part III covers programmer/system communications. Chapter 7 introduces the basic functions performed by any command or job control language. Subsequent chapters present specific examples, including MS-DOS (Chapter 8), UNIX (Chapter 9), IBM's DOS/VSE (Chapter 10), and IBM's OS/JCL (Chapters 11 and 12). The section ends with a discussion of compilers, linkage editors, loaders, and libraries (Chapter 13). For the typical programmer, a relatively small subset of a command or job control language is adequate for everyday use. Thus, only selected features are covered; the intent is to illustrate programmer/system communications and not to present an exhaustive course in JCL.

Clearly, few students will actually use all these job control and command languages. A suggested approach is to read Chapter 7 carefully, select one language for in-depth study, complete several "programming" exercises using that language, and then read, compare, and contrast one or two others. All four job control and command languages are summarized in the Appendix.

In Part IV we turn to case studies of several operating systems. First, (in Chapter 14) we consider MS-DOS (PC-DOS) as an illustration of a basic, single-user system. A key element in many multiple-user systems is virtual memory; thus the essentials of segmentation, paging, and virtual memory are covered next (Chapter 15). Chapter 16 returns to the case study approach, overviewing UNIX.

Chapters 17 through 19 are related. In Chapter 17, the operating principles of the IBM System/370 computer family are introduced. Next, two very different operating systems designed to work in this environment are discussed—DOS/VSE in Chapter 18, and OS/VS2 in Chapter 19. A major point of emphasis will be the impact of a machine's architecture on its operating system's design.

Part V turns to current operating system topics. First, in Chapter 20, we'll consider large-scale virtual machine systems, building on concepts learned in Chapters 17, 18, and 19. VM/SP, IBM's current mainframe standard, will serve as an example. Increasingly, computer and communication technologies are merging, so we'll cover networks and network operating systems in Chapter 21. Finally, in Chapter 22, we'll trace the evolution of system software from an application routine, to a utility, to an operating system feature, using data base management as an example.

Assumed Background

Before starting this text, you should know how to program in at least one language and have a solid understanding of computer fundamentals and terminology. Knowledge of assembler language would help but is not essential. A reasonable grasp of the relationship between binary and hexadecimal is assumed; if your number system skills are rusty, read Appendix A. Because the book emphasizes applications rather than operating system theory, no mathematics beyond algebra is required.

Summary

You'll find a brief summary at the end of each chapter. Read it carefully. If you come across something you don't understand, reread the relevant chapter material. You should also find the summaries a useful preexamination review.

Only a few concepts were introduced in this first chapter. An operating system is a hardware/software interface that, on larger systems, serves as a resource manager. The operating system is the application programmer's primary interface with the computer. The balance of the chapter presented an overview of the text.

Key Words

Following each chapter's summary is a list of key words. You should know the meanings of each of these words; if you don't, you've missed something and should reread the relevant material. This chapter was introductory, so no key words are listed, although you should have a rough sense of what an operating system is.

Exercises

Each chapter ends with a set of exercises. These subjective questions are designed to help you review the chapter material and to force you to think about key concepts. Often, you will be asked to relate two or more ideas. Occasionally, a question will require that you look beyond or extrapolate from the chapter material. Take the time to write out answers to these exercises.

1. What, in general, is an operating system?

2. An operating system presents a user or an application programmer with

a "friendly" hardware interface. What does this mean? Why is it important?

3. An operating system, particularly on a large computer, is a resource manager. What resources are managed? Why does it make sense to use the operating system as a resource manager?

4. Give several reasons why future computer professionals should study operating systems.

I

Basic System Resources

C H A P T E R
2

Hardware

Main Memory

Physical Memory Devices

A computer's **main memory** holds binary digits, or **bits** (see Appendix A for a review of number system concepts). Almost any device that can assume either of two states can serve as storage, but most computers use integrated circuit memory (Fig. 2.1). A small computer might contain enough memory to store thousands of bits; a large machine might store millions. The difference is one of degree, not function.

Most main memory is random access memory (RAM). The programmer (through a program, of course) can read or write RAM; its contents are easy to change. Usually, this flexibility is an advantage. Sometimes, however, it makes sense to record key software or data in more permanent, read-only memory (ROM). A good example of a ROM-based program is the BASIC language interpreter found in many microcomputers. As the name implies, ROM can be read, but not written.

A single bit can hold either a 0 or a 1. Generally, however, the contents of memory are envisioned as groups of bits called bytes and words. A **byte** contains enough bits (usually eight) to represent a single character. For example, the ASCII code for a capital A is 01000001. Within main memory, the letter A would be stored by recording that bit pattern in a single byte (8 bits).

Bytes are fine for storing characters but are too small to hold a meaningful number. Most computers are able to manipulate a group of bytes called a **word**. Some small computers have 8-bit words. Other, more powerful machines work with 16-bit (2-byte), 32-bit (4-byte), and even 64-bit words.

Thus we have a memory hierarchy (Fig. 2.2). The basic unit of storage is the bit. Bits are grouped to form bytes, which in turn are grouped to form words. In one application, a given word might hold a binary number. In another, that word's bytes might hold individual characters, or a program instruction.

Addressing Memory

A typical microcomputer contains 128,000 (128K[1]) or more bytes or words, while a large mainframe may have millions! A given element of data might be stored in any one of them. If the processor needs a particular data element, how does it find the byte or word that holds it?

Each physical storage unit is assigned a unique **address**. On most computers, the bytes or words are numbered sequentially—0, 1, 2, and so on. The processor accesses a specific memory location by referencing its

---

[1] The suffix K, which stands for kilo, means 1024. Thus, a computer with 128K bytes of main memory contains 131,072 actual memory locations.

address. For example, if the processor needs the data stored in byte 1048, it asks memory for the contents of byte 1048. Since there is only one byte 1048, the processor gets the right data. Depending on the computer, bytes or words are the basic addressable units of memory. Data move between the processor and main memory a byte or a word at a time.

Fig. 2.1   The main memory of most computers is composed of integrated circuit chips.

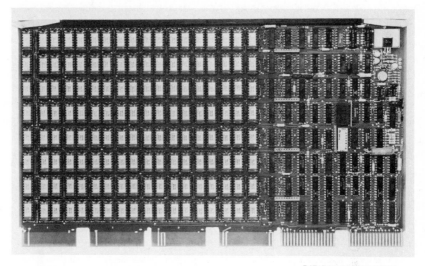

DATARAM CORPORATION

Fig. 2.2   In a computer's main memory, bits are combined to form bytes, and bytes, in turn, are combined to form words. This example shows a 32-bit or 4-byte word.

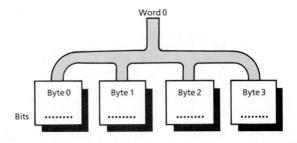

The Processor

The **processor**, often called the central processing unit (CPU) or main processor, is the component that manipulates data. A processor can do nothing without a program to provide control; whatever intelligence a computer has is derived from software, not hardware. The processor manipulates data stored in main memory under the control of a program stored in main memory (Fig. 2.3).

A **program** is a series of **instructions**, each of which tells the computer to perform one of its basic functions: add, subtract, multiply, divide, compare, copy, start input, or start output. Each instruction has an operation code and one or more operands (Fig. 2.4). The operation code specifies the function to be performed, and the operands identify the memory locations that are to participate in the operation. For example, the instruction in Fig. 2.4 tells the computer to add the contents of memory locations 1000 and 1002.

The processor contains four key components (Fig. 2.5). The **instruction control unit** fetches instructions from main memory. The **arithmetic**

Fig. 2.3   The processor manipulates data stored in main memory under control of a program stored in main memory.

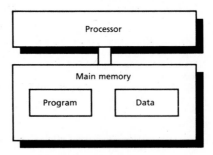

Fig. 2.4   An instruction is composed of an operation code and one or more operands. The operation code tells the computer what to do. The operand or operands identify the addresses of the data elements to be manipulated.

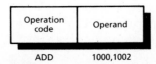

Fig. 2.5   A processor contains four key components.

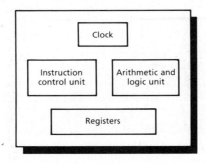

and logic unit consists of the circuits that add, subtract, multiply, and so on (the computer's instruction set). It executes instructions. **Registers** are temporary storage devices that hold control information, key data, and intermediate results. The **clock** generates precisely timed electronic pulses that synchronize the other components.

Machine Cycles

Exactly how do a computer's internal components work together to execute instructions? Let's use a model of a simple computer system (Fig. 2.6) to illustrate a few **machine cycles**. Begin with the processor. In addition to the clock, it contains an instruction control unit, an arithmetic and logic unit, and several registers, including an instruction counter, an instruction register, and a work register called the accumulator. The computer's other major component, main memory, holds program instructions and data values. Note that each main memory location is assigned an address.

The process starts when the clock generates a pulse of current which activates the instruction control unit. Its job is to decide what the machine will do next. The computer is controlled by program instructions, and the instructions, remember, are stored in main memory. The address of the next instruction to be executed is found in the instruction counter (Fig. 2.6a). The instruction control unit checks the instruction counter, finds the address, and fetches the next instruction, placing it in the instruction register (Fig. 2.6b). Fetching an instruction from memory takes time, giving the instruction control unit an opportunity to increment the instruction counter to point to the next instruction (Fig. 2.6b).

Next, the instruction control unit activates the arithmetic and logic unit, which executes the instruction stored in the instruction register (Fig.

2.6c). Note that, following execution of the instruction, a data value is copied from main memory to the accumulator register.

Once again, the clock "ticks." Thus, it's back to the instruction control unit, where the next machine cycle begins (Fig. 2.6d). Referring to the instruction counter, the instruction control unit fetches the next instruction and copies it into the instruction register (Fig. 2.6e). Again, note that the instruction register now points to the next instruction.

The arithmetic and logic unit gets control and executes the instruction in the instruction register (Fig. 2.6f); thus a data value from memory is added to the accumulator. The next clock pulse takes us back to the instruction control unit. As before, the instruction counter points to the next instruction, which is fetched and copied into the instruction register. The instruction control unit then activates the arithmetic and logic unit, which executes the instruction.

Fig. 2.6   A computer executes instructions by following a basic machine cycle.

a. As our example begins, main memory holds both program instructions and data. The instruction register points to the first instruction to be executed.

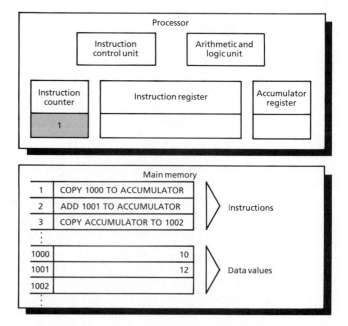

b. In response to a fetch command from the instruction control unit, the first instruction is copied from memory and stored in the instruction register. Note that the instruction counter points to the next instruction.

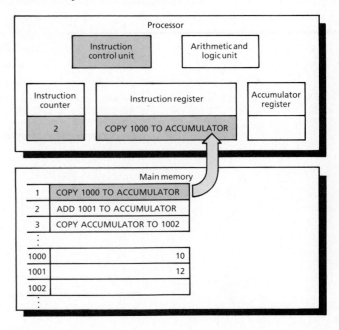

c. Next, the arithmetic and logic unit gets control, and executes the instruction in the instruction register. Thus, a data value is copied from main memory and loaded into the accumulator register.

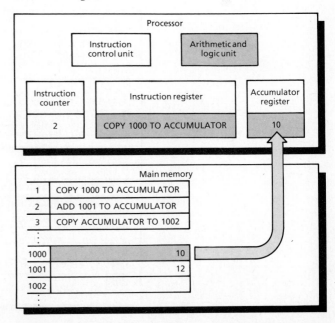

d. As the next cycle begins, the instruction control unit regains control and looks to the instruction register for the address of the next instruction.

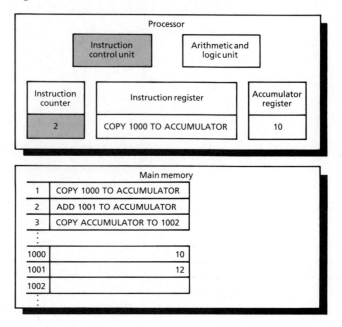

e. The next instruction is fetched and copied into the instruction register. Note that the instruction counter points to the next instruction.

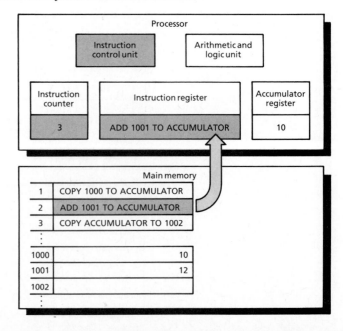

f. The arithmetic and logic unit executes the instruction in the instruction register. Two values are added, and their sum is placed in the accumulator register.

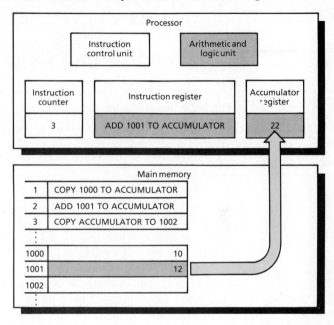

Fig. 2.7   The basic machine cycle is repeated over and over again, until all the instructions in the program have been executed.

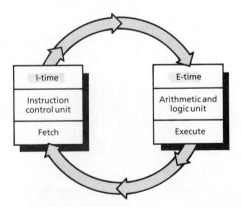

An instruction is fetched by the instruction control unit during **I-time**, or instruction time, and executed by the arithmetic and logic unit during **E-time**, or execution time (Fig. 2.7). This process is repeated over and over until the program is finished. The clock drives the process, generating pulses at precisely timed intervals. The rate at which those clock pulses are generated determines the computer's operating speed.

Input and Output Devices

Input and output devices provide a means for people to access a computer. The basic **input** device on most small computer systems (Fig. 2.8) is a keyboard. As characters are typed, they are stored in main memory and then copied from memory to the basic **output** device, a display screen. In effect, the screen serves as a window on memory, allowing the user to view its contents.

The image displayed on a screen is temporary; it fades as soon as the power is cut. By routing the output to a printer, a permanent copy (called a hard copy) is obtained. Character printers print one character at a time, usually at rates varying from 30 to perhaps 180 characters per second. The speed is fine for a few pages of output, but it's much too slow for volume printing. An option to use a line printer which, as the name implies, prints line by line instead of character by character. Rates of 1000 lines per minute (and more) are common. Page printers, which churn out complete pages at a time, are even faster. For more compact output or long-term storage, there is computer output microfilm (COM). Computers are not limited to displaying characters, of course; graphic output is also possible. A plotter generates hard-copy graphic output.

Fig. 2.8   A typical computer system. Input is provided by a keyboard. Output goes to the screen or to the printer.

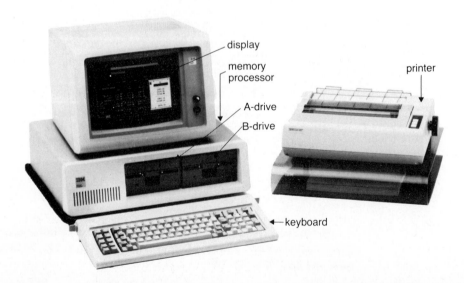

Punched cards were among the first computer input media. The standard card is composed of eighty columns, each divided into twelve rows. Characters are recorded as patterns of holes in a column; for each possible row/column position, there either is or is not a hole. A card reader converts the hole patterns to electronic form. Note the similarity between a card's hole/no hole patterns and binary.

Several common input media rely on magnetic properties. For example, the characters on the bottom of most checks are printed with a special magnetic ink called MICR (magnetic ink character recognition), and can be read electronically. Another banking medium is the magnetic stripe card. The strip of magnetic tape holds such data as a customer's account number and credit limit, and is read much like sound recording tape.

Other media are read optically. For example, consider standardized test forms. Students use a black pencil to mark their answers. The white paper reflects light; the black spots reflect much less; variations in the intensity of the reflected light can be converted to an electronic pattern. OCR (optical character recognition) equipment uses the same principle to read typed or even handwritten material. Bar codes, such as the Universal Product Code (UPC) printed on most supermarket packages, can be read at a checkout station or by a hand-held scanner.

Often, terminals are linked to a central computer by cables or communication lines. A "dumb" terminal is simply a keyboard and a display screen. An intelligent terminal contains its own memory and processor and can perform many data processing functions independently. Other special-purpose terminals are designed for specific functions. Examples include automatic bank teller terminals and supermarket checkout stations.

Perhaps the most natural way of communicating with a computer is by voice. Voice response (output) is already used in such mundane applications as children's toys and video games. Due to the tremendous variety of human speech patterns, voice recognition (input) is much more difficult, but significant advances have been made.

Secondary Storage

There are numerous problems with main memory. For one thing, it's expensive, and the supply on most machines is limited. Another problem is volatility; main memory loses its contents when the power is cut. **Secondary storage** is a fast, accurate, inexpensive, high-capacity, nonvolatile extension of main memory.

Diskette

The most common microcomputer secondary storage medium is **diskette** or floppy disk (Fig. 2.9), a thin circular piece of flexible polyester coated with a magnetic material. Data are recorded on one or both flat surfaces. A diskette drive works much like a record turntable. The round hole in the center of the disk allows the drive mechanism to engage and spin it; an access mechanism, analogous to the tone arm, reads and writes the surface through the window visible near the bottom of Fig. 2.9.

The data are recorded on a series of concentric circles called tracks (Fig. 2.10). The access mechanism steps from track to track, reading or writing one at a time. The tracks are subdivided into sectors; it is the contents of a sector that move between the diskette and main memory. To distinguish the sectors, they are addressed by numbering them sequentially—0, 1, 2, and so on.

When a program instruction requesting diskette input is encountered, the processor sends a control signal to the drive. In response, the drive spindle is engaged, and the disk begins to spin, quickly reaching a constant rotational speed (Fig. 2.11a). Next, the access mechanism is moved to the track containing the desired data (Fig. 2.11b). The time required to bring the drive up to speed and position the access mechanism is called seek time. Remember that data are transferred between the diskette and main memory one sector at a time. The desired sector may be anywhere on the track. The time required for the sector to rotate to the access mechanism (Fig. 2.11c) is called rotational delay.

Fig. 2.9   The most popular microcomputer secondary storage medium is diskette.

Courtesy: 3M Company

Fig. 2.10   Data are recorded on a series of concentric circles called tracks.
                    The tracks, in turn, are subdivided into sectors. Data move
                    between the disk surface and main memory a sector at a time.

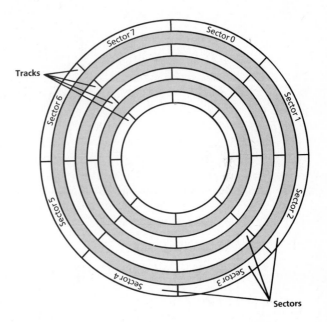

Hard Disk

Although diskette is quite fast, data access still means a delay of at least a fraction of a second. Many common personal computer applications involve only limited disk access, so the delay is hardly noticeable. On other applications, however, waiting can be intolerable. The solution is often a **hard disk**.

A diskette drive spins only when data are being read or written. The drive must be brought up to operating speed before the read/write heads can be moved and the data accessed, and that takes time. A hard disk, in contrast, spins constantly. Since it is not necessary to wait for the drive to reach operating speed before moving the access mechanism, seek time is significantly reduced, often to a few thousandths of a second. Further improvements are gained by spinning the disk more rapidly (1000 revolutions per minute or more), which reduces rotational delay. Data stored on hard disk can be accessed far more rapidly than data stored on diskette. Another advantage of hard disk is its storage capacity. A typical double-sided diskette might hold 360,000 characters. A hard disk for a microcomputer system might store 20 to 30 million characters.

Fig. 2.11   Reading a sector from disk.

a. First, the disk drive is brought up to operating speed.

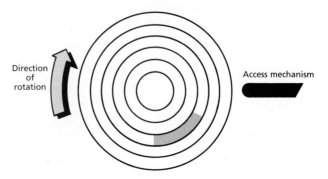

b. Next, the access mechanism is positioned over the track that holds the desired data. The time required to perform steps a and b is called seek time.

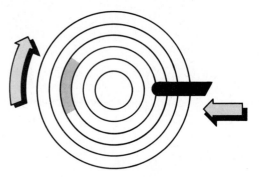

c. Finally, the system must wait until the desired sector rotates to the read/write head (rotational delay) before the data are transferred into main memory.

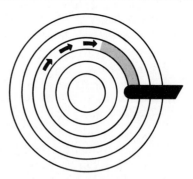

Although single-surface **disks** do exist, particularly on small systems, most large computers use disk packs consisting of several recording surfaces stacked on a common drive shaft (Fig. 2.12). Typically, each surface has its own read/write head. The heads are arrayed on a single, comblike access mechanism; they all move together. Imagine, for example, that the access mechanism is positioned over track 30. The top read/write head will access track 30 on surface 0. Moving down, surface by surface, the second head will be over track 30 on surface 1, the third over track 30 on surface 2, and so on. One position of the access mechanism corresponds to one track on each surface. This set of tracks is called a cylinder.

Accessing disk begins with seek time. The access mechanism is moved to a selected cylinder, and a selected head is activated. The system is now looking at a single track. Next, the desired data rotate to the read/write head—rotational delay. Finally, the data are read and transferred into the computer.

On some hard disks, tracks are divided into fixed-length sectors, and data move between the disk's surface and main memory a sector at a time. Other hard disks, particularly on large mainframes, are track addressed, with tracks subdivided into physical records or blocks. A physical record can be any length, from a single byte to a full track; the physical record length (or block size) is chosen to fit the application. Data are transferred between secondary and main storage a block at a time.

Application programs process logical records; generally, a logical record holds the data needed by a single program iteration. Because physical I/O operations are relatively slow, two or more logical records are often blocked to form a single physical record (Fig. 2.13). On input, the physical

Fig. 2.12   On a disk pack, each surface has its own read/write head. The heads are arrayed on a single, comblike access mechanism. Thus, they all move together.

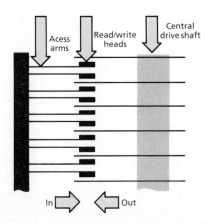

Fig. 2.13   Because physical I/O is relatively slow, several logical records are
                     often blocked to form a single physical record. Thus, a single
                     physical I/O operation can support several logical I/O operations.

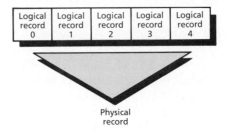

record is transferred into main memory. Individual logical records are then
extracted, one by one, and processed by the program; note that several
logical records might be processed before the next physical input operation
takes place. On output, logical records are collected to form a block in main
memory, and physical output is postponed until the block is full.

Given the tremendous capacity of a disk pack, losing one, through
human error, fire, flood, or similar disaster, can destroy a great deal of
important data. In most large computer centers, the data are regularly
backed up by copying them. Should a disk pack be lost, the **backup** copy is
used to restore its contents.

Other Secondary Media

The least expensive secondary storage medium is magnetic cassette, the
same cassette tape used to record music. Data are output to a tape recorder.
By playing the recording back, the material is restored to main memory.
Cassettes are inexpensive and compact, but they are also relatively slow and
error prone. They are used on some small home computer systems or for
archival storage.

Magnetic tape (similar to reel-to-reel recording tape) is a common
backup medium. Accessed through high-speed drives, tape is fast, with data
transfer rates comparable to disk. Its storage capacity is high, and a reel of
tape is inexpensive. Unfortunately, data can be read or written only in a
fixed sequence, which limits tape to a few applications.

The original secondary storage device was magnetic drum. As the name
implies, a drum is a cylinder coated on the outside surface with the same
magnetic material that coats disk and tape. Data are stored on parallel
tracks that encircle the surface. Each track has its own read/write head.
Since no head movement is required, there is no seek time—magnetic

drum is very fast. However, compared to disk, drum has limited storage capacity and is expensive.

One of the newest secondary storage media is video disk. These disks are read and written by a laser beam; there is no physical contact between the recording surface and the read/write mechanism. Fast, accurate, compact, and easy to use, video disk has a promising future.

Accessing Secondary Storage

Because of its storage capacity, a single disk can hold hundreds of programs or the data for dozens of different applications. If you are a computer user, however, you want a particular program, and you want to access a particular set of data. How does the computer find the right program or the right data?

Start by reviewing how data are stored on disk. The surface is divided into tracks, which, in turn, are divided into sectors or blocks. The tracks are numbered sequentially. The outer track is 0. Moving toward the disk's center, the next track is 1, then 2, and so on. The sectors (or blocks) on a track are also numbered sequentially, starting with 0. Track 5, sector 8 is a particular sector; track 5, sector 9 is a different sector; and track 6, sector 8 is yet another one. Each sector has a unique track/sector address; each physical record has a unique track/block address.

When a program is stored on disk, it is normally recorded in a set of consecutive sectors or blocks. Thus, if the program starts on track 3, sector 0, you can assume it's continued on track 3, sector 1, and so on. If the computer can find a program's beginning, it can find the entire program.

How does the system determine where a particular program begins on disk? A portion of the first track is set aside to hold a **directory** (Fig. 2.14). When the program is first written to disk, it is assigned a name. The program's name is then recorded in the directory, along with the track and sector (or track and block) address where it begins. Later, to retrieve the program, a user enters the program's name. Given a name, the computer reads the directory, searches for the name, finds the address where the program begins, and reads the program.

Data are accessed in much the same way. The data for a given application are grouped to form a file. Each file is assigned a name. The file name and the address of its first sector or block are recorded in the disk's directory. Because the data that make up a file are normally stored consecutively, knowing the file's start address allows the system to find its other blocks or sectors.

Some hard-disk systems support an optional search-by-key feature. In addition to the normal block number, a logical key (for example, a social security number) is recorded with each physical record. During seek time, the access mechanism is positioned over the selected cylinder, and a selected read/write head is activated. Normally, the track is then searched by count for a particular sector or block. When the search-by-key feature is utilized, the track is searched for a particular logical key.

Fig. 2.14   The programs and files stored on a disk are listed in the disk's
                     directory.

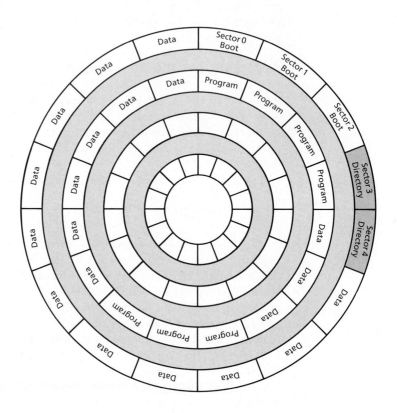

Secondary storage is an extension of main memory, not a replacement
for it. A computer cannot execute a program stored on disk unless it is first
copied into main memory, nor can it manipulate data stored on a secondary
medium until they have been copied into main memory. Main memory
holds the current program and the current data; secondary storage is long-
term storage.

The input and output devices described earlier provide human access
to the computer system; taken together, they are sometimes called the
computer's front end. Secondary storage is a machine readable medium.
Data are stored in a form convenient to the computer and can be read and
written only by the machine; taken together, a computer's secondary storage devices form its back end. The only way people can access the data
stored on a disk is by instructing the computer to read them into main
memory and then write them to the screen.

Linking the Components

You know that data are stored in a computer as patterns of bits. Within a given machine, the patterns are consistent; for example, if the code for the letter A is 01000001, this pattern, and *only* this pattern, will be used to represent an A.

The rule does not apply to input, output, or secondary storage devices, however. On a keyboard, each key generates one character. A printer represents characters as patterns of dots or positions on a print wheel. A card reader interprets patterns of holes punched in a card. An optical device reads light intensity, while a disk drive records and reads magnetized spots. Each peripheral device represents or interprets data in its own unique way, and the signals used by a device may or may not match the signals stored inside the computer. If these dissimilar devices are to communicate, translation is necessary. This is the function of the **interface** board.

Consider, for example, a keyboard. When a key is pressed, an electronic signal is sent to the keyboard's interface. In response, the interface generates the code that represents the character inside the computer, and transfers the coded data into main memory (2.15a). Change the device to a printer (Fig. 2.15b). As output begins, the data are stored in memory as binary-coded characters. The printer, we'll assume, requires a dot pattern. Clearly translation is necessary. The coded characters are sent to the printer's interface, which translates the computer's binary codes to printer form.

The printer and the keyboard are different; the signals that physically control them and the electronic patterns they use to represent data are device dependent. However, because the device-dependent tasks are assigned to interface boards, both can be attached to the same computer. On input, an interface translates external signals into a form acceptable to the computer. Output signals are electronically converted from the computer's internal code to a form acceptable to the peripheral device. Because they are electronically different, a printer and a keyboard require different interface boards.

Secondary storage devices are linked to the system through interfaces, too. The interface physically controls the disk drive, accepting seek, read, and write commands from the processor, positioning the access mechanism, and managing the flow of data between the disk surface and main memory. Because the disk drives attached to a given computer are virtually identical, a single interface often controls two or more peripherals. Consequently, only one drive can be active at a time.

Many interfaces contain buffers. A **buffer** is temporary memory or storage used to adjust for the speed differential between adjacent devices. For example, if you've ever waited for a lengthy paper to print, you know that a printer is much slower than a computer. If waiting for the printer is a problem, add a buffer to your printer interface. Then, instead of the computer sending the contents of main memory directly to the printer, it can send the information to the buffer at computer speed. Subsequently, as the

Fig. 2.15   The functions of an interface board.

a. Input from the keyboard enters the interface and is converted to the computer's internal form.

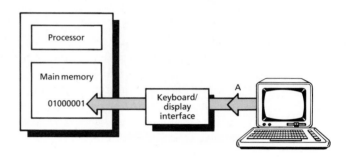

b. Data stored in main memory are sent to the printer interface, converted to printer form, and output.

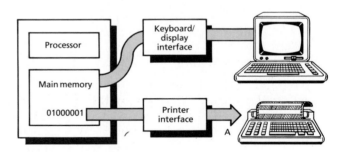

characters are dumped from the buffer to the printer at printer speed, you can use the computer for some other task.

Assigning one interface to each device is reasonable on a microcomputer system. However, on a large system with hundreds of peripherals, this approach is simply unworkable. Instead, input and output devices are linked to a large computer system through channels and control units.

Certain functions (for example, deciding where the next byte can be found or stored in memory and counting the characters transferred to or from an external device) are common to almost all types of input and output. On a microcomputer, they are performed by each interface; in effect, they are duplicated for each device on the system. On larger machines, these common functions are assigned to data **channels** (Fig. 2.16).

Note that a channel handles device-independent functions. What about such device-dependent functions as interpreting magnetic patterns or mov-

Fig. 2.16   On a large computer system, peripheral devices are linked to the system through a channel and an I/O control unit.

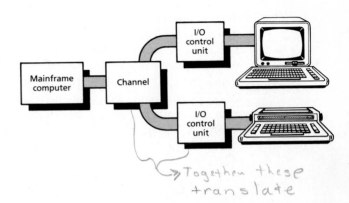

Together these translate

ing a disk's access mechanism? They are implemented through **I/O control units** or interface units. Each physical device has its own control unit. The channel communicates with the computer in the computer's language; the control unit communicates with the external device on the device's terms; the channel and the control unit, working together, translate.

A typical large computer system may have three or four channels, with numerous control units attached to each one. Some channels overlap or multiplex the operation of several slow input and output devices. Other selector channels link dozens of secondary storage devices to the system, often "selecting" one high-speed device at a time and serving as a simple data path between it and the computer. When a given data transfer is complete, the channel is then free to select another secondary storage device. With channels and control units, hundreds of input and output devices can access the computer through only a few easy-to-control data paths.

Summary

A computer is a binary machine. Its memory stores bits. Generally, memory is grouped into bytes, or words, or both (depending on the system), and each basic storage unit is assigned an address. Using this address, the processor can read or write selected bytes or words.

The processor consists of a clock, an instruction control unit, an arithmetic and logic unit, and registers. Once a program is stored in main memory, the processor can execute it. During I-time, the instruction control unit fetches an instruction from main memory; during E-time, the arithmetic and logic unit executes that instruction. Precisely timed electronic pulses generated by the clock drive this basic machine cycle.

People access a computer through its input and output devices. We briefly considered several common I/O devices and media.

Because of its cost, limited capacity, and volatility, main memory cannot be used for long-term or for volume storage. Secondary storage is a solution. The most popular microcomputer medium is diskette. Data are stored on the disk's surface on a series of concentric circles called tracks. The tracks are subdivided into sectors. On input, the contents of one sector are copied from disk to main memory; on output, one sector moves from memory to the disk's surface. To access disk, it is first necessary to bring the drive up to operating speed and then move the access mechanism over the track containing the desired data (seek time). Additional time is lost waiting for the desired sector to rotate to the read/write head (rotational delay).

Unlike diskette, a hard disk spins constantly; thus a major component of seek time is eliminated. Because hard disk rotates faster than diskette, it has less rotational delay. Hard disk has more storage capacity, too. Often, several surfaces are stacked on a single drive shaft to form a disk pack. A disk pack normally has one read/write head per surface, with the heads grouped on a single access mechanism. One position of the access mechanism defines a cylinder consisting of one track on each surface. On many hard disks, tracks are divided into sectors. On others, tracks are divided into physical records or blocks, with the block size chosen to fit the application.

Because data can be so valuable, disk packs are normally backed up. Magnetic tape is a common backup medium. The first secondary storage medium was magnetic drum. Video disk shows promise for the future.

A single disk can contain numerous programs and data files. To distinguish them, a directory is maintained. The directory identifies the programs and data files and indicates the track and sector (or track and block) address where each one begins. Given the address of the first sector, the other sectors can be located.

Secondary storage is an extension of main memory. The computer cannot execute a program until it has been loaded into main memory, nor can it process data until they have been copied into main memory.

Each peripheral device is electronically different, but the computer always deals with a common code. An interface serves to bridge this gap. A buffer can help to adjust for the speed differential between adjacent devices. On larger computers, each peripheral device is linked to a control unit, the control units are plugged into channels, and the channels are connected to the computer. The channel performs device-independent tasks; those functions unique to a given peripheral device are assigned to the control unit.

Key Words

address	directory	I-time
arithmetic and	disk	machine cycle
logic unit	diskette	main memory
backup	E-time	output
bit	hard disk	processor
buffer	input	program
byte	instruction	register
channel	instruction	secondary storage
clock	control unit	word
control unit (I/O)	interface	

Exercises

1. Computers manipulate *binary* data and execute *binary* instructions. Why binary?

2. Distinguish between reading and writing memory. Distinguish between ROM and RAM.

3. Distinguish between physical memory and its contents.

4. Relate the terms bit, byte, and word.

5. How is a computer's main memory addressed? Why is addressing memory important?

6. Draw a sketch showing the key components of a processor. Add blocks representing main memory, a program, and data.

7. Explain what happens during a computer's basic machine cycle.

8. What are registers? Where are they located? Why are they needed?

9. How are input/output and secondary storage devices similar? How are they different?

10. Why is secondary storage necessary?

11. Distinguish between cylinders, tracks, and sectors. Distinguish between sectors and blocks.

12. Briefly explain the process of reading data from or writing data to disk.

13. Distinguish between diskette and hard disk. What advantages are associated with using hard disk?

14. What is the purpose of a disk's directory? Why is it needed?

15. What is the purpose of an interface? Why are interfaces needed?

16. Distinguish between a microcomputer interface and the channel/control unit used on mainframes. How are they similar? How are they different?

17. Why do computer manufacturers use channels and control units instead of simple interface boards on large computer systems?

18. What is a buffer? Why are buffers used?

19. Briefly distinguish between a selector channel and a multiplexer channel. Why does it make sense to use different types of channels to link I/O devices and secondary storage devices to a computer?

20. Exercise 6 asked you to sketch a computer's internal components. Add channels, control units, I/O devices, and secondary storage devices to your sketch.

C H A P T E R

3

Software and Data

Hardware and Software

A computer is a machine (hardware) that processes data under control of a stored program. All three elements—the hardware, the data, and the software—must be present or the system cannot function. In Chapter 2 we discussed hardware. In this chapter we turn our attention to software and data.

We begin with a simple fact—software and data are stored on the hardware; they exist as nothing more substantial than patterns of bits, electronic impulses, that can be destroyed or changed in far less than the blink of an eye. One pattern of bits might represent a machine-level instruction. Another might hold EBCDIC or ASCII coded data. Yet another might hold a pure binary integer, or a floating-point number. Hardware is physical; software and data are logical.

Software

Instructions

A **program** is a series of instructions that guides a computer through a process. Each **instruction** tells the machine to perform one of its basic functions: add, subtract, multiply, divide, compare, copy, request input, or request output. The processor fetches and executes a single instruction during each machine cycle. A typical instruction (Fig. 3.1) contains an **operation code** that specifies the function to be performed and a series of **operands** that specify the memory locations or registers holding the data to be manipulated. For example, the instruction

ADD 3,4

tells a hypothetical computer to add registers 3 and 4.

Because a computer's instruction set is so limited, even simple logical operations call for several instructions. For example, imagine two data

Fig. 3.1   An instruction is composed of an operation code and one or more operands. The operation code tells the computer what to do. The operand or operands specify the addresses of the data elements to be manipulated.

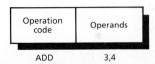

Operation code	Operands
ADD	3,4

Fig. 3.2   Because a computer's main memory stores bits, the program
                     must exist in binary form. These four instructions are needed to
                     add two numbers on an IBM mainframe computer.

```
0101100000110000110000000000000000

0101100001000000110000000000000100

0001101000110100

0101000000110000110000000000001000
```

values stored in main memory. To add them on many computers, both
values are first loaded (or copied) into registers, the registers are added, and
then the answer is stored (or copied) back into main memory. That's four
instructions: LOAD, LOAD, ADD, and STORE. If four instructions are
needed to add two numbers, imagine the number of instructions in a
complete program.

   A computer is controlled by a program stored in its own main memory.
Because main memory stores bits, the program must exist in binary form.
Figure 3.2 shows the binary, machine-level instructions needed to load two
numbers into registers, add them, and store the answer in memory. If
programmers had to write in **machine language** there would be very few
programmers.

Programming Languages

One option is to write instructions in an **assembler language**; for example,
Fig. 3.3 shows how two numbers might be added in IBM mainframe assembler. The programmer writes one mnemonic (memory-aiding) instruction
for each machine-level instruction. AR (for add registers) is much easier to
remember than the equivalent binary operation code: 00011010. L (for
load) is much easier to remember than 01011000. The operands use labels,
such as A, B, and C, instead of numbers to represent main memory addresses, and that simplifies the code, too.

   Unfortunately, there are no computers that can directly execute assembler language instructions. Writing mnemonic codes may simplify the programmer's job, but computers are still binary machines and require binary
instructions. Thus, translation is necessary. An assembler program (Fig.
3.3) reads a programmer's **source code**, translates the source statements to
binary, and produces an **object module**. Because the object module is a
machine-level version of the programmer's code, it can be loaded into
memory and executed.

   An assembler language programmer writes one mnemonic instruction

Fig. 3.3   An assembler program reads a programmer's mnemonic source
                        statements, translates each one to a single machine-level
                        instruction, and then combines them to form an object module.

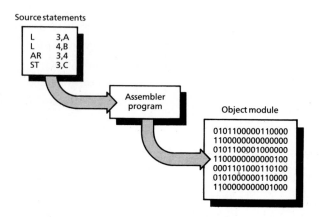

for each machine-level instruction. Because of the one-to-one relationship
between the language and the machine, assemblers are machine dependent,
and a program written for one type of computer won't run on another. On a
given machine, assembler language generates the most efficient programs
possible, and thus is often used to write operating systems and other system
software. However, when it comes to application programs, machine dependency is a high price to pay for efficiency, so application programs are
rarely written in assembler.

A computer needs four machine-level instructions to add two numbers,
because that's the way a computer works. Human beings shouldn't have to
think like computers. Why not simply allow the programmer to indicate
addition and assume the other instructions? For example, one way to view
addition is as an algebraic expression:

C = A + B

Why not allow a programmer to write statements in a form similar to
algebraic expressions, read those source statements into a program, and let
the program generate the necessary machine-level code (Fig. 3.4)? That's
exactly what happens with a **compiler**. Compare the binary instructions in
Figs. 3.3 and 3.4; they're identical.

Many compiler languages, including FORTRAN, BASIC, Pascal, PL/1,
and ALGOL, are algebraically based. The most popular business-oriented
language, COBOL, calls for statements that resemble brief English-language
sentences (Fig. 3.5). Note, however, that no matter what language is used,
the objective is the same. The programmer writes source code. An assembler program accepts mnemonic source code and generates a machine-level

Fig. 3.4

A compiler reads a programmer's source statements, translates each one to one or more machine-level instructions, and then combines them to form an object module.

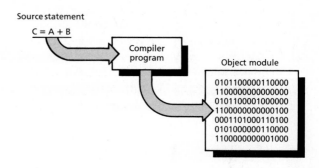

object module. A FORTRAN compiler accepts FORTRAN source code and generates a machine-level object module. A COBOL compiler accepts CO-BOL source code and generates a machine-level object module.

What's the difference between an assembler and a compiler? With an assembler, each source statement is converted to a single machine-level instruction. With a compiler, a given source statement may be converted to any number of machine-level instructions.

An option is to use an **interpreter**. An assembler or a compiler reads a complete source program and generates a complete object module. An interpreter, on the other hand, works with one source statement at a time, reading it, translating it to machine level, executing the resulting binary instructions, and then moving on to the next source statement. Both com-

Fig. 3.5

The most popular business-oriented language is COBOL. As with other compiler languages, COBOL statements are translated into a machine-level object module.

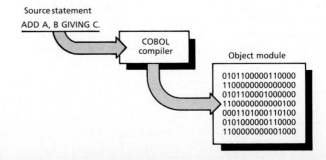

pilers and interpreters generate machine-level instructions, but the process is different.

Each language has its own syntax, punctuation, and spelling rules, so a Pascal source program is meaningless to a COBOL compiler or a BASIC interpreter. However, no matter what language is used, the objective is the same: defining a series of steps to guide the computer through a process.

With traditional assemblers, compilers, and interpreters, the programmer defines a *procedure* telling the computer exactly how to solve a problem. However, with a modern, **nonprocedural language** (sometimes called a fourth-generation or declarative language), the programmer simply defines the logical structure of the problem and lets the language translator figure out how to solve it. Examples include Prolog, Focus, SQL, and Lotus 1-2-3.

Libraries

Picture a programmer writing a large routine. As source statements are typed, they are manipulated by an editor program and stored on disk. Because large programs are rarely written in a single session, the programmer will eventually stop working and remove the disk from the drive. Later, when work resumes, the disk is reinserted, and new source statements are added to the old ones. That same disk might hold other source programs and even routines written by other programmers. It's a good example of a source statement **library** (Fig. 3.6).

Fig. 3.6   Source statements are typically typed, manipulated by an editor, and stored on a source statement library. If changes are necessary, the programmer can read the original statements from the library, change or delete them, add new statements, and update the library. Eventually, the source statements are compiled and an object module is created.

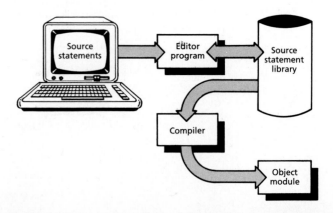

Fig. 3.7

Object modules can be stored on a library, too. Because an object module is a binary, machine-level routine, there is no inherent difference between one produced by an assembler and one produced by a FORTRAN compiler, so both can be stored on the same library.

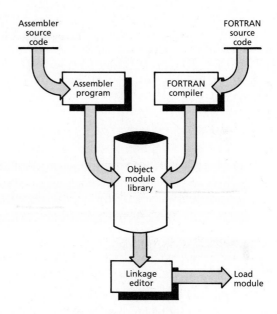

Eventually, the source program is completed and compiled. The resulting object module might be loaded directly into main memory, but more often, it is stored on an object module library (Fig. 3.7). Because object modules are binary, machine-level routines, there is no inherent difference between one produced by an assembler and one produced by a FORTRAN compiler (or any other compiler for that matter). Thus, object modules generated by different source languages can be stored on the same library.

Some object modules can be loaded into memory and executed. Others, however, include references to subroutines that are not part of the object module. For example, imagine a program that simulates a game of cards. If, some time ago, another programmer wrote an excellent subroutine to deal cards, it would make sense to reuse that logic.

Picture the new program after it has been written, compiled, and stored on the object module library (Fig. 3.8). The subroutine that deals cards is stored on the same library. Before the program is loaded, the two routines must be combined to form a **load module** (Fig. 3.9). An object module is a machine-language translation of a source module, and may include references to other subroutines. A load module is a complete, ready-to-execute program with all subroutines in place. Combining object modules to form a

Fig. 3.8   In this example, the just created object module is incomplete
because it includes a reference to an independent subroutine.

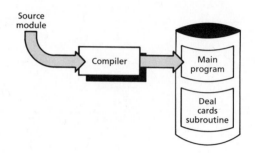

load module is the job of the **linkage editor** or **loader** (Fig. 3.10). A
linkage editor prepares a complete load module and copies it to a library for
immediate or eventual loading. A loader, on the other hand, simply creates
a load module in main memory and gives it control.

Reentrant Code

Many programs modify themselves as they run, changing key data values
and even executable instructions. Imagine two users concurrently accessing
the same program. Any attempt to share the code would be doomed because changes made by one user could have unforeseen consequences for
the other. If the program can modify itself, there must be two copies in
memory, one for each user.

Fig. 3.9   Before the program can be loaded and executed, the object
modules for the main program and the subroutine must be
combined to form a load module.

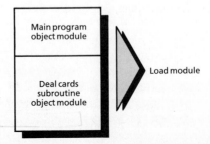

$T Q 2$

Fig. 3.10   The linkage editor combines object modules to form a complete, ready-to-execute load module.

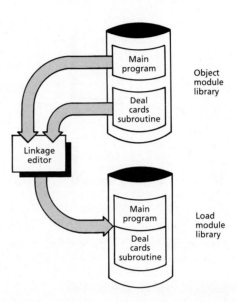

$T Q \;\; \rightarrow$ A **reentrant** program or program module does *not* modify itself. Consequently, since the code does not change, two or more programmers can share the same logic. Often, the secret to creating reentrant code is breaking the program into two components: a logic segment and a data segment (Fig. 3.11). The data segment belongs to an individual user and can be modified as the program runs. The logic segment, on the other hand, consists of program instructions that cannot be changed. Given such segmentation, it is possible to assign each of several users their own data segments and allow them to share a single logic segment (Fig. 3.12). Avoiding duplication of program logic can save a great deal of main memory space.

An operating system is composed of system software modules that

Fig. 3.11   One way to achieve reentrant code is to divide a program into separate logic and data segments. As the program runs, the contents of the data segment can change, but the reentrant logic segment cannot.

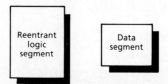

Fig. 3.12   Given reentrant code, it is possible for several users to share the
same logic segment. This saves main memory space.

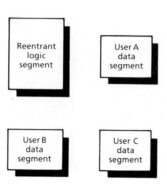

support application programs. On a large system, several applications may
execute concurrently. It makes little sense to include multiple copies of the
same support logic; thus, almost by definition, an operating system contains shared, reentrant code.

Data

Data Management

Like software, data are stored on hardware as patterns of bits. Simply
storing the data is not enough, however. A typical computer system, even a
small one, can have dozens of disks and tapes, each holding data for dozens
of different applications. For any given application, one and only one set of
data will do. We must be able to store, locate, and retrieve the specific data
needed by a given program. That is the concern of **data management**.

A single diskette can hold numerous programs, or data for several
different applications, or both. For a given application, one and only one set
of data will do, and finding the right data is much like finding the right
program. There are differences between accessing programs and accessing
data, however. When a program is needed, all its instructions must be
loaded into memory. Data, on the other hand, are processed selectively, a
few elements at a time. Thus, it is not enough merely to locate the data; we
must be able to distinguish the individual data elements, too.

Data Elements

A **data element** is a single, meaningful unit of data, such as a name, a social
security number, or a temperature reading. Most computers can store and
manipulate pure binary integers, floating-point numbers, decimal numbers,

Fig. 3.13   The simplest data structure is a list. In this example, commas separate the individual data elements, and a semicolon marks the end of the list.

```
12,84,65,49,193,8,17,33;
```

and character or string data. (See Appendix A for a review of these data types.)

Data Structures

The key to retrieving data is remembering where they are stored. If the data elements are stored according to a consistent and well-understood structure, it is possible to retrieve them by remembering that structure.

The simplest **data structure** is a list. For example, data for a program that computes an average might be stored as a series of numbers separated by commas (Fig. 3.13). The commas distinguish the individual data elements.

Most programming languages support a more complex data structure called an array (Fig. 3.14). Each array element holds one data value. Each

Fig. 3.14   Most programming languages support a more complex data structure called an array. Individual cells are assigned a number or numbers, and data values are inserted, manipulated, and extracted by referencing those numbers.

1,1	1,2	1,3	1,4	1,5
71	38	29	90	70
2,1	2,2	2,3	2,4	2,5
91	13	56	77	20
3,1	3,2	3,3	3,4	3,5
68	18	54	63	56
4,1	4,2	4,3	4,4	4,5
12	38	68	39	74
5,1	5,2	5,3	5,4	5,5
82	80	35	98	61

element is assigned a unique identifying number or numbers, and individual data elements can be inserted, extracted, or manipulated by referencing those numbers. For example, in the array pictured in Fig. 3.14, elements are identified by a row number and a column number, and row 1, column 3 (element 1,3) contains the value 29. Once an array has been filled, it can be written to disk, tape, or any other secondary medium and later read back into memory for processing.

Consider a program that generates name and address labels. For each label, we need a name, a street address, a city, a state, and a zip code. If we needed only a few labels, we might store the data in a list, but separating the elements would soon become tedious. An option is to set up an array of names and addresses, with each row holding the data for a single label. The only problem is that the entire array must be in memory before the individual elements can be accessed, and main memory space is limited. Thus, even with an array, we could generate relatively few labels.

A better solution is to organize the data as a **file** (Fig. 3.15). All computer data begin as patterns of bits. On a file, the bits are grouped to form characters. Groups of characters, in turn, form meaningful data elements called fields. A group of related fields is a record; the file is a set of related records. For example, in a name and address file, an individual's name is a field. Each record holds a complete set of data for a single individual (a name, a street address, and so on). The file consists of all the records.

Fig. 3.15   Characters are grouped to form fields. Fields are grouped to form records. A file is a group of related records.

	Name	Street address	City	State	Zip code
	Melinda Atkins	142 Maple St.	Oxford	Ohio	450781718
	Charles Baker	713 Main Street	Cincinnati	Ohio	457033304
	Thomas Bates	42 South Blvd.	Atlanta	Georgia	352170315
	Lisa Campanella	8 Tower Square	San Jose	California	953214450
	Shen Chan	State Route 77	Binghamton	New York	127561495
	Tomas Garcia	473 Dixie Highway	Lexington	Kentucky	434101236
	⋮	⋮	⋮	⋮	⋮
	Arthur White	Northside Mall	Orlando	Florida	214504372
	Character				
	Field	Field	Field	Field	Field
	Record				

File

The data in a file are processed record by record. Normally, the file is stored on a secondary medium such as disk. Programs are written to read a record, process its fields, generate the appropriate output, and then read and process another record. Because only one record is in main memory at a time, very little memory is needed. Because many records can be stored on a single disk, a great deal of data can be processed in this limited space.

Access Techniques

How can a computer locate specific records in a file? The key to many storage and retrieval techniques is the **relative record number**. Imagine a string of 100 records. Number the first one 0, the second 1, the third 2, and so on. The numbers indicate a given record's position relative to the first record in the file. The file's first record (relative record 0) is at "start of file plus 0"; its second record is at "start of file plus 1," and so on.

Now, store the records on disk (Fig. 3.16); to keep our initial example simple, we'll store one per sector. Number the sectors relative to the start of the file—0, 1, 2, and so on. Note that the relative record number, a logical concept, and the relative sector number, a physical location, are identical. Given a relative record number, it is possible to compute a relative sector number. Given a relative sector number, it is possible to compute a physical disk address.

Assume a file begins at track 30, sector 0, and that one logical record is stored in each sector. As Fig. 3.17 shows, relative record 0 is stored at track 30, sector 0, relative record 1 is at track 30, sector 1, and so on. Where is relative record 10? Track 30, sector 10. In our example, the relative record number indicates how many sectors away from the beginning of the file the record is stored. The file starts at track 30, sector 0. Relative record 10 is stored 10 sectors away, at track 30, sector 10.

We might complicate matters by storing two or more logical records in each sector, or by creating a file extending over two or more tracks. While

---

Fig. 3.16   A relative record number indicates a record's position relative to the first record in a file. Relative sector numbers are generated by counting from the physical file's first sector. Given a relative record number, it is possible to compute a physical disk address.

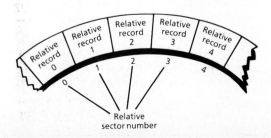

Fig. 3.17   Given the start of a file address (from open) and a relative record
                       number, a physical disk address can be computed.

Relative record number	Actual location on disk	
	Track	Sector
0	30	0
1	30	1
2	30	2
3	30	3
4	30	4
5	30	5
6	30	6
7	30	7
8	30	8
9	30	9
10	30	10
.	.	.
.	.	.
.	.	.

we won't discuss the details, in either case it is still possible to develop a
simple algorithm to compute a record's physical location, given its relative
record number. Many different algorithms are used. Some allow records to
be stored or retrieved sequentially. Others allow individual records to be
accessed in random order. Let's examine a few common **data access** techniques.

Imagine preparing meeting announcements for a club. You need a set
of mailing labels, and each member's name and address is recorded on an
index card. Probably the easiest way to generate the labels is to copy the
data from the first card, turn to the second card and copy it, and so on,
processing the records sequentially, from the beginning of the file to the
end.

Magazine publishers face the same problem with each new issue, but
need mailing labels for tens of thousands of subscribers. Rather than using
index cards, they store customer data on disk or magnetic tape, one record
per subscriber. The easiest way to ensure that all labels are generated is to
process the records in the order in which they are stored, proceeding
sequentially from the first record in the file to the last. To simplify handling,
the records might be presorted by zip code or a mailing zone, but the basic
idea of processing the data in physical order still holds.

How does this relate to the relative record number concept? A relative
record number indicates a record's position on the file. With sequential
access, processing begins with relative record 0, then moves to relative
record 1, 2, and so on. Accessing data sequentially involves little more than
counting. For example, imagine a program has just finished processing

relative record 14. What is the next record? Obviously, relative record 15. Simply by counting records, it is possible to read them, or write them, in physical order.

Processing records in sequence is not always acceptable. For example, when a subscriber moves, his or her address must be changed in the file. Searching for that subscriber's record sequentially is like looking for a telephone number by starting with the first page of the telephone book and reading line by line. That's not how we use a telephone book. Instead, knowing the records are stored in alphabetical order, we quickly narrow our search to a portion of a single page, and then begin reading the entries, ignoring the bulk of the data. The way we use a telephone book is a good example of direct, or random, access.

A disk drive reads or writes one sector at a time. To randomly access a specific record, all the programmer must do is remember the address of the sector that holds the record and ask for it. The problem is remembering all those disk addresses. One solution is to maintain an index of the records. Again, we'll use the name and address file as an example. We want to access individual customer records by name. As the file is created, records are written, one at a time, in relative record number order. Additionally, as each record is written, the customer name and the associated relative record number are recorded in an array or index (Fig. 3.18). After the last record has been written to disk and its position recorded on the index, the index is itself stored.

Once the index has been created, it can be used to find individual records. Assume, for example, that Susan Smith has changed her address. To record her new address on the file, a program could:

1. read the file index,
2. search the index for her name,
3. find her relative record number,
4. compute the disk address, and read her record,

Fig. 3.18   A file index can help when records must be accessed directly.

Key	Relative record
Atkins, Melinda	0
Baker, Charles	1
Bates, Thomas	2
Campanella, Lisa	3
Chan, Shen	4
Garcia, Tomas	5
.	.
.	.
.	.

5. change her address, and

6. rewrite the record to the same place on disk.

Note that this specific record is accessed directly, and that no other records in the file are involved.

The basic idea of direct access is assigning each record an easy-to-remember, logical key, and then converting that key to a relative record number. Given this relative location, a physical address can be computed, and the record accessed. Using an index is one technique for converting keys to physical addresses. Another is to pass a numeric key to an algorithm and compute a relative record number.

Not all data access techniques rely on relative *record* numbers; in fact, some computer experts consider the very concept of a record an unnecessary anachronism left over from the days of punched cards. On many modern operating systems, most notably UNIX, there are no records. Instead, data stored on disk are treated as simple strings of characters or bytes, and no other structure is imposed. On such systems, programmers address data by relative *byte* number (the same way they address main memory).

Data base Management

There are problems with traditional data management. Many of these result from viewing applications independently. For example, consider payroll. Most organizations prepare their payrolls by computer because using a machine instead of a small army of clerks saves money. Thus, the firm develops a payroll program to process a payroll file. Inventory, accounts receivable, accounts payable, and general ledger are similar applications, so the firm develops an inventory program, an inventory file, an accounts receivable program, an accounts receivable file, and so on. Each program is independent, and each processes its own independent data file.

Why is this a problem? For one thing, different applications often need the same data elements. For example, schools generate both bills and student grade reports. View the applications independently. The billing program reads a file of billing data, and the grade report program reads an independent file of grade data. The outputs of both programs are mailed to the students' homes; thus, student names and addresses must be redundantly recorded on both files. What happens when a student moves? Unless both files are updated, one will be wrong. Redundant data are difficult to maintain.

Data dependency is a more subtle problem. There are many different file organizations, each has its own rules for storing and retrieving data, and certain tricks of the trade can significantly improve the efficiency of a given program. If the programmer takes advantage of these efficiencies, the program's logic becomes dependent upon the physical structure of the data. When a program's logic is tied to its physical data structure, changing that

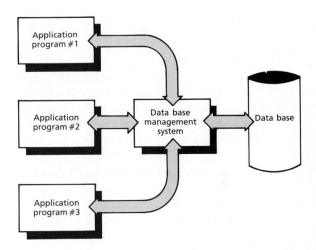

Fig. 3.19   Many of the problems associated with traditional data access techniques can be solved by using a data base.

structure will almost certainly require changing the program. As a result, programs using traditional access methods can be difficult to maintain.

The solution to both problems is organizing the data as a single, integrated **data base**. The task of controlling access to all the data can then be concentrated in a centralized data base management system (Fig. 3.19).

How does a centralized data base solve the data redundancy problem? All data are collected and stored in a single place; consequently, there is one and only one copy of any given data element. When the value of an element (an address, for example) changes, the single data base copy is corrected. Any program requiring access to this data element gets the same value, because there is only one value.

How does a data base help to solve the data dependency problem? Since the responsibility for accessing the physical data rests with the data base management system, the programmer can ignore the physical data structure. As a result, programs tend to be much less dependent upon their data and are generally much easier to maintain.

Summary

A program is a series of instructions that guides a computer through a process. Each instruction tells the machine to perform one of its basic functions. Because computers are binary machines, the program stored in a computer's main memory must be in binary form.

An assembler programmer writes one mnemonic instruction for each machine-level instruction. A compiler reads source statements, translates each one into one or more machine-level instructions, and combines them to form an object module. An interpreter works with one source statement at a time, translating it and executing the resulting machine-level code before moving on to the next instruction. With a nonprocedural language, the programmer defines the logical structure of the problem and lets the translator program solve it.

Source code is stored on a source statement library. An assembler or compiler reads the source code and stores the resulting object module on an object module library. A linkage editor or loader combines object modules to form a load module. An object module is a machine-level translation of a programmer's source code that may include references to other subroutines. A load module is a complete, ready-to-execute program.

The key to retrieving data is remembering where they are stored. Often, the secret is storing them in a well-defined structure. The simplest data structure is a list. Most programming languages support arrays; individual data elements are identified by numbering the array's cells.

In a file, individual characters are grouped to form fields, fields are grouped to form records, and a set of related records forms the file. Accessing the data on a file involves reading and writing individual records. Often, the key to finding a specific record is its relative record number. The records in a file are numbered sequentially, with each relative record number indicating the record's position relative to the first one in the file. Given its relative record number, it is possible to compute a record's physical location.

With sequential access, data are stored and retrieved in a fixed order, essentially by counting records. With direct or random access, individual records can be retrieved without regard for their positions on the physical file. Not all data access techniques rely on relative record numbers, however. Some treat the data stored on disk as simple character or byte strings and use relative byte values to address them.

With traditional data management, because different applications often require the same data, certain data elements may be stored redundantly. Also, a program's logic can be too closely linked to the physical structure of its data. The solution is to collect all the organization's data in a centralized data base. With a data base, there is only one copy of each data element, so the data redundancy problem is eliminated. Because every program must access data through a data base management system, programs are insulated from the physical data structure; thus, data dependency is reduced.

Key Words

assembler language	instruction	object module
compiler	interpreter	operand
data access	library	operation code
data element	linkage editor	program
data management	load module	reentrant
data structure	loader	relative record
data base	machine language	number
file	nonprocedural	source code
	language	

Exercises

1. Without a program to provide control, a computer is little more than an expensive calculator. Do you agree? Why, or why not?

2. Relate the idea of an instruction to a computer's basic machine cycle.

3. Why are programming languages necessary?

4. Distinguish between an assembler and a compiler.

5. Distinguish between a compiler and an interpreter.

6. What is a library? Why are libraries useful?

7. Distinguish between a source module, an object module, and a load module.

8. When a program is accessed, all its instructions are accessed. Data, on the other hand, are accessed selectively. Explain.

9. What is a data element? Describe several different types of data elements.

10. What is a data structure? Why are data structures important?

11. Briefly relate the terms character, field, record, and file.

12. Briefly explain the relative record concept.

13. Distinguish between sequential and direct access. Relate both techniques to the relative record concept.

14. Some modern operating systems don't even recognize records, treating data stored on disk as simple strings of bytes. What advantages might you expect from such an approach? What disadvantages?

15. What is a data base? Why are data bases useful?

CHAPTER

4

Linking the Components

Linking Internal Components

Bus Lines

A computer is a system, with data and instructions flowing between its components in response to processor commands. Clearly, those components must be physically linked. Inside a computer, speed is essential. Thus, internal components are normally linked by **bus** lines. A bus is a ribbonlike set of parallel wires that can carry several bits at a time.

Some bus lines transmit power. Others carry instructions, data, addresses, or commands. On some computers, a single bus might serve two or more purposes; on others, the data, address, and command buses are separate. Basically, however, a computer's internal components are linked by bus lines.

Word Size

Communication between components is greatly simplified if they are electronically similar. Thus, on most systems, the internal components are designed around a common **word** size. For example, on a 32-bit computer, the processor manipulates 32-bit numbers, main memory and the registers store 32-bit words, and data and instructions move between the components over 32-bit bus lines.

A computer's word size affects its processing speed, memory capacity, precision, instruction set size, and cost. Let's consider speed first. A 32-bit bus contains 32 wires, and thus can carry 32 bits at a time. A 16-bit bus has only 16 parallel wires, and thus can carry only 16. Because the wider bus moves twice as much data in the same amount of time, the 32-bit machine is clearly faster. Generally, the bigger the word size, the faster the computer.

Memory capacity is also a function of word size. To access main memory, the processor must transmit over a bus the address of a desired instruction or data element. On a 32-bit machine, a 32-bit address can be transmitted. The biggest 32-bit number is roughly 4 billion in decimal terms; thus the processor can access as many as 4 billion different memory locations. On the other hand, a 16-bit computer transmits a 16-bit address, limiting it to roughly 64,000 memory locations. Generally, the bigger its word size, the more main memory a computer can access.

There are 16-bit microcomputers that access considerably more than 64K bytes of memory. How is that possible? A 16-bit machine can access more than 64K if addresses are broken into two or more parts and transmitted during successive machine cycles. Each cycle takes time, however, so memory capacity is gained at the expense of processing speed.

Next, consider the size of the numbers each machine can manipulate. Registers generally hold one word. The processor's internal circuitry is usually most efficient when manipulating numbers one word in length. A 32-bit mainframe adds 32-bit numbers; a 16-bit machine adds 16-bit numbers. Clearly, the machine with the bigger word size is more precise. While the 16-bit machine may be able to add two 32-bit numbers, it will need several machine cycles to do so, once again sacrificing speed.

What about instructions? They, too, must move from main memory to the processor over a bus. A 32-bit bus can carry a bigger instruction than a 16-bit bus. The bigger instruction size means more bits are available for the operation code. A machine with a 6-bit op code can have only 64 different instructions, while a machine with an 8-bit op code can have as many as 256 different instructions.

Word size also influences a system's cost. Most 8-bit machines are priced well under $1000, while more powerful 16-bit micros sell for $2,000 or more. A typical 16-bit minicomputer costs about $10,000, a 32-bit mainframe sells for roughly $100,000, and most 64-bit supercomputers exceed $1 million. Generally, a bigger word size means a faster, more precise machine with greater main memory capacity, a larger, more varied instruction set, and a higher price tag.

I - time
Know E - time

Machine Cycles

Perhaps the easiest way to envision how the various components of a computer are linked is to follow, in detail, a typical **machine cycle**. Consider the computer pictured in Fig. 4.1a. Note that a single bus line links the processor, the registers, and main memory. The system registers hold key control information and are not, normally, available to the application programmer. The work registers can be used by the programmer for computations or addressing.

TQ → During instruction time, or I-time, the instruction control unit fetches the next instruction from main memory. The address of the next instruction is found in the instruction counter. The instruction control unit extracts this address and sends it as part of a fetch **command** over the bus to the memory controller (Fig. 4.1a). The memory controller accepts the command, reads the requested memory location, and copies its contents onto the bus (Fig. 4.1b). This takes time, giving the instruction control unit an opportunity to increment the instruction counter to point to the *next* instruction. Meanwhile, the current instruction moves over the bus and into the instruction register (Fig. 4.1c).

TQ → During E-time, control flows to the arithmetic and logic unit, which executes the instruction in the instruction register (Fig. 4.1d). Assume it calls for loading a main memory word into a work register. Responding to the instruction, the arithmetic and logic unit issues, again over the bus, a command to fetch the contents of a specified main memory location (Fig. 4.1e). As before, the memory controller reads the requested word and copies the contents onto the bus. Thus, the data flow into a work register (Fig. 4.1f).

TQ → Note carefully how the components are coordinated. Instructions, addresses, and data flow over the bus in response to commands issued by the

Fig. 4.1   A machine cycle.

a. Obtaining the address of the next instruction from the instruction counter, the
instruction control unit sends a fetch command to main memory.

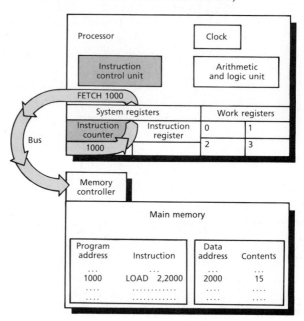

b. The memory controller responds to the fetch command by copying the contents
of the requested memory location onto the bus.

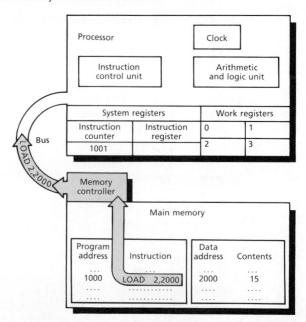

c. The instruction moves over the bus and into the instruction register.

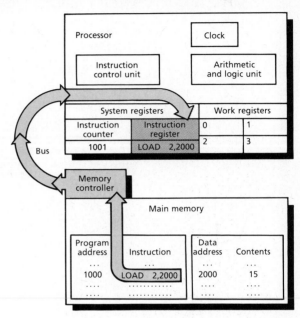

d. During E-time, the arithmetic and logic unit executes the instruction in the instruction register.

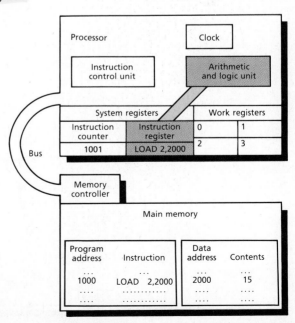

e. The instruction calls for copying data from memory into a register. Thus, the arithmetic and logic unit sends a fetch comand to main memory.

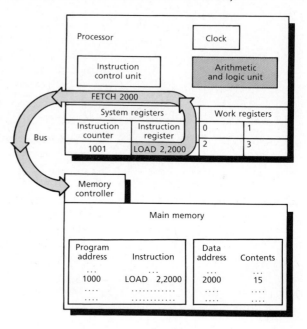

f. The main memory controller responds by copying the contents of the requested memory location onto the bus. The data value then flows over the bus and into a work register.

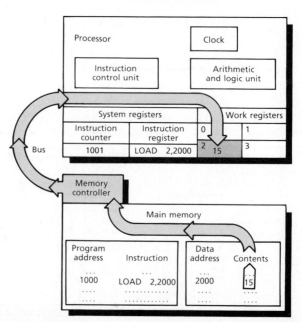

processor. Controlling everything, of course, are the clock's precisely timed pulses.

TQ →   Not all instructions can be executed in a single machine cycle. For example, contrast an instruction that adds the contents of two registers with one that adds two values stored in main memory. In the first case, the data are already in the processor. In the second case, the arithmetic and logic unit will have to fetch both values before adding them, and that takes time. Adding two registers might call for a single machine cycle. Adding memory contents to a register might take two machine cycles, while adding two memory locations might require four. More complex instructions (such as multiplying two decimal numbers) might consume a dozen or more.

TQ →   Recently, several firms have announced reduced instruction set computers (RISC technology). The idea is simple. Instead of offering a complete instruction set (for example, one including binary, decimal, floating-point, and string operations) the number of available instructions is reduced and the hardware is optimized to execute each of them in one or two machine cycles. While not ideal for every application, reduced instruction set computers offer significant advantages for such compute-bound tasks as engineering graphics and simulation.

Architectures

Not all computers are designed in exactly the same way. Computer scientists use the term **architecture** to describe the relationships between a computer's components. Let's investigate.

Single-bus Architecture

Most microcomputers are constructed around a motherboard (Fig. 4.2), a metal framework containing a series of slots linked, through a bus, to an 8- or 16-bit processor (Fig. 4.3). Memory is added by plugging a memory board into one of the open slots (Fig. 4.4). Additional boards tie input, output, and secondary storage devices to the system. The components pictured in Fig. 4.4 are linked by a common bus; this arrangement is called **single-bus architecture** (Fig. 4.5). All communications between components flow over this single bus.

Interfaces

Because the electronic signals controlling a keyboard/display unit, a printer, and a diskette drive are different, each peripheral device has its own **interface**. One side of the interface communicates with the computer, using internal codes (Fig. 4.6). The other side is device dependent, communicating with the external device in its own terms. The basic function of the interface is translation.

Fig. 4.2

A microcomputer is constructed around a metal framework called a motherboard. Typically, the processor and related components are mounted on the motherboard, and a bus links the processor to a series of slots that are used to attach other boards to the system.

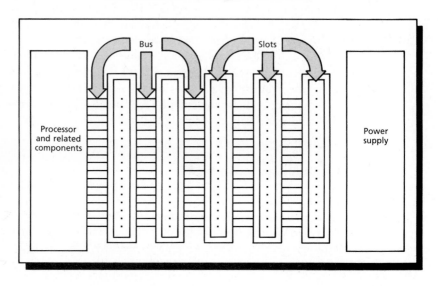

Fig. 4.3

A schematic drawing showing a processor and a motherboard. A bus links the processor with a number of slots into which components can be plugged.

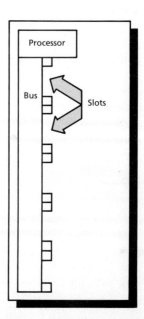

Fig. 4.4

Input devices, output devices, and secondary storage devices are added to the system by plugging the appropriate interface into an open slot and then running a cable from the external device to the interface.

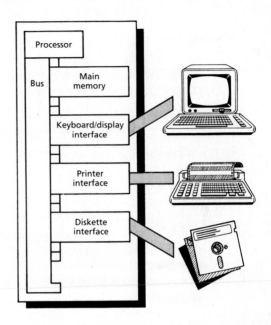

TO ∿

Fig. 4.5

A typical microcomputer uses a single-bus architecture, with all internal components linked by a single bus line.

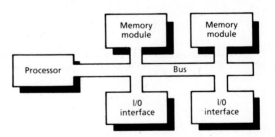

Fig. 4.6

The basic function of an interface is to translate between internal and external data forms.

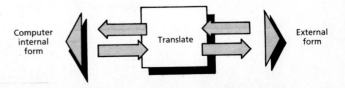

For example, the letter A is represented physically both as a key on a keyboard and as a dot pattern on a printer. When a user types *A*, an electronic pulse enters the keyboard/display interface where it is translated to the binary code that represents an *A* inside the computer. Later, on output, this same code is sent to a printer interface, where it is translated to the electronic signals needed to form the proper dot pattern. Note that the computer always uses the same binary code, no matter what peripheral device is involved. To the processor all peripherals look alike.

Channels and Control Units

Microcomputers are designed for single users, so single-bus architecture is reasonable. A mainframe with a 32-bit processor, a million or more bytes of main memory, scores of secondary storage devices, and numerous input and output devices is much too powerful and expensive to dedicate to a single user, however. Consequently, mainframes often execute several programs concurrently. A mainframe's basic machine cycle is identical to a microcomputer's—its processor still fetches and executes one instruction at a time. How can such a machine execute two or more programs concurrently? The key is freeing the main processor from responsibility for controlling I/O.

Controlling input and output involves such logical functions as selecting the path over which the data are to flow, counting characters, and computing main memory addresses. Because the main processor is the only source of logic on a microcomputer system, the processor must directly control each input and output operation. While it is controlling I/O, the processor is not available to execute application program instructions, but given the nature of a microcomputer system, this is a minor problem.

Fig. 4.7   On a mainframe, device-independent functions are assigned to a channel, and device-dependent functions are assigned to an I/O control unit.

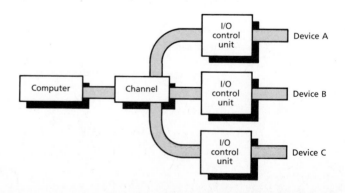

TQ →
TQ →   Most mainframes assign the task of controlling I/O to **channels** (Fig. 4.7). A channel is a micro- or minicomputer with its own processor. Thus it can perform logical functions in parallel with the computer's main processor, freeing the main processor to do other things.

Some I/O functions are device dependent; for example, controlling the movement of an access arm is a disk problem, while converting characters to a dot pattern is unique to a dot matrix printer. Other tasks, such as selecting a data path, counting characters, and computing main memory addresses, are common to all input and output operations, no matter what

TQ →   peripheral device is involved. The channel handles these device-*independent*
TQ →   functions, while the device-*dependent* functions are assigned to an I/O control unit. Each physical device has its own control unit.

Multiple-bus Architecture

Single-bus architecture creates a number of problems on a multiple-user system. Channel communication is one of the easiest to visualize. A channel moves data between main memory and a peripheral device. The computer's processor manipulates data in main memory. Allowing a channel

#7 →   and a processor to simultaneously access memory won't work on a microcomputer system, because the single-bus architecture provides only one

TQ →   physical data path. Simultaneous access requires independent data paths, so most mainframes use **multiple-bus architecture** (Fig. 4.8).

Start with a channel. Typically, two bus lines link it with the computer (Fig. 4.8a). As an input or output operation begins, the main processor sends a "start I/O" command over the command bus to the channel's processor. In response, the channel assumes responsibility for the input or output operation, establishing a link with the external device and controlling the transfer of data into main memory over the data bus (Fig. 4.8b). (Note that the *channel's* memory serves as a buffer between the peripheral

Fig. 4.8   Many mainframes use multiple-bus architecture.

a. The main processor starts an I/O operation by sending a signal to the channel.

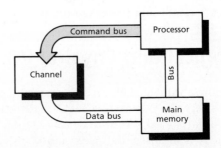

b. The channel assumes responsibility for the I/O operation, and the processor turns its attention to another program.

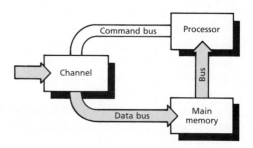

c. The channel sends an interrupt to the processor to signal the end of the I/O operation.

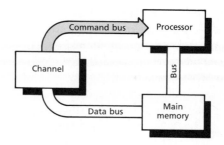

device and *main* memory.) Meanwhile, the main processor can turn its attention to another program.

The channel is an independent, asynchronous device with its own processor. It controls the I/O operation. Because the channel and the computer are independent, the main processor has no way of knowing when the I/O operation is complete unless the channel's processor tells it. Thus as the last character of data flows across the channel, the channel processor sends the main processor an electronic signal called an **interrupt** (Fig. 4.8c). When it receives the interrupt, the main processor knows the requested I/O operation has been completed, and can take appropriate action. We'll consider the interrupt process in detail in later chapters.

Logical and Physical I/O

Picture a sequential file on disk. Imagine a program designed to process the file's records. Whenever a READ statement is executed, the programmer expects the next record to be copied from disk into main memory. What exactly is meant by the "next" record? It's a logical concept. In effect, the programmer is saying, "Get me the next record, and I don't care what physical steps are involved." It's not that easy. The data must be copied from one device to another, and that involves considerable logic.

Primitives

#9 → Peripheral devices are controlled by interfaces or control units that are limited to a few **primitive** operations. For example, a disk interface or control unit can:

1. move the access mechanism to a specific track (seek),
2. read a specific sector, or
3. write a specific sector.

TQ → Because printers, tape drives, and terminals are so different, they are controlled by different sets of primitive operations, and thus by different interfaces. Interfaces and control units execute special programs, called I/O or channel programs, that consist of primitive commands.

Open

TQ → Because computers and their peripherals are physically independent, their electronic signals must be carefully synchronized before they can begin communicating. Often, an initial electronic link is established by exchanging a set of prearranged protocol signals at **open** time. After a device is officially opened, the computer knows it exists and knows how to communicate with it.

TQ → Often, open involves more than simply establishing communication with a peripheral device. For example, a single disk can hold hundreds of programs and data files. For a given application, only one program and only one set of data will do. How does the system select the right program or the right data file?

#10 { The files stored on a disk are identified by name in the disk's directory (see Chapter 2). On a given system, the directory is always stored in the same place (for example, track 0, sector 2). Once initial contact with the disk drive has been established, the open logic can issue the primitive commands to read the directory (seek track 0, read sector 2). Once the directory is in memory, the open logic can search it for the file's name. Recorded along with the file name is the disk address where the file begins. Given the address of a file's first sector, the location of its other sectors can be computed.

Accessing Data

TQ { What steps are involved in physically accessing the data? What primitive functions are available to the disk control unit? Essentially, there are three:

T Q {
1. seek to a track,
2. read a sector, or
3. write a sector.

Primitive functions of disk control unit.

The concept of the "next" record is meaningless at this level. To find data physically on disk, you must specify a track and issue a seek command, and then specify a sector and issue a read command. The programmer is concerned with **logical I/O**. The device is limited to **physical I/O**. How can this gap be bridged?

The process starts when the application program issues a logical I/O request. The problem is converting this logical request into a series of primitive physical I/O operations. Often, the key is the relative record number.

A relative record number indicates a record's position relative to the beginning of a file. How does the system know where the file begins? One function of the open logic was reading the disk's directory, searching it for the file's name, and extracting the file's start address. In general, once a file has been opened, the location of any record on that file can be computed by using the appropriate relative record number.

Once again, imagine a program reading data sequentially. As the program begins, the file is opened. The disk address of its first record is now known. The file's first record is relative record 0; its second record is relative record 1, and so on. Accessing individual records involves little more than counting them. For example, imagine that relative record 5 has just been read. Clearly, the "next" record is relative record 6. Where is it physically located? Given the start of file address (from open), and knowing that the desired record is at "start of file plus 6," its disk address can be computed and the necessary primitive commands issued.

Now, picture a direct access application. A program needs data for student number 123456. In some way, that student number must be converted to a relative record number. One option is to use a randomizing algorithm. Another is to store a table of student numbers and their associated relative record numbers and do a table look-up. Once the student number has been converted to a relative record number, the process of computing a disk address, given the start of file address, is easy. Given the disk address, the necessary primitive commands can be issued.

Of course, few programmers communicate directly with peripheral devices at a primitive level. Generally, the responsibility for translating a programmer's logical I/O requests to physical commands is assigned to the operating system (Fig. 4.9). Because there are so many data access techniques available, some mainframe computers assign application-dependent portions of this translation process to special subroutines called **access methods** (Fig. 4.10), keeping only application-*independent* logic in the operating system. An access method is added to a program load module by the linkage editor (Fig. 4.11); thus, application-dependent I/O logic occupies main memory only when the application program occupies main memory. Another option is to assign responsibility for all data base access to a data base management system.

Once a record's physical location has been determined, the process of communicating with the peripheral device can begin. Typically, the access method identifies the necessary primitive commands, sets up a channel

Fig. 4.9   Often, responsibility for converting a programmer's logical I/O requests into primitive physical commands is assigned to the operating system.

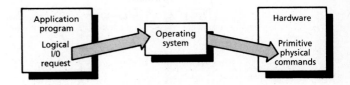

Fig. 4.10   On many mainframe computers, application-dependent portions of the logical-to-physical I/O conversion are handled by an access method.

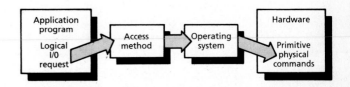

Fig. 4.11   Access methods are added to a program load module by the linkage editor.

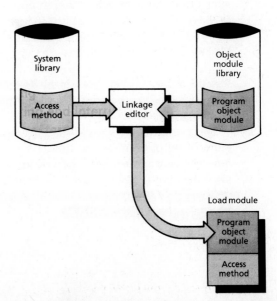

Fig. 4.12   This figure summarizes the process of converting a logical I/O
                     request to primitive physical commands.

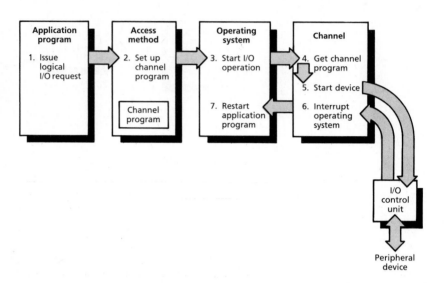

program, and calls the operating system. The operating system then sends a
"start I/O" signal to the channel, which accesses main memory, finds the
channel program, and transfers it to the I/O control unit. Once the data
have been transferred, the channel notifies the operating system through an
interrupt, and the program can resume processing. The elements involved
in this operation are summarized in Fig. 4.12.

Many students are surprised to learn that a task as apparently simple as
reading data from disk can be so complex. In fact, the complexity associated
with physical I/O is one of the major reasons why operating systems and
systems software came into being. Remember the basic function of an
operating system: to present the programmer with a relatively friendly
interface. Physical I/O is one of those rough spots in the hardware.

Access methods were among the first system programs, and input/
output control forms the core of most modern operating systems. We are,
however, getting ahead of ourselves. In the chapters that follow, we'll study
key operating system concepts in some detail. An operating system is a
resource manager—its job is to manage the hardware, software, and data
resources of a computer system. The intent of Chapters 2, 3, and 4 was to
provide you with a summary of these resources and a feel for how they fit
together.

Summary

#1 → A computer's internal components are linked by bus lines. On most computers, the internal components are designed around a common word size. The choice of a word size affects a computer's speed, memory capacity, precision, instruction set size, and cost. Sometimes, memory capacity and
TO → precision can be increased by sacrificing processing speed.

A microcomputer is constructed around a metal framework called a motherboard. Features are added by plugging memory boards and various interface boards into available slots; the number of slots limits the number of peripherals that can be added. Typically, each peripheral device requires its own interface board.

Mainframes often support multiple concurrent users. Rather than wasting the main processor's time controlling input and output, the responsibility for I/O is transferred to a channel, which communicates with the external device, handling a number of device-independent functions. Those tasks that depend on the external device are assigned to control units. Because a channel contains its own processor, it can work simultaneously with the main processor. When a channel completes an I/O operation, it notifies the main processor by sending it an electronic signal called an
#7 → interrupt. For a channel and a main processor to simultaneously access the same main memory, independent data paths are needed. Thus, most mainframes use multiple-bus architecture.

An I/O control unit executes primitive commands to physically control a peripheral device. These primitive commands are given to the control unit in the form of an I/O or channel program.

The first step in accessing a peripheral device is opening it. When a shared device such as disk is opened, the open logic establishes a data path, reads the disk's directory, searches for the file name, and extracts the file's disk address. Given the address of the file's first sector, the location of any data in the file can be computed from a relative record number. Few programmers actually deal with primitive I/O operations. Instead, they assign responsibility for translating logical I/O requests to physical form to the operation system, an access method, or a data base management system.

Key Words

access method	control unit	open
architecture	interface	physical I/O
bus	interrupt	primitive
channel	logical I/O	single-bus
channel program	machine cycle	architecture
command	multiple-bus	word
	architecture	

Exercises

1. How are a computer's internal components physically linked?

2. On most computers, all internal components are designed around a common word size. Why?

3. Explain how a computer's word size affects its processing speed, main memory capacity, precision, and instruction set size.

4. What is meant by a computer's architecture?

5. In describing a microcomputer's architecture, we used the terms motherboard, slot, and bus. Relate them.

6. On a typical microcomputer system, each input, output, and secondary storage device has its own interface. Why?

7. Distinguish between single-bus architecture and multiple-bus architecture.

8. On a mainframe computer, channels and control units are used instead of simple interfaces. Why? *To allow simultanious operation of CPU & I/o devices.*

9. What is a primitive operation? *Peripheral device commands*

10. Briefly explain what happens when a file is opened.

11. Distinguish between logical and physical I/O.

12. On small computers, responsibility for converting logical I/O requests to physical commands is assigned to the operating system, while on large mainframes, access methods are often used. Why?

PART

II

Basic Operating System Concepts

CHAPTER
5

Single-user Systems

KEY IDEAS

The single-user environment
Communicating with the user
  The command processor
  The command language
  Shells
Communicating with the hardware
  The input/output control system
  The file system
  Memory allocation
  Interrupts
The boot
Efficiencies
  Speed disparity
  Scheduling
  Other run-time savings
Utilities

The Single-user Environment

Most microcomputers are used by one person at a time. Resources include perhaps 256K of main memory, a keyboard, a display, a printer, and one or two diskette drives; a hard disk and a modem are popular options. Resource allocation conflicts are rare simply because there is only one user. Personal computers are inexpensive, so machine efficiency is only a minor concern. Thus, microcomputer operating systems generally stress ease of use.

Let's examine the ease-of-use criterion. Imagine a program that selects a number between 1 and 10 and gives the user three chances to guess it. The essential logic might involve ten or twelve instructions. At that level, however, the game would be so *unfriendly* that only the programmer could play it. To improve the program so that anyone can play, the programmer might add instructions to display explanations and directions, trap errors, and otherwise lead the user through the game. Those added instructions make the program both larger and more complex.

The program's size is the key concern. Microcomputers contain limited main memory. If the operating system is too large, there won't be enough memory left to hold a meaningful application program. Thus, the designers of microcomputer operating systems must balance ease of use with memory space. Keep this objective in mind as we examine the essential functions of a single-user operating system.

Communicating with the User

The Command Processor

Computers are not intelligent. Before the operating system can perform one of its functions, the person using the computer must tell it what to do. The user, much like a military officer, issues orders. The operating system responds like a sergeant, gathering the necessary resources, and carrying out each command. The operating system module that accepts, interprets, and carries out commands is the **command processor** (Fig. 5.1).

The command processor consists of a number of modules, each of which performs a single task (Fig. 5.2). For example, one module contains the instructions that guide the computer through the process of copying a program from disk and loading it into main memory. Another contains the instructions that transfer control of the computer to that program.

The Command Language

The programmer or user communicates with the command processor through a **command language**, generally typing simple, one-word commands, such as LOAD (load a program from disk), RUN (execute the program stored in main memory), FORMAT (format a disk), COPY (copy a

Fig. 5.1 The operating system module that accepts, interprets, and carries out commands is called the command processor.

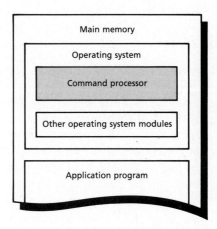

Fig. 5.2 The command processor is composed of a number of program modules, each of which performs a single, logical function.

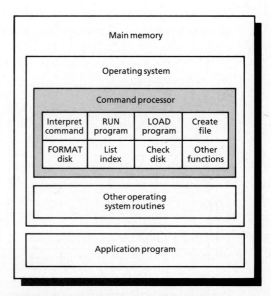

file), and so on. The command processor interprets each command and gives control to the appropriate functional module.

For example, consider the task of loading and executing a program. As the process begins, a prompt (for example, A>) is displayed on the screen. In response, the user types

LOAD MYPGM

and presses the enter key (Fig. 5.3a). The command flows into main memory, where the command processor evaluates it. Recognizing a *LOAD* command, the command processor transfers control to its program loading module (Fig. 5.3b), which reads the requested program from disk. Once the program is loaded, the command processor gets control again, displays another prompt, and waits for the next command (Fig. 5.3c).

The next command, we'll assume, is

RUN

It tells the operating system to execute the application program stored in main memory. Following a *RUN* command, the command processor gives

---

Fig. 5.3   The operating system is responsible for loading an application
                     program and giving it control.

a. Responding to the operating system's prompt, a user types a load command. The
        command processor then interprets the command.

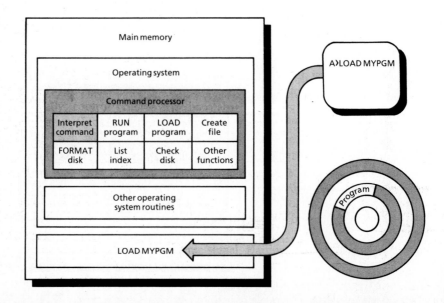

b. The command says to load a program. Thus, the command processor's program loading module gets control.

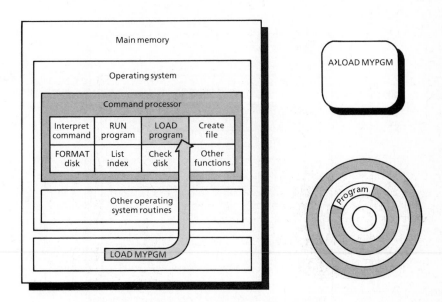

c. After the program is loaded, the command processor gets control, displays its prompt, and waits for the next command.

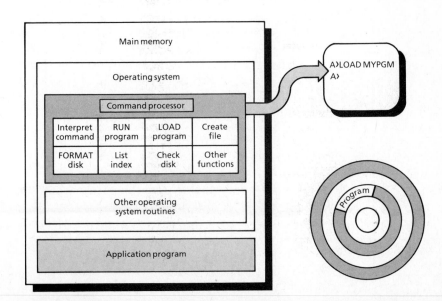

d. The next command tells the operating system to run the program in memory. Thus the command processor gives control to the module that starts the application program.

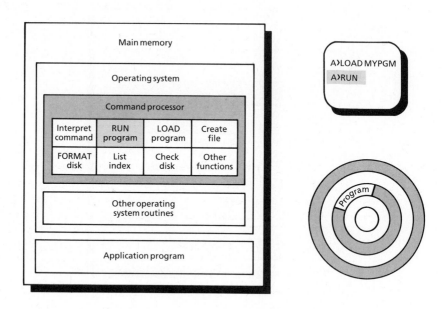

control to the module that starts the application program (Fig. 5.3d). When the application program is finished executing, it gives control back to the command processor, which displays a prompt and waits for the next command.

Many command languages include a batch feature. For example, imagine a payroll application in which input data are sorted and then processed by a payroll program. The commands to perform these functions might include:

SORT TIMEDATA
LOAD PAY
RUN
PRINT CHECKS

Payroll is run weekly; thus the same four commands must be typed once a week. An option is to create a **batch file** consisting of the four commands. Given such a file, the application can be run by typing a single command, such as

PAYROLL

The command processor will search the system disk for a batch file named *PAYROLL*, read the file, and then carry out the specified commands in order.

On most microcomputers, the command processor is the operating system's main control module, accepting commands, interpreting them, and determining which lower level modules are needed to carry them out. Those lower level modules communicate directly with the hardware. When they are done, they return control to the command processor, which displays a prompt and waits for the next command. Such systems are said to be **command driven**.

Shells

One way to visualize the command processor is as a **shell** surrounding the operating system (Fig. 5.4). Programmers and users communicate with the shell through commands. The shell, in turn, interprets the commands and uses various operating system functions to access the hardware.

Most microcomputer operating systems include a standard shell consisting of a command processor that interprets standard commands. Often, this standard shell is replaced or augmented by a custom shell. For example, while skilled programmers might be quite comfortable with cryptic commands, a nontechnical user might find them intimidating. A custom shell designed for nontechnical users might display available commands as visual images or icons (for example, an open file drawer for *SAVE*, or a wastebasket for *DELETE*), and allow the user to select a command by pointing to its image. Another common approach is to list commands in a menu.

Fig. 5.4 The command processor is sometimes called a shell. The shell insulates the user or programmer from the operating system modules that communicate directly with the hardware.

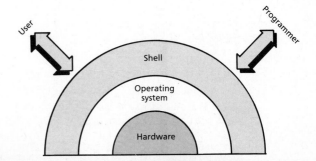

While a custom shell can make a computer easier to use, it occupies more main memory and consumes more processor time than a standard shell. For many users, however, the advantages are worth the cost. If you check a current list of the most popular commercial software packages you'll see a few custom shells in among the spreadsheets, word processors, and data base managers.

Communicating with the Hardware

The basic purpose of any operating system is to insulate users and programmers from the hardware. Simply put, there is a great deal of logic involved in communicating with hardware. Rather than forcing everyone to replicate this logic every time hardware access is necessary, it makes sense to write a single set of routines, place them in the operating system, and allow users and programmers to call them.

The Input/Output Control System

For example, consider the problem of accessing data on disk. A disk drive is limited to a few primitive operations, including:

1. Seek to a track.
2. Read a sector from that track.
3. Write a sector to that track.

The only way to read a program or a set of data from disk into main memory is to send the drive a series of **primitive commands** asking it to seek and read the contents of one or more sectors. Note that the disk drive must be told exactly where to position the read/write mechanism, and exactly which sectors to read.

Where do these commands come from? On a computer, the only sources of intelligence or logic are the human user and software. Imagine if you had to communicate at a primitive level. If your program needed data stored on track 20, sectors 8 and 9, you would have to tell the system to:

SEEK 20
READ 8
SEEK 20
READ 9

All you want, however, are the data; the primitive hardware details associated with accessing them are (or should be) the computer's concern. That's where the operating system comes into play. Most contain an **input/output control system**, or **IOCS** (Fig. 5.5), that generates the necessary primitive commands.

Fig. 5.5

#6

Most operating systems also contain an input/output control system. The IOCS is the module that communicates directly with the peripheral equipment.

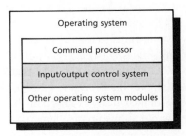

Our example was based on accessing disk. The input/output control system communicates with the computer's other peripherals, too. Each device is controlled by its own unique set of primitive commands. Application programs issue logical requests to start input or to start output. The input/output control system accepts these logical I/O requests and generates the primitive commands needed to control physically a peripheral device (Fig. 5.6).

Establishing communication with an external device involves more than just generating primitive commands, however. For example, whenever two hardware components (such as a computer and a disk drive) communicate with each other, their electronic signals must be carefully synchronized. Synchronization involves exchanging a predetermined set of signals called a **protocol**. Starting or checking protocol signals is a tedious process usually assigned to the operating system.

Other problems arise from the difference between logical and physical data structures. For example, imagine a program written to process a series of 56-byte logical records stored on disk. A disk is physically accessed one sector at a time, and a typical sector size is 512 bytes. Storing one 56-byte

Fig. 5.6

The application program passes logical I/O requests to the input/output control system, which interprets each request and generates the primitive commands needed to control the physical I/O operation.

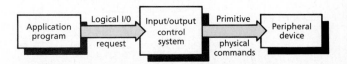

logical record in each 512-byte physical sector means wasting 456 bytes per sector. Clearly, wasting that much space is unacceptable.

The solution is **blocking** the data, storing several logical records in each sector (Fig. 5.7). A physical record is the unit of data transferred between an external device and main memory by a single physical I/O operation. A logical record is the unit of data referenced when a program issues a single logical read or write instruction. On output, the input/output control system collects logical records, builds a block or sector in main memory, and starts a physical output operation when a block is filled. On input, the IOCS reads a physical block or sector and, one by one, in response to read instructions, extracts logical records and makes them available to the application program.

Some applications involve lengthy records. For example, the academic history of a college senior might not fit in a single 512-byte sector (Fig. 5.8). In this case the logical record (a single student's grade history), is bigger than the physical record (a single sector). Thus, a single logical read calls for two or more physical input operations, while a single logical write means two or more physical writes. The input/output control system accepts logical I/O requests from an application program, performs whatever physical I/O operations are necessary to obtain the requested data, either selects or combines the physical data to form a logical record, and returns the logical record to the application program.

Not all operating systems work with records. Some view data on disk as simple strings of bytes. Instead of requesting logical records by relative record number, the application program requests a number of bytes starting with a relative *byte* address, and then superimposes on that string whatever data structure it wishes. The operating system's input/output control system accepts logical I/O requests and performs the physical I/O operations

Fig. 5.7   Better utilization of disk space can be achieved by blocking data, storing several logical records in a single sector (physical record).

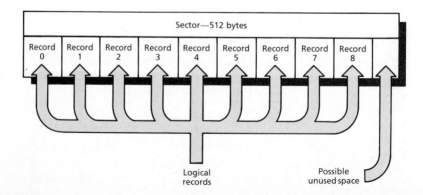

Fig. 5.8   Sometimes, a logical record can be bigger than a single physical sector.

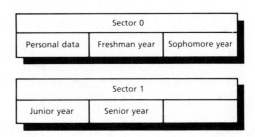

needed to carry them out, translating relative byte locations and lengths to specific track and sector addresses.

The File System

Given a file's start address, the location of any record or byte in the file can be computed by using its relative record or relative byte number. However, a disk can hold hundreds of different files and programs. How does the system know where a particular file begins? The location of every file stored on a disk can be found by searching the disk's directory (Fig. 5.9). This task is performed by the **file system**.

#8

A program is a special type of file. The process of loading one begins with a command, such as

LOAD SPACEWAR

The command processor interprets the command and transfers control to the program-loading module. That module, in turn, calls the file system, which reads the directory. Since a disk directory is always stored in the same sector or sectors (usually track 0, sector 1 or 2), the file system knows where to find it.

Once the directory is in main memory, the file system can search it. Each program is identified by name; note that *SPACEWAR* is the third entry. Following the program's name is its physical location (in other words, the track and sector holding its first instructions). Using this information, the file system can generate the seek and read commands needed to copy the program into memory.

When a program is first written to disk, its name and physical location are recorded in the directory. To retrieve the program, the directory is read and searched for the name, the program's physical location is extracted, and

Fig. 5.9　　　　The directory found on each disk is the key to accessing programs
and files by name. To load a program, the operating system reads
the directory, searches it by name, extracts the desired file's
location, and then issues the primitive commands to read it.

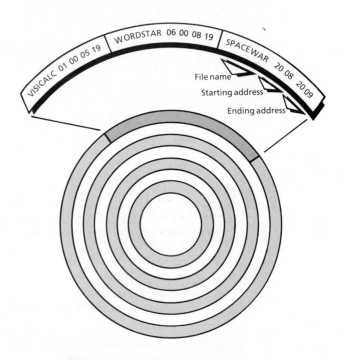

the necessary primitive commands are issued. The file system manages the
directory and generates primitive commands.

Programs are normally saved and loaded in response to operating system commands. Data files, on the other hand, are created and accessed by
programs. To create a new file or find an existing file, the programmer
codes an **open** instruction. When a file is opened, the file system gets
control, reads the directory, finds the directory entry for an old file or
creates a directory entry for a new file, and notes the file's start address for
subsequent use. Generally, when a program is finished with a file, the file is
closed. In response to a **close** instruction, the file system updates the
directory to indicate such information as the file's length and ending address. Programs are saved and loaded; files are opened and closed; records
are read and written.

The file system is also responsible for allocating space on disk. Ideally,
when a file is created, its data are stored in a series of consecutive sectors,
but because many different files share the same disk, this is not always
possible. For example, imagine a file created on Wednesday and updated on
Thursday. Wednesday's data might occupy consecutive sectors, but data

belonging to some other file might lie between Wednesday's data and Thursday's data. The file system bridges this gap.

Often, a table of sectors identified by relative sector number is maintained on disk (Fig. 5.10). When a file is created, the file system records the number of its first sector in the directory. When that first sector is filled, the disk allocation table is searched, and the next available sector is identified and allocated to the program. (In our example, available sectors are identified by a 0 table value.) Note that the next available sector may or may not be physically adjacent to the first one.

To link the sectors, the second sector's number is recorded in the first sector's table entry. Follow the chain of **pointers** in Fig. 5.10. The directory tells us that file A starts in sector 6. The table entry for sector 6 points to sector 7; sector 7's entry points to sector 9; and sector 9's table entry points to sector 12. Because sector 12's table entry holds a sentinel value, it marks the end of the file. Not all file systems use 0 to mark free sectors and -1 as a sentinel value, but this example gives you a sense of how disk allocation techniques work.

One potentially confusing point is the difference between the file system and the input/output control system. Generally, the IOCS is the module that communicates *directly* with peripheral devices at a primitive level.

#9 →

Fig. 5.10   Many operating systems use a table of sectors to allocate disk space. Sectors belonging to a particular file are linked by pointers. A zero table entry might indicate an unallocated sector. The table is itself stored on disk.

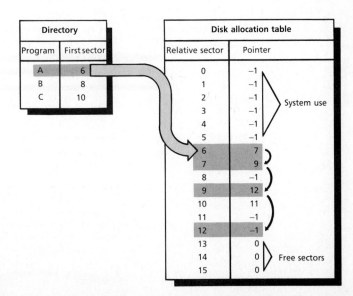

The file system, on the other hand, performs such logical functions as managing the directory and allocating disk space. The file system uses the IOCS to read and write the directory, the disk allocation table, and data sectors.

Memory Allocation

The operating system is a collection of software modules that, among other things, loads application programs and supports them as they run. Clearly, the operating system must itself occupy memory. Generally, the first few hundred bytes of memory are set aside to hold key operating system control information (Fig. 5.11). Next come the input/output control system and the file system, followed by the command processor. The remaining main memory is called the **transient area**; this is where application programs are loaded.

Some operating system modules, such as the ones that control physical I/O, directly support application programs as they run, and thus must be **resident**. Others, such as the module that formats disks, are used only occasionally, and thus can be **transient**. Transient modules reside on disk and are read into memory when needed. Given that main memory space is limited, keeping only essential logic resident is a good idea.

Loading application programs is not always as simple as it seems. The amount of space needed by a program can change as it runs. For example, some programs make use of **overlay** structures. The idea of overlays developed during the second generation, when the amount of available memory was quite limited. The problem, in a nutshell, was how to fit a 32K program onto a 16K machine. The solution was breaking the program into modules.

For example, imagine a program with four 8K modules (Fig. 5.12a). Module 1 holds the main control logic and key data common to the entire

Fig. 5.11   The various operating system modules occupy main memory. Generally, the control information starts in low memory (byte 0), while the transient area occupies high memory.

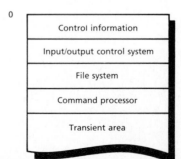

Fig. 5.12 • With overlay structures, only the necessary portions of a program are kept in main memory.

a. The complete program consists of four modules.

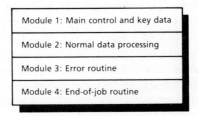

Module 1: Main control and key data

Module 2: Normal data processing

Module 3: Error routine

Module 4: End-of-job routine

b. Under normal conditions, only modules 1 and 2 are in memory.

Module 1

Module 2

ℬ 13

c. When errors are encountered, module 3 overlays module 2.

Module 1

Module 3

d. At end-of-job, only modules 1 and 4 are needed.

Module 1

Module 4

program. Module 2 processes valid input data. Occasionally, errors or un-usual data values call for the logic in module 3. Module 4 generates end-of-program statistics, and thus is needed only when the program terminates.

Clearly, module 1 must remain in memory at all times. If no errors are encountered, there is no need for module 3. If an error occurs, module 3's logic must be executed, but modules 2 and 4 are superfluous. Thus, as the program begins, modules 1 and 2 are in main memory (Fig. 5.12b). When an error is encountered, module 3 is read into memory, overlaying module 2 (Fig. 5.12c). It stays in memory until the next valid set of data is read; at that time module 2 replaces it. Finally, just before the program ends, module 4 overlays 2 or 3 (Fig. 5.12d) and generates its statistics.

Memory is not nearly so limited on modern microcomputers, but overlays are still used. Some programming languages support a chain function that allows new programs or subroutines to be loaded in response to program-generated requests, and many commercial programs use overlays for special features.

Because the amount of memory required by a program can change as it runs, the operating system maintains a table of unused space. When a program issues a chain or overlay request, it transfers control to the operating system, which scans its free memory list, determines if there is adequate space to hold the new module, allocates the space, and reads the module into memory (the process is just like loading a program). Finally, the operating system returns control to the application program.

Sometimes, the resident operating system is itself partially overlaid. When an application program is running, it needs the support of the input/output control system, the file system, and some of the command processor's functions, but has little or no use for other command processor features. Often, part of the command processor occupies high memory (Fig. 5.13). If extra space is needed, those functions can be overlaid. Of course, when the program finishes executing, the command processor must be read back into memory.

Fig. 5.13   Some operating systems store all or part of the command processor in high memory. If necessary, the transient area can be expanded to overlay these operating system modules.

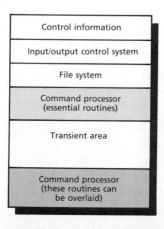

Interrupts

A computer's processor and main memory are synchronized by the processor's clock; thus, communication involves no special problems. A computer and its peripheral devices, on the other hand, are asynchronous. They function independently.

The computer, of course, is in charge and can always initiate communications with a peripheral. Before an external device can talk to the processor, however, it must get the processor's attention. On most computers, peripherals establish communication with the processor by sending an electronic signal called an **interrupt**. When hardware senses an interrupt, it saves the control information needed to resume processing the current program, and transfers control to an operating system module.

Interrupts can also be generated by software. The operating system contains support modules that are utilized by application programs. For a programmer to call a particular support module, he or she would have to know a great deal about the operating system's structure. As an option, most systems allow the programmer to store key control information in a register and issue an interrupt. As a result, the operating system's interrupt handler routine gets control, reads the register's contents, and transfers control to the module responsible for the requested service. Once the operating system is finished, control is returned to the application program.

On many computers, interrupts also allow the machine to sense, and thus react to, errors. When a hardware component fails, an interrupt transfers control to the operating system, which attempts to recover. If a program tries an illegal operation, such as a zero divide, the operating system might display an error message or generate a dump before terminating the program.

An interrupt is an electronic signal that is sensed by hardware, which responds by (1) saving the control information needed to resume the current program and (2) transferring control to the operating system. At this point, the interrupt itself ends. The operating system handles the interrupt. Eventually, assuming no unrecoverable errors, control is returned to the program that was executing at the time the interrupt occurred. We'll consider interrupts in more detail in subsequent chapters.

The Boot

Loading and executing a program starts with a command that the operating system reads and interprets. Clearly, the operating system must be in memory before the command is issued. How does it get there? On some systems, the operating system is stored in read-only memory. ROM is permanent; it keeps its contents even when the power is lost. A ROM-based operating system is always there.

However, on most computers, main memory is composed of RAM, or random access memory. RAM is volatile; it loses its contents when the power is cut. Thus, each time the computer is turned on, the operating system must be loaded. Unfortunately, we can't simply type a command, such as LOAD OS, and let the operating system take care of loading itself. Why not? When the computer is first turned on, main memory is empty. If the operating system is not yet in memory, it can't possibly read, interpret, and carry out commands.

Fig. 5.14   Loading the operating system.

a. When the computer is first turned on, hardware automatically reads the boot program from the first few sectors of a disk.

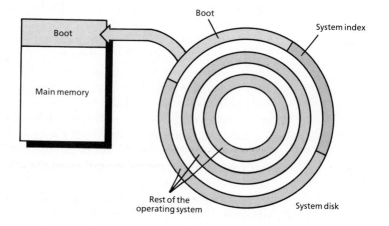

b. The boot routine contains the instructions that read the rest of the operating system from disk into memory.

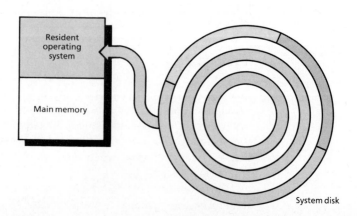

#15

TQ

Typically, the operating system is stored on disk. The idea is to copy it into memory. This objective is achieved by a special program called a **boot** (Fig. 5.14). Generally, the boot is stored on the first sector (or two) of a disk. Hardware is designed to read this sector automatically whenever the power is turned on (Fig. 5.14a). The boot consists of only a few instructions, but they are sufficient to read the rest of the operating system into memory (Fig. 5.14b); note how it is seemingly "pulled in by its own bootstraps." Now, a user can type the commands to load and execute an application program.

Efficiencies

In addition to serving as an interface between hardware and software, an operating system also manages the computer's resources, ensuring that they are used efficiently. While efficiency is less crucial on a microcomputer than on an expensive mainframe, there are a few **resource management** techniques that are common to single-user systems.

Speed Disparity

The fact that a computer is running an application program does not necessarily mean it is being used efficiently. For one thing, there is a tremendous **speed disparity** between the computer and its peripheral devices.

This concept is best illustrated by an example. Imagine a program that reads a sector from disk, executes 100 instructions, and then writes a sector to disk (Fig. 5.15). Our computer is capable of executing 1 million instructions per second, so those 100 instructions occupy only 0.0001 seconds of the processor's time. A high-speed disk can seek and access a single sector in a few milliseconds; let's use 0.0010 seconds for the read and write operations. Total program cycle time is 0.0021 seconds, of which 0.0020

Fig. 5.15   The speed disparity between a computer and its peripheral devices has a significant impact on system efficiency.

Read 1 sector	0.0010 sec
Execute 100 instructions	0.0001 sec
Write 1 sector	0.0010 sec
Total cycle time	0.0021 sec

Wait time: $\dfrac{0.0020}{0.0021} = 0.9524$, or 95.24%

seconds (over 95 percent of the total) are spent waiting for I/O. Any technique that reduces the number of physical input and output operations will significantly improve system efficiency.

One approach is to use **multiple buffers**. For example, imagine that each sector assigned to a program holds ten logical records. Set up two buffers, each large enough to hold one sector. As the program begins, both buffers are filled and the first logical record is made available to the application program (Fig. 5.16). The program processes the first logical record and requests a second one. Again, the record is made available to the application program; note that no physical I/O is needed.

The program continues processing data from the first buffer (Fig. 5.17). Eventually, the buffer is exhausted. Thus, the operating system turns to buffer number two and concurrently issues a physical read. While the external device is doing its (relatively) slow thing, the computer is processing data from the second buffer, thus significantly reducing wasted time. When buffer two is exhausted, data from the by now full first buffer are processed while the second buffer is replenished.

Scheduling

Microcomputer users tend to focus on a single application, such as word processing, spreadsheets, or program development. However, many small business systems execute a variety of programs, computing payroll, then updating inventory, then generating accounting reports, and so on. On such computers, job-to-job transition can be a problem.

Before any program can be run, disks must be selected, the printer loaded with the proper forms, and other **setup** tasks completed. This takes time. One consequence of wasted time might be paying the operator overtime; another is poor utilization of a piece of relatively expensive capital equipment, the computer. A partial solution is **scheduling**.

For example, consider four programs with varying printer paper requirements (Fig. 5.18). Running these jobs in the given sequence means

Fig. 5.16   If more than one buffer is used, data in one can be processed while the other buffer is being replenished.

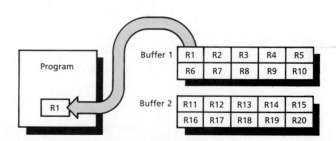

Fig. 5.17 This flowchart illustrates the essential logic of multiple buffering.

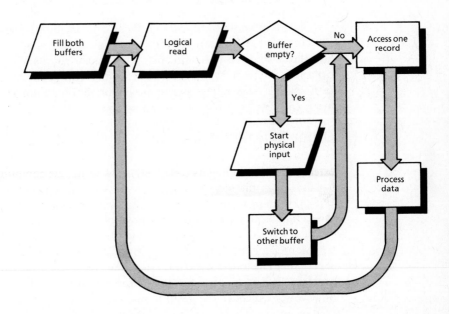

Fig. 5.18 Scheduling jobs to take advantage of common setups can save time.

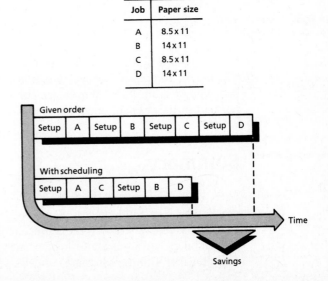

Job	Paper size
A	8.5 x 11
B	14 x 11
C	8.5 x 11
D	14 x 11

changing the paper four times. If programs with similar requirements are grouped, however, the same work can be done with only a single forms change, yielding a significant reduction both in total setup time and total elapsed time.

Not all program combinations are so obvious, but the idea of grouping similar tasks to take advantage of common setups is a good one. Scheduling also allows an operator to anticipate a program's requirements, for example, collecting program B's resources as program A runs. As we'll discover in the next chapter, scheduling is far more important on a multiple-user system, but it can help on single-user systems, too.

Other Run-time Savings

Setup is not the only source of wasted time on a computer. Consider, for example, compilation. Once a program is debugged, compilation, the conversion from programmer language to machine language, simply produces the same output over and over again. A better choice is storing the object module on disk, and then loading and executing it.

Many programs process a great deal of data, and thus run for quite some time. The longer a program runs, the greater the risk that an electrical problem, data error, or some other failure will interrupt the run. Often, the only way to recover the results is to rerun the program, and that's an obvious waste of computer and user time. Checkpoints can minimize this problem.

The basic idea is to dump a program's intermediate results to secondary storage at regular intervals—perhaps every ten minutes. Often, the entire program is dumped. Should an error occur, the program is restarted at the last checkpoint. With a checkpoint every ten minutes, at most ten minutes of work will be lost.

Utilities

Most operating systems incorporate a set of **utility** routines. Included are assemblers, compilers, linkage editors, loaders, line editors, sort routines, debugging features, library management routines, and many more. While not part of the resident operating system, they are invaluable.

Summary

Users communicate with an operating system through a command language. The command processor accepts, interprets, and carries out the commands. One way to view the command processor is as a shell separating programmers and users from those portions of the operating system that communicate with the hardware. Sometimes, custom shells are substituted

TΦ

for the standard shell. Most microcomputer operating systems are command driven.

Communicating with input and output devices is difficult because each is controlled by its own primitive commands. The input/output control system (IOCS) accepts logical I/O requests, performs necessary physical I/O operations, and either extracts or builds the requested logical records. Sometimes, this involves blocking and deblocking. Sometimes, a logical record is larger than a single physical record.

Files and programs are accessed by name through the file system. Each file is recorded in a disk directory. The file system reads the directory, searches it by file name, and extracts the file's start address. Programs are loaded or saved in response to commands. Data files are opened and closed in response to program instructions. The input/output control system communicates with the physical devices; the file system manages the directory and allocates disk space.

TΦ

The resident portion of the operating system normally occupies low memory. Following the resident operating system is a transient area where application programs and operating system transients are loaded. Because the amount of memory used by a program can vary as the program runs, the operating system must keep track of available memory. We briefly covered overlay structures and explained how portions of the operating system can be overlaid.

TΦ

An interrupt is an electronic signal that causes the computer to stop the current program, save its control information, and transfer control to the operating system. After the interrupt is handled, the program that was executing when the interrupt occurred resumes processing.

Because a computer's main memory is volatile, the operating system must be loaded each time the computer is turned on. The routine that loads the operating system is called a boot.

Multiple buffering helps to adjust for the speed disparity between a computer and its peripherals. Scheduling can help to reduce time lost to setup operations. Checkpoints can help minimize the amount of processing lost when a program fails. In addition to its resident modules, most operating systems include several utility routines.

Key Words

batch file	input/output	protocol
blocking	control system	resident
boot	interrupt	resource
checkpoint	IOCS	management
close	logical I/O	scheduling
command driven	multiple buffering	setup
command language	open	shell
command	overlay	speed disparity
processor	physical I/O	transient
file system	pointer	transient area
	primitive	utility
	command	

Exercises

1. Briefly describe the single-user environment. Why is it important to understand an operating system's environment before studying its features?

2. Because a microcomputer's main memory is limited, microcomputer operating systems contain only essential features. Three common modules are a command processor, an input/output control system, and a file system. Briefly explain why each of these modules is *essential* to a typical microcomputer user.

3. What is a command language? What is a batch command file?

4. Many microcomputer operating systems are command driven. What does this mean?

5. A command processor is sometimes called a shell. Why? Distinguish between a standard shell and a custom shell.

6. What functions are performed by the input/output control system?

7. Distinguish between logical I/O and physical I/O. Distinguish between a physical record and a logical record.

8. What functions are performed by the file system?

9. Briefly distinguish between the input/output control system and the file system.

10. What happens when a file is opened? What happens when a file is closed?

11. Sketch the main memory layout of a typical microcomputer operating system.

12. Distinguish between resident and transient modules.

13. Briefly explain overlay structures.

14. What is an interrupt? Why are interrupts important?

15. What is a boot? Why is a boot needed?

16. Briefly describe the speed disparity between a computer and its peripheral devices. Why is this speed disparity important?

17. Briefly explain multiple buffering.

18. What is a utility?

CHAPTER
6

Multiple-user Systems

The Multiple-user Environment

Microcomputers are inexpensive, so efficiency is generally not a major concern. Mainframes, on the other hand, are quite expensive, and their potential computing power should not be wasted. Thus, efficient resource utilization is crucial on a mainframe.

Given the speed disparity between a computer and its peripherals, input and output operations significantly affect efficiency. For example, picture a computer with a single program in memory. The program cannot process data it doesn't yet have, and success cannot be assumed until an output operation is finished, so the program waits for input or output. Since the program controls the computer, the computer waits, too. Typically, computers spend far more time waiting for input and output than processing data, and that's inefficient.

Why not put two programs in memory? Then, when program A is waiting for data, the processor can turn its attention to program B (Fig. 6.1). And why stop at two programs? With three, even more otherwise wasted time is utilized (Fig. 6.2). Generally, the more programs in memory, the greater the utilization of the processor.

Note that, although several different programs are in memory, only one is active at a time. The processor fetches and executes a single instruction during each machine cycle. If the processor can execute only one *instruction* at a time, it cannot possibly work on more than one *program* at a time. Simultaneous means "at the same instant." No processor can execute two or more programs simultaneously. Concurrent means "over the same time period." A processor can certainly execute two or more programs concurrently.

The advantage of concurrently executing multiple programs is obvious: more work can be done in the same time on the same computer. However,

Fig. 6.1   With two programs in main memory, the processor can switch its attention to program B when program A is waiting for input or output.

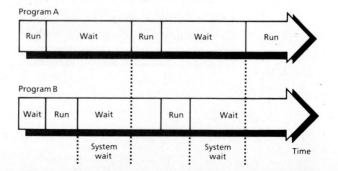

Fig. 6.2 With programs in main memory, even more wait time can be utilized.

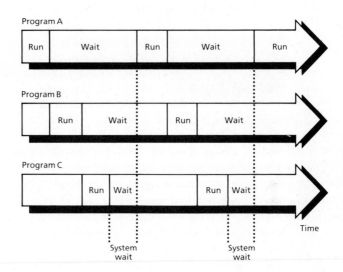

while a mainframe's resources are substantial, they are limited and, with two or more concurrent users, conflicts over processor time, memory space, and peripheral device allocation are inevitable. When these conflicts occur, they must be resolved. Since human operators cannot function at computer speeds, key decisions must be made by the computer itself. Because the operating system serves as a hardware/software interface, it's an ideal place to implement resource management.

Multiprogramming

The two most popular approaches to resource management are **multiprogramming** and time-sharing. Let's consider multiprogramming first. Originally developed to support batch processing applications (such as payroll, accounts payable, accounts receivable, and general ledger), multiprogramming operating systems take advantage of the fact that such programs are generally I/O bound. The key measures of effectiveness are **throughput** (run time divided by elapsed time) and **turnaround** (the time between job submission and job completion).

We covered single-user operating systems in Chapter 5. The essential components included a command processor, an input/output control system, a file system, and a transient area. On a multiprogramming system, the transient area is subdivided to hold several independent programs. However, users, programmers, and operators must still communicate with the operating system and programs must still access peripheral devices and files, so the basic functions are still needed. A multiprogramming operating system builds on this base, with resource management added to the operating system modules you've already studied.

Memory Management

If memory is to hold multiple programs, memory space must be managed. The simplest approach, **fixed-partition memory management** (Fig. 6.3), divides the available space into fixed-length **partitions** each of which can hold one program. Partition sizes are generally set when the system is booted. Note that the memory allocation decision is made before the fact, in other words, before the actual amount of space needed by a given program is known. Imagine a 32K program. If the partition size is 256K, fully 224K will be wasted when that program runs. Fixed-partition memory management wastes space. Its major advantage is simplicity.

Under **dynamic memory management**, the transient area is treated as a pool of unstructured free space (Fig. 6.4). When the system decides to load a particular program, a **region** of memory just sufficient to hold it is allocated from the pool. Because a program gets only the space it needs, relatively little is wasted.

Dynamic memory management does not, however, completely solve the wasted space problem. Assume, for example, that a 120K program has just finished executing (Fig. 6.5). If there are no 120K programs available, the system might load a 60K program and a 50K program. Note that 10K remains unallocated. If there are no 10K or smaller programs available, the space will simply not be used. Over time, little chunks of unused space will be spread throughout memory—**fragmentation**.

Most load modules are addressed relative to their first byte, with, for example, an access method being "so many" bytes away from the load module's entry point. Thus, although the load module can be placed anywhere in memory, it must occupy contiguous space. Taken together, the

Fig. 6.3   Under fixed partition memory management, the available main memory space is divided into a series of fixed-length partitions.

| Operating system |
| Partition A |
| Partition B |
| Partition C |
| Partition D |

Fig. 6.4 Under dynamic memory management, the transient area is treated as a pool of unstructured free space.

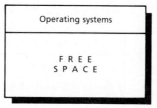

unused fragments of memory might represent enough space to hold a complete program, but because they are noncontiguous, they cannot be used.

There is no law that requires load modules to be contiguous. An alternative is to break a program into logical **segments**, assigning addresses relative to segment entry points, and loading the segments into *non*contiguous memory (Fig. 6.6). Programmers tend to segment their programs anyway, with key functions viewed as separate problems to be independently solved and then linked, so segmentation makes logical sense.

Another approach is to divide programs into fixed-length **pages**, addressing memory relative to the start of a page, and loading pages into noncontiguous memory. The basic difference between segmentation and paging is that segments follow the logic of the program, while the fixed page size is selected to optimize memory allocation.

TQ

Fig. 6.5 Over time, dynamic memory management leaves small fragments of unused space spread throughout memory.

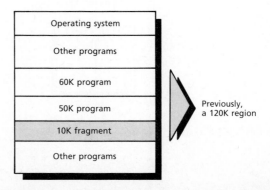

Fig. 6.6   Under segmentation, a program is broken into several segments.
                     Because the instructions and data within a segment are addressed
                     relative to the *segment's* beginning address, a program's segments
                     can be loaded into noncontiguous memory.

Operating system
Other programs
Program A, segment 1—10K
Other programs
Program A, segment 2—20K
Other programs

You know a processor can execute only one instruction at a time. Why,
then, must an entire program be in memory before processing can begin?
Under **virtual memory**, programs are divided into pages or segments and
stored on disk, and only essential modules are read into main memory.

Consider, for example, the computer system sketched in Fig. 6.7a.
Main memory (called *real* memory) is large enough to hold four pages.
Three programs are stored on virtual memory (disk). As we begin, the first

Fig. 6.7   Under virtual memory, only necessary portions of a program are
                     stored in real memory.

a. As we begin, the first page, A-0, is read from virtual into real memory.

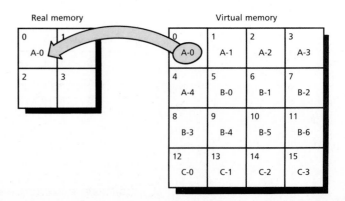

b. Eventually, as additional pages are read, real memory is filled.

Real memory

0	1
A-0	B-0
2	3
C-0	A-1

Virtual memory

0	1	2	3
A-0	A-1	A-2	A-3
4	5	6	7
A-4	B-0	B-1	B-2
8	9	10	11
B-3	B-4	B-5	B-6
12	13	14	15
C-0	C-1	C-2	C-3

c. To make room in real memory, an inactive page is copied back to virtual.

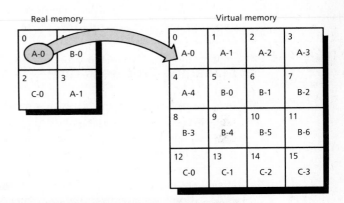

d. A new page is then read into real memory.

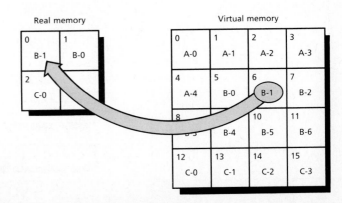

page in program A (page A-0) is copied into real memory and starts to execute. Soon it requests an I/O operation and drops into a wait state; thus the first page in program B (page B-0) is loaded.

Eventually memory comes to resemble Fig. 6.7b, with all real pages filled. Assume program A has just requested input. Program B is next in line, but its next instructions are on page B-1, which is not yet in real memory. The processor cannot execute instructions residing on virtual memory. Thus, page B-1 must be copied into real memory.

Program A has moved on to its second page, and no longer needs page A-0. Thus the operating system sends page A-0 back to virtual memory (Fig. 6.7c), and copies page B-1 into the vacated real page (Fig. 6.7d). Now, the instructions on page B-1 can be executed. By swapping pages between virtual and real memory, numerous concurrent programs can be executed in a limited amount of real-memory space.

Simply allocating space is not enough, however. When multiple programs share main memory, they must be protected from each other. Generally, the operating system keeps track of the space assigned to each program. If a program attempts to modify (or sometimes even to read) the contents of memory locations that don't belong to it, hardware generates an interrupt and gives control to the operating system, which (usually) terminates the program.

Key field in pscw

Managing Processor Time

Imagine several programs occupying memory. Some time ago, program A requested data from disk (Fig. 6.8). The input operation was assigned to a channel, and the processor turned to program B. Assume the input operation has just been completed. Both programs are ready to run. Which one gets the processor? Computers are so fast that a human operator cannot effectively make such real-time choices. Instead, the processor's time is managed by an operating system module called the **dispatcher.**

TQ →

#6

Fig. 6.8   With multiple concurrent users, it is possible that two or more programs will be ready to execute at the same time. When this happens, an operating system module must resolve the conflict, deciding which program goes first.

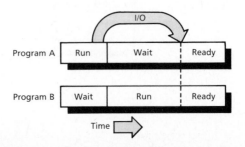

Fig. 6.9   Often, the dispatcher looks for a ready program by checking partitions in fixed priority order. For example, with two partitions, the program in the foreground is always checked before the program in the background.

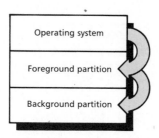

The dispatcher uses an algorithm to select the next program. For example, consider a system with two fixed-length partitions known as the **foreground** and the **background** (Fig. 6.9). The dispatcher checks the program in the foreground partition first; if it's ready, it gets control. Only if the foreground program is still waiting does the dispatcher check the background partition. The foreground has high priority; the background, low priority.

This idea can be extended to larger systems, with the dispatcher checking partitions in a fixed order until a ready program is found. The first partition checked has highest priority; the last, lowest priority. The only way the low-priority program can get control is if all the higher priority partitions are waiting.

There are a number of control fields that must be maintained in support of each active program. Often, a **control block** is created to hold each partition's flags, constants, and variables (Fig. 6.10). These control blocks might be linked by pointers or stored in a table. The dispatcher determines which program is to be given control by following a chain of pointers from control block to control block, or by moving through the table entries from top to bottom.

It is also possible to implement more complex priority schemes. For example, a program's priority can be set by a job control or command language statement, or computed dynamically, perhaps taking into account such factors as program size, time in memory, I/O device requirements, and other measures of the program's impact on system resources. The dispatcher can then search control blocks in priority order.

Interrupts

How does the operating system know when to switch from one program to another? The key is I/O. A program loses control of the processor when it starts an input or output operation and is eligible to regain control when

Fig. 6.10   A control block is created to hold key control information for
                    each partition. Often these control blocks are stored in a table or
                    linked by pointers. The dispatcher looks for a ready program by
                    following the pointers from control block to control block.
                    Clearly, the first control block on the chain has highest priority.

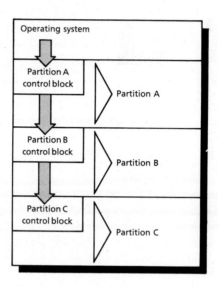

that operation is completed. If the operating system is to decide which
program goes next, it must know when input or output operations begin
and end. **Interrupts** mark these events.

Follow the steps in Fig. 6.11. When an application program needs data,
it issues an interrupt (Fig. 6.11a). In response, hardware transfers control
to the operating system's **interrupt handler** routine. Once it gets control,
the interrupt handler drops the application program into a wait state (Fig.
6.11b) and calls the input/output control system to start the I/O operation.
Finally, control goes to the dispatcher, which starts another application
program (Fig. 6.11c).

Later, when the I/O operation is finished, the channel issues an interrupt (Fig. 6.11d). Once again the interrupt handler gets control (Fig. 6.11e)
and resets the program needing data to a ready state. Then it transfers
control to the dispatcher, which starts an application program (Fig. 6.11f).
Note how interrupts mark the beginning and end of each I/O operation, and
thus alert the operating system that control can be transferred to another
program.

An interrupt is an electronic signal. Hardware senses the signal, saves
key control information for the currently executing program, and transfers
control to the operating system. The operating system handles the inter-

Fig. 6.11   The key to managing the processor's time is recognizing when
                 input and output operations begin and end. Generally, these
                 crucial events are signaled by interrupts.

a. The program requests the operating system's support by issuing an interrupt.

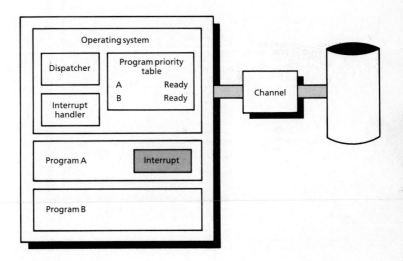

b. Following the interrupt, the interrupt handler routine gets control and sets the
program to a wait state.

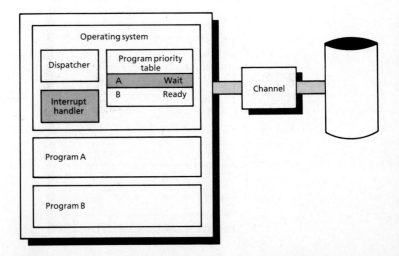

c. After the interrupt handler starts the requested input or output operation, the dispatcher gives control to another application program.

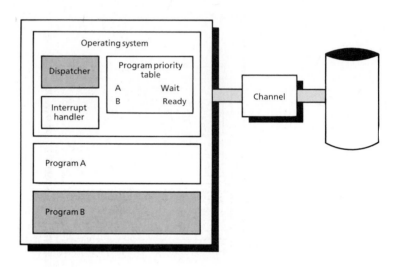

d. Eventually, the channel signals the end of the I/O operation by sending the computer an interrupt.

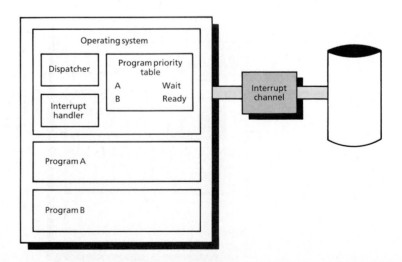

e. Following the interrupt, the interrupt handler gets control and resets program A to a ready state.

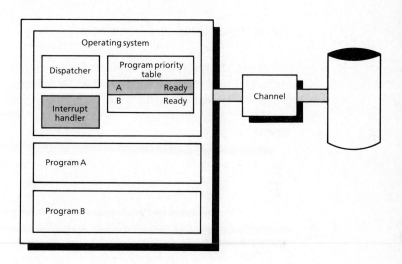

f. Finally, the dispatcher selects an application program and gives it control of the processor.

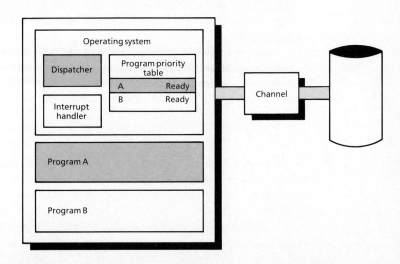

rupt. The dispatcher then starts an application program. Eventually, the program that was executing at the time of the interrupt resumes processing. Note that the interrupt is merely a signal. Distinguish between the interrupt itself and the logic that handles it.

Peripheral Device Allocation

What would happen if two programs were to take turns writing to the same printer? The output would be useless. Or imagine two programs sending primitive commands to the same tape drive. Quite possibly, neither one would get the right data. Access to peripheral devices must be carefully managed.

One possible consequence of poor resource management is **deadlock**. Imagine a computer with one tape drive and one printer. Program A controls the drive, while B has the printer. After running for a time, A requests the printer, but it's in use. Next, B gets control and requests the tape drive, but it's in use. Two programs each control a resource needed by the other. Neither can continue until the other gives in, but neither is willing to give in. That's deadlock.

One solution is prevention; some operating systems will not concurrently load a program unless all its resource needs (including peripheral devices and main memory space) can be guaranteed. More sophisticated operating systems allow some deadlocks to occur, sense them, and take corrective action.

Scheduling and Queuing

Processor management is concerned with the internal priorities of programs already in main memory. As a program finishes processing and space becomes available, which program is loaded into memory next? This decision typically involves two separate modules, a **queuing** routine and a **scheduler**.

As programs enter the system, they are placed on a queue by the queuing routine (Fig. 6.12). When space becomes available, the scheduler selects a program from the queue and loads it into main memory (Fig. 6.13). Generally, the first program on the queue is loaded first, but more sophisticated priority rules can be used.

Sometimes, more than one queue is maintained. Often, a program is placed on a particular queue based on its resource needs; for example, programs requiring magnetic tape or special printer forms can be separated from those calling for more normal setup. By grouping programs with similar resource needs, they can be scheduled to take advantage of common setups.

Clearly distinguish between a program's internal and external priorities. Once a program is in main memory, the dispatcher uses its internal priority to determine its right to access the processor. An external priority

Fig. 6.12   When a program first enters a multiprogramming system, a queuing routine copies it to a queue on secondary storage.

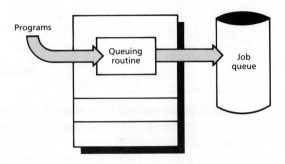

#11

has to do with getting the program into memory in the first place. Until the program is in memory, it has no internal priority. Once in memory, its external priority is no longer relevant.

Spooling

The value of multiprogramming is that more programs can be run in the same amount of time. If the turnover rate of those programs can be increased, even greater efficiencies can be realized. For example, imagine a system with five concurrent programs. Assume each one occupies memory for ten seconds. As soon as a program finishes executing, another one replaces it; thus, the computer can run thirty programs a minute. If each program's run time could be reduced to five seconds, sixty programs could run in that same minute.

Fig. 6.13   Later, when space becomes available, the scheduling routine loads a program from the queue into main memory.

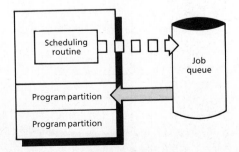

Picture a program that generates payroll for 1000 employees. Reading 1000 time cards takes at least two minutes. Printing 1000 checks takes a few minutes more, so the program will need at least four or five minutes to run. But what if the slow card reader and printer were replaced by a disk? A disk drive is much faster, so the program would run in much less time. Consequently, memory would be freed for another program much more quickly.

That's the essential idea behind **spooling**. Even with multiprogramming, it's common for all application programs to be waiting for I/O. When this happens, the processor has nothing to do. During these idle periods, the operating system's spooling module reads data from such slow devices as card readers or terminal keyboards and stores them on a high-speed medium such as disk, even before the program needing those data has been loaded into memory. Later, when the program is loaded, its input data can be read from disk. On output, data are spooled to disk and later dumped to the printer. Because the application program deals only with high-speed I/O, it finishes processing much more quickly, thus freeing space for another program.

A Multiprogramming Operating System

A multiprogramming operating system begins with the same basic functions as a single-user operating system (Fig. 6.14). Generally, several tables and control blocks occupy low memory, followed by an input/output control system, a file system, and a command processor. Next comes logic to

Fig. 6.14   A typical multiprogramming operating system contains modules to perform all the functions shown in this diagram.

System control tables and other control information		
Input/output control system	File system	Command processor
Memory manager	Memory protection	Dispatcher
Interrupt handler	Device allocation routine	Deadlock manager
Queuing routine	Scheduler	Spooler
Transient area—application programs		

manage the system's resources, including memory management and memory protection routines, a dispatcher, an interrupt handler, device allocation modules, logic to deal with or prevent deadlocks, a queuing routine, a scheduler, and a spooler. Keep this overview of the operating system in mind when we study the components in more detail in Part IV.

Time-Sharing

Time-sharing systems are different. Users enter brief transactions through slow keyboard terminals. Applications tend to be interactive. Programs are usually small and process relatively little data. Perhaps the most important measure of effectiveness is **response time**, the elapsed time between entering a transaction and seeing the first character of the system's response appear on the screen.

Roll-in/Roll-out

Picture a typical time-sharing application. Transactions (a single program statement, a line of input data, or a command) are typed through a keyboard. In most cases, very little actual processing is required. Typing is slow; two transactions per minute is the best most people can do. To the computer, each user represents a string of brief, widely spaced processing demands.

   As a transaction is processed, the system knows that considerable time will pass before that user's next transaction arrives; thus the work space can be rolled out to secondary storage, making room for another application in main memory (Fig. 6.15a). Later, when the first user's next transaction arrives, his or her work space is rolled back in (Fig. 6.15b). On most time-sharing systems, such **roll-in** and **roll-out** techniques are used to manage main memory space.

Fig. 6.15   Many time-sharing systems rely on roll-in and roll-out techniques to manage main memory space.

a. When the system finishes processing a transaction, the user's work space is rolled out to disk.

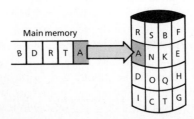

b. Later, when the user's next transaction enters the system, the work space is rolled back in.

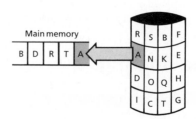

Time-slicing

Imagine you have just spent twenty minutes typing the data for a statistical analysis program. Each data element was one brief transaction; your work to this point certainly fits the assumptions of a typical time-sharing application. Your last transaction, however, is different. It's a command telling the system to process the data. It causes the computer to begin a computational routine that can easily run for two or three minutes. While your transaction is processed, every one of the other users on the system will have to wait, and, given the system's need to maintain good response time, that's intolerable.

The solution is **time-slicing**. Each program is restricted to a maximum "slice" of time, perhaps 0.1 second. Once a program gets control, it runs until one of two things happen. If the program requires input or output before exhausting its time slice, it calls the operating system and "voluntarily" drops into a wait state, just like a multiprogramming application. If, however, the program uses up its entire time slice, a timer interrupt transfers control to the operating system, which selects the next program.

If more than one program is ready to resume processing, which one gets control? Often, a **polling** algorithm supplies the answer. Imagine a table of program control blocks (Fig. 6.16). Starting at the top, the operating system's dispatcher checks the first program's status. If it's ready, it gets control. If not, the dispatcher moves on to the second control block.

Assume this second program is ready. It gets control, but, in no more than a single time slice, the dispatcher will have to select another program. The last program to have control was number two. Thus, the search begins with the third table entry; note that program two is now at the end of the line. Eventually, the dispatcher works its way through the entire table. At this point, it returns to the top and repeats the process. Program two will get another shot only after every other program has a chance.

There are alternatives to simple round-robin polling. Two (or even more) tables can be maintained, with high-priority programs on the first one and background or low-priority routines on the second. Another option is to place multiple references to critical programs on the table, thus giving them several chances to claim the processor on each polling cycle.

Fig. 6.16   A time-sharing dispatcher selects the next program by polling all programs in memory.

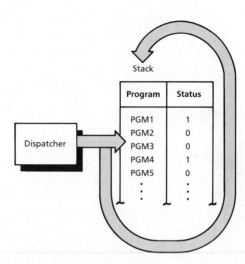

Some systems use a variation of multiprogramming's priority search rule, recomputing priorities every second or two. A common priority algorithm is to divide actual run time by elapsed memory residency time; the limit of this computation is 1, and that's considered low priority. The more processor time a program uses, the worse its priority becomes; thus, compute-bound tasks tend to drop to the end of the line.

Time-sharing and Interrupts

Do time-sharing systems handle interrupts? Certainly. External devices still communicate with the processor, programs still need the operating system's support, and program and hardware failures still occur. An interrupt represents a transition point—an opportunity to transfer control to another program. On a multiprogramming system, the dispatcher follows a priority algorithm after any interrupt, no matter what program had control when the interrupt occurred. On a time-sharing system, the program that was processing at the time of the interrupt normally resumes processing until it either issues its own interrupt or exceeds its time limit.

Allocating External Devices

External device allocations can be quite dynamic on a multiprogramming system, with a given program asking for almost any imaginable combination. Consequently, a multiprogramming operating system must contain considerable logic to prevent or deal with device allocation conflicts.

Most time-sharing systems rely on defaults to minimize this exposure. Each user has a keyboard and a screen that serve as standard input and output devices, a work space that is rolled in and rolled out between disk and main memory, and a certain amount of disk space to hold programs and files. Spooling is often used for printed output. Generally, peripheral device requests beyond these default limits must be approved by the system manager before they are needed. Defaults simplify both application programming and the operating system's device allocation and deadlock routines, but they also limit the programmer's flexibility.

External Priority

A programmer who decides to work on a time-sharing system either walks to the computer center or dials the computer's telephone number. If no terminal is available or the line is busy, programming is postponed. On a time-sharing system, equipment availability determines external priority. A high-priority user can be assigned a personal terminal, and to ensure quick response, this terminal can be polled several times in each polling cycle. Otherwise, scheduling and external priorities are not factors on time-sharing systems. Scheduling is a batch concept.

Driving an Operating System

An operating system is a large program consisting of numerous functional routines. An excellent way to visualize an operating system is to start with its main control module. To identify the main control module, imagine a time when no application programs are active. What must happen before the next program gets control? On single-user systems, a command must be issued; thus, they are command driven. On multiprogramming systems, an interrupt must be processed; most are interrupt driven. Time-sharing systems use a polling algorithm to select the next program; they are generally poll driven.

Summary

Because a mainframe computer is much faster than its peripheral devices, it generally spends more time waiting for I/O than processing data. One solution is to load two or more programs into main memory and allow the processor to execute them concurrently. With multiple programs competing for the computer's limited resources, conflicts are inevitable. Most are resolved by the operating system.

Multiprogramming operating systems were initially developed for large batch applications. Important measures of effectiveness include throughput and turnaround.

The simplest form of memory management divides main memory into fixed-length partitions and loads one program in each one. Greater efficiency can be achieved by using dynamic memory management, segmentation, or paging. With virtual memory management, programs are stored on disk, and only active portions are loaded into main memory. Another operating system responsibility is preventing one program from destroying another's memory space.

When two or more programs are ready to use the processor, a dispatcher routine selects the next program by following a priority algorithm. Interrupts mark the beginning and end of input and output operations, alerting the system that control can be transferred to another program.

Peripheral devices must be carefully managed. Deadlock occurs when two programs each control a resource needed by the other, but neither is willing to give up its resource. Some operating systems are designed to prevent deadlock; others sense deadlock and take corrective action.

When programs enter a multiprogramming system, they are stored on a queue. Later, when memory space becomes available, a scheduler selects the next program from the queue and loads it into memory. To improve the turnover rate of programs, data are often spooled from slow-speed devices to disk, and then read from disk into the program. On output, results are spooled to disk and eventually dumped to the printer.

Figure 6.14 is a good visual summary of the basic functions of a multiprogramming operating system.

Time-sharing is used for interactive applications. The key measure of system effectiveness is response time. Because the time between successive transactions is usually quite lengthy, memory space can be managed by roll-in and roll-out techniques.

To eliminate the risk of one program tying up the system and forcing all other users to wait, time-slicing is used to manage the processor's time. Often, the dispatcher follows a polling algorithm to determine which program gets the processor next. External device allocation and external priority are not as significant on a time-sharing system as they are on a multiprogramming system.

Most single-user systems are command driven. Most multiprogramming systems are interrupt driven. Most time-sharing systems are poll driven.

Key Words

background	fragmentation	roll-in
control block	interrupt	roll-out
deadlock	interrupt handler	scheduler
dispatcher	multiprogramming	segment
dynamic memory	page	spooling
management	partition	throughput
fixed-partition	polling	time-sharing
memory	queuing	time-slicing
management	region	turnaround
foreground	response time	virtual memory

Exercises

1. Generally, the more programs in memory, the greater the utilization of the processor. Explain why this is so.

2. Time-sharing and multiprogramming use different measures of system effectiveness. Briefly explain how these measures of effectiveness influence an operating system's design.

3. Distinguish between fixed-partition memory management, dynamic memory management, segmentation, and paging.

4. What is virtual memory? How can virtual memory help improve throughput?

5. Why is memory protection necessary?

6. What does the dispatcher do? What are control blocks, and why are they necessary? Relate these two ideas.

7. What is an interrupt? Explain the relationship between interrupts and the dispatcher.

8. Distinguish between an interrupt and the logic that handles the interrupt.

9. What is deadlock?

10. Explain how the queuing routine and the scheduler work together to load application programs.

11. Distinguish between a program's internal priority and its external priority.

12. What is spooling? How does spooling help throughput and turn-around? *Simultous perpherial operations online .*

13. Compare roll-in/roll-out to multiprogramming memory management. In particular, compare roll-in/roll-out and virtual memory. How are they similar? How are they different?

14. What is time-slicing? Why is it necessary on a time-sharing system?

15. Multiprogramming systems are generally interrupt driven, while most time-sharing systems are poll driven. Why?

Command and Job Control Languages

CHAPTER
7

Command Languages

K E Y   I D E A S

Command language functions
Identifying users
Identifying programs
Specifying device requirements
Run-time intervention
Sources of commands
Learning a command language

Command Language Functions

An operating system is an interface between a computer's programs or users and its hardware (Fig. 7.1). Programs request operating system support by issuing interrupts. People communicate directly with the operating system by typing **commands** or **job control language** statements. The operating system coordinates and manages resources; the command language provides guidance and direction.

Identifying Users

One key operating system function is identifying users. On time-sharing or interactive systems, a person normally begins a session by typing a user number and a password. Most batch jobs start with a job control language statement that identifies the application and the responsible programmer or user.

User identification is an essential security feature. Computer resources are expensive, and the data and software stored on a computer can be crucial to an organization, so unauthorized access must be denied. Additionally, user identification can serve as a basis for setting priorities or for limiting access. For example, in an academic system, a faculty ID might give a professor high priority and the right to access any student's work space, while a student ID would restrict the user to standard priority and his or her own work space.

Identifying Programs

A second major function is identifying programs. Normally, operating system routines and utilities, application programs, compilers, editors, and other support routines are assigned names. It's the user's responsibility to

Fig. 7.1   Users communicate with an operating system through commands or job control language statements.

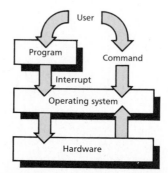

specify, through the command language, the name of the program or routine to be executed. On interactive systems, the command often consists of little more than the program name, followed, perhaps, by some run-time options. On a batch system, several different programs might be identified on a series of job control statements, with the order of the statements indicating the order in which the programs are to be run.

Specifying Device Requirements

The user also specifies peripheral device requirements through the command language. This is often a minor concern on interactive systems, which tend to rely on default device assignments, but it can be significant on a batch system. Generally, a batch user is expected to define each program's peripheral device needs through job control language statements. Given a list of device needs, the operating system can determine if the necessary resources are available before loading a program.

Most batch and interactive systems allow users to name and set access limits on files. Some operating systems allocate disk space dynamically, as programs request it. Others expect job control statements to specify the required number of cylinders, tracks, sectors, or blocks, or even absolute disk addresses.

Run-time Intervention

Finally, most command languages support run-time intervention. The simplest example is a control break on a single-user system; if a program gets into an endless loop or begins generating clearly invalid results, the programmer can usually stop it by simultaneously pressing control and break (or some other combination of keys). The result is an interrupt that terminates the program and transfers control to the operating system.

Run-time intervention can be considerably more complex on a multiple-user system. Many support an automatic time-out feature that terminates long-running programs; often a command language parameter sets expected run time. Occasionally, an unexpected "hot" job enters the system and demands immediate attention. When this happens, the operator must be able to override normal priorities. Occasionally, jobs or sessions must be canceled; once again the command language provides a means.

Sources of Commands

Users and programmers are the most common sources of operating system commands. On interactive systems, single-line commands are typed as work progresses. On batch systems, a series of commands, called a **job stream**, is prepared and submitted before the first program is loaded (Fig. 7.2). Job stream commands identify the user, define (in order) the programs to be run, and request peripheral device support for each program.

Fig. 7.2   On batch processing systems, a series of commands often enters
                      through the job stream.

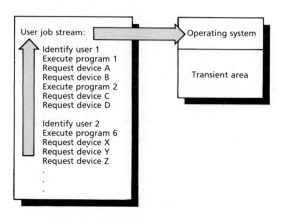

The operator's console is a second source of commands (Fig. 7.3). At the
start of the day, the operator boots the system by following initial program
load (IPL) procedures to set such key variables as default main memory
space allocations, internal priority rules, system device assignments, the
system date and time, and others. As the system runs, other commands are
used to halt, terminate, or load a program, check the status of the system,
identify a user, and, in general, control the flow of work. At the end of the
day, other commands allow the operator to shut down the system.

   Generally, software belongs to the programmer, while the operator
controls the hardware. Where do the data fit? Many large organizations
assign responsibility for secondary storage space, data maintenance,
backup, security, and accessibility to a data base administrator. Other sys-

Fig. 7.3   The system operator enters real-time commands through the
                      system console.

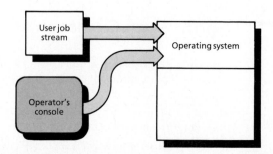

Fig. 7.4   On many systems, the data base administrator's or super user's
console is yet another source of commands.

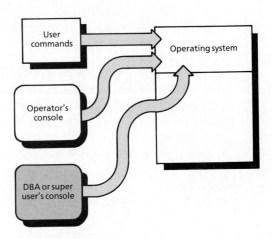

tems identify a super user who has overall responsibility for managing the
entire system. The data base administrator's or super user's console represents a third source of commands (Fig. 7.4).

Imagine if every user were given access to a complete set of system
commands. Be honest: wouldn't you be tempted to cancel a friend's program as a joke if you had the opportunity? The set of commands available
to a user is often quite limited. The operator, on the other hand, can issue
all user commands plus several others, such as cancel a program, change a
user's priority, postpone a batch job, and so on. The system administrator
represents yet a higher level of control. Often this individual is empowered
to issue any user command, any operator command, and several others as
well. Thus, the complete command language is available only to the system
administrator, the operator is limited to a subset, and users to a still smaller
subset.

Learning a Command Language

Perhaps the best way to learn a command language is to issue some commands. The next six chapters are designed to help you do exactly that.
Chapter 8 introduces the command language for a popular microcomputer
operating system, MS-DOS (or PC-DOS). Chapter 9 investigates UNIX and
its command language. Most MS-DOS and UNIX commands are interactive,
so Chapters 8 and 9 are written as tutorials. Chapter 10 presents a batch job
control language for IBM's DOS/VSE operating system. Perhaps the best
known batch job control language, IBM's OS/JCL, is covered in Chapters 11

and 12. Part III ends (Chapter 13) with a discussion of libraries and the linkage editor, using OS/JCL examples.

Most job control and command languages are quite "rich," with features that allow a skilled expert to do just about anything. However, the average programmer needs only a small subset of a command language. The intent of these chapters is to focus on that small subset. Ideally, you should be able to read a chapter, gain an appreciation for a command language, complete some exercises, and learn enough to begin using a system. As your skill increases, of course, you will find it necessary to consult a reference manual to learn more advanced features.

It is unlikely that anyone but a future system programmer will use, on a regular basis, all four command languages. Thus, a good approach is to select one or two for in-depth study. Carefully read about the command languages you (or your instructor) have selected, and work through the tutorial or complete the end-of-chapter programming exercises. Read the other chapters. Note how the other command languages are similar to, and yet different from, the ones you are studying.

The material in this brief chapter is general and relates to all command languages. Much of Chapter 13 is also general and should be read carefully; specific examples are clearly identified and can be skipped by those who choose not to study OS/JCL. Near the end of the book, you'll find a series of appendices summarizing these four command and job control languages. You should find these appendices useful references.

Summary

People communicate with an operating system through a command or job control language. Command language statements identify users, identify programs to be executed, request peripheral device support, name files, set access limits on files, and request secondary storage space. Other commands allow operators, programmers, and users to intervene as a program runs.

The most common sources of commands are users and programmers. Time-sharing commands are entered interactively, as work progresses. Batch commands are prepared before any programs are loaded and submitted to the operating system through the job stream. Operator commands enter the system through the operator's console. A third source is the data base administrator's or super user's console. Often, only the super user has access to a complete set of commands, with the operator limited to a subset and users to a still smaller subset.

Key Words

command	job control language	job stream

Exercises

1. Identifying users is not a major problem on single-user systems. Why not?

2. Why must multiprogramming and time-sharing users be identified?

3. Generally, users or the operator must issue commands identifying the program or programs to be executed by a computer. Why?

4. Distinguish between interactive commands and batch commands. Hint: the key is timing.

5. Deadlocks were introduced in Chapter 6. Relate a user's requests for peripheral device support to the deadlock concept.

6. Why is the ability to intervene as a program runs an important command language feature?

7. Many systems limit users to a subset of the command language. Why?

8

MS-DOS Commands

K E Y   I D E A S

MS-DOS
Getting started
 Formatting a disk
The file system
 File names
 Directories
 Path names
 Viewing a directory
 Creating directories
 Creating files
 Changing directories
 Manipulating files
Pipes, filters, and redirection
Batch files
Other useful commands

MS-DOS

Since its release in the fall of 1981, the IBM personal computer, better known as the PC, has become an industry standard. Its operating system, PC-DOS, was developed for IBM by Microsoft Corporation. It, too, has become a standard and is available in a generic version called MS-DOS. IBM PCs run PC-DOS; compatible microcomputers from other suppliers run MS-DOS; the two operating systems are functionally identical.

The general form of an MS-DOS **command** is shown in Fig. 8.1. The **default drive** and the system **prompt** are displayed by the operating system. The user responds by typing a command name followed by necessary **parameters**. A **delimiter**, usually a space, separates the command from the parameters, and, if there are several, the parameters from each other.

Some MS-DOS commands are **resident**; in other words, they reside in main memory whenever the operating system is loaded. Others are **transient**; they remain on disk and are read into memory only when needed. Resident commands can be issued even if the system disk is not in a drive; transient commands cannot.

This introduction to MS-DOS commands is presented as a tutorial. Don't just read it. Instead, find an IBM PC or compatible computer, and, as you read about a command, enter it and see for yourself how the computer responds.[1] You'll need a copy of MS-DOS or PC-DOS (version 2.0 or

---

[1] The examples in this chapter were run on a Zenith Data Systems Z-100 personal computer under MS-DOS Version 2.

Fig. 8.1　　　All MS-DOS commands follow this general format.

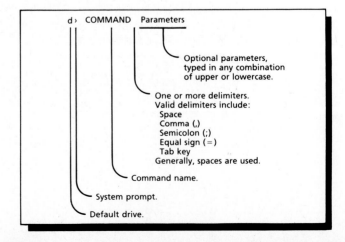

higher) and a blank diskette. Later, you'll find Appendix B a useful reference.

Getting Started

Main memory is volatile. Thus, when a computer is first turned on, the operating system is not in memory. Instead, it resides on disk, and must be loaded before any commands can be issued. Start with the DOS disk in drive A (the leftmost or top drive). When you switch on the computer, hardware automatically reads, from disk, a routine called the **boot**, which, in turn, loads the rest of the operating system. (If the computer is already running, simultaneously pressing Ctrl, Alt, and Del has the same effect.) Try it.

Once the operating system is loaded, it issues two commands: *DATE* and *TIME* (Fig. 8.2). When asked to "Enter new date:", you have two choices. One is simply to press return and accept the default date (1-01-1980). The second is to type the current date and *then* press return. When asked to "Enter new time:", you have the same choices. (For now, press return in response to both commands; we'll set the date and time later.) MS-DOS stamps every file it creates or modifies with the date and time. Many programming languages include features that get the date and time

Fig. 8.2   Once it's loaded, MS-DOS issues two commands: *DATE* and *TIME*. The last line on this screen shows the standard system prompt.

```
MS-DOS Version 2.11
Copyright (C) 1981,82,83 Microsoft Corp.
Current date is Tue 1-01-1980
Enter new date:
Current time is 0:00:12.24
Enter new time:

A>
```

from the operating system. If you don't set them correctly, they won't be reported correctly.

Note the last line in Fig. 8.2. It reads

A>

That's the standard system prompt. The default drive is A; unless it is told otherwise, the operating system will expect to find programs, routines, and data files on the disk in drive A. The greater-than symbol (>) is the prompt; it means MS-DOS is waiting for you to enter the next command. Let's change the default drive. Type *B:* (Fig. 8.3). Use either upper or lowercase; it doesn't matter which because MS-DOS converts everything to uppercase. Press return. Note that the next prompt reads

B>

The default drive is now B. Type *A:*, and press return. The default drive should be A again.

When we first booted the system, we accepted the default date and time. Let's correct them. The first step is to issue a *DATE* command (Fig. 8.4). Following the command, *DATE*, are the parameters month, day, and year, separated by dashes or hyphens. The month must lie between 1 (or 01) and 12; the day must lie between 1 and 31. Years between 1900 and

---

Fig. 8.3   To change the default drive, type a drive letter followed by a
colon.

```
MS-DOS Version 2.11
Copyright (C) 1981,82,83 Microsoft Corp.
Current date is Tue 1-01-1980
Enter new date:
Current time is 0:00:12:24
Enter new time:

A>B:

B>A:

A>
```

Fig. 8.4   The *DATE* command allows a user to check and/or set the system
                      date.

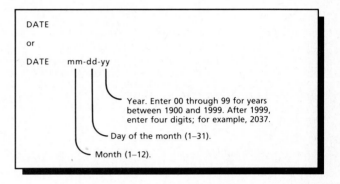

1999 can be typed as two-digit (87) or four-digit (1987) numbers; years
after 2000 (or before 1900) must be typed as four-digit numbers (2037). If
you type a bad date, the system responds with an error message. Simply
reenter the date correctly.

There are two ways to enter a *DATE* command. If you type *DATE* and
then press return, the system will display its version of the current date and
ask you to enter a new one. If you respond by pressing return again, the
system will continue to use its current date. To change the date, type a new
one. An option is to enter *DATE*, a space, and then type the new date before
pressing return; for example,

DATE 07-04-88

If it's given a date, the operating system won't prompt you to enter a new
one.

The *TIME* command is similar (Fig. 8.5). If you type *TIME*, the system
displays its current time and prompts you to enter a new value. Hours are
based on 24-hour military time; for example, 10 a.m. is 10, and 3 p.m. is 15.
Generally, you should enter the time to the nearest minute; few applications require greater accuracy. If you type hours and minutes (separated by
a colon), the values of seconds and hundredths of a second are set to zero.

Try a few *DATE* and *TIME* commands. They can be typed in any order.
Use any combination of upper and lowercase letter (remember, MS-DOS
converts everything to uppercase). Lie to the computer; it doesn't care. Of
course, you should set the date and time correctly before actively using the
system, but the computer will accept whatever you tell it.

Some applications require a particular version of MS-DOS. The version
number was displayed when the system was booted, but that first line may

Fig. 8.5   The *TIME* command allows a user to check and/or set the system
                      time.

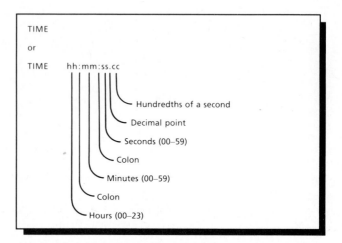

have scrolled off the screen by now. To view the version number, type

VER

There are no parameters. In response, the system displays its version number.

Formatting a Disk

Later in the chapter you'll need a work disk. Before a disk can be used, it must be formatted. The formatting process writes a pattern of sectors on the disk surface, records a copy of the boot routine on the first sector, and initializes control information. Let's use the MS-DOS *FORMAT* command (Fig. 8.6) to format a disk.

The simplest form of the command consists of a single word: *FORMAT*. It's transient, so the format routine must be read into memory. The default drive is A and no parameters are specified; thus MS-DOS will expect to find both the format routine and the disk to be formatted in drive A. However, if your system has two drives, it makes more sense to insert the blank disk in drive B and format it there. Try typing

FORMAT B:

The parameter *B:* identifies drive B. Because the default drive is A, *FORMAT* will be read from the disk in drive A. Because the first parameter identifies

Fig. 8.6   The *FORMAT* command allows a user to format a disk.

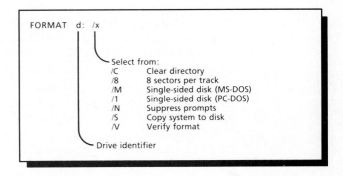

```
FORMAT   d:  /x


                        Select from:
                        /C        Clear directory
                        /8        8 sectors per track
                        /M        Single-sided disk (MS-DOS)
                        /1        Single-sided disk (PC-DOS)
                        /N        Suppress prompts
                        /S        Copy system to disk
                        /V        Verify format
                      Drive identifier
```

drive B, the disk in drive B will be formatted. Figure 8.7 shows the system messages generated by the format routine.

Several optional parameters are summarized in Fig. 8.6. Unless it is told otherwise, *FORMAT* initializes a double-sided disk with nine sectors per track, yielding 360K bytes of storage. Some of the options change this default. Coding */S* records a copy of the operating system on the new disk.

Fig. 8.7   The *FORMAT* command generates its own prompts to guide a
                      user through the process of formatting a disk.

```
A>FORMAT B:

                        FORMAT version 2.10
            Copyright (C) 1984, Zenith Data Systems Corporation

Insert new disk in drive B
and press RETURN when ready.

Enter desired volume label (11 characters,
RETURN for none)? DOSDEMO

      362496 bytes total disk space
      362496 bytes available on disk

Do you wish to format another disk (Y/N)?N
A>
```

The File System

File Names

The MS-DOS file system allows a user to identify, save, and retrieve files by name. (A program is a type of file.) A **file name** (Fig. 8.8) is composed of the name itself and an optional extension. The name consists of from 1 to 8 characters. A few file names are reserved by the system, and delimiters may not be used; otherwise, just about any combination of characters you can type is legal. The file name is separated from its 1- to 3-character extension by a period. Some extensions have special meaning to the operating system; they are summarized in Fig. 8.8. The extension is sometimes used to identify a version of a program or data file; for example, *VITA.1*, *VITA.2*, and so on.

Fig. 8.8   This figure summarizes the rules for defining a file name.

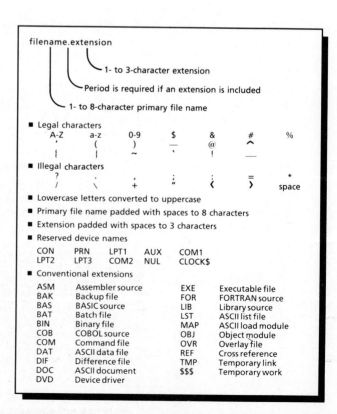

Directories

When a file is created, the operating system records its name and starting address in the disk's **directory** (Fig. 8.9). Later, when the file is retrieved, the operating system reads the directory and searches it by file name. Early versions of MS-DOS kept track of all the files stored on a disk in a single directory. Starting with version 2.0, however, Microsoft implemented a much more flexible hierarchical directory structure.

Imagine, for example, that a work disk holds several different types of files. Letters and other correspondence are generated by a text editor. Chapters for a book are output by a word processor. BASIC programs form another group of files.

With only a single directory, references to all these different types of files will be mixed together. To find a program, the operating system will have to search the entire directory. More significantly, so will the user. Picture a disk with 40 or 50 files. If you forget a name, there's a good chance you'll never see that file again.

Fig. 8.9 A file's name and starting address are recorded in the disk directory.

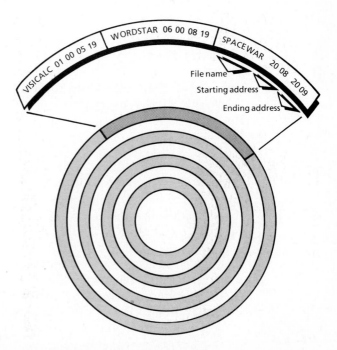

Fig. 8.10   Current versions of MS-DOS support a highly flexible inverted
                                 tree directory structure.

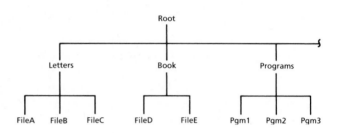

When a disk is formatted, a single **root directory** is created. Current
versions of MS-DOS allow a user to add special files called **subdirectories**.
For our example, we might define three: *LETTERS*, *BOOK*, and *PROGRAMS*
(Fig. 8.10); a directory name is just like a file name without an extension.
All correspondence could then be recorded under *LETTERS*, book chapters
under *BOOK*, and BASIC programs under *PROGRAMS*. This structure
makes it much easier to keep track of the files.

Path Names

With subdirectories, however, you need more than a simple file name to
find a file. For example, it is possible to have a file named *PAY* recorded
under two different directories. A reference to *PAY* would thus be ambiguous—which *PAY* do you mean? To identify a file, you need a complete **path
name** (Fig. 8.11); for example,

\LETTERS\PAY

The first back slash (on an IBM PC keyboard, the back slash key is just
above and to the left of the space bar) references the root directory. The
second back slash separates the directory name from the file name. Thus, to
find *PAY*, start with the root directory, find a subdirectory named *LETTERS*,
and search the subdirectory for the file name.

It is possible to divide a subdirectory into lower level directories. For
example, Fig. 8.12 shows *LETTERS* broken into three subdirectories. One,
CLUB, is further subdivided into *ROTARY* and *JCC*. To retrieve a letter
named *MEMBER.3* from the *ROTARY* subdirectory, code

\LETTERS\CLUB\ROTARY\MEMBER.3

Fig. 8.11   This figure summarizes the rules for defining path names.

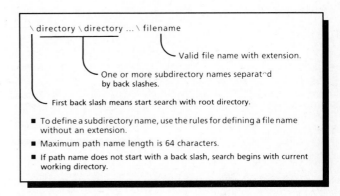

Note how the path name leads from directory to directory until, finally, you reach the desired file.

At first glance, subdirectories seem to complicate rather than simplify accessing files. In practice, people rarely use such lengthy path names. Instead, they select a working directory and allow the operating system to add the directory names needed to complete a path name. Later in the chapter, you'll learn how to select a working directory.

Viewing a Directory

Before you begin creating and manipulating directories, it might be wise to look through an existing one. There are numerous programs and files on the MS-DOS disk; start by getting a general idea of its contents. Type a

Fig. 8.12   Directories can be subdivided into lower level subdirectories.

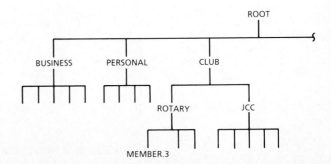

Fig. 8.13   The check disk (*CHKDSK*) command checks a disk's directory
                    and reports on its contents.

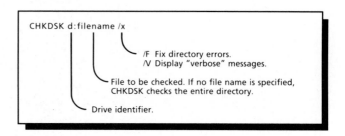

```
CHKDSK d:filename /x

                        /F  Fix directory errors.
                        /V  Display "verbose" messages.

                    File to be checked. If no file name is specified,
                    CHKDSK checks the entire directory.

                Drive identifier.
```

check disk (*CHKDSK*) command (Fig. 8.13)

CHKDSK

This command is transient, so you'll notice a slight delay as the routine is
read from disk. Because there are no parameters, MS-DOS will check the
disk in the default drive. The output is shown in Fig. 8.14. You now know

Fig. 8.14   The check disk command reports on the contents of the desig-
                    nated disk.

```
A>CHKDSK

        322560 bytes total disk space
         23552 bytes in 2 hidden files
        228352 bytes in 34 user files
         70656 bytes available on disk

        327680 bytes total memory
        301488 bytes free

A>
```

Fig. 8.15   The directory (*DIR*) command displays a directory's contents.

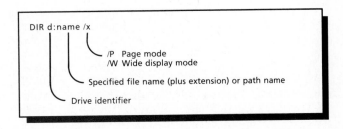

how many files are stored on the MS-DOS disk and how much free space remains.

Next, look at the names of the programs stored on that disk. Type a directory (*DIR*) command (Fig. 8.15)

DIR

It's resident, so the operating system will respond much more quickly. Because there are no parameters, MS-DOS will look to the disk in drive A. Part of the output is shown in Fig. 8.16; the complete MS-DOS directory is too big to fit on a single screen. For each file, you can see a file name and extension, the file size, and the date and time the file was created.

Are any of these files subdirectories? To find out, type a *TREE* command (Fig. 8.17)

TREE

It's transient. (How can you tell?) In response, MS-DOS reads the directory and displays only directory paths. As Fig. 8.18 shows, the MS-DOS disk contains only a root directory.

Creating Directories

Let's use a make directory (*MKDIR*) command (Fig. 8.19) to create a few subdirectories on the work disk you just formatted. Start with *LETTERS*. The work disk is in drive B. The default drive is A, so you'll have to identify the output drive. To create a directory named *LETTERS* on drive B, code

MKDIR B:\LETTERS

The back slash (\) indicates that *LETTERS* is a subdirectory of the root directory (Fig. 8.20). Use similar commands to create two more directories:

Fig. 8.16   The MS-DOS directory is too big to fit on a single screen.

COMP	COM	3656	10-24-84	3:23p
RECOVER	COM	2295	11-21-83	3:29p
RDCPM	COM	4925	1-06-84	3:04p
SEARCH	COM	4054	11-01-83	4:31p
TREE	COM	1791	10-09-84	2:24p
APPLY	COM	1945	9-27-84	8:42a
CIPHER	COM	153	1-31-83	3:21p
SORT	EXE	1632	11-01-83	3:34p
MORE	COM	4364	11-21-83	2:52p
MAP	COM	3599	10-26-84	10:24a
FIND	EXE	10624	11-03-83	4:07p
ASSIGN	COM	16746	9-07-84	10:35a
PSCIDS	COM	1367	11-09-83	3:04p
PSCOKI	COM	1369	5-04-84	2:10p
PSCTS315	COM	1396	11-14-83	3:03p
PSCP920	COM	816	11-18-83	3:04p
PSCMX80	COM	1456	11-08-83	3:02p
PSCMPI	COM	1394	11-08-83	3:03p
ANSI	SYS	1963	10-22-84	9:31a
MDISK	DVD	1293	7-17-84	8:57a
BACKUP	EXE	14976	4-16-83	4:10p
BACKUP5	EXE	14976	4-16-83	4:10p

34 File(s)   70656 bytes free

A>

Fig. 8.17   The *TREE* command displays the directory paths on the specified disk.

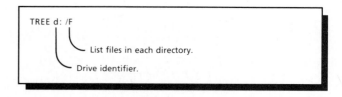

```
TREE d: /F
```
List files in each directory.
Drive identifier.

Fig. 8.18   Note, near the bottom of this screen, that MS-DOS has no
subdirectories.

```
TREE        COM    1791    10-09-84    2:24p
APPLY       COM    1945     9-27-84    8:42a
CIPHER      COM     153     1-31-83    3:21p
SORT        EXE    1632    11-01-83    3:34p
MORE        COM    4364    11-21-83    2:52p
MAP         COM    3599    10-26-84   10:24a
FIND        EXE   10624    11-03-83    4:07p
ASSIGN      COM   16746     9-07-84   10:35a
PSCIDS      COM    1367    11-09-83    3:04p
PSCOKI      COM    1369     5-04-84    2:10p
PSCTS315    COM    1396    11-14-83    3:03p
PSCP920     COM     816    11-18-83    3:04p
PSCMX80     COM    1456    11-08-83    3:02p
PSCMPI      COM    1394    11-08-83    3:03p
ANSI        SYS    1963    10-22-84    9:31a
MDISK       DVD    1293     7-17-84    8:57a
BACKUP      EXE   14976     4-16-83    4:10p
BACKUP5     EXE   14976     4-16-83    4:10p
          34 File(s)       70656 bytes free

A>TREE

No sub-directories exist

A>
```

Fig. 8.19   The make directory (*MKDIR*) command creates a new directory.

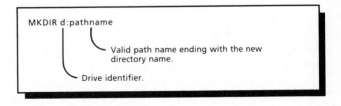

Fig. 8.20

This screen shows the commands to create three subdirectories. The *DIR* command near the bottom of the screen shows that the subdirectories have been created.

```
A>MKDIR B:LETTERS

A>MKDIR B:BOOK

A>MKDIR B:PROGRAMS

A>DIR B:

    Volume in drive B is DOSDEMO
    Directory of B:\

LETTERS      <DIR>    3-26-86   1:41p
BOOK         <DIR>    3-26-86   1:41p
PROGRAMS     <DIR>    3-26-86   1:42p
             3 File(s)    359424 bytes free

A>
```

BOOK and *PROGRAMS*. When you're finished, type a directory command

DIR B:

As Fig. 8.20 shows, three subdirectories have been added to the work disk's root directory.

    MKDIR creates a directory. To remove a directory, code an *RMDIR* command.

Creating Files

Most files are created by programs, such as the MS-DOS line editor, compilers and interpreters, word processors, spreadsheet programs, and data base managers. Another option is to copy an existing file. When MS-DOS carries out a *COPY* command (Fig. 8.21), it reads the file specified in the first parameter (the source file), and copies it to the file described in the second parameter (the destination file).

    One of the simplest ways to create a file is to copy the data from the console. For example, type

COPY CON B:\LETTERS\JIM

Fig. 8.21   The *COPY* command copies one or more files from a source to a
                     destination.

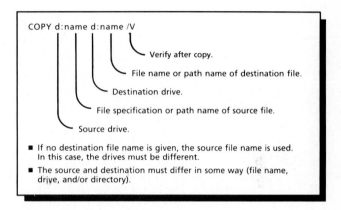

```
COPY d:name d:name /V
```
- Verify after copy.
- File name or path name of destination file.
- Destination drive.
- File specification or path name of source file.
- Source drive.

■ If no destination file name is given, the source file name is used.
  In this case, the drives must be different.

■ The source and destination must differ in some way (file name,
  drive, and/or directory).

The first file name, *CON*, stands for the console. To MS-DOS, it means
input data will be typed through the keyboard. After you enter the command, the cursor will appear directly under the command line (you'll see
no prompt). Simply type whatever you want. When you reach the end of a
line, press return. When you've typed all your lines, press function key F6
and then return; that's the *COPY* command's sentinel value.

Copy several files from the console and store them under the subdirectories created earlier (you can see some examples near the top of Fig. 8.22).
Type anything you want; file contents are not crucial to this exercise. If you
prefer, use the BASIC interpreter to create a few BASIC programs and store
them under directory *PROGRAMS,* use your favorite word processor to
create a few text files and store them under directory *BOOK,* and copy a few
LETTERS files from the console.

Some operating systems require a programmer or user to specify a file's
size when creating it. That's not necessary under MS-DOS. We'll investigate
how MS-DOS dynamically allocates disk space in Chapter 14.

Changing Directories

Now that the work disk holds some directories and files, let's investigate it.
Start with a check disk command

CHKDSK B:

Clearly, the work disk contains three directories and several files (Fig.
8.22). Next, type

DIR B:

Fig. 8.22

Near the top of this screen, you can see the last two copy operations. The check disk command's output shows that five user files have been added to the work disk.

```
A>COPY CON B:\PROGRAMS\PGM1.BAS
REM     This is a BASIC remark or comment.
REM     This is another one.
^Z
            1 File(s) copied

A>COPY CON B:\BOOK\CHAPTER 1.DR1
It was a dark and rainy night.
^Z
            1 File(s) copied

A>CHKDSK B:
Volume DOSDEMO          created Mar 26, 1986 1:41p

362496  bytes total disk space
     0  bytes in 1 hidden files
  3072  bytes in 3 directories
  5120  bytes in 5 user files
354304  bytes available on disk

327680  bytes total memory
301488  bytes free

A>
```

Only the three directories (the contents of the root directory) are listed (Fig. 8.23). How can you view the contents of the *LETTERS* directory? Type

DIR B:\LETTERS

Your screen should look something like the bottom half of Fig. 8.23 (your file names may be different, of course).

Look carefully at Fig. 8.23. Directory *LETTERS* contains two unusual files: (.) and (..). The single dot refers to the directory itself; the double dot is a reference to its parent.

Finally, type a *TREE* command

TREE B:

Fig. 8.23   The first directory command lists the contents of the root
directory. The second command lists the contents of
subdirectory *LETTERS*.

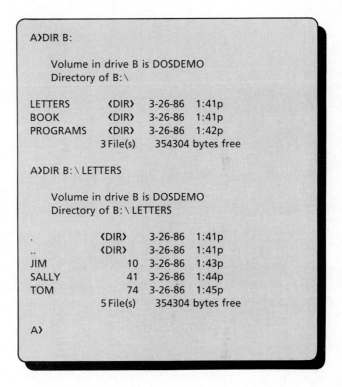

```
A>DIR B:

    Volume in drive B is DOSDEMO
    Directory of B:\

LETTERS          <DIR>    3-26-86   1:41p
BOOK             <DIR>    3-26-86   1:41p
PROGRAMS         <DIR>    3-26-86   1:42p
              3 File(s)      354304 bytes free

A>DIR B:\LETTERS

    Volume in drive B is DOSDEMO
    Directory of B:\LETTERS

.                <DIR>    3-26-86   1:41p
..               <DIR>    3-26-86   1:41p
JIM                 10    3-26-86   1:43p
SALLY               41    3-26-86   1:44p
TOM                 74    3-26-86   1:45p
              5 File(s)      354304 bytes free

A>
```

As Fig. 8.24 shows, the root directory contains three subdirectories, none of
which hold lower level directories.

The root directory is the current **working directory**. Let's shift to a
different working directory. Type a change directory (*CHDIR*) command
(Fig. 8.25); for example,

CHDIR B:\LETTERS

Now type

DIR B:

The output should resemble the bottom half of Fig. 8.23. If you don't
specify a directory, MS-DOS starts with your current working directory.
The change directory command allows you to specify a working directory.

Fig. 8.24   The root directory contains three subdirectories, none of which
                       holds lower level directories.

```
A)TREE B:

DIRECTORY PATH LISTING FOR VOLUME ???????????

Path: \LETTERS
Sub-directories: None

Path: \ BOOK
Sub-directories: None

Path: \ PROGRAMS
Sub-directories: None

A)
```

Manipulating Files

Earlier, you copied text from the console to a disk file. More generally,
already existing files are copied. The *COPY* command's first parameter
specifies a source file; the second parameter identifies the destination. If
drive designators are prefixed to a parameter, a file on one disk can be
copied to another. If a file name is specified for the destination file, the new
file name is used; if not, the source file name is assigned to the destination

Fig. 8.25   The change directory (*CHDIR*) command changes the current
                       working directory.

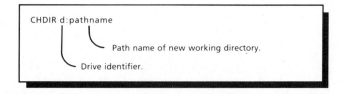

file. For example,

COPY \LETTERS\TOM B:

copies a file named *TOM* from drive A to drive B and assigns it path name *\LETTERS\TOM* while

COPY \LETTERS\TOM \LETTERS\TAMMY

reads file *TOM*, makes another copy on drive A, and assigns it path name *\LETTERS\TAMMY*.

Special **wild card** characters allow a user to generalize the parameters. A question mark (?) represents any single character; for example, the file name

TERM.?

identifies *TERM.1*, *TERM.2*, *TERM.C*, and any other file named *TERM* with a 1-character extension. An asterisk (*) represents multiple characters; for example,

TERM.*

stands for every file named *TERM* with a 1-, 2-, or 3-character extension, including *TERM.1*, *TERM.V6*, and *TERM.ABC*.

Imagine you've been working on a BASIC program. Your source module is called *MYPGM.BAS*; the object module is *MYPGM.OBJ*. You want to copy both. You have two options. One is to issue two *COPY* commands. The other is to reference *MYPGM.** or *MYPGM.???*. Seeing the wild card characters, MS-DOS will look for all files that fit; thus a single command will copy both.

Wild card characters are particularly useful for making backup copies of selected files or an entire disk. For example,

COPY *.* B:

will copy every file on the disk in drive A to the disk in drive B, while

COPY *.BAS B:

will copy every file with extension *BAS* (generally, BASIC programs) from drive A to drive B.

Occasionally, you'll want simply to rename a file or assign it to another directory without actually copying it. Use a *RENAME* command. To remove a file, use an *ERASE* command.

To display a file's contents on the screen, you could code a *COPY* command with *CON* as its second parameter; for example,

COPY B:\LETTERS\JIM CON

An option is to code a *TYPE* command, such as

TYPE B:\LETTERS\JIM

TYPE reads the specified file and displays it on the screen.

A program is a special kind of file. Executable programs are assigned extensions *COM* or *EXE*. To load and execute a program, simply type its file name (with or without its extension) as though it were a command. If no extension is given, MS-DOS will look for a resident command with the specified name. If it finds none, it will search for the file name with a *.COM* extension, then for a *.EXE* file, and finally for a *.BAT* file. (We'll consider batch files shortly.)

Pipes, Filters, and Redirection

Many MS-DOS commands assume a standard input or output device; for example, the directory command sends its output to the screen. By using **redirection** parameters (Fig. 8.26), a user can change those defaults.

Let's consider a few examples. To print a copy of drive B's directory, code

DIR B: >PRN

To print the MS-DOS directory, code

DIR >PRN

Fig. 8.26

Many MS-DOS commands and filters deal with standard input and output devices. Special redirection parameters allow a user to change to a specified file or device.

Parameter	Meaning	Example
<	Change source to a specified file or device	<MYFILE.DAT
>	Change destination to a specified file or device	>PRN
>>	Change destination, usually to an existing file, and append new output to it	>>HOLD.DAT
I	Pipe standard output to another command or to a filter	DIR I MORE

To copy drive A's directory to a file on drive B, code

DIR >B:DFILE

If a program you have written expects its input from the standard input device (the keyboard), and for testing purposes, you want to get input data from a text file, code something like

MYPGM <B:TESTDATA.1

It's much easier than modifying the program and recompiling it.

A **filter** is a special type of command. It accepts input from the standard input device, modifies (or filters) the data in some way, and sends the results to the standard output device. For example, *SORT* (Fig. 8.27) accepts data from the keyboard, sorts the data values into alphabetical or numerical sequence, and outputs the sorted data to the screen. Of course, with redirection, you can override or change the standard input device, output device, or both. For example, to sort the contents of a file and display the result on the screen, code

SORT <MYFILE.DAT

To sort a file and store the output in a different file, code

SORT <MYFILE >RESULT

The *MORE* command (Fig. 8.28) is another useful filter. It sends output to the terminal one screen at a time. *MORE* is generally used with pipes.

A **pipe** causes one command's standard output to be used as the standard input to another command. Pipes are designated by a vertical line (I); on an IBM PC, press shift and the back slash key. For example, try displaying the MS-DOS directory. Type

DIR

Fig. 8.27   The function of the *SORT* filter should be obvious.

```
SORT /x
      L  /R    Means reverse sort, or descending order.
         /+n   Means sort field starts at position n.
```

Fig. 8.28   The filter *MORE* reads text from the standard input device and
                      displays it one screen at a time.

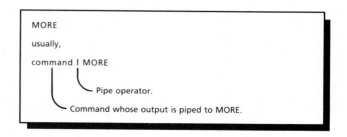

Fig. 8.29   *MORE* displays data one screen at a time.

```
Volume in drive A has no label
Directory of A:\

COMMAND     COM    18128     10-18-84      9:43a
FORMAT      COM    12912     10-23-84      1:47p
CONFIGUR    COM    19724      5-03-84     10:33a
MODE        COM     8669     10-23-84      9:01a
CHKDSK      COM     6468     11-21-83      3:34p
EDLIN       COM     8080     11-21-83      2:01p
PRINT       COM     6303      9-07-84      1:14p
SYS         COM     2189      1-16-84     12:53p
DISKCOPY    COM    14592     10-23-84      1:45p
DISKCOMP    COM     1598     10-23-84      1:50p
DEBUG       COM    12484      4-04-84      9:20a
FC          EXE     2585     11-21-83      2:10p
COMP        COM     3656     10-24-84      3:23p
RECOVER     COM     2295     11-21-83      3:29p
RDCPM       COM     4925      1-06-84      3:04p
SEARCH      COM     4054     11-01-83      4:31p
TREE        COM     1791     10-09-84      2:24p
APPLY       COM     1945      9-27-84      8:42a
CIPHER      COM      153      1-31-83      3:21p
--More--
```

The first several file names will scroll off the screen before you have time to read them. Now type

DIR | MORE

The directory command's standard output will be routed to the *MORE* filter rather than directly to the screen. *MORE* will display one screen and then wait until you press enter before displaying the next one (Fig. 8.29).

Try another experiment. Sort the MS-DOS directory, and then display it one screen at a time. It's easy. Just code

DIR | SORT | MORE

Note that the data are displayed one screen at a time in alphabetical order (Fig. 8.30).

Fig. 8.30   If the MS-DOS directory is piped through *SORT* and then through *MORE*, the output is displayed one screen at a time in alphabetical order. Note that even descriptive messages and summary lines are sorted.

```
          36 File(s)     68608 bytes free
     Directory of A: \
     Volume in drive A has no label

%PIPE1      $$$        0     3-26-86    1:58p
%PIPE2      $$$        0     3-26-86    1:58p
ANSI        SYS     1963    10-22-84    9:31a
APPLY       COM     1945     9-27-84    8:42a
ASSIGN      COM    16746     9-07-84   10:35a
BACKUP      EXE    14976     4-16-83    4:10p
BACKUP5     EXE    14976     4-16-83    4:10p
CHKDSK      COM     6468    11-21-83    3:24p
CIPHER      COM      153     1-31-83    3:21p
COMMAND     COM    18128    10-18-84    9:43a
COMP        COM     3656    10-24-84    3:23p
CONFIGUR    COM    19724     5-03-84   10:33a
DEBUG       COM    12484     4-04-84    9:20a
DISKCOMP    COM     1598    10-23-84    1:50p
DISKCOPY    COM    14592    10-23-84    1:45p
EDLIN       COM     8080    11-21-83    2:01p
FC          EXE     2585    11-21-83    2:10p
FIND        EXE    10624    11-03-83    4:07p
--More--
```

Pipes, filters, and redirection are powerful tools. As you become more experienced with MS-DOS, you'll find many uses for them.

Batch Files

While most MS-DOS applications are interactive, you will occasionally encounter a need to issue the same set of commands over and over again. For example, the manuscript for this book was written on a word processor called Word Perfect. Loading Word Perfect requires four commands: *DATE*, *TIME*, *B*: (the data disk's default drive), and *A:WP* (where *WP* is the program name). Typing those same commands every day is annoying. An option is to create a **batch file**.

The normal boot procedure includes *DATE* and *TIME*, but nothing else. Ideally, we'd like to replace the normal procedure with our own boot sequence that includes all four commands. We can do it by creating an *AUTOEXEC.BAT* file. (The extension *BAT* means batch.) When the computer is booted, the operating system searches the default drive's directory for a file named *AUTOEXEC.BAT*. If such a file exists, MS-DOS reads it and issues its commands in order. If not, the standard boot sequence is followed.

To create an *AUTOEXEC.BAT* file, use the text editor or simply copy the commands from the console; for example,

COPY CON B:AUTOEXEC.BAT

(The sentinel value, remember, is function key F6.) The commands you type will be stored on a batch file on drive B. Subsequently, when the system is booted with that disk in the default drive, the commands in *AUTOEXEC.BAT* will replace the standard boot sequence. You may not have Word Perfect, but consider creating an *AUTOEXEC.BAT* file for your favorite software package.

An expansion board with a battery-operated clock is a popular option on many personal computer systems. If your system is equipped with a clock, you can obtain the current date and time from it rather than from the keyboard by creating an *AUTOEXEC.BAT* file. Check your expansion board user's guide for details.

Other types of batch files can be created, too. For example, imagine a payroll application that calls for entering data to a verification program, sorting those data, processing the data through a payroll program, and, finally, printing the checks. Four programs must run to complete this application. Week after week, the same four programs must be run in the same order. Instead of expecting an operator to enter the necessary commands, a better approach is to create a batch file; for example,

ECHO Insert payroll data disk in drive B.
VERIFY

SORT <B:TIMEDATA >B:TIMESORT
PAYROLL
CHECKS

This file of commands might be called *PAY.BAT*. To run the complete payroll application, the operator enters a single line

PAY.BAT

MS-DOS will respond by reading the batch file and carrying out the commands in order.

The *ECHO* command is new. It displays comments or messages on the screen. Another use for *ECHO* is turning on or off the printing of other commands. Normally, when a command is issued it is displayed on the screen. Adding *ECHO OFF* suppresses this display; adding *ECHO ON* reactivates it. The default is *ON*.

Other Useful Commands

MS-DOS is a powerful operating system, and we have barely scratched the surface of its command language. However, assuming you have actually tried the commands described in this chapter, you should be able to read the reference manual and determine how to use additional commands on your own. For example, *COMP* compares two files and is used to verify a copy operation; *DISKCOPY* copies an entire disk, track by track; *DISK-COMP* compares the contents of two disks. Another useful command, *RECOVER*, allows you to salvage at least portions of a file from a disk that contains bad sectors. Find an MS-DOS or PC-DOS reference manual and read about the *RECOVER* command.

We've already considered two filters: *MORE* and *SORT*. Another filter, *CIPHER*, encrypts or decrypts data given a key word. A fourth filter, *FIND*, searches the standard input stream or, using redirection, a file, for a specified series of characters. Although it isn't a filter, the clear screen (*CLS*) command is useful. If you can't guess what it does, try it.

Many applications generate graphic output. If you'd like to print a copy of what appears on the screen, use the *GRAPHICS* command (it's available in PC-DOS, but not in MS-DOS). Simply type *GRAPHICS*, press return, and then load your application program. The graphics command loads a copy of a graphics routine immediately after the operating system. With this routine in place, pressing Shift-PrtSc sends the contents of the screen to the printer in graphics mode rather than character mode. You must have a graphics printer, and it will run slowly, but you'll get a very nice graphic image.

Finally, consider the *PRINT* command. It places one or more text files in a print queue. The contents of the queue are then printed in the background, in parallel with other MS-DOS commands; in other words, as the printer prints, you can type other commands and work on other applications concurrently. Once you learn how to use the *PRINT* command, you will never again be willing to wait for the printer.

Summary

This chapter introduced the MS-DOS command language. The basic structure of a command was illustrated and the difference between resident and transient commands explained. We then turned to normal boot procedures and introduced *DATE* and *TIME*, the default drive, the standard system prompt, and the *VER* command. Next, we formatted a disk.

The file system is a key element of MS-DOS. We considered the rules for defining file names, discussed hierarchical directory structures, the root directory, and subdirectories, and described path names. Using the MS-DOS disk as an example, we introduced *CHKDSK*, *DIR*, and *TREE* commands.

The next step was creating several directories and files on the work disk formatted earlier. Using *MKDIR*, we created three directories. Next, we added several files to the work disk and used *DIR* and *TREE* to verify their presence. *CHDIR* allowed us to change our working directory. Later, we used wild card characters to copy multiple files, and introduced the *TYPE* command.

Many commands and utilities expect input from the standard system input device and send output to the standard system output device. Redirection allows a user to substitute files or other devices for these standard devices. Filters are routines that accept data from a standard input device, modify them, and send the results to a standard output device. Filters are often used with pipes. We considered *MORE* and *SORT*, and combined them to generate some interesting output.

When faced with a need to issue the same set of commands again and again, a user can create a batch file. *AUTOEXEC.BAT* files replace the system's normal boot procedure. Other batch files can be used for repetitive applications. To invoke the commands in a batch file, simply code the file's name as though it were a command.

The chapter ended with a brief overview of several other MS-DOS commands. For a more detailed summary of command formats, see Appendix B.

Key Words

batch file	file name	root directory
boot	filter	*SORT*
CHDIR	*FORMAT*	subdirectory
CHKDSK	*MKDIR*	*TIME*
command	*MORE*	transient
COPY	parameter	*TREE*
DATE	path name	*TYPE*
default drive	pipe	*VER*
delimiter	prompt	wild card
DIR	redirection	working directory
directory	resident	

References

1. IBM and Microsoft (1983). *Disk Operating System, Version 2.10.*
2. King, Richard Allen (1983). *The IBM PC-DOS Handbook.* Berkeley, California: Sybex, Inc.
3. Zenith Data Systems and Microsoft (1984). *MS-DOS, Version 2.*

Exercises

1. If you haven't already done so, work through the chapter tutorial.

2. Describe the general form of an MS-DOS command. What are parameters? What are delimiters?

3. Distinguish between resident and transient commands.

4. Why is it important to set the date and time before using a system?

5. What is the significance of the default drive?

6. Why must a diskette be formatted before use?

7. What is the significance of a file name extension?

8. Briefly describe a hierarchical directory structure. What advantages does it offer over a simple linear structure?

9. Distinguish between a path name and a file name.

10. Distinguish between creating a directory and creating a file.

11. Distinguish between the root directory and a working directory.

12. What are wild card characters? Why are they useful? Why can't they be part of a file's legal name?

13. Briefly explain redirection.

14. What are filters? What are pipes? Briefly explain how they work together.

15. What is a batch file? Why are batch files useful?

16. If you normally use a particular application program such as a word processor or a spreadsheet, create an *AUTOEXEC.BAT* file of the commands needed to boot it.

17. Create a set of directories to help keep track of your MS-DOS text files or programs. Add your existing files to the directory (rename them).

CHAPTER

9

UNIX Commands and Utilities

UNIX

UNIX was developed at Bell Laboratories, a division of AT&T, in the 1970s. Largely the work of two individuals, Ken Thompson and Dennis Ritchie, the system's main thrust was providing a convenient working environment for programming. Today, it is an important standard that has influenced the design of many modern operating systems. For example, current releases of MS-DOS incorporate numerous UNIX features. Experienced programmers consider UNIX simple, elegant, and easy to learn. Beginners, on the other hand, sometimes find it terse, and not very friendly.

UNIX commands are processed by a **shell** that lies between the user and the resident operating system (Fig. 9.1). The shell is not really part of the operating system, so it can be changed. Professional programmers might choose a technical shell. Beginners might prefer selecting commands from a menu or by pointing at pictures (icons). The idea of a command processor that is independent from the operating system was an important UNIX innovation.

Two shells are in common use. The standard shell, sometimes called the **Bourne shell**, was developed at Bell Laboratories. A second, the **C shell**, is related to the C programming language. They are similar; in fact, you can follow the chapter tutorial and complete the end-of-chapter exercises using either one. As you become more experienced, you will want to write shell programs; at that point, the differences become significant.

Figure 9.2 shows the general form of a UNIX command. The system **prompt** (often, a dollar sign for the Bourne shell or a percent sign for the C shell) is displayed by UNIX. Command names are generally terse (*ed* for editor, *cp* for copy a file), but meaningful. One or more spaces separate the command name from the options. If they are included, the options are usually preceded by a minus sign to distinguish them from the arguments. Most options are designated by a single lowercase letter, and more than one can be coded. One or more spaces separate the options from the arguments, which generally consist of one or more file names.

Fig. 9.1   UNIX commands are processed by a shell that lies between the user and the resident operating system.

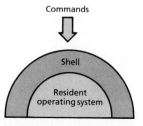

Fig. 9.2   The general form of a UNIX command.

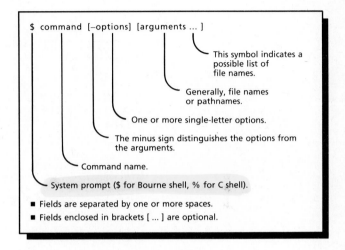

```
$ command [–options] [arguments ... ]
```
                                        This symbol indicates a
                                        possible list of
                                        file names.

                                    Generally, file names
                                    or pathnames.

                                One or more single-letter options.

                            The minus sign distinguishes the options from
                            the arguments.

                        Command name.

                    System prompt ($ for Bourne shell, % for C shell).

■ Fields are separated by one or more spaces.
■ Fields enclosed in brackets [...] are optional.

Unlike MS-DOS, UNIX is a multiple-user operating system, with high-speed hard disk replacing diskettes. Because disk access is so fast, the distinction between transient and resident modules is largely transparent to the user. Also, given the storage capacity of hard disk, users normally share the same pack.

This introduction to UNIX commands and utilities is presented as a tutorial. The examples were run on a Digital Equipment Corporation MicroVax computer under the Bourne shell. Don't just read it. Instead, find a UNIX system, and as you read about a command enter it and see for yourself how the computer responds. You'll need a user name and a password; see your instructor or your system's super user. Later, you'll find Appendix C a useful reference.

Logging On

Usually, a system administrator or super user is responsible for such start-up procedures as booting the system and setting the date and time, so the UNIX user can ignore these tasks. When you sit down at a terminal, the system should be up and running.

Every UNIX session begins with a request for a **login name** and a **password** (Fig. 9.3). In response to the first prompt, type your login name and press return. Next, you'll be asked for your password. Type it and press return; for security reasons, passwords are never displayed.

On some systems, you'll be expected to select your own password the first time you log on. Use any combination of up to eight keyboard charac-

Fig. 9.3

Normally, your system's super user will assign you a login name and a password. This screen shows a normal log on sequence and illustrates several commands.

```
login: bill
password:

Welcome to UNIX!

$passwd
Changing password for bill
Old password:
Type new password:
Retype password:
$date
Tues Jul 15 10:32:15 EST 1986
$who am i
bill        tty1 Jul 15 10:21
$
```

ters. UNIX prefers relatively lengthy passwords and may ask you to try again if you suggest less than six characters.

Figure 9.3 shows a normal logon sequence, and then illustrates several commands. Use the *passwd* utility (Fig. 9.4) to change your password. The *date* utility (Fig. 9.5) displays the system date and time. To identify users currently logged on your system, type *who* (Fig. 9.6). A user working on more than one project may have two or more login names, and that can be

Fig. 9.4

Use the *passwd* utility to change your password.

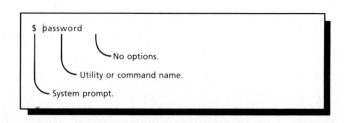

```
$ password
              └── No options.
          └── Utility or command name.
      └── System prompt.
```

Fig. 9.5   The *date* utility displays the system date and time.

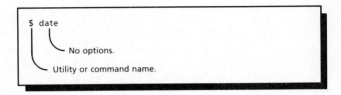

confusing. The command

who am i

displays his or her current login name.

The *write* utility (on some systems, it's *talk*) allows two users to exchange real-time messages, while *mail* sends and receives electronic mail. Many larger UNIX systems feature an on-line reference manual. To obtain a description of any utility, code *man* followed by the utility name. For example,

man who

displays a description of the *who* utility. Because of space limitations, microcomputer versions of UNIX may not support *man*.

Two shells, the Bourne shell and the C shell, are considered UNIX standards; on most systems, one of them is started after logon. While the examples in this text will work under either shell, you can select one. To activate the Bourne shell, type *sh*; to switch to the C shell, type *csh*.

Fig. 9.6   The *who* utility displays the names of users currently logged on the system.

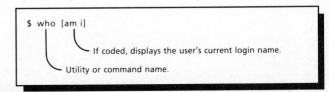

The File System

File Names

The UNIX **file system** allows a user to identify, save, and retrieve files by name. (A program is a type of file.) A **file name** (Fig. 9.7) consists of from 1 to 14 characters. Don't use slashes (/), and avoid starting a file name with a minus sign or hyphen; otherwise, virtually any combination of characters is legal. Note that UNIX distinguishes between uppercase and lowercase; *A* and *a* are different. If you include a period, the characters following it are considered the file name **extension**. The extension is significant to some compilers and to the linkage editor; otherwise, it's simply part of the file name. An **invisible file**'s name starts with a period; invisible file names are not normally displayed when a directory is listed.

Directories

Imagine a user who maintains several different types of files. Letters and other correspondence are generated by a text editor, chapters for a book are output by a word processor, and C programs form another group. Dozens, perhaps even hundreds of different users will have similar needs. Keeping track of all those files in a single **directory** is almost impossible. Instead, UNIX uses a flexible hierarchical directory structure (Fig. 9.8).

The structure begins with a **root directory**. Growing from the root are several "children." Some hold references to utilities and other system rou-

Fig. 9.7   The rules for defining UNIX file names.

```
filename.extension

         Optional. Portion of file name following period.

         Period (optional).

         1–14-character file name.
         (Note: includes period and extension if coded.)
```

■ Suggested characters include A-Z, a-z, 0-9, comma (,), and underscore (_).
■ Avoid using slash (/) characters in file name.
■ Don't start a file name with a minus sign (–).
■ UNIX distinguishes between uppercase and lowercase.
■ If you include a period in the file name, the characters following the period form the extension.
■ The period and the extension count against the 14-character limit.
■ You can code more than one period.

Fig. 9.8   UNIX uses a hierarchical directory structure.

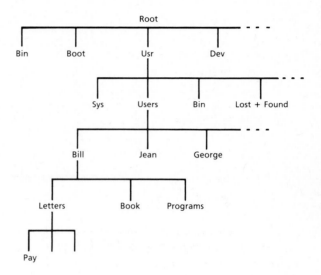

tines. One, *usr*, contains several children of its own, one of which, *users*, holds all the user directory names. Note that *bill* is *users* child, a grandchild of *usr*, and a great grandchild of the root directory. Under *bill* come subdirectories to hold letters, book chapters, and programs. Incidentally, a directory is a special type of file, so the rules for naming directories and files are the same.

Pathnames

With all these directories, however, we need more than a simple name to find a file. For example, it is possible to have files named *pay* recorded under two different directories. A reference to *pay* would thus be ambiguous—which *pay* do we mean? To identify a file, we need a complete **pathname** (Fig. 9.9); for example,

/usr/users/bill//letters/pay

Look at Fig. 9.8, and follow the pathname. The first slash (/) indicates the root directory. Move down to *usr*, then *users*, then *bill*, then *letters*, and finally to the file.

At first glance, subdirectories seem to complicate rather than simplify accessing files. In practice, however, people rarely use such lengthy pathnames. Instead, when you log on, UNIX selects your **home directory** (its name usually matches your login name) as your initial **working directory**.

Fig. 9.9   Because UNIX uses a hierarchical directory structure, you must
                               specify a complete pathname to identify uniquely a file.

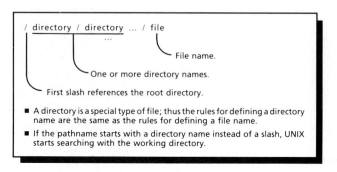

Unless it is told otherwise, the operating system searches for files starting
with your working directory; thus,

letters/pay

is all you need to find file *pay*. Later in the chapter, you'll see how to change
working directories.

Viewing a Directory

Before we begin creating and manipulating directories, let's look through
some existing ones. Start by printing or displaying your working directory.
Just type

pwd

and then press return; the results are shown in Fig. 9.10 (your working
directory name will be different).

Even if this is the first time you've logged on, your home directory
should contain a few files. To view their names, type an *ls* (list directory)
command (Fig. 9.11)

ls -a

The output is shown in Fig. 9.12 (your output may differ). The file names
that begin with a period are usually invisible; had the *-a* option not been
coded, they would not have been listed.

Two files, (.) and (..) are particularly interesting. The single period
stands for the working directory; the double period is a synonym for its
parent. They are useful shorthands for writing pathnames.

Fig. 9.10   The *pwd* (print working directory) command displays the pathname of your current working directory. Note: on your UNIX system, your working directory may have a different pathname.

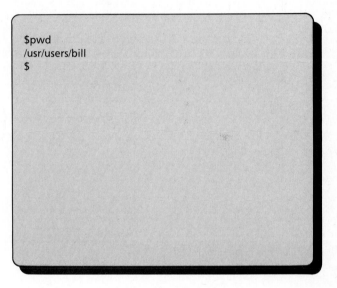

```
$pwd
/usr/users/bill
$
```

Fig. 9.11   The list directory *(ls)* command displays, normally in alphabetical order, the names of the files in the specified directories. If no directories are coded, the contents of the current working directory are listed.

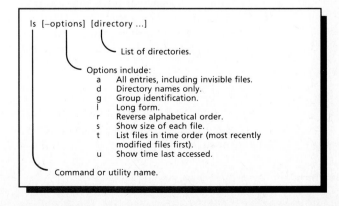

```
ls  [–options]  [directory ...]
                            └─── List of directories.

         Options include:
               a    All entries, including invisible files.
               d    Directory names only.
               g    Group identification.
               l    Long form.
               r    Reverse alphabetical order.
               s    Show size of each file.
               t    List files in time order (most recently
                    modified files first).
               u    Show time last accessed.
         Command or utility name.
```

Fig. 9.12   Following an *ls* command, the names of the files in the referenced
                        directory are listed in alphabetical order.

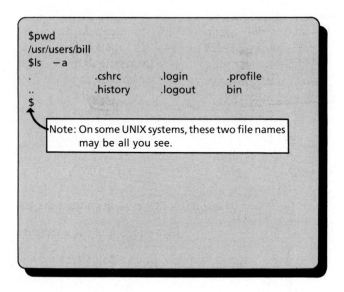

Try a few variations; some sample results are shown in Fig. 9.13. For
example, code

ls

with no options. File names beginning with a period should no longer
appear. In fact, on many systems, absolutely nothing is displayed because
initially there are no regular files. If you ask for a list of files, and there are
none, UNIX displays nothing, not even a "directory empty" message. To
experienced programmers, that makes sense. A beginner might find such
terseness a bit intimidating, however.

To list only directories, code a *d* option

ls -d

Next, take a look at the long form

ls -l

Fig. 9.13   Experiment with the *ls* command, coding several options.

```
$pwd
/usr/users/bill
$ls   -a
  .               .cshrc        .login        .profile
  ..              .history      .logout       bin
$ls
bin
$ls   -d
  .               ..

$ls   -l
total  1
d rw x r- x r - x   2 bill      24 Mar 25  05:05 bin
$ls   -1a
total  9
d rw x r- x r - x   3 bill      512 Apr 14  10:02 .
d rw x r- x r - x  68 root     1536 Mar 26  16:32 ..
- rw x r- x r - x   1 bill      414 Mar 25  05:05 .cshrc
- rw x r- x - - -   1 bill      588 Mar 25  10:07 .history
- rw x r- x r - x   1 bill      245 Mar 25  05:05 .login
- rw - r- - - - -   1 root       44 Mar 26  16:33 .logout
- r x wr- x r - x   1 bill      103 Mar 25  05:05 .profile
d rw x r- x r - x   2 bill       24 Mar 25  05:05 bin

$
```

Finally, list everything, including invisible files, in long form

ls -la

To indicate more than one option, simply code all the option letters one after another.

A long-form line shows a file's owner, size, and the date and time it was most recently modified. The first 10 characters indicate the file type and its access permissions (Fig. 9.14). The file can be an ordinary file (data or a program), a directory, or a special file that corresponds to an input or output device. Three sets of permissions are included—one for the file's owner, a second for users in the owner's group, and a third for all other users. Based on the recorded values, a given user or group can be granted read (r), write (w), or execute (x) permission, or any combination. A minus sign indicates no permission. To change access permissions, use the *chmod* utility.

Fig. 9.14   The first 10 characters in a long-form directory line indicate the
file's type and access permissions. Use *chmod* to change them.

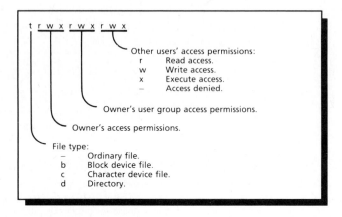

Creating Directories

Let's create three subdirectories under our home directory. Type a make
directory command (Fig. 9.15)

mkdir letters book programs

Note that the command is followed by a list of directory names separated by
spaces. UNIX will respond by creating the requested directories, but will
not display a confirmation message (after all, you didn't tell it to).

To find out if the directories actually were created, type

ls -d

The output is shown in Fig. 9.16. Compare it with Fig. 9.14; clearly, the
three directories now exist.

The *mkdir* utility creates a directory. Use *rmdir* to remove or delete one.

Fig. 9.15   Directories are created by the make directory (*mkdir*) utility.

```
mkdir  directory...

            One or more directory names.
```

Fig. 9.16   After a make directory command is executed, a directory list
                       should reveal the new directories' names.

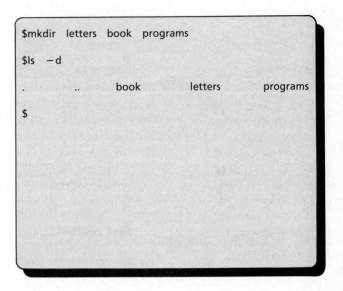

```
$mkdir  letters  book  programs

$ls   −d

.              ..          book          letters          programs

$
```

Changing Working Directories

The *ls* command lists the contents of the current working directory. You
can use a *cd* command (Fig. 9.17) to change the current working directory.
For example, code

cd /

The slash identifies the root directory. UNIX will display no confirmation
message, but the root directory will be your new working directory. Now

Fig. 9.17   Use a *cd* (change directory) command to switch to a new working
                       directory.

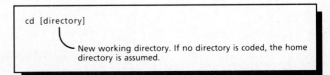

```
cd [directory]
```
New working directory. If no directory is coded, the home
directory is assumed.

code

ls -a

The output (on the author's system) is shown in the top half of Fig. 9.18.
    Next, switch to a lower level, or child, directory. Type

cd /usr/users

On many UNIX systems, *users* contains each user's home directory. Once
again, list your working directory's contents; the output (on the author's
system) is shown in the bottom half of Fig. 9.18.
    Finally, move back to your home directory. Type

cd

Fig. 9.18   This screen shows the contents of the root directory and of
                    directory *users* on the author's UNIX system. You may see a
                    different list of files on your system.

```
$cd   /
$ls   — a
    .              .profile      etc          save         verify.log
    ..             TEST          flp          sys          vmunix
    .cshrc         bin           fverify      test
    .hostabbr      boot          lib          tmp
    .login         core          lost + fnd   tp
    .logout        dev           mnt          usr

$cd   /usr/users
    .              datacom3      jj2eossa     mb52ossb     rw42ossa
    ..             datacom4      jk3rossb     md4gossa     sk4ossa
    ab2bossb       db5nossb      jm1xossb     m19nossa     sn0bossb
    ab7cossa       dc1zossb      jm6bossb     mt7nossb     sr6dossa
    ac7sossa       dg44ossb      jm8vossb     mv3oossb     sr71ossb
    bac            d12nossb      jm0sossb     nr5hossa     st7vossa
    bc9gossb       dw00ossa      jw6wossa     pa31ossa     sw3kossb
    bd41ossb       dw1gossa      kc1uossb     pb1possb     tb8hossa
    bh5tossa       er8oossa      kc4iossb     pg4nossb     tg3uossb
    bill           es19ossb      kg0xossa     ph7oossb     tw6sossa
    c136ossa       guest         kr6fossb     rb2aossb     tr41ossa
    dat            hp1qossa      ks9kossb     rh22ossa     wsd
    datacom1       jd8vossb      lt9fossa     rs6iossa

$
```

with no options or arguments. To verify that you've returned to your home directory, type a *pwd* (print working directory) command. Once again, list the directory's contents.

Creating Files

Most files are created by programs, such as editors, compilers, interpreters, word processors, spreadsheets, and data base managers. Most UNIX systems incorporate both a line editor (*ed*) and a powerful full-screen "visual" editor (*vi*). While an in-depth discussion of its features is beyond the scope of this book, we can use *vi* to create a few simple files. First, however, let's change the current working directory to *letters*. It's a subdirectory of your home directory, which, if you've been following the tutorial, is your current working directory. Unless you specify otherwise, UNIX always assumes that a file reference starts with the current working directory, so

cd letters

changes the working directory to *letters*.

Start by requesting the visual editor (Fig. 9.19). For example, to create (in the working directory) a file named *tom*, code

vi tom

Except for a message at the bottom, the screen should go blank. The visual editor has two operating modes: command and insert. As you begin, you're in command mode. (We'll cover only a few essential commands.) To enter insert mode, press the *i* key. You'll get no confirmation, but you should be able to begin entering text. (Note: you may have to tell *vi* your terminal type—check with your instructor or your system administrator.)

Type anything you want. When you're done, exit insert mode by pressing the escape key (or on some systems, a function key), and then type *:wq* (for write quit). Some systems accept a pair of capital Zs as a command to exit *vi*. You should see a system prompt indicating that you're back in the

Fig. 9.19   The visual editor (*vi*) can be used to create text files and source
                      modules.

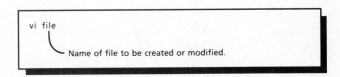

Fig. 9.20   This screen shows the message displayed by the visual editor
after it has created a file.

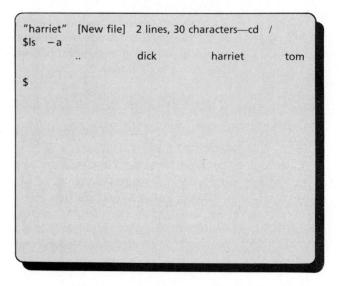

shell. Type an *ls* command to verify that the file is on disk. Repeat this
procedure to create two more files named *dick* and *harriet* (Fig. 9.20).

Some operating systems require a programmer or user to specify a file's
size when creating it. That's not necessary under UNIX. We'll investigate
how UNIX dynamically allocates disk space in Chapter 16.

Manipulating Files

Now that you've created some files, let's manipulate them. For example, the
concatenate (*cat*) utility (Fig. 9.21), displays the contents of selected files.

Fig. 9.21   Use the concatenate (*cat*) utility to display the contents of one or
more files.

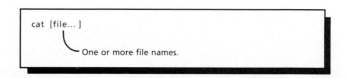

To display *tom*, code

cat tom

The file should appear on your screen. To list the contents of more than one file, code a series of file names; for example,

cat tom dick harriet

produces something like the output shown in Fig. 9.22. (You should see whatever you typed through *vi*.)

Imagine that a file named *resume* contains enough data to fill several screens. If you code

cat resume

much of the data will scroll off the screen before you can read it. To display the file's contents one screen at a time, code

more resume

Fig. 9.22
The word concatenate means "to join together." Thus, if several file names follow a *cat* command, the contents of all the files are displayed one after another.

```
$cat  tom  dick  harriet
Hi, Tom!
Go ahead, Richard.
Make my day.
This is a file
named harriet.
$
```

Press the space bar to view another screen, or the delete key to end the program. The *more* utility is not available on all versions of UNIX. If your system doesn't have *more*, you might be able to suspend a display by pressing control-s, and resume the display by pressing control-q.

Your current working directory is *letters*. Switch back to your home directory by coding

cd

Now try

cat harriet

You should get an error message. Try

cat letters/harriet

You should get valid output. Why? List your working directory

ls -a

Do you see a file named *harriet*? No. However, the directory *letters* does appear. If you follow a path from your current directory, through *letters*, you'll find *harriet*.

To copy a file, use the copy (*cp*) utility (Fig. 9.23). For example, code

cp letters/dick book/chapt.2

Now,

cat book/chapt.2

Fig. 9.23   To copy a file, use the copy (*cp*) utility.

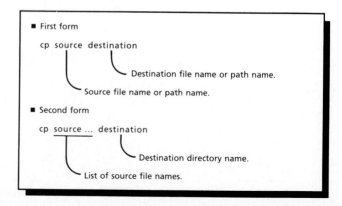

Fig. 9.24   When a file is copied, its name appears in the new directory.

```
$cd
$cp   letters/dick   book/chapt.2
$cat   book/chapt.2
Go ahead, Richard.
Make my day.
$ls   −a     book
.               ..                       chapt.2
$
```

should display the contents of the newly created file (Fig. 9.24). List the directory

ls -a book

File *chapt.2* should appear in the list.

The same file can be referenced in more than one directory by creating a link (Fig. 9.25). For example, code

ln letters/harriet book

Fig. 9.25   The same file can be referenced in more than one directory by creating a link.

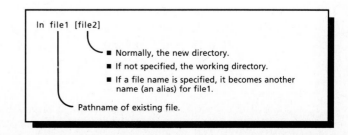

followed by

ls -a book

and compare the output to Fig. 9.24. You should see a new entry in the list. Copy duplicates a file. Link does not; it merely assigns another name to the same file by creating a new directory entry.

To rename a file, code an *mv* (move) command. To delete a file, code an *rm* (for remove link) command. If a file has multiple links, *rm* will not delete it; you'll still be able to access it through other links. When you remove the last link to a file, however, it's gone.

Wild card characters make it easy to reference a number of related file names. A question mark (?) represents any single character; for example, the file name

term?

expands to *term1*, *term2*, *termc*, and any other file named *term* followed by any single character. An asterisk (*) represents multiple characters; for example,

term*

stands for *term1*, *term.v6*, *term.abcdefgh*, and any other file named *term* followed by any combination of from 1 to 10 characters (the limit, remember, is 14).

Imagine you've been working on a C program. Your source module is called *mypgm.c*; the object module is *mypgm.o*. You want to copy both. You have two options. One is to issue two *cp* commands. The other is to reference *mypgm.** or *mypgm.?*. Seeing the wild card characters, the shell will look for all files that fit; thus a single wild card name references both.

Pipes, Filters, and Redirection

Many UNIX utilities and commands assume a standard input or output device; for example, *cat* sends its output to the screen, while *vi* gets its input from the keyboard. By using **redirection** operators (Fig. 9.26), a user can tell the shell to change those defaults.

Let's use *cat* to illustrate this feature. You already know that a *cat* command followed by a file name displays the contents of the file. Try coding *cat* with no options

cat

Since no inputs or outputs are specified, the shell assumes the standard input and output devices (the keyboard and the screen). Thus, whatever

Fig. 9.26   Many UNIX commands and filters deal with the standard input
                         and output devices. Redirection operators and pipes allow a user
                         to change to a specified file or device.

Parameter	Meaning	Example
⟨	Change source to a specified file or device	⟨myfile
⟩	Change destination to a specified file or device	⟩tempfile
⟩⟩	Change destination, usually to an existing file, and append new output to it	⟩⟩master.pay
|	Pipe standard output to another command or to a filter	cat file1|sort

you type is simply echoed back to the screen. Try typing a few lines (Fig.
9.27). Press return at the end of each line; when you're finished, press
control-D (the end-of-file sentinel value). Some UNIX systems echo line by
line; others display all the output only after you press control-D; in either
case, data are copied from the standard input to the standard output device.

Fig. 9.27   This series of *cat* commands illustrates redirection.

```
$cat
The quick brown fox
jumped over the lazy dog.
The quick brown fox
jumped over the lazy dog.
^D
$cat >book/intro
There was a young man from Nantucket
who ...
^D
$ls   -a   book
.             ..                    chapt.2           intro
$
```

Redirect that output. Type

cat >book/intro

followed by several lines of text (Fig. 9.27). Press control-D when you're finished. Now, list your directory

ls -a book

You should see the new entry.

A **filter** accepts input from the standard input device, modifies (or filters) the data in some way, and sends the results to the standard output device. For example, consider *sort* (Fig. 9.28). It's a utility that reads input from the specified file or files (or the standard input device), sorts them into alphabetical or numerical sequence, and outputs the sorted data to the screen. It can also be used as a filter.

A **pipe** causes one utility's standard output to be used as another utility's standard input. Pipes are designated by a vertical line (|). For example, earlier in the chapter, you coded

cat tom dick harriet

Repeat that command. Now, try

cat tom dick harriet | sort

As the bottom half of Fig. 9.29 shows, the standard output has been routed through *sort*, and the file contents are displayed, line by line, in alphabetical order.

Fig. 9.28   The *sort* utility can be used by itself or as a filter.

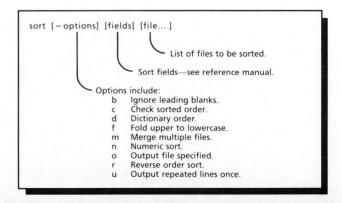

Fig. 9.29   With pipes, one utility's standard output becomes another
utility's standard input.

```
$cat  tom  dick  harriet
Hi, Tom!
Go ahead, Richard.
Make my day.
This is a file
named harriet.

$cat  tom  dick  harriet  |  sort
Go ahead, Richard.
Hi, Tom!
Make my day.
named harriet.
This is a file
```

UNIX utilities can be viewed as tools. Each one performs a single function. Instead of writing a massive program to perform a series of functions, it makes sense to use the existing tools. Pipes, filters, and redirection make it easy to link programs and utilities. As you become more experienced with UNIX, you'll find many uses for them.

Incidentally, most utilities send error messages to the standard error device—usually, the screen. The shell does not redirect error messages. Thus, they won't be lost in an output file or down a pipe.

This marks the end of the chapter tutorial. When you're ready, log off the system by pressing control-D. An option is to type a *logout* command.

Shell Scripts

Many data processing applications are run daily, weekly, or at other regular intervals. Others, for example, a program test, are repeated many times. When such applications are run, a set of commands must be issued. Repeating the application means repeating the commands. Retyping the same commands over and over again is annoying and error prone. An option is to write a **shell script**.

A shell script is a file that consists of a series of commands. (It's much like an MS/DOS BAT file.) The shell is actually a highly sophisticated, interpretive programming language, with its own variables, expressions, sequence, decision, and repetitive structures. Writing shell scripts is beyond the scope of this book, but it is a powerful UNIX feature that you will eventually want to learn more about.

Other Useful Commands

We have barely scratched the surface of the UNIX command language. However, assuming you have actually tried the commands described in this chapter, you should be able to read a reference manual or a UNIX textbook and determine how to use additional commands on your own. For example, check *lpr*. It sends the contents of a file to the line printer. Then check *pr*. This filter prepares output for the line printer, adding page headers, page numbers, and so on. Try using pipes to direct the output from *cat*, through *pr*, and then to *lpr*.

We've already mentioned the visual editor, *vi*. Several other utilities transform text prepared under *vi* into printable form. For example, *nroff* formats text, *troff* prepares output for a phototypesetter, *eqn* sets up equations, *tbl* formats tables, and *spell* checks for spelling errors. Learn to use them; they are powerful tools.

Some tasks, for example, printing the contents of a file or performing a lengthy compile, can be time-consuming. Instead of idly waiting for such a process to finish executing, you can take advantage of UNIX's multiprogramming capability and run it in the **background**. While it runs, the terminal is free to support another program.

To run a program in the background, type an ampersand (&) at the end of the command line; for example,

lpr names &

Usually, the shell starts a command as soon as you enter it, and then waits for it to terminate before displaying the next prompt. The ampersand tells the shell to start the process, immediately display a process identification number, and give you another prompt (see Chapter 16 for additional details). Respond by typing your next command. To check the status of your background command, type a process status (*ps*) command.

Two other utilities support communications between systems. Call UNIX (*cu*) is a terminal emulator that allows a user to dial a remote computer and access it. UNIX-to-UNIX copy (*uucp*) transfers files between UNIX systems.

Summary

UNIX commands are processed by a shell. The basic structure of a command was illustrated, and normal logon procedures introduced. The *passwd* utility can be used to change a password; the *date* utility displays the system date and time, and *who* displays a list of users logged on the system.

The UNIX file system allows a user to store, retrieve, and manipulate files by name. The rules for defining file names were explained. Because UNIX uses a hierarchical directory structure, a pathname must be specified to completely identify a file. The *pwd* command displays the current working directory's pathname. You used *ls* to list a directory's contents, trying several different options. Next, you used *mkdir* to create three directories and experimented with the change directory (*cd*) command. Finally, you used the visual editor (*vi*) to create some files, and manipulated those files with *cat*, *cp*, and *ln* commands.

Many UNIX utilities and commands assume the standard input or output device. Redirection tells the shell to change these defaults. A filter accepts data from the standard input device, modifies them in some way, and sends the results to the standard output device. Pipes allow a user to link utilities and other programs, treating the standard output generated by one as the standard input for another. The *sort* utility was used to illustrate pipes and filters.

Many data processing jobs are run frequently. Thus, the same set of commands must be entered again and again. An option is to write a shell script. The chapter ended with a brief overview of several other UNIX commands and a discussion of background processing.

Key Words

background	filter	prompt
Bourne shell	home directory	redirection
C shell	invisible file	root directory
cat	login name	shell
cd	*ls*	shell script
cp	*mkdir*	*sort*
date	password	*vi*
directory	*passwd*	*who*
extension	pathname	wild card
file name	pipe	working directory
file system		

References

1. Bourne, S.R. (1983). *The UNIX System*. Reading, Massachusetts: Addison-Wesley Publishing Company.
2. Brown, P.J. (1984). *Starting with UNIX*. Reading, Massachusetts: Addison-Wesley Publishing Company.
3. Sobell, Mark G. (1984). *A Practical Guide to the UNIX System*. Menlo Park, California: The Benjamin Cummings Publishing Company, Inc.

Exercises

1. If you haven't already done so, work through the chapter tutorial.

2. What is a shell? Relate the UNIX shell to the command processor introduced in Chapter 5.

3. Describe the general form of a UNIX command.

4. Chapter 8 discussed MS-DOS. Typically, start-up procedures included booting the operating system and setting the date and time. A UNIX user can ignore these tasks, but must provide a login name and a password. Why are these two operating systems so different?

5. Briefly describe a hierarchical directory structure. What advantages does it offer over a simple linear structure?

6. Distinguish between a pathname and a file name.

7. Distinguish between the root directory, your home directory, and your working directory.

8. Explain the significance of the (.) and (..) file names. What do they mean? Why are they useful?

9. Distinguish between creating a directory and creating a file.

10. When you log on, your home directory is your working directory. Why would you want to change that?

11. What are wild card characters? Why are they useful? Why can't they be part of a file's legal name?

12. Briefly explain redirection.

13. What are filters? What are pipes? Briefly explain how they work together.

14. What is a shell script? Compare a shell script to an MS-DOS batch file.

15. What is the advantage of running selected programs in the background?

CHAPTER

10

DOS/VSE Job Control Language

KEY IDEAS

DOS/VSE
Job control language
The JOB statement
The EXEC statement
   Compiling and link editing
   Cataloging programs
I/O control
   The ASSGN statement
Other job control functions
Cataloged procedures

DOS/VSE

During the computer's second generation, such accounting applications as payroll, accounts receivable, accounts payable, and general ledger were dominant. These applications run on a scheduled basis; thus most second-generation systems were batch oriented. Punched cards were the standard input medium. Programmers prepared decks of cards containing program statements and data, and submitted them to a computer operator along with detailed instructions for running them. The operator scheduled the work and returned the results later.

IBM's 1964 announcement of the System/360 computer series heralded the arrival of the third generation. The application base remained relatively constant, but multiprogramming significantly changed the operator's job. Using written instructions to control several applications concurrently is almost impossible. Thus, it became necessary to insert control statements into the job stream.

IBM's disk operating system (DOS) was written to support small- and medium-size computer systems. Initial versions were limited to two concurrent programs; today's DOS/VSE (for virtual storage extended) can handle up to five application programs plus the resident operating system. Its job control language is straightforward. As you read, remember that DOS JCL was developed with punched cards and batch processing in mind.

Job Control Language

Chapters 8 and 9 presented two interactive command languages. DOS/VSE **job control language** (JCL) is different because DOS/VSE is *not* an interactive operating system. On an interactive system, commands are issued as the work progresses. On a batch system, all commands must be prepared before the first one is submitted.

Under DOS/VSE, programmers or users prepare complete **jobs** consisting of instructions, data, and JCL statements. A job might contain almost any number of related programs; for example, a data verification program, a sort program, a payroll program, and a check writing program might form a payroll job. To a programmer or a user, a complete job is a single unit of work. Once prepared, jobs are submitted to a computer operator, who combines them with other jobs to form a **job stream** (Fig. 10.1).

Look carefully at the job stream pictured in Fig. 10.1. Clearly, the payroll job and the inventory job are different, and, even though they might be submitted together, they must be kept separate. Job separation and identification are essential job control language functions. Within a job, programs must be identified; thus, program identification is a second job control language function. As a program runs, certain default peripheral device assignments can be assumed, but any deviations from these defaults must be clearly communicated to the operating system; this is a third job

Fig. 10.1   On batch processing systems, program instructions, data, and control statements enter through the job stream.

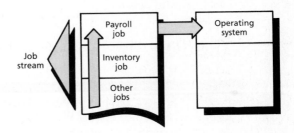

control language function. Finally, a number of options are communicated through command statements.

Figure 10.2 shows the general form of a DOS job control language statement. The two slashes (//) in positions 1 and 2 must be coded. Position 3 must be blank. Following one or more blanks is an **operation**: JOB (job identification), EXEC (program identification), ASSGN (device assignment), or OPTION. One or more blanks separate the operation from the **operands**. A few statements call for **options**; they are separated from the operands by one or more blanks. Note that blanks serve as field separators.

Because DOS/VSE JCL is a batch command language, the tutorial approach of Chapters 8 and 9 is inappropriate. Instead, the various commands will be introduced one by one, with several complete examples illustrating typical jobs. The nature of batch JCL makes it particularly important that you complete the end-of-chapter exercises.

Fig. 10.2   The general form of a DOS job control language statement.

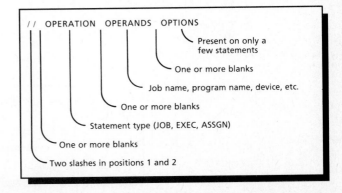

Incidentally, the job control language described in this chapter is a subset of the DOS system command language. Any job control statement can be entered through the operator's console. Additionally, the operator has a set of system initialization and job control commands that cannot be submitted through the job stream.

The JOB Statement

#1 → Jobs are separated and identified by **JOB statements** (Fig. 10.3). The two slashes (//) must appear in positions 1 and 2. One or more blanks separate the slashes from the keyword JOB. The **job name** is chosen by the programmer to identify the job. Accounting information is optional, although some installations may require it.

A job name consists of from 1 to 8 characters. The first one must be a letter; otherwise, any combination of letters and digits is valid. It makes sense, however, to use meaningful job names. For example, a programmer named Sue might code

        //   JOB   SUE

To distinguish jobs, she might choose

        //   JOB   SUE1
                  .
                  .
                  .
        //   JOB   SUE2

and so on. Often, jobs are assigned a prefix followed by a sequence number; for example,

        // JOB PCOO15

Fig. 10.3   The general form of a DOS JOB statement.

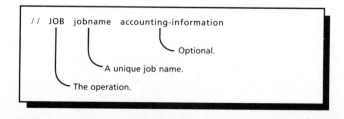

might identify the production control department's fifteenth job. An option is to choose a functional job name, such as

```
//    JOB PAYROLL
```

Every job submitted to a DOS/VSE system must begin with a JOB statement.

The EXEC Statement

Programs are identified by **EXEC** (execute) **statements** (Fig. 10.4). Once again, the statement begins with two slashes in positions 1 and 2. One or more blanks separate the slashes from the key word EXEC. Additional blanks separate the command from the **program name**, which identifies a load module stored in a library.

It should be noted that the program name bears absolutely no relationship to the job name. Like the job name, it consists of from 1 to 8 alphanumeric characters, but there the similarity ends. A job name serves to identify a job being run on the computer right now; when the job ends, the job name ceases to exist. A program name, on the other hand, serves to identify a program on a system library. When the current job terminates, the program still exists, ready, perhaps, to be included in another job.

A job is composed of one or more **job steps**. For example, consider the job illustrated in Fig. 10.5. In the first step, labor data are read into an edit program that eliminates certain data entry errors. The good data are sorted, and the sorted data are then read, along with a master year-to-date-earnings file, into a payroll program. The final job step is an audit program that prepares reports for the accounting department. The job ends with a /& statement. Each job step is one program. Each program requires its own EXEC statement. When DOS reads

```
// EXEC PAYEDIT
```

it loads a copy of program PAYEDIT into memory.

Fig. 10.4   The general form of a DOS EXEC statement.

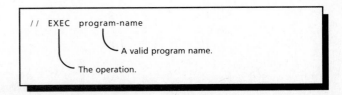

```
// EXEC  program-name
              └── A valid program name.
        └── The operation.
```

Fig. 10.5   Jobs start with a JOB statement. Programs are identified by EXEC
                         statements. A single job might involve several programs.

```
// JOB      PAYROLL
// EXEC     PAYEDIT
// EXEC     SORT
// EXEC     PAYROLL
// EXEC     PAYAUDIT
/&
```

Note that the job and the third program are both named PAYROLL
(Fig. 10.5). That's perfectly legal, but it's pure coincidence. The operating
system doesn't care; we could have coded

// JOB MELVIN

and still referenced the same programs.

Compiling and Link Editing

DOS assumes the program referenced in an EXEC statement is stored on a
library in load module form. The first step in creating a load module is
compilation. A compiler is a program that converts source statements into
an object module. Like any program, the compiler is loaded by the operating system when an EXEC statement references it; for example, the commands to compile a COBOL program are shown in Fig. 10.6. The **/* statement** marks the end of the source module. The **/& statement** marks the

Fig. 10.6   Compiling a COBOL source program calls for these DOS JCL
                         statements.

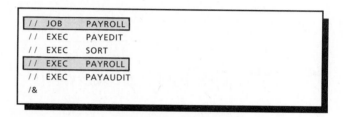

```
// JOB      TEST1
// EXEC     COBOL

         ▷  COBOL source statements

/*
/&
```

Fig. 10.7   The OPTION statement allows a programmer to specify run-time options.

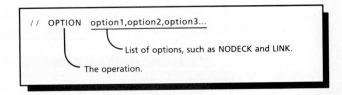

```
//  OPTION   option1,option2,option3...

                              List of options, such as NODECK and LINK.

                  The operation.
```

end of the job. The output will include a listing, compiler error messages, and an object module.

Once a clean assembly or compilation is obtained, the programmer will almost certainly want to test the program. This requires a new job control statement, the **OPTION statement** (Fig. 10.7). Many options can be coded; we won't attempt to cover them all. One, **LINK**, is particularly important, however. It tells the compiler to write the object module to a file where it can be accessed by the linkage editor program and converted to a load module.

For example, Fig. 10.8 shows a COBOL compile, link edit, and execute job. Note that the OPTION statement precedes the associated EXEC state-

Fig. 10.8   Testing a program calls for three job steps—compile, link edit, and execute. The OPTION statement tells the compiler to write the object module to a system file where the linkage editor can find it.

```
//  JOB        DAVIS1
//  OPTION     LINK
//  EXEC       COBOL

          COBOL source module

/ *
//  EXEC       LNKEDT
//  EXEC

          Data

/ *
/ &
```

ment. In this example, the OPTION statement provides information for the COBOL compiler. Note also the last EXEC statement. No program name is specified. When the program name field is blank, DOS selects the load module most recently created by the linkage editor.

TO → The /* statements mark the end of the source module and the end of the job stream data. By convention, programs treat /* statements as sentinel values. To DOS, they are null commands; the operating system basically ignores them. Some programmers use them to separate job steps.

#4 → Because the compile, link edit, execute sequence is so common, DOS/VSE has incorporated a special **GO option** on the EXEC statement (Fig. 10.9). It implies an automatic link edit and execute after the program has been compiled. Serious compiler or linkage editor errors will terminate the job, of course.

Cataloging Programs

An EXEC statement must reference a load module stored on the system's core image library; under DOS, they are called **phases**. To add a program to the library, the programmer must provide a phase name by coding a **PHASE statement**. Figure 10.10 illustrates the commands needed to assemble a program, link it, and catalog the resulting load module to the core image library. Once a load module is on the core image library, executing it requires only the following control statements:

```
// JOB WHATEVER
// EXEC MYPGM
     } data
/*
/&
```

The PHASE statement's second operand (Fig. 10.10) is an asterisk (*). It indicates that the phase is to be loaded in the first available spot in its

---

Fig. 10.9 A DOS/VSE programmer can invoke the compile, link edit, and execute sequence by adding a GO parameter to the EXEC statement.

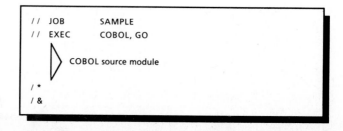

```
//  JOB        SAMPLE
//  EXEC       COBOL, GO

      >   COBOL source module

/ *
/ &
```

Fig. 10.10

An OPTION CATAL statement tells the linkage editor to catalog the load module to the core image library under the specified PHASE name.

CIL

```
//  JOB        PGM14
//  OPTION     CATAL
    PHASE      MYPGM,*
//  EXEC       ASSEMBLY,        → Load module in
                                      core
    ▷  Assembler source module

/ *
//  EXEC       LNKEDT
//  EXEC
    ▷  Data

/ *
/ &
```

Fig. 10.11

Subroutine names are passed to the linkage editor through INCLUDE statements. The specified subroutines are added to the main program as the linkage editor builds a load module.

```
//  JOB        NAME
//  OPTION     CATAL
    PHASE      PGMA,*
//  EXEC       ASSEMBLY

        ▷  Assembler source module

/ *
    INCLUDE    SUBR1
    INCLUDE    SUBR2
//  EXEC       LNKEDT
//  EXEC
        ▷  Data

/ *
/ &
```

partition. The load address can be specified in a number of different ways, but that's a detail we won't explore. Note that position 1 of the PHASE statement is blank. It isn't a standard job control statement. Instead, it's an input parameter to the linkage editor program.

Programs often include subroutines, standard headers, and other previously written logic. Under DOS, these external references are specified in **INCLUDE statements**; for example, Fig. 10.11 shows an assembly followed by a link edit step that adds two subroutines to the main program. The subroutines must be stored on a relocatable library in object module form. The cataloged phase will include the main program and the two subroutines. The INCLUDE provides input to the linkage editor; thus position 1 (at least) is blank.

I/O Control

Under DOS, every physical I/O device attached to a system is assigned a **symbolic name**. Programmers read input data through SYSIPT, send print lines to SYSLST, handle tapes through (perhaps) SYS006, and so on. As long as the programmer is willing to accept his or her installation's standard symbolic names, no additional job control language statements are needed.

DOS programmers must code a **DTF** (Define The File) for each file accessed by program. The DTF sets key parameters and specifies an access method. For example, DTFCD defines a card file; DTFPR, a print file; DTFMT, a magnetic tape file; DTFSD, a sequential file on disk; and DTFDA, a direct access file. Many other combinations of device and access method could be cited.

Fig. 10.12 shows a simple assembly language program containing a DTFCD. The DTF has three parameters. The DEVADDR is the symbolic name of the physical I/O device. IOAREA1 is the label of an 80-character region of main memory set aside to hold an input record, and EOFADDR is the address (label) of the instruction to be executed when the end-of-file marker (/*) is sensed. In this example, the device address (SYSIPT) is the standard system input device (usually a card reader or a keyboard). This program could be run with no job control references to I/O devices.

Other parameters that might be coded in a DTF include: block size, the name of a second I/O area for dual-buffer I/O, label types, the file type (input or output), record form on devices where this can be a variable, logical record length, information identifying a direct access or indexed sequential key, and many others.

The ASSGN Statement

Occasionally, a programmer may wish to change a standard device assignment. Assume, for example, that a DTFMT (magnetic tape) refers to DEVADDR = SYS010, a particular tape drive. As the programmer enters the computer center, that drive has already been assigned to a two-hour job,

Fig. 10.12 The DOS programmer defines file linkages by coding DTF instructions. This program segment shows a simple assembly routine containing a DTF.

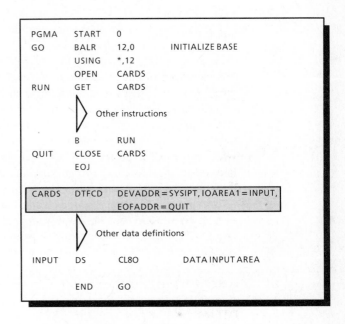

```
PGMA     START    0
GO       BALR     12,0          INITIALIZE BASE
         USING    *,12
         OPEN     CARDS
RUN      GET      CARDS

                  Other instructions

         B        RUN
QUIT     CLOSE    CARDS
         EOJ

CARDS    DTFCD    DEVADDR = SYSIPT, IOAREA1 = INPUT,
                  EOFADDR = QUIT

                  Other data definitions

INPUT    DS       CL80          DATA INPUT AREA

         END      GO
```

but another drive is free. By using an **ASSGN statement** (Fig. 10.13), the programmer can change SYS010 from its standard device assignment to another device *for one job step only.*

To understand the ASSGN statement, it is useful to know how external devices are addressed on an IBM computer. All peripherals are attached to the system through channels. Each channel is assigned a one-digit number;

Fig. 10.13 A programmer can change a standard device assignment by coding an ASSGN statement.

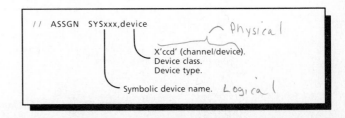

```
// ASSGN SYSxxx,device
```
Physical

X'ccd' (channel/device).
Device class.
Device type.
Symbolic device name. Logical

each device is assigned a two-digit hexadecimal number ranging from a minimum of 00 to a maximum of FF (255 in decimal). The system address of any peripheral device is simply its channel number followed by its device number. For example, 008 represents device 08 on channel 0; 00E is channel 0, device 14 (0E in hex); 181 is channel 1, device 81; 281 is channel 2, device 81, and so on.

If SYS010 is the symbolic name of device 180, and device 181 is free, the programmer can change to device 181 by placing an ASSGN statement in front of the relevant EXEC (Fig. 10.14). The change in assignment holds for one job step only; for example, in Fig. 10.14, after PROGRAM3 terminates, the standard assignment is once again in effect.

In many batch installations, programmers are not allowed in the computer room. How, then, can they know which tape drive, disk drive, printer, or card reader is free? Perhaps more to the point, do programmers really care which specific tape drive supports a program? Although some devices are equipped with important special features, generally, all a programmer wants is a device to read input or write output, and one tape drive, or disk drive, or printer is pretty much like any other.

Newer versions of DOS allow a progammer to specify device classes on an ASSGN statement. For example, if any tape drive will do, the programmer might code

// ASSGN SYS005,TAPE

The system will assign logical device SYS005 to the first available tape drive. Likewise,

// ASSGN SYS014,DISK

represents a request for the first available disk drive. Other valid classes include: READER, PRINTER, PUNCH, DISKETTE, CKD (cylinder/track addressed disk), and FBA (fixed-block architecture disk).

Fig. 10.14   These commands show how SYS010 can be changed from its standard device assignment to channel 1, device 81. Note that an ASSGN statement changes a device assignment for a single job step.

```
//  JOB        P148
//  ASSGN      SYS010,X'181'
//  EXEC       PROGRAM3
    .
    .
    .
```

It is not unusual for a computer center to have several different models of tape drives, disk drives, card readers, or printers. The programmer can, of course, always request a device by its channel/device address, but there is a middle road—the device type can be specified. For example,

// ASSGN SYSLST,3211   *Printer (Physical)*

Logical

assigns logical device SYSLST to the first available 3211 printer, but will not consider a 1403 printer, while

// ASSGN SYS008,2400T9

assigns the first nine-track 2400 tape drive, and avoids the seven-track 2400 tape drive. Using device class or device type assignments can save the programmer work.

Other Job Control Functions

Most DOS progammers use very little job control beyond the few statements we've already discussed. JOB and EXEC statements are, of course, essential. An OPTION statement is needed to compile and test a program. Once testing is completed, load modules must be cataloged to a core image library, and that calls for OPTION, PHASE, and possibly one or more INCLUDE statements. Occasionally, an ASSGN statement is needed to change a standard device assignment. That's about all the average programmer really needs. Other job control functions are usually left to experts.

Since the purpose of this chapter is to cover some of the more commonly used features of DOS/VSE job control language, we won't spend much time discussing the lesser used statements. Instead, we'll briefly describe some the average programmer may occasionally encounter.

Most magnetic tape and direct access files are created with labels. The DLBL statement provides information for writing and/or checking direct access labels; the TLBL statement performs the same functions for magnetic tape labels. The LBLTYP statement tells the linkage editor how much main storage space is to be set aside for label processing.

A single direct access volume (one disk pack, for example) can hold numerous files. To prevent the accidental destruction of data, the physical location of a new file must be carefully controlled. Often, a system manager allocates space for a file by coding an EXTENT statement. Creating a file on a direct access device often requires both an EXTENT and a DLBL statement.

Under DOS, programmers can set several "user program switch indicators" by coding a UPSI statement. The switches indicate key conditions at the start of a program run, and are tested by standard assembly language statements.

Cataloged Procedures

Once a program has been successfully compiled and tested, it is ready to be placed into production. A final compilation and link edit produces a load module that is assigned a phase name and placed on a library. From this point, the compilation and link edit steps are no longer necessary. Instead, the load module or phase is simply loaded into main memory and given control.

Earlier in the chapter, we considered a payroll job (Fig. 10.5). It consisted of four programs: a data edit routine, a sort, the payroll program, and an auditing program. As a minimum, this job would require a JOB statement and four EXEC statements. Additionally, several ASSGN statements and, perhaps, other control statements might be needed. The list of job control commands can easily stretch to 20 or more on multiple-step jobs.

Rather than submit scores of control statements every time a production job is run, a programmer can create a **cataloged procedure**, a special library entry consisting of nothing but control statements. Given a cataloged procedure, all the necessary control statements can be invoked by a single EXEC statement (Fig. 10.15). For example, assume that a procedure named PAYSYS holds all the job control for the payroll job. Only three statements

```
// JOB PAYROLL
// EXEC PROC-PAYSYS
/&
```

will be needed to run payroll. When DOS encounters the EXEC statement, it reads PAYSYS from the procedure library and, in effect, inserts the procedure into the job stream. A single EXEC statement referencing a cataloged

---

Fig. 10.15   Cataloged procedures containing all the job control language
statements for repetitive jobs can be defined and stored on a
procedure library. When a cataloged procedure is named on an
EXEC statement, its JCL statements are inserted into the job
stream.

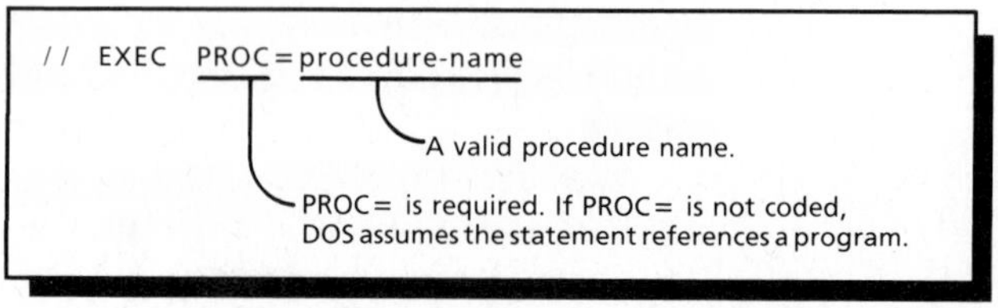

```
// EXEC  PROC=procedure-name
                         A valid procedure name.
              PROC= is required. If PROC= is not coded,
              DOS assumes the statement references a program.
```

procedure might be equivalent to dozens of individual job control language statements.

Summary

This chapter covered many of the basic features of IBM's disk operating system job control language (DOS JCL). A job is a single unit of work consisting of one or more related programs. JOB statements separate and identify jobs. EXEC statements specify the load modules to be loaded and executed. A single JOB statement may be followed by more than one EXEC, each of which marks a single job step.

To compile and test a program, the programmer must inform the system that the load module produced by the linkage editor is to be loaded and executed. This is done through an OPTION statement. Given a LINK option, the assembler or compiler writes the object module to a system file. The linkage editor reads the object module and prepares a load module. Following an EXEC with no program name, the load module is loaded and executed. Under DOS/VSE, the programmer can achieve the same result by coding a GO option on the EXEC statement for the compiler.

In a production environment, programs are usually run by loading and executing a load module directly from a library, bypassing the lengthy assemble (or compile) and link edit steps. Under DOS, these library load modules are called phases. To catalog a phase to the core image library, the programmer codes a CATAL option. CATAL implies LINK.

Each cataloged phase must be given a unique name through a PHASE statement. Additional subroutines and other precoded modules can be specified through INCLUDE statements. The PHASE and INCLUDE statements provide information to the linkage editor; their first position must be blank. The other job control statements—JOB, EXEC, ASSGN, and OPTION—must begin with two slashes (//) in positions 1 and 2. Position 3 (at least) must be blank.

Each peripheral device on a DOS system is assigned a symbolic name. Each combination of a physical device and an access method has its own DTF (Define The File). A program's physical device assignments are specified in its DTFs. A programmer can change a physical device assignment for the current job step by coding an ASSGN statement. Often, programmers specify a device type or a device class rather than a specific physical device.

For the average programmer, these few control statements are enough. In most DOS installations, other less commonly used features of DOS job control are left to specialists.

A cataloged procedure is a set of precoded job control language statements stored on a library and accessed by name through a single EXEC statement. Cataloged procedures are commonly used on production systems.

A detailed summary of DOS JCL can be found in Appendix D.

Key Words

ASSGN statement	job control	option
cataloged	language	OPTION statement
procedure	job name	phase
DTF	job step	PHASE statement
EXEC statement	JOB statement	program name
GO option	job stream	symbolic name
INCLUDE	LINK	/* statement
statement	operand	/& statement
job	operation	

Exercises

1. What functions are performed by a JOB statement?

2. Distinguish between a job and a job step.

3. What functions are performed by an EXEC statement?

4. Explain the purpose of the GO option on a DOS/VSE EXEC statement.

5. Explain the process of cataloging a load module to the core image library. Start with a source module.

6. What is the purpose of a DTF?

7. What function is performed by an ASSGN statement?

8. What is a cataloged procedure?

9. Use DOS JCL statements to compile, link edit, and execute a program written in the language of your choice.

10. Catalog the program you wrote for Exercise 9 to the core image library. Then, run it.

11. Write, in the language of your choice, a series of programs to perform the following functions:
    a. Read data from the standard input device and create a sequential file on disk.
    b. Read the sequential disk file, sort the records into sequence, and create a new file of sorted data on disk.
    c. Read the sorted records and print them.

    Use a sort utility or a language sort feature, or write your sort routine. Catalog all three programs to the core image library. Then, prepare a series of JCL statements to run the three programs.

IBM OS/JCL: JOB and EXEC Statements

K E Y   I D E A S

OS/JCL
  Jobs and job steps
  Cataloged procedures
  JCL statement format
JOB statements
  Accounting information
  The programmer name
  The CLASS parameter
  The TIME parameter
  The REGION parameter
  The MSGLEVEL parameter
  Defaults
  Other JOB parameters
  Continuing a JCL statement
EXEC statements
  The COND parameter
  Other EXEC parameters

OS/JCL

IBM's disk operating system was designed for relatively small computers. With no more than five application programs, techniques such as assigning each I/O device a specific symbolic name or requiring a file specialist to allocate direct access space are (or, in the late 1960s, were) acceptable. IBM's full operating systems, including the virtual memory systems available on current hardware, can support many more concurrent application programs. On such large systems, additional software support is essential. Because these operating systems are larger and more complex, IBM's OS/JCL is considerably more complex than DOS/JCL.

There are three basic JCL statements:

1. **JOB statements** separate and identify jobs. Secondary functions include passing the system accounting and priority information.
2. **EXEC**, or execute, **statements** identify the programs to be executed.
3. **DD**, or data definition, **statements** define, in detail, the characteristics of each peripheral device used by the job.

Here in Chapter 11, we'll discuss JOB and EXEC statements; DD statements will be covered in Chapter 12. We'll focus on those job control language features used by a typical programmer.

Jobs and Job Steps

Consider the compile, link edit, and execute sequence diagrammed in Fig. 11.1. To the programmer, all these steps constitute a single **job** and produce a single set of output. To the system, however, three distinct programs must be executed. The programmer sees a job consisting of several programs. The computer sees a series of programs, each of which represents a single **job step**.

A job must begin with a JOB statement and can contain almost any number of job steps. Each job step requires one EXEC statement. Within a job step, one DD statement must be coded for each peripheral device accessed by the program.

A compile, link edit, and execute job involves three steps. The compiler reads source statements from a terminal and a macro library, prints a listing, and writes an object module to disk. The linkage editor gets its input from the object file created by the first job step and, perhaps, from a subroutine library. Output goes to the printer and to a disk file where a copy of the load module is stored. This load module is the program for the third job step. The program reads data from a disk file and sends its output to the printer and to another disk file.

The JCL needed to support this job is outlined in Fig. 11.2. As you read

Fig. 11.1   An apparently simple compile, link edit, and execute job
                    involves all these peripheral devices and programs.

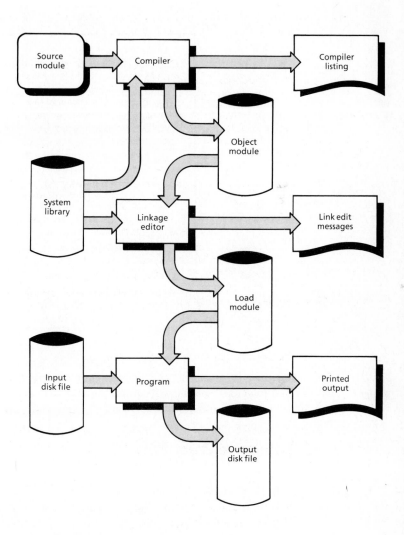

the outline, remember two points:

1. To the computer, each job step is independent.
2. One DD statement must be provided for each input and output
   device.

The first statement identifies the job. Statements 2, 6, and 10, the three
EXEC statements, mark the start of the three job steps. DD statements
identify the peripheral devices needed by each job step.

Fig. 11.2   A compile, link edit, and execute job calls for all these job control
                                 language statements.

---

1. A JOB statement.
2. An EXEC statement for the compiler.
3. A DD statement for the object module file.
4. A DD statement for the printer.
5. A DD statement for the source module.
6. An EXEC statement for the linkage editor.
7. A DD statement for the object module file. This is the same
   file described in statement 3, but, because this is a different job step
   a separate DD statement is needed.
8. A DD statement for the load module.
9. A DD statement for the printer.
10. An EXEC statement for the load module.
11. A DD statement for the load module. This is the same file created
    in the previous job step (statement 8), but, once again, this is a
    new step.
12. A DD statement for the disk input file.
13. A DD statement for the disk output file.
14. A DD statement for the printer.

Note particularly statements 3 and 7. They describe the *same* file. Why
are both DDs necessary? Statement 3 defines the object module file for the
first job step. Statement 7 defines the object module file for the second job
step. To the computer, each job step is independent.

Cataloged Procedures

One compile, link edit, and execute job is much like any other. Thus, each
time a program is tested, the programmer must repeat the same commands.
Typing the same commands again and again is tedious and error prone. An
option is to reference a **cataloged procedure**.

A cataloged procedure is a set of precoded JCL statements, stored on a
library and added to the job stream by the operating system. Figure 11.3
outlines the JCL for a compile, link edit, and execute job using a cataloged
procedure. When it reads the EXEC statement, the operating system
searches the procedure library, obtains a copy of the procedure's JCL, and
inserts the statements into the job stream. The programmer can focus on
JCL unique to the job; all the repetitive code is in the procedure.

Later, after we've looked at a few JCL statements, we'll analyze a typical
cataloged procedure.

Fig. 11.3   A cataloged procedure is a library file containing precoded JCL statements. Given a cataloged procedure, a compile, link edit, and execute job calls for only a few JCL statements.

1. A JOB statement.
2. An EXEC COBOL, or EXEC FORTRAN, or some other EXEC statement referencing the appropriate cataloged procedure.
3. A DD statement for disk input.
4. A DD statement for disk output.
5. A DD statement for printer output.

JCL Statement Format

When IBM's job control language was first released, punched cards were the standard input medium. Cards are prepared on a keypunch. A typical keypunch can record capital letters, the digits 0–9, and several punctuation marks. Thus, JCL statements are written using this limited character set.

The basic format of a JCL statement is shown in Fig. 11.4. Job names, step names, and DD names are chosen by the programmer. They consist of

Fig. 11.4   The general form of an OS/JCL statement.

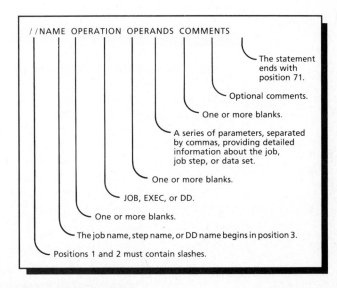

```
//NAME OPERATION OPERANDS COMMENTS
```

- The statement ends with position 71.
- Optional comments.
- One or more blanks.
- A series of parameters, separated by commas, providing detailed information about the job, job step, or data set.
- One or more blanks.
- JOB, EXEC, or DD.
- One or more blanks.
- The job name, step name, or DD name begins in position 3.
- Positions 1 and 2 must contain slashes.

from 1 to 8 letters, digits, or national characters (@, $, #); the first character may not be a digit. The operation field must be JOB, EXEC, or DD. The operands consist of a series of **parameters** separated by commas; we'll discuss numerous parameters in this and the next chapter. Comments are optional.

Note carefully that blanks are used to separate fields. Stray blanks are the beginner's most common JCL error. They will be interpreted as field separators. For example, coding

```
// STEP2  EXEC  COBOL
```

will result in a strange error message—there is no such operation as STEP2 (only JOB, EXEC, and DD are valid). You know what you mean, but the computer doesn't. Try

```
//STEP2  EXEC  COBOL
```

with no blanks between the // and the name field.

JOB Statements

The function of a JOB statement (Fig. 11.5) is to identify and mark the beginning of a job, thus separating it from other jobs. A unique **job name** is required. It must start with a letter or a national character; otherwise, any combination of from 1 to 8 letters, digits, and national characters is legal. In many computer centers, job names are assigned by the operating system, thus eliminating the risk that two or more jobs might have the same name.

Accounting Information

The job name and the operation (JOB) are the only required fields. One important secondary function is to pass information to an accounting routine. **Accounting information** is coded as the first parameter in the oper-

Fig. 11.5   The general form of a JOB statement.

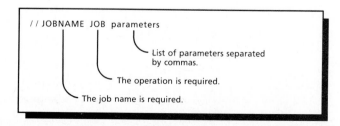

ands field. For example, the statement

//JOB396   JOB   1234

indicates that the cost of running job JOB396 is to be charged against account 1234. Often, multiple accounting **subparameters** are coded. For example,

//MU435   JOB   (1234,875)

might mean that job MU435 is to be charged against account number 1234, user number 875. Subparameters are separated by commas.

Note the use of parentheses. When more than one subparameter is coded, parentheses are required. Also, note the position of the accounting information—it's always the first parameter. Accounting information is a **positional parameter**. Its meaning is determined by its relative position in the operands field.

The exact content of the accounting field is up to the installation; each computer center can define its own accounting subparameters. Note that the subparameters are also positional.

The Programmer Name

On a pure batch system, programmers assemble JCL statements, source statements, and data to form a complete job, submit it to the system, and come back for the results a few hours later. To simplify programmer identification, the **programmer's name** is coded in second positional parameter; for example,

//MU098   JOB   (2987,235),DAVIS

or

//MU1735   JOB   (2195,235),'W.S. DAVIS'

Code up to 20 letters or digits. You can also include a single period. The apostrophes are needed when special characters, such as commas, blanks, or additional periods, are part of the programmer's name. Your computer center may have a preferred format. Note that the programmer's name is separated from the accounting information by a comma.

The CLASS Parameter

One way to improve the efficiency of a batch system is to carefully schedule the work by grouping jobs with similar resource needs. Often, the task of grouping jobs is simplified by assigning them to classes. For example, a class A job might need only the standard input and output devices, while jobs calling for multiple-part paper might be assigned to class B, and those needing magnetic tape might fall into class C. A programmer indicates a job's class by coding a **CLASS parameter**; for example,

//MU741 JOB (3984,444),SMITH,CLASS=A

CLASS is a **keyword parameter**. It derives its meaning not from its position, but from the key word CLASS.

The TIME Parameter

Most multiprogramming systems automatically cancel a program caught in an endless loop after a reasonable time has passed. The data for setting the timer must come from somewhere. Often, the source is a **TIME parameter** (Fig. 11.6). For example,

TIME=(5,30)

asks for 5 minutes and 30 seconds of processor time, while

TIME=(5) or TIME=5 or TIME=(5,0)

request exactly five minutes. Note the parentheses. When the first subparameter alone is coded, they can be skipped; however, when more than one subparameter is coded, parentheses must be used.

Minutes and seconds are positional subparameters; in other words, they are defined by their relative positions. Minutes come first; seconds come second. For example, to request exactly 30 seconds, code

TIME=(,30)

The comma indicates the absence of the positional subparameter for minutes.

Fig. 11.6   The TIME parameter sets a run-time limit on the job.

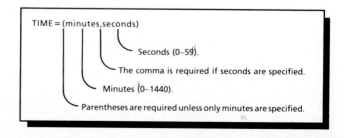

CLASS and TIME are themselves keyword parameters. The keywords CLASS and TIME give them meaning independent of their position. For example, the following JOB statements are all legal:

```
//X14  JOB  (345,86),JONES,CLASS=C,TIME=2
//Z135 JOB  (296,25),'A. SMITH',TIME=(,30),CLASS=B
//AB31 JOB  (940,45),THOMAS,CLASS=B,TIME=(1,15)
```

The accounting information must come first, followed by the programmer name. They are positional parameters, deriving their meaning from their relative positions. Because CLASS and TIME are keyword parameters, they can be coded in any order.

The REGION Parameter

On some systems, a job's priority is determined, in part, by the amount of space it requires. The programmer can request space by coding a **REGION parameter**. Space is allocated in 2048- (2K-) byte blocks; for example,

```
REGION=128K
```

The MSGLEVEL Parameter

Programmer-coded JCL statements, the JCL statements included in a cataloged procedure, and messages indicating the operating system's actions are valuable to the programmer, but once the program is released, they are meaningless to users. The **MSGLEVEL** (message level) **parameter** (Fig. 11.7) allows the programmer to select which JCL and device allocation messages are to be printed. For example,

```
MSGLEVEL=(1,1)
```

Fig. 11.7   The MSGLEVEL parameter specifies which JCL statements and operating system messages are to be printed.

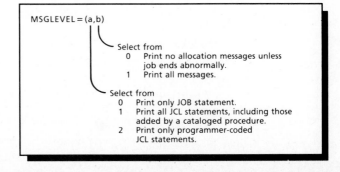

means to print everything, while

MSGLEVEL=(0,0)

means print only the JOB statement unless the job fails, and

MSGLEVEL=(1,0)

instructs the system to print all JCL statements but to skip allocation messages.

Note that parentheses were included in all three examples. Why? How many subparameters were coded? In each case, two. You must use parentheses any time more than one subparameter is coded.

Defaults

Instead of requiring numerous parameters each time a job is submitted, most computer centers rely on **defaults**. If the programmer fails, for any reason, to code a particular parameter, the system assumes a value. Often, only accounting information, the programmer's name, and the job class are required. Defaults are based on the job class with, for example, all CLASS-A jobs assigned a 64K region and a 30-second time limit, while CLASS-B jobs get 128K and a 2-minute time limit. To override a default, simply code the appropriate parameter.

Other JOB Parameters

Other parameters, all keyword in nature, allow the programmer to specify such things as job priority, run type, condition code limits, and restart options. We won't attempt to cover them here; when a need arises, check with a system programmer or look them up in a JCL manual.

Continuing a JCL Statement

Consider the following JOB statement:

```
//C1234567    JOB  (3998,659),'A.B. JONES',CLASS=A,
//                 TIME=(5,30),REGION=128K
```

It's too long to fit on a single line, and thus must be continued. The rules for continuing a JCL statement are:

1. Interrupt the field after a complete parameter or subparameter, including the trailing comma, has been coded. (In other words, stop after any comma.)
2. Optionally code any nonblank character in position 72. Position 72 can be left blank; the continuation character is optional.

3. Code slashes (//) in positions 1 and 2 of the continuation line.
4. Continue coding in any position from 4 through 16. Position 3 must be blank and coding must be resumed no later than position 16.

In other words, just break after a comma and resume coding on the next line. The same rules hold for any type of JCL statement.

EXEC Statements

An EXEC statement (Fig. 11.8) marks the beginning of a job step. Its purpose is to identify the program (or cataloged procedure) to be executed. The **step name** is optional; the rules for coding a step name are the same as the rules for coding a job name. The first parameter must be a program or procedure name; for example,

    // EXEC PGM=SORT6

or

    // EXEC PROC=COBOL

The keyword **PROC** may be skipped; for example,

    // EXEC COBOL

If a program is referenced, **PGM** must be coded.

When a cataloged procedure is referenced, the operating system searches the procedure library and replaces the programmer's EXEC state-

---

Fig. 11.8   The general form of an EXEC statement.

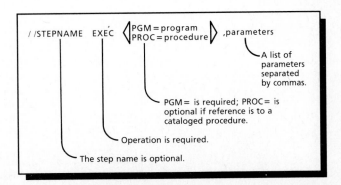

ment with a set of precoded JCL; for example, Fig. 11.9 shows the JCL added to the job stream to replace

// EXEC FORTRAN

The final EXEC statement's program name

PGM=*.LKED.SYSLMOD

looks a bit confusing. The asterisk (*) is a **backward reference**. It tells the operating system to look at a previous JCL statement. Which one? Find the step named LKED. Then, find the DD statement in that step named SYSLMOD. This reference tells the operating system to "execute the program created in job step LKED and stored on data set SYSLMOD."

The programmer coded a cataloged procedure. The procedure itself contained, in this case, three EXEC statements, each calling for a specific program. References to specific programs contain the keyword PGM.

Often, the program or cataloged procedure name is the only parameter coded on an EXEC statement. There are other EXEC parameters, however.

The COND Parameter

When you submit a job containing compiler errors, the result is usually a listing followed by a message indicating that the link edit and go steps were skipped. This makes sense—why bother with subsequent steps if the first one is wrong? But how does the operating system know that the last two steps should be skipped?

You may have noticed something called a severity code on your compiler listing. Warnings are worth 4 points; simple errors, 8; severe errors, 12

Fig. 11.9   The cataloged procedure FORTRAN inserts a number of JCL statements into the job stream.

//FORT	EXEC	PGM=IEYFORT
//SYSPRINT	DD	parameters (printed output)
//SYSLIN	DD	parameters (object module output)
//LKED	EXEC	PGM=IEWL, other parameters
//SYSLIB	DD	parameters (system library)
//SYSLMOD	DD	parameters (load module output)
//SYSPRINT	DD	parameters (printed output)
//SYSUT1	DD	parameters (work space)
//SYSLIN	DD	parameters (object module input)
//GO	EXEC	PGM=*.LKED.SYSLMOD,...

points. A program containing severe errors will almost certainly not run. The compiler passes the highest severity code to the system by placing a condition code in a register. The operating system can check this condition code prior to loading and executing a job step, skipping the step if the condition code is not acceptable.

The programmer sets the limits for this comparison through a **COND** (condition) **parameter** (Fig. 11.10). For example,

COND=(12,LE,FORT)

says that if 12 is less than or equal to the actual condition code returned by job step FORT, the present step is to be skipped.

Run through that logic again. Assume the COND parameter appears in the following EXEC statement:

//LKED EXEC PGM=IEWL,COND=(12,LE,FORT)

The step named LKED will be *bypassed* if 12 is less than or equal to the actual condition code returned by job step FORT. The logic is a bit unusual, so be careful. When comparing a variable and a constant, most program-mers code the variable first. On the COND parameter, the *constant* is coded first, making the logic seem to read backward. The fact that a match leads to a negative decision, skipping a step, adds to the confusion.

The safest way to handle COND logic is to read it as it's coded, from left to right—the step is skipped if some constant meets a certain condition with respect to the actual condition code returned by a prior job step. Incidentally, the third positional subparameter (the step name of the prior

---

Fig. 11.10   The COND parameter allows a programmer to specify run-time
                        conditions under which a job step is to be skipped.

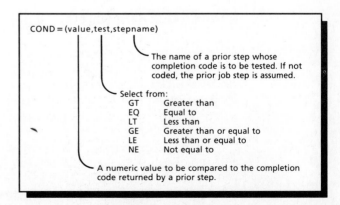

job step) can be skipped; if a step name is not coded, the most recently completed step is assumed.

The legal comparisons are summarized in Fig. 11.10. In the FORTRAN cataloged procedure (Fig. 11.9), COND parameters are normally added to the EXEC statements for both the link edit and go steps. The statement

```
//LKED  EXEC  PGM=IEWL,COND=(8,LE,FORT)
```

tells the operating system to skip the LKED step if 8 is less than or equal to the actual condition code returned by the FORT job step. The statement

```
//GO  EXEC  PGM=*.LKED.SYSLMOD,COND=(4,LT,FORT)
```

places a similar restriction on the GO step.

Multiple conditions can be coded in a single COND parameter; for example,

```
COND=((8,LE,FORT),(4,LT,LKED))
```

means that this step is to be skipped if 8 is less than or equal to the actual condition code returned by FORT *or* if 4 is less than the actual condition code returned by LKED. Note the parentheses; JCL punctuation can be tedious.

You can take advantage of the COND parameter in your own programs, too. For example, imagine a series of programs that screen input data, process those data, and report the bad data found by the first program. What if there are no bad data? There is no point to running the third program. Why not count errors in that first program, and pass the count to the operating system through a return code? Then, the parameter

```
COND=(0,EQ,SCREEN)
```

on the final program's EXEC statement would cause the step to be skipped if "0 is equal to the condition code returned by SCREEN."

Other EXEC Parameters

Other EXEC parameters allow the programmer to pass accounting information to a job step or set a dispatching priority for the step. Some parameters can be coded on the JOB statement or on an EXEC statement. For example, the programmer has the option of specifying a time limit, a region size, restart options, and other conditions for the complete job or for each job step independently.

Programmers often encounter a **PARM parameter** in a cataloged procedure. For example, in the FORTRAN procedure,

```
//  EXEC  FORTRAN,PARM.FORT='NODECK,LIST'
```

the PARM parameter informs the FORT job step (the compiler) that no object deck is to be punched and that a listing is to be printed. Detailed information on the meaning of parameters for any compiler language can be found in the programmer's guide to that language.

A detailed summary of the JOB and EXEC statement parameters is found in Appendix E. Coverage of OS/JCL will continue in Chapter 12.

Summary

The chapter began with an overview of the three OS/JCL statements: JOB, EXEC, and DD. The basic format of any JCL statement was described. Each job submitted to the system must begin with a JOB statement. A job consists of one or more job steps, each of which begins with an EXEC statement. Each EXEC statement references a single program or a cataloged procedure. Within a job step, one DD statement is coded for each input or output device accessed by the program. A cataloged procedure is a set of precoded JCL statements stored on a library and added to the job stream when the procedure name is referenced.

On a JOB statement, the job name must be coded. In the operands field, the first two positional parameters are, respectively, accounting information and the programmer's name. Key word parameters include CLASS, TIME, REGION, and MSGLEVEL. Often, the programmer codes only accounting information, a programmer name, and a CLASS parameter; default values are used for the other parameters.

The step name field on an EXEC statement is optional. Following the operation, either a PGM or a PROC parameter must be coded. (If a procedure is referenced, the key word PROC can be skipped.) By coding a COND parameter, a programmer can instruct the operating system to skip a job step depending on the return code from a previous job step. A PARM parameter can be used to pass run-time information to a program. Certain parameters, such as TIME and REGION, can be coded on the JOB statement or on an EXEC statement. If coded on the JOB statement, they affect every job step; if coded on an EXEC statement, they affect only that step.

The DD statement will be covered in Chapter 12.

Key Words

accounting	EXEC statement	PGM parameter
information	job	positional
backward	job name	parameter
reference	JOB statement	PROC parameter
cataloged	job step	programmer name
procedure	keyword parameter	REGION
CLASS parameter	MSGLEVEL	parameter
COND parameter	parameter	step name
DD statement	parameter	subparameters
default	PARM parameter	TIME parameter

Exercises

1. Distinguish between a job and a job step. How are JOB and EXEC statements related to jobs and job steps?

2. What is a positional parameter? Give some examples.

3. What is a keyword parameter? Give some examples.

4. What does MSGLEVEL=(1,1) mean?

5. What is a cataloged procedure? Why are cataloged procedures used?

6. Explain default options.

7. Code a JOB statement. Use the job name of your choice, your course number as an accounting information parameter, and your own name. Request 90K of memory, 1 minute and 30 seconds of processor time, and job class Q. Don't print any allocation messages. Print only the JCL you code.

8. Code an EXEC statement referencing cataloged procedure COBOL. Skip this step if STEP1 returned a condition code of 100.

9. Compile, link edit, and execute a program written in the language of your choice. Use a cataloged procedure, and print all JCL statements, including those added by the procedure. Read through the JCL, and determine the purpose of each statement. In the exercises following Chapter 12, you will be asked to interpret each DD statement parameter.

10. Write, in the language of your choice, a series of three programs to perform the following functions:
   a. Read data from punched cards or a terminal (the standard input device) and create a sequential file on disk.
   b. Read the sequential file, sort the records, and create a new disk file to hold the sorted data.
   c. Read and print the sorted records.

   Use a sort utility or a language sort feature, or write your own sort routine. At this point, obtain a clean compilation for each program. We'll add the JCL needed to run them at the end of Chapter 12.

CHAPTER

12

IBM/OS JCL:
DD Statements

External Device Linkage

Many second-generation programs were designed to communicate with specific input and output devices. When software is device dependent, changing hardware often means reprogramming, and that's expensive. Thus, device independence became an important part of IBM's System/360-370 design philosophy.

Device independence means a programmer can change peripherals with minimum effort and minimum program revision. On an IBM mainframe, the keys are data control blocks and DD statements. Data control blocks are coded inside a program and contain only those parameters that must be known before the program is loaded. Physical devices are defined outside the program in DD statements. Programs and their peripherals are not linked until load time.

Data Control Blocks

In assembly language, one **data control block** (DCB) is coded for each file accessed by a program. The DCB sets up a series of constants and addresses describing the characteristics of the physical and logical records. For example,

```
INPUT  DCB  MACRF=GM,DSORG=PS,DDNAME=LINES,                    C
            other-parameters
```

defines a sequential file. The MACRF (macro form) and DSORG (data set organization) parameters, taken together, specify an access method. The DDNAME is the link to a DD statement. Other possible parameters include the logical record length, block size, record form, buffering technique, recording density, and many others. The MACRF, DSORG, and DDNAME must be coded within the program; other parameters can appear either in the program DCB or on the DD statement.

Figure 12.1 shows a simple read and print program. The DCBs are highlighted. The DSORG and MACRF parameters define the access methods. The EODAD (end-of-data address) parameter specifies the address of the end-of-data routine.

The EXEC statement references a cataloged procedure—ASMFCLG (assemble, link edit, and go). The assembler creates an object module containing two data control blocks. The access methods are added to the load module (Fig. 12.2) by the linkage editor *before* the program is executed.

DD Statements

Once the load module is complete, the program can be executed. The instruction

```
OPEN (SCREEN,INPUT)
```

Fig. 12.1

One data control block is coded for each file accessed by a program. The physical device is specified outside the program in a DD statement.

```
//JOB121     JOB            (2398,34),DAVIS, CLASS = A
//           EXEC           ASMFCLG
//SYSIN      DD             *

            STARTUP         MACRO FOR REGISTER CONVENTIONS
            B       GO      BRANCH TO EXECUTABLE CODE

LINEOUT     DC      CL1''   SPACE FOR INPUT AND OUTPUT DATA
LINEIN      DS      CL80
            DC      CL40

*                           DATA CONTROL BLOCKS
*
SCREEN      DCB     MACRF = GM,DSORG = PS,
                    DDNAME = DATAIN,EODAD = QUIT

PRINTER     DCB     MACRF = GM,DSORG = PS,DDNAME = LINE

*                           START OF PROGRAM -- FILE OPEN
*
GO          OPEN (SCREEN, INPUT)
            OPEN (PRINTER, OUTPUT)

*                           READ AND PRINT LOOP
*
RUN         GET     SCREEN, LINEIN
            PUT     PRINTER, LINEOUT
            B       RUN

*                           END OF PROGRAM ROUTINE
*
QUIT        CLOSE (SCREEN, PRINTER)
            STOP            END OF PROGRAM MACRO
/*

//LINE       DD      parameters
//DATAIN     DD      parameters
/*
//
```

Fig. 12.2   Based on the data control block MACRF and DSORG parameters,
                         the linkage editor selects an access method and links it to the
                         program load module.

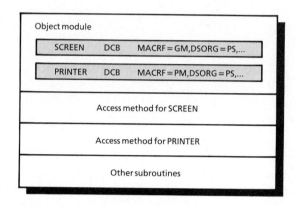

references a data control block labeled SCREEN (Fig. 12.3). The DCB's
DDNAME parameter points to a **DD statement** named DATAIN, which
specifies a physical device. Likewise, the instruction

OPEN (PRINTER,OUTPUT)

establishes linkage to a specific physical output device via the DDNAME
parameter coded in the DCB named PRINTER.

Fig. 12.3   The link to a specific physical device is established at OPEN time.

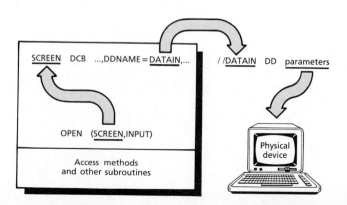

Note carefully the timing of major events in this sequence. The program data control block is written by the programmer *before* compilation. Thus, it is input to the compiler and included in the object module. The linkage editor uses DCB parameters to select an access method. Actual linkage to a physical device is postponed until *run time*, when the OPEN instruction is executed. Thus, switching physical devices can be accomplished by changing a job control language statement. Because JCL statements are *not* part of the load module, devices can be changed without recompiling the program.

In COBOL, a data control block is built from a SELECT...ASSIGN clause in the ENVIRONMENT DIVISION and from several DATA DIVISION clauses such as BLOCK CONTAINS, LABELS ARE, and others. The DDNAME is part of the SELECT...ASSIGN clause, with

SELECT DATAIN ASSIGN TO UT-S-SCREEN.

pointing to

//SCREEN DD parameters

In FORTRAN, a DCB is created for each device number referenced in a READ or WRITE statement. Sequential access is assumed unless a FILE statement specifies otherwise. The DDNAME is built from the device number, with, for example,

WRITE (6, 15) A,B,C

pointing to data control block

label DCB DDDNAME=FT06F001

which references

//FT06F001 DD parameters

A DD statement's parameters define a specific physical device. The balance of this chapter explains how.

Unit Record Hardware

Unit record hardware includes such devices as card readers, printers, and terminals. They work with unit records—lines, cards, screens, and so on. There is no blocking, all records are the same length, and there is no distinction between logical and physical records. Providing input or dealing with output is the programmer's responsibility; no special operator instructions are necessary. Printers and terminals display different line lengths, and not all card readers are restricted to standard 80-column cards, but, aside from record length, the only variable is the physical device.

The UNIT Parameter

The **UNIT parameter** (Fig. 12.4) specifies the input or output device. One option is coding an actual unit address. Every peripheral attached to an IBM system is identified by a three-digit hex number. For example, if a printer is device 8 on channel 0, its unit address is 008, and the DD statement

//PRINTER DD UNIT=008

references it. The unit address form implies that no other device will do; given the DD statement illustrated above, if device 008 is busy, or for some other reason not available, the program must wait to be loaded. This form of the UNIT parameter is rarely used.

If a programmer wants a 3211 printer, and any 3211 printer will do, a device type can be specified; for example,

//OUTS DD UNIT=3211

The program can be loaded and run as soon as *any* 3211 printer is free. A 2501 card reader can be requested by coding UNIT=2501; a 2520 card-read punch is requested by coding UNIT=2520. If a system has more than one of a particular device, specifying a device type is less restrictive than specifying a unit address.

A third choice is referencing a group name. For example, the DD statement

//XYZ DD UNIT=READER

might be a request for any available card reader, be it a 2501, a 2520, or a 3505. It's the most general form of the UNIT parameter, and thus the most frequently used. An installation can define its own group names, although PUNCH, READER, CONSOLE, and PRINTER are almost standard.

Fig. 12.4   The UNIT parameter defines a physical device.

```
UNIT = device

      └─ Select from:
            Unit or device address (channel/device address)
            Device type (2501, 3330, etc.)
            Group name (READER, PRINTER, etc.)
```

Note that there are no blanks in "UNIT=READER." Blanks, remember, are field separators.

The DCB Parameter

Generally, because a unit record's length rarely, if ever, changes, the logical record length is defined in the program DCB. However, some variation is possible. For example, many screens can be switched from an 80-character to a 40-character line. If 80-character logical records are defined inside the program, switching to 40 characters means recompilation.

There is an alternative: **DCB parameters** can be coded on the DD statement (Fig. 12.5). For example, replacing

```
//SCREEN  DD  UNIT=CONSOLE,DCB=LRECL=80
```

with

```
//SCREEN  DD  UNIT=CONSOLE,DCB=LRECL=40
```

changes the logical record length without recompiling the program. DCB subparameters can be coded within the program data control block or on the DD statement.

Note that LRECL=40 is not enclosed in parentheses. Why not? Because it's a *single* subparameter, and when only one is coded, parentheses are not needed.

Data control block subparameters are merged into the program DCB at open time. Parameters coded in the program will not be changed even if the DD's version is different—hard-coded information takes precedence. If a

---

Fig. 12.5   DSORG, MACRF, and DDNAME must be coded in the program data control block. Other DCB subparameters can be coded on the DD statement.

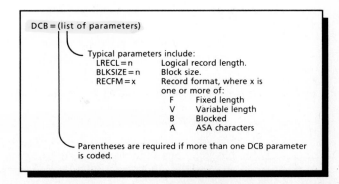

```
DCB = (list of parameters)
           Typical parameters include:
           LRECL = n           Logical record length.
           BLKSIZE = n         Block size.
           RECFM = x           Record format, where x is
                               one or more of:
                               F     Fixed length
                               V     Variable length
                               B     Blocked
                               A     ASA characters
           Parentheses are required if more than one DCB parameter
           is coded.
```

programmer anticipates changing the basic record format, the volatile parameters should be coded in the DD statement.

Both UNIT and DCB are keyword parameters; they can be coded in any
order.

Magnetic Disk

Magnetic disk is the most common secondary storage medium. Some disks
store data in sectors or fixed-length blocks. Others allocate space a track at
a time and allow the programmer to vary the record format to fit the
application. Logical records can be almost any length, and can even vary
within a file. Additionally, they can be blocked or unblocked. Also, disk
space is a limited resource. On an IBM mainframe, the programmer must
estimate the amount of space needed before creating a file.

People can't read the data stored on disk. A human operator is unlikely
to load already-punched cards into a card punch, or used paper onto a
printer, but it's quite possible that disk space previously allocated to one
program might be reused by another, thus destroying the old data. Rather
than trusting to chance, a programmer must carefully specify the disposition of a disk file.

Disk is a shared resource, with numerous files and programs stored on
a single pack (or volume). Since disk can only be read electronically,
directory entries identifying the individual files must be recorded on the
surface. Also, packs can be dismounted and stored off-line. Thus, volumes
must be clearly identified, both visually and electronically, if an operator is
to mount the right one.

UNIT and DCB

As with unit-record equipment, a disk drive is referenced through a UNIT
parameter; for example, UNIT=181 means channel 1, device 81. The de-
vice-address form is rarely used. Direct access devices are most often requested by device type (2311, 2314, 3330, 3340, and so on). For example,

UNIT=3330

is a request for any 3330 disk drive.

Disk is frequently used to store intermediate results. To simplify requesting temporary work files, many installations set aside some direct
access space that a programmer can reference with a group name such as
SYSDA or WORK1.

A disk data control block is just like a unit record data control block.
On disk, records can be fixed or variable in length and blocked or unblocked; thus additional DCB subparameters are needed. A few are summarized in Fig. 12.5.

The DISP Parameter

The **DISP**, or disposition, **parameter** (Fig. 12.6) tells the system what to do with a disk file. The first positional subparameter describes the file's status before the job step is executed. If a file is to be created, it's NEW. An existing file is OLD. Some, a library for example, might be concurrently accessed (but not modified) by more than one program. Such files are shared (SHR). Disposition MOD allows a program to add more data to an existing file.

The second subparameter specifies system action following normal job step completion. If there is no further need for the data, the programmer can DELETE them. KEEP means that the file will be retained. If the data are needed by a subsequent step within the same job, the programmer can PASS them. The file can be entered on a catalog (CATLG) and retained, or removed from a catalog (UNCATLG) and deleted.

The proper disposition might be different following *abnormal* job termination; the third DISP subparameter can be DELETE, KEEP, CATLG, or UNCATLG. If the third subparameter is not coded, the normal termination disposition is assumed.

To create a file, pass it to another job step, and delete it in the event of serious error, code

DISP=(NEW,PASS,DELETE)

If a file is to be created and, normally, cataloged but in the event of an error

Fig. 12.6   The disposition (DISP) parameter specifies the file's status both before and after the program runs.

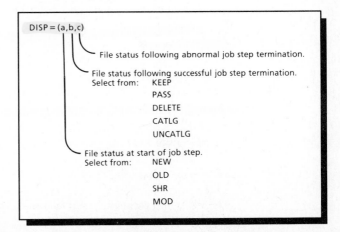

kept for study or possible restart, code

DISP=(NEW,CATLG,KEEP)

A temporary work file needed only for the life of the job step would have, as part of its DD statement,

DISP=(NEW,DELETE)

which is equivalent to

DISP=(NEW,DELETE,DELETE)

The DSNAME Parameter

To simplify retrieving cataloged or passed data sets, the programmer can give a file a unique name by coding a **DSNAME**, or DSN, **parameter**. A valid data set name consists of from one to eight letters, numbers, or national symbols, and must begin with a letter or a national symbol. Data set names can be qualified; for example,

DSNAME=MU.USERDATA.SAN1

indicates that a data set named SAN1 appears on an index named USER-DATA, and that this index can be located by referring to a master index named MU. Each level of qualification must exist as an index in the system catalog.

Temporary life-of-job files are assigned data set names beginning with an ampersand (&); for example,

DSNAME=&&TEMP

To avoid confusing them with assembly language macro parameters, temporary data set names normally begin with a double ampersand. Incidentally, the term **data set** was coined by IBM to encompass both traditional files and libraries.

The VOLUME Parameter

The **VOLUME**, or **VOL**, **parameter** specifies a particular disk volume (or pack). Each volume has a unique serial number. To request pack number MU1234, a programmer would code

VOL=SER=MU1234

The VOLUME parameter is coded only if the application demands a specific disk volume.

Note carefully the difference between UNIT and VOLUME. The UNIT parameter specifies a disk *drive*. The VOLUME parameter identifies the *pack* that is to be mounted on that drive.

The SPACE Parameter

It makes little sense to load and execute a program when adequate direct access space is not available. Thus, programmers are required to estimate their space requirements through a **SPACE parameter** (Fig. 12.7).

Space can be requested in tracks, cylinders, or blocks. The first positional subparameter identifies the unit; the second indicates the number of units. For example,

SPACE=(TRK,20)

is a request for 20 tracks, while

SPACE=(CYL,14)

asks for 14 cylinders, and

SPACE=(200,10)

asks for ten 200-byte blocks.

Fig. 12.7   A SPACE parameter indicates the amount of direct access space a file will need.

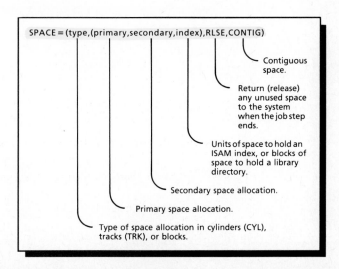

Estimating space requirements is not always easy. To ensure sufficient space, a programmer might be tempted to request more than the program needs, thus tying up a limited resource. Fortunately, another option is available. The parameter

SPACE=(TRK,(10,2))

requests a *primary* allocation of 10 tracks, and a *secondary* allocation of 2 tracks. Should the initial 10 tracks be filled, an additional 2 will be allocated, if available. If those 2 are filled, 2 more are allocated. The system will make a maximum of 15 secondary allocations; thus, the parameter coded above could represent as many as 40 tracks (10, plus 2 times 15).

The primary space allocation is made before the program is loaded. The secondary allocation is filled on an as-needed, if-available basis *after* the job step begins executing. A job step may be canceled for insufficient direct access space, even though its primary and secondary requests are more than adequate, if space is not available at the time of the secondary request. It is to the programmer's advantage to make the primary space estimate as accurate as possible.

Note that the primary and secondary subparameters are enclosed in parentheses. Both deal with the number of units of direct access space, and thus should be treated as a single entity. (In effect, the primary and secondary allocations are *sub*-subparameters. When two or more sub-subparameters are coded, a set of inner parentheses is needed.)

Requesting too much space can tie up a limited resource. The programmer can return unused space to the system at the end of a job step by coding a RLSE (release) subparameter; for example,

SPACE=(CYL,(5,1),RLSE)

It's a positional subparameter that must follow the primary and secondary allocations.

To optimize disk input and output, space is sometimes requested in contiguous units. The parameter

SPACE=(TRK,(5,2),RLSE,CONTIG)

asks for five contiguous tracks, with a secondary request for two more, and returns unused space to the system at the conclusion of the job step. Without RLSE, this parameter would be coded

SPACE=(TRK,(5,2),,CONTIG)

Note the extra comma indicating the absence of a positional subparameter.

Some Examples

Figure 12.8 shows several examples of DD statements to create and retrieve disk data sets. If a data set has been cataloged or passed by a prior step, it can normally be retrieved by coding only the DDNAME and DISP parame-

Fig. 12.8   This figure shows some examples of complete DD statements to create and retrieve disk files.

```
1.  Creating a temporary data set on the system work pack.

//DISK          DD  DSNAME = &&TEMP,UNIT = SYSDA,
//                  DISP = (NEW,PASS),SPACE = (CYL,5),
//                  DCB = (LRECL = 120,BLKSIZE = 2400,
//                  RECFM = FB)

2.  Creating a cataloged data set on a specific volume.
//RECS          DD  DSN = MU.USERDATA.SAN4,UNIT = 3330,
//                  VOL = SER = MIAMI3,DISP = (NEW,CATLG),
//                  SPACE = (TRK,(20,5),RLSE,CONTIG),
//                  DCB = (LRECL = 155,RECFM = FB,
//                  BLKSIZE = 1550)

3.  Creating a kept data set.

//KEEPIT        DD  SPACE = (CYL,(10,2),RLSE),
//                  DCB = (RECFM = FB,LRECL = 72,BLKSIZE = 720),
//                  VOL = SER = MYPACK,DISP = (NEW,KEEP),
//                  DSNAME = MYDATA,UNIT = 3330

4.  Retrieving a passed data set.

//DATA          DD  DSNAME = &&TEMP,DISP = (OLD,DELETE)

5.  Retrieving a cataloged data set.

//STUFF         DD  DSN = MU.USERDATA.SAN4,DISP = OLD

6.  Retrieving a kept data set that has not been cataloged requires UNIT
    and VOLUME parameters in addition to DSNAME and DISP.

//DDNAME        DD  DSNAME = MYDATA,UNIT = 3330,
//                  VOL = SER = MYPACK,DISP = (OLD,KEEP)
```

ters. Other parameters, including the data control block parameters, can be found in the directory entry for cataloged data sets and the operating system tables for passed data sets; thus they need not be recoded.

Magnetic Tape

Once the most common secondary storage medium, magnetic tape is now used largely for backup and to transmit data or programs between computer centers. Tape and disk have a great deal in common. Both support a variety of record lengths and record formats. Neither is human-readable; thus both require careful labeling, cataloging, and attention to post-job disposition.

There are also some important differences. On disk, a typical volume holds a number of files or data sets. On tape, one volume per file is the general rule, but it is not unusual for a large file to spill over onto a second or third tape. Thus, the programmer must be able to request multiple volumes and (perhaps) multiple drives to mount those volumes.

Disk is generally an in-house medium, with all the drives and packs under control of the computer center. Tape, on the other hand, is often used to transfer data between centers. This "foreign interface" can create problems because not all computer centers use the same tape. Some record data on seven tracks; some use nine tracks; others use ten. The recording density can vary, too. Finally, there are many different types of tape labels.

The programmer must communicate to the system, through DD parameters, the unique characteristics of a given tape file before the system can access that tape.

UNIT and DCB

The UNIT parameter defines the physical device. A programmer can choose to specify a drive's channel/device address, but this is rarely done. Many computer centers define one or more device classes, such as TAPE, TAPE9, or TAPE7. For example,

UNIT=TAPE9

might represent a request for a tape drive able to handle nine-track tapes, while

UNIT=TAPE7

might be a request for a drive that can work with seven-track tapes.

The device type is the most commonly used form for magnetic tape. Figure 12.9 shows the device types that have been defined for IBM's 2400 series tape drives; for example, to request a nine-track 800-bpi drive, code

UNIT=2400-4

Other models have similar device types.

Let's pause for a moment and clear up a possible point of confusion. The UNIT parameter is a request for a physical drive. It says nothing about the tape that might be mounted on that drive. Later we'll encounter the DCB density subparameter, and you'll be tempted to ask, "Didn't I already specify the density in the UNIT parameter?" The answer is no! You requested a drive that was capable of handling tape recorded at a certain density.

Fig. 12.9   This table shows the device type designations for IBM's 2400
                       series tape drives. Other models have similar device types.

Device type	Description
2400	9-track, 800 bpi (bytes per inch)
2400-1	7-track, no data conversion
2400-2	7-track with data conversion
2400-3	7-track, 1600 bpi
2400-4	7-track, 800 and 1600 bpi
2400-5	2420 model 5, 1600 bpi

Occasionally, a multiple volume data set may require more than one
tape drive. The unit count subparameter follows the device type; for example,

UNIT=(2400-3,3)

asks for three nine-track 1600-bpi drives. Both subparameters are positional; the device type must be coded first, the unit count second. The
parameter

UNIT=(3,2400)

which is *incorrect*, is a request for 2400, model 3 tape drives. Positional
parameters derive their meaning from their relative positions. If the unit
count subparameter is not coded, a single unit is assumed.

To save system time and eliminate lengthy waits by a program already
in memory, tape mount messages are normally given to the operator as the
job step is about to be loaded. Occasionally, when probable errors or other
special processing characteristics make the tape's use questionable, it makes
sense to postpone tape mounting until OPEN time. Coding

UNIT=(2400,2,DEFER)

requests two nine-track, 800-bpi tape drives and postpones mounting; the
DEFER option is a third positional subparameter. To postpone mounting a
single 1600-bpi tape, code

UNIT=(2400-3,,DEFER)

The extra comma indicates a missing positional subparameter. Positional
subparameters, to belabor a point, derive their meaning from their relative
positions. DEFER is the *third* positional subparameter.

Fig. 12.10   Because magnetic tape can be recorded at several different densities, the DCB sometimes contains a DEN subparameter.

```
DCB = (DEN = n,...)

           Select from:
              0   7-track, 200 bpi
              1   7-track, 556 bpi
              2   9-track, 800 bpi
              3   9-track, 1600 bpi
              4   6250 bpi
```

Tape and disk have similar DCB parameters; LRECL, BLKSIZE, and RECFM are most common. Additionally, the DEN (density) subparameter specifies the tape's recording density (Fig. 12.10). Why bother with a density code when density seems to be a part of the UNIT parameter? The UNIT parameter defines the physical device, not the volume that is mounted on that device. For example,

DCB=(BLKSIZE-750,DEN=3,LRECL=75,RECFM=FB)

defines fixed-length, blocked records, 75 bytes in length, stored in 750-byte blocks (ten logical records) on 1600-bpi tape.

DISP and DSNAME

Disk and tape dispositions are, for all practical purposes, identical. The DSNAME parameter provides a convenient mechanism for retrieving a cataloged or passed data set.

VOLUME

Changing a disk pack is time-consuming. Thus, in many computer centers disks are permanently mounted. Consequently, the VOLUME parameter is rarely needed.

Magnetic tape is different. Tape volumes are stored off-line and mounted only when needed. Thus, the volume serial number is almost always specified; for example,

VOL=SER=MIAMI5

Note that SER is a keyword subparameter.

To request multiple tape volumes, code a list of serial numbers; for example,

VOL=SER=(MO1,MO2,MO3,MO4)

asks for four different tapes. A request for four volumes might be accompanied by a UNIT parameter requesting four drives

UNIT=(TAPE,4)

On the other hand, if the tape volumes are to be accessed one after another, a single drive might do.

The programmer can request a scratch or work tape by omitting the VOLUME parameter. Some installations prefer a more specific request, such as

//TAPE DD UNIT=2400-3,VOL=SER=SCRTCH,...

The VOLUME parameter is used to generate tape mount messages. The message

MOUNT TAPE SCRTCH ON DEVICE 182

is an obvious request for a scratch tape.

The LABEL Parameter

The **LABEL parameter** (Fig. 12.11) specifies both the label type and the relative position of the file on the volume. Normally, one file is stored on each tape, but a volume can hold more than one. The sequence number is

Fig. 12.11   Magnetic tape is used to transfer data between computer centers. Because different computer centers sometimes follow different labeling standards, the LABEL parameter may be needed.

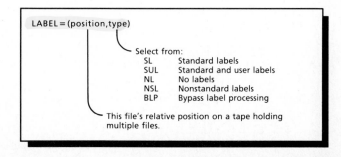

```
LABEL = (position,type)

                          Select from:
                          SL      Standard labels
                          SUL     Standard and user labels
                          NL      No labels
                          NSL     Nonstandard labels
                          BLP     Bypass label processing

                          This file's relative position on a tape holding
                          multiple files.
```

the desired file's relative position on the tape—1 for the first file, 2 for the second, and so on. Valid label types are summarized in Fig. 12.11. Standard labels are created and checked by the operating system; user labels and nonstandard labels must be checked by a programmer routine (if they are checked at all). The "bypass label processing" option implies that labels are present, but for some reason, they are not to be processed.

To create a new, single-volume tape file with standard labels, code

LABEL=(1,SL)

or

LABEL=(,SL)

The lone comma indicates the absence of the first positional parameter, which is assumed to be 1. On a new tape data set, the OPEN macro creates a label; on an existing data set, the OPEN checks the label to determine if the proper file has been mounted.

Standard labels are typically a default, so the LABEL parameter can often be skipped. Remember, however, that magnetic tape is used to transfer data or programs between computer centers, and not all centers follow

Fig. 12.12   This figure shows some examples of complete DD statements to create magnetic tape files.

```
   1.  Create and pass a temporary data set.

   //TAPE         DD  UNIT = 2400 – 3, VOL = SER = WX2453,
   //                 DCB = (LRECL = 145, BLKSIZE = 2900,
   //                 RECFM = FB), LABEL = (,SL),
   //                 DISP = (NEW, PASS), DSN = &&T

   2.  Create and catalog a permanent data set.

   //MAG1         DD  UNIT = 2400 – 4, LABEL = (,SL), DSN = TT,
   //                 VOL = SER = A572, DCB = (RECFM = FB,
   //                 BLKSIZE = 1200, LRECL = 120, DEN = 3),
   //                 DISP = (NEW, CATLG)

   3.  Use a scratch tape.

   //SCRATCH      DD  DISP = (NEW, DELETE), DSNAME = &&WORK,
   //                 DCB = (BLKSIZE = 104, LRECL = 52, RECFM = FB),
   //                 LABEL = (,SL), UNIT = 2400 – 3,
   //                 VOL = SER = SCRTCH
```

TQ ?

the same standard. Thus, programmers should be familiar with the LABEL parameter.

The DUMMY Parameter

Loading tapes is time-consuming. Often, particularly during program testing, a programmer may choose to bypass tape mounting by coding a **DUMMY parameter**.

//DATA DD DUMMY,UNIT=2400,...

TQ → DUMMY must be the first parameter in the operands field. Later, the job can be resubmitted without the DUMMY parameter.

Some Examples

Figure 12.12 shows several examples of DD statements for creating files on magnetic tape.

System Input and Output

A great deal of I/O takes place through relatively few devices. On some systems, a terminal keyboard and screen are the standards. On others, spooling routines create temporary disk files to insulate application programs from such slow devices as keyboards, card readers, and printers. Default parameters are often used to access these standard system input and output devices.

For example, the **system input** device is normally accessed by a statement such as

//SYSIN DD *

The asterisk indicates that the data follows "this" DD statement in the job stream. There is nothing sacred about SYSIN; it's just a DDNAME. The programmer can use any DDNAME for the system input device, as long as it matches the name coded in the program's internal data control block. Many compilers and utilities use SYSIN to reference the system input device.

To spool data to the **system output** device, code

//SYSOUT DD SYSOUT=A

or

//SYSPRINT DD SYSOUT=A

Device A generally implies eventual printer output. For punched card output, code

```
//SYSPUNCH  DD  SYSOUT=B
```

SYSOUT, SYSPRINT, and SYSPUNCH are common DDNAMEs; you can use any name you wish. An installation can choose its own symbols to indicate the various system devices.

Many installations limit the amount of system output space available to a program. You can override this limit by coding a SPACE parameter

```
//SYSPRINT  DD  SYSOUT=A,SPACE=(CYL,(5,2))
```

Job Step Qualification

Often, two or more DD statements, each in a different job step but still within the same job, are assigned the same DDNAME. For example, on a compile, link edit, and go job, both the compiler and the go step often get input from the system input device. Thus, both can contain a

```
//SYSIN  DD  *
```

statement. To distinguish these two statements, the DDNAMEs are often qualified (Fig. 12.13). The FORTRAN procedure contains three job steps: FORT (the compiler), LKED (the linkage editor), and GO (the program load module). FORT.SYSIN is the name of a DD statement attached to the

Fig. 12.13   When the same DDNAME occurs more than once in a cataloged procedure, qualify the DDNAMEs by preceding them with their step names.

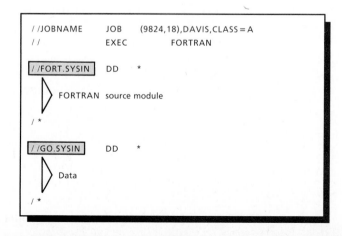

first job step. GO.SYSIN is attached to the GO step. Qualified DDNAMES can be used only within a cataloged procedure.

Libraries

A library can contain numerous programs and data files. Each program or file is a member of the library. To access a given member, code a member name as part of the DSNAME (Fig. 12.14). For example, to access a file named TIME from the PAYROLL library, code

DSNAME=PAYROLL(TIME),DISP=OLD

Let's turn our attention to loading programs. For such system software as compilers, the linkage editor, and utilities, no library reference is needed. Private libraries, however, must be identified by the programmer. For example, assume that MYPGM is stored on MYLIB. The two statements

```
//         EXEC   PGM=MYPGM
//STEPLIB   DD     DSNAME=MYLIB,DISP=SHR
```

tell the system to "load and execute MYPGM, which is found on MYLIB."

The DDNAME *must be* STEPLIB and the STEPLIB DD statement must *immediately* follow the EXEC statement. The DSNAME defines the library name. DISP=SHR indicates that the contents of the library will not be modified. Note that the member name is not specified; the EXEC statement defines it.

Code a **STEPLIB statement** following each EXEC that references a program on a private library. If a multistep job calls for several programs from the same library, a single **JOBLIB statement** can replace several STEPLIBs. The JOBLIB statement follows the JOB statement and precedes the first EXEC. A JOBLIB statement defines a library for all steps in the job.

Fig. 12.14   To access a single library member, code the member name as part of the DDNAME.

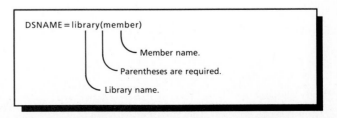

Other JCL Statements

A PROC statement is used to assign default values to symbolic parameters in a cataloged procedure. A null statement (//) is sometimes used to mark the end of a job. A comment starts with //*, followed by anything at all. Comments can be inserted at any point in the job stream.

Summary

Perhaps the best way to summarize what you have learned about IBM OS/JCL is to work through an example. Figure 12.15 shows a flowchart for a multistep job. The first job step reads data through the system input device and edits them. The output is written to a temporary disk file. The edit program is stored on a private library. Step two sorts the data to tape. In the third job step, the tape file is merged with a master file on disk; errors are written to another tape, and, at the end of the job step, both tapes are cataloged. Finally, an error processing routine is compiled, link edited, and executed. The JCL to support this job is shown in Fig. 12.16. Incidentally, all of the STEPLIB statements could have been replaced by

//JOBLIB DD DSN=MU.USERPGM.SAN,DISP=SHR

Read through the statements one by one and be sure you understand what each parameter means. If you can do that, you'll have a solid understanding of OS/JCL. See Appendix C for a summary of the parameters.

Fig. 12.15 This flowchart shows the job steps and physical devices needed to support a four-step master file update application.

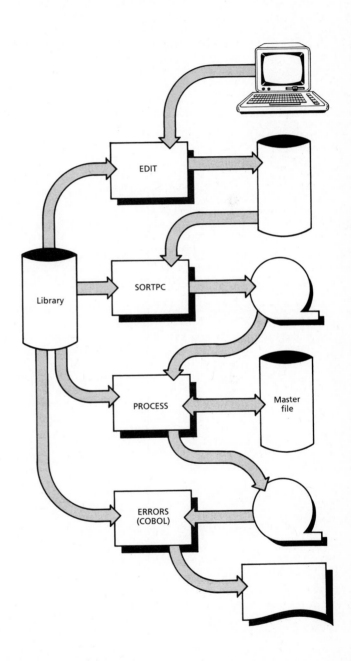

Fig. 12.16

Read through the JCL in this complete example, making sure you understand what each parameter means.

```
//MYJOB      JOB       (9182,222),'W.S. DAVIS',CLASS = A

//STEP1      EXEC      PGM = EDIT
//STEPLIB    DD        DSN = MU.USERPGM.SAN,DISP = SHR
//OUTS       DD        DSNAME = &&TEMP,
//                     UNIT = SYSDA,DISP = (NEW,PASS),
//                     SPACE = (TRK,(10,2,RLSE),
//                     DCB = (LRECL = 80,
//                     BLKSIZE = 800,RECFM = FB)
//SYSIN              DD      *

           ▷ Data

/*

//SECOND    EXEC       SORTPC
//SORTIN     DD        DSN = &&TEMP,DISP = (OLD,DELETE)
//SORTOUT  DD         DSNAME = MYOUTS,UNIT = 2400 – 3,
//                     VOL = SER = R712,
//                     LABEL = (,SL),DISP = (NEW,PASS),
//                     DCB = (LRECL = 80,
//                     BLKSIZE = 800,RECFM = FB)
//* THE NEXT TWO STATEMENTS DEFINE THE SORT FIELDS.
//SYSIN      DD      *
     SORT FIELDS = (1,5,CH,A)
/*        THE FIELD STARTS IN POSITION 1, IS 5 POSITIONS LONG,
//*       AND HOLDS CHARACTER DATA WHICH ARE TO BE SORTED
//*       INTO ASCENDING ORDER.

//THIRD     EXEC       PGM = PROCESS
//STEPLIB    DD        DSN = MU.USERPGM.SAN,DISP = SHR
//TAPEIN     DD        DSN = MYOUTS, DISP = (OLD,CATLG)
//MASTER    DD         DSN = MU.USERDATA.SAN5,
//                     DISP = (OLD,KEEP)
//TAPEOUT  DD          DSN = MYERRS,UNIT = 2400 – 3,
//                     VOL = SER = E712,LABEL = (,SL),
//                     DISP = (NEW,CATLG),DISP = (LRECL = 80,
//                     BLKSIZE = 1200,RECFM = FB)

//LAST      EXEC       COBOL
//COB.SYSIN      DD      *

           ▷ COBOL source module

/*
//TAPEIN     DD        DSN = MYERRS,DISP = (OLD,KEEP)
//
```

Key Words

data control block	DSNAME parameter	STEPLIB statement
data set	DUMMY parameter	system input
DCB parameter	JOBLIB statement	system output
DD statement	LABEL parameter	UNIT parameter
DDNAME	SPACE parameter	VOLUME parameter
DISP parameter		

Exercises

1. Explain how a program is linked to a physical I/O device under operating system/360-370.

2. Explain the relationship between a program DCB and the DCB parameter on a DD statement.

3. Code a UNIT parameter to reserve three 2400-series tape drives with 800-bpi capacity. Don't mount the tapes until open time.

4. Code a DD statement DCB parameter for a magnetic tape file holding fixed-length, blocked records. Logical records are 50 characters long, and the blocking factor is 50. It's a 1600-bpi tape.

5. Code a space parameter to reserve 20 contiguous cylinders. Allow for additional cylinders, requesting two at a time. Return unused cylinders to the system at the end of the job step.

6. Code a DD statement to create a 1600-bpi tape, serial number MY-TAPE. Catalog the tape if the job step ends normally; otherwise, keep the tape for analysis. For simplicity, the tape's serial number and catalog name should be the same. Records are 125 characters each, blocked in groups of 20; all records are the same length. Use standard labels.

7. Code a DD statement for a temporary work data set on the system direct access device (SYSDA). Get ten tracks. Request secondary tracks in a group of two. They do not have to be contiguous, but do return unused tracks to the system at the end of the job step. Logical records are 100 bytes each and should be blocked in groups of 30. The data set is to be passed to a subsequent job step.

8. Explain why a JOBLIB or STEPLIB statement is necessary when executing a program stored on a private library.

9. Exercise 9 in Chapter 11 asked you to compile, link edit, and execute a program. Refer to the JCL generated by that cataloged procedure, and interpret each DD statement parameter.

10. Exercise 10 in Chapter 11 asked you to write and test a series of three programs. Add the JCL needed to run those three programs as a single job.

11. Briefly explain the difference between compilation time, link edit time, and run time. Why is this difference significant?

12. Why is it valuable to postpone physical device assignments until run time?

Your instructor may assign additional JCL exercises.

Libraries and the Linkage Editor

KEY IDEAS

Program libraries
  Compile, link edit, and execute
Compilers and source statement libraries
  Creating a library
  Adding members to a library
  Using private source statement libraries
Object modules
  Creating an object module library
  Adding object modules to a library
Load modules
  The linkage editor
  The primary object module
  System libraries
  Private libraries
  Load module libraries
The loader

Program Libraries

Once you learn the essentials of a job control or command language, your next major interface with the operating system often involves libraries. During program development, code may be maintained on a source statement library. Common subroutines are found on object module libraries. Production programs are stored on load module libraries.

This chapter explains the differences between source, object, and load modules, and illustrates (using IBM OS/JCL) the basics of library management. The key is understanding what happens. Given a sense of the underlying concepts, it is relatively easy to determine how to create and access libraries on almost any system.

Much of the material in this chapter is general and, with a few changes in terminology, can be applied to almost any computer system. Other material is IBM-specific. For those who do not use an IBM computer, the vendor-specific material is clearly identified.

Compile, Link Edit, and Execute

A programer's source statements are translated into object form by a compiler or an assembler. A linkage editor then converts the object module into a load module. This compile, link edit, and execute sequence (Fig. 13.1) is basic; you probably memorized it in your first computer course. But, what exactly is a source module? an object module? a load module? And, *why* is this sequence necessary?

Generally, a **source module** is a set of program statements written in a source language such as COBOL, FORTRAN, Pascal, or assembler. No computer can directly execute source statements; they must first be translated into machine-level code by a compiler or an interpreter. A compiler accepts a complete source program, and generates a complete object module. An interpreter accepts a single source statement, translates it to machine level, executes the resulting code, and then turns to the next source statement. Interpreters are popular on microcomputers and time-shared systems, and are often used by casual programmers. Professionals are more likely to use compilers.

An **object module** is pure binary, machine-level code. Most are incomplete, however, containing references to other object modules such as access methods and subroutines; thus, they cannot be loaded and executed. Instead, several object modules must first be linked to form a complete **load module**. The program that links object modules to form a load module is called (at least by IBM) the **linkage editor**.

The program flow illustrated in Fig. 13.1 is oversimplified, because the process of compiling and link editing a program involves several **libraries** (Fig. 13.2). Let's analyze the compile, link edit, and execute steps one by one, and consider the nature of each of these libraries.

Fig. 13.1   Programs typically pass through a compiler and the linkage
                       editor before they are ready to execute.

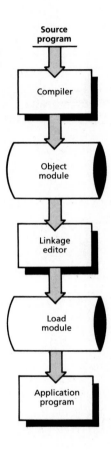

Fig. 13.2   The compile, link edit, and execute sequence involves both
                       system and private libraries.

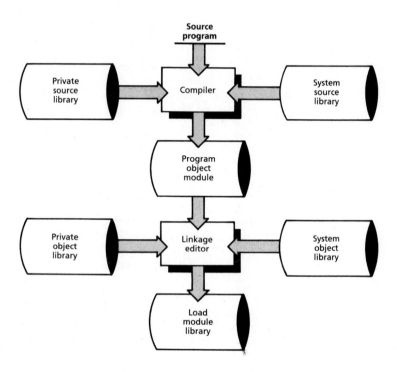

Compilers and Source Statement Libraries

Source modules are written by programmers in a source language. The statements may be keypunched, thus creating a source deck. More often, they are entered through a terminal under control of a text editor and stored in electronic form on disk.

The source code as prepared by the programmer is normally incomplete. For example, an assembler language program may contain **macros**. Before the program can be assembled, each macro must be expanded into one or more source statements. (Look at an assembler listing; the source statements generated by macros are preceded by plus signs.) System macros, such as OPEN, CLOSE, GET, and PUT, are stored on a system **source statement library** (Fig. 13.2). Private macros are stored on private source statement libraries.

Most languages support source statement libraries. For example, to merge prewritten code into a program, a COBOL programmer can code a

COPY statement; in PL/1, the command is INCLUDE. The compiler builds a complete source module, combining the programmer's source code with other code from system and/or private source statement libraries, before compiling the code.

For example, imagine that a systems analyst working on a payroll application has defined the employee time record as a COBOL data structure and, using a utility program, has stored the source code on a COBOL source statement library (Fig. 13.3). Once it's on the library, a programmer can access it by inserting a COPY statement at the appropriate spot in the source program. As the COBOL compiler scans the source code, it replaces COPY statements with library code (Fig. 13.4). Once all the COPY statements have been expanded, the source module is complete, and compilation can begin. An assembler program expands macros in precisely the same way.

Fig. 13.3   Source code is placed on a source statement library by a utility program.

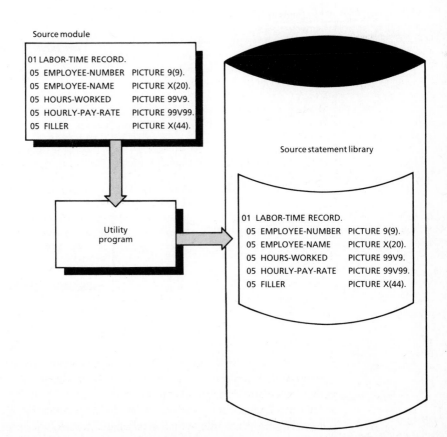

Fig. 13.4   When a compiler encounters a reference to a source statement
library, it replaces the reference with the library code.

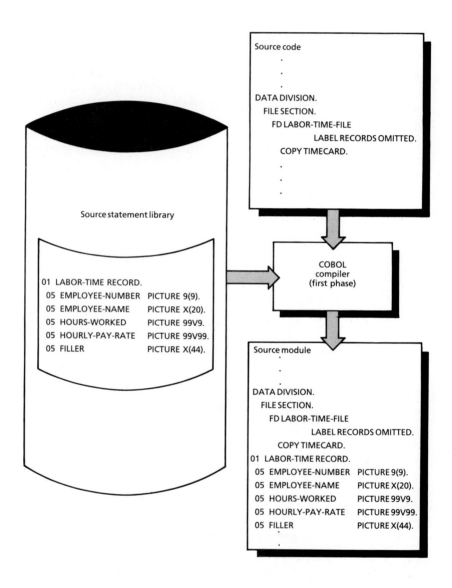

A private source statement library contains "home-grown" macros and
customized source code. A system source statement library contains more
widely used source code (I/O macros, for example). The compiler combines
source statement library entries with the programmer's source code to
produce a source module, which is translated to machine-level object code.

Creating a Library (IBM OS/JCL)

A library is a special type of file consisting of a **directory** and several **members** (Fig. 13.5). The members can be source modules, object modules, load modules, or data. The members' names and absolute disk addresses are listed in the directory. If, for example, a programmer requests member TAX on a library named PAYROLL, the operating system will find the library, read the directory, search it, and access the requested member. IBM calls this library structure a **partitioned data set** (PDS).

The basic difference between a regular data set (a file) and a partitioned data set is the PDS directory. When creating a library, the programmer must tell the system how much space to allocate to the directory by coding a positional subparameter on the SPACE parameter (Fig. 13.6). The directory subparameter defines the number of 256-byte blocks that are allocated to the directory; each block identifies five (at most six) members.

For example, assume you are about to create a library. You have estimated that ten cylinders will be needed to store about sixty programs. Because each directory block can list, conservatively, five programs, you'll need twelve blocks. To create the library, code

```
//PDS   DD   DSNAME=MYLIB,DISP=(NEW,CATLG),UNIT=3330,
//           VOL=SER=MYPACK,SPACE=(CYL,(10,,12)),
//           DCB=(LRECL=80,BLKSIZE=400,RECFM=FB)
```

Fig. 13.5   A library is a type of file that consists of a directory and several members. IBM calls this library structure a partitioned data set.

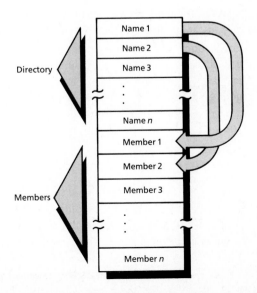

Fig. 13.6   To indicate the amount of space to be allocated to a partitioned
                       data set's directory, code a positional subparameter on the
                       SPACE parameter.

```
SPACE = (type,(primary,secondary,directory))

                                       Number of 256-byte
                                       directory blocks.
```

Twelve directory blocks are specified; space for them is taken from the ten
primary cylinders. There is no secondary space allocation.

   Note that the logical record length (LRECL) is set to 80 bytes. Compilers and linkage editors originated when punched cards were the standard
input medium. Even today, many installations maintain old program decks,
and some continue to use punched cards as a source of library members or
as a library backup. Because disk can support any logical record length, it
makes sense to accommodate the less flexible medium.

   On an IBM computer, a DD statement cannot stand on its own; as a
minimum, a JOB statement and a single EXEC must accompany the DD
that defines the library. One way to create an empty library is to run a
dummy program named **IEFBR14**. A system utility, it consists of a single
instruction, a branch to register 14. (In COBOL terms, that branch is
equivalent to STOP RUN; in FORTRAN, it's STOP; in BASIC, END.) Figure
13.7 illustrates a job that creates an empty partitioned data set using
IEFBR14. When the "program" is loaded, the operating system allocates
space for the PDS and starts the program. IEFBR14 immediately quits. In
effect, this utility fools the system into doing some work.

Fig. 13.7   To create an empty partitioned data set, run a program named
                       IEFBR14.

```
//        JOB     ....
//        EXEC    PGM = IEFBR14
//PDS     DD      DSNAME = MYLIB,DISP = (NEW,CATLG),
//                UNIT = 3330, VOL = SER = MYPACK,
//                SPACE = (CYL,(10,,12)),
//                DCB = (LRECL = 80,RECFM = FB,BLKSIZE = 400)
/*
```

Adding Members to a Library (IBM OS/JCL)

Once the library exists, adding members to it is relatively easy. If source statements are entered through a text editor, the output can be written to a designated source statement library. An option is to prepare a source deck (or an electronic source module on disk or tape), and then use a utility program to copy it to the library.

The utility program most often used to add members to a source statement library on an IBM mainframe computer is called **IEBGENER**. It's also used to copy disk files for system backup and to display the contents of a file as a debugging aid. The utility has options that allow a programmer to copy records selectively and to reformat output. IEBGENER is a very useful utility.

Assume a programmer wants to add a source module named MAST-FILE to the library we just created (MYLIB). Figure 13.8 shows the JCL statements needed to run the IEBGENER utility. The program requires certain DDNAMEs. The input data set must be called SYSUT1. Output must go to SYSUT2. A SYSPRINT DD statement allows the program to write messages to the printer; it is required. Finally, SYSIN allows optional parameters to be passed to the program. Because this application calls for no optional features, we coded DUMMY.

Look carefully at the SYSUT2 DD statement. Note the DSNAME

DSNAME=MYLIB(MASTFILE)

MYLIB is the name of a partitioned data set. MASTFILE is a member name.

Fig. 13.8   Use a utility, such as IEBGENER, to add a source module to a library.

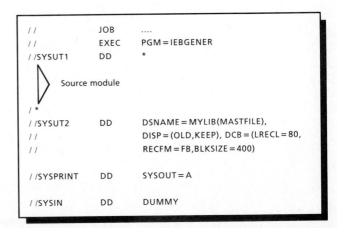

```
//              JOB      ....
//              EXEC     PGM = IEBGENER
//SYSUT1        DD       *

        Source module

/*
//SYSUT2        DD       DSNAME = MYLIB(MASTFILE),
//                       DISP = (OLD,KEEP), DCB = (LRECL = 80,
//                       RECFM = FB,BLKSIZE = 400)

//SYSPRINT      DD       SYSOUT = A

//SYSIN         DD       DUMMY
```

Remember the directory at the beginning of the PDS? When the member is added to the library, an entry under the name MASTFILE is made in the directory. In the future, the member can be retrieved by this name. The member name must be enclosed in parentheses and must immediately follow the DSNAME. The rules for defining a member name are the same as the rules for defining a data set name. Note: Assuming that DCB parameters were defined when the library was created, the DCB on the SYSUT2 statement in Fig. 13.8 would not be needed.

Using Private Source Statement Libraries (IBM OS/JCL)

Once members have been added to a private source statement library, how can a programmer access them? Compiling or assembling a program involves several input and output data sets that are normally defined in a cataloged procedure. For example, Fig. 13.9 shows the JCL statements generated by the compile-only cataloged procedure ASMFC. One statement is of particular interest:

XXSYSLIB DD DSNAME=SYS1.MACLIB,DISP=SHR

Fig. 13.9   The cataloged procedure for the assembler program, ASMFC.
Statements preceded by // are coded by the programmer. Those
beginning with XX are part of the cataloged procedure.

```
//               JOB      ...
//               EXEC     ASMFC
XXASM            EXEC     PGM=IEUASM
XXSYSLIB         DD       DSNAME=SYS1.MACLIB,DISP=SHR

XXSYSUT1         DD       ...
XXSYSUT2         DD       ...
XXSYSUT3         DD       ...
XXSYSPRINT       DD       SYSOUT=A
XXSYSPUNCH       DD       SYSOUT=B
XXSYSGO          DD       DSNAME=&&LOADSET,
XX                        SPACE=(400,(100,20)),
XX                        DISP=(OLD,PASS),UNIT=SYSDA,
XX                        DCB=(LRECL=80,
XX                        BLKSIZE=400,RECFM=FB)
//ASM.SYSIN      DD       *

            Source code

/*
```

It defines the system macro library, SYS1.MACLIB, and thus tells the assembler where to find such system macros as GET, PUT, OPEN, CLOSE, DCB, and so on. To use a private library simply change this statement; for example,

```
//              EXEC   ASMFC
//ASM.SYSLIB   DD     DSN=MYLIB,DISP=SHR
```

Coding an explicit **SYSLIB** statement overrides the cataloged procedure, replacing the standard SYSLIB statement with the one provided by the programmer.

What if both system and private macros are needed? To identify two (or more) source statement libraries, code

```
//              EXEC   ASMFC
//ASM.SYSLIB   DD     DSN=SYS1.MACLIB,DISP=SHR
//             DD     DSN=MYLIB,DISP=SHR
```

Note that the second DD statement has no DDNAME. The last name encountered, SYSLIB, still holds; the two libraries are concatenated. When it encounters a macro, the assembler will search SYS1.MACLIB. If the macro is not found, the assembler will search MYLIB. Additional libraries can be concatenated by attaching additional unnamed DD statements; the order of the DD statements determines the order in which the libraries will be searched.

Object Modules

Compilers and assemblers generate object modules. An object module contains machine-level code, but is normally incomplete and thus cannot be loaded and executed. For example, most input and output operations involve calling an access method. A given access method might appear in hundreds of different programs, and recompiling the same code again and again is a waste of time. Instead, access methods are stored in object module form and added to the application program *after* compilation.

To cite another example, consider a subroutine such as the FORTRAN SQRT function. The programmer codes

```
X = SQRT(Y)
```

and, after the instruction is executed, expects to find the square root of Y in the field called X. It isn't quite that simple; the square root is actually estimated in a fairly complex subroutine. The subroutine could be stored as a FORTRAN source module, copied into each program that references SQRT, and recompiled, but that would be very inefficient. Instead, the SQRT function is stored as an object module.

A compiler works with source code. Certain key logical elements, such as access methods and standard subroutines, do not exist at the source level. Thus, there is no way for the *compiler* to incorporate this essential logic into an object module. Consequently, the object module will refer to logic that simply is not there—an unresolved **external reference**. As it builds an object module, the compiler generates a table of unresolved external references and places it at the beginning of the object module (Fig. 13.10). This **external symbol dictionary** (the **ESD**) is used by the linkage editor as it builds a load module.

Creating an Object Module Library

Physically, there is no difference between a source statement library and an **object module library**; in fact, on some systems, it is possible to mix source and object modules on the same library. Under IBM DOS/VSE, the object module library is called the relocatable library. The term linkage library is sometimes used on an IBM OS system. It is possible to have both private and system object module libraries (Fig. 13.11), with the "most recently compiled" object module perhaps being viewed as a special case.

Fig. 13.10   An object module's external references are listed in its external symbol dictionary.

External symbol dictionary	
Symbol	Location
MAIN	Known
SEQAM	?
SUBRI	?

Object code

MAIN _____

         .
         .
         .

     CALL SEQAM
         .
         .
         .

     CALL SUBR1
         .
         .

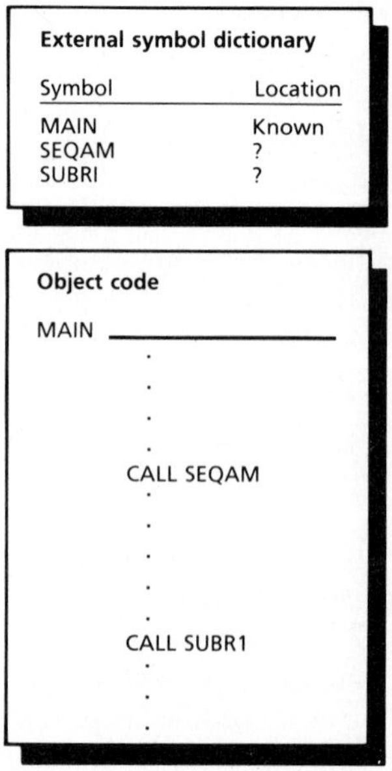

Fig. 13.11   The linkage editor can access both system and private object
module libraries.

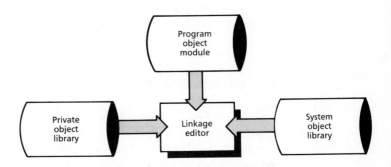

Adding Object Modules to a Library (IBM OS/JCL)

Object modules are generated by compilers. To add an object module to a
library, you must control the compiler's output. For example, Fig. 13.9
shows the JCL statements generated by the cataloged procedure ASMFC
(compile only). Earlier, we considered the SYSLIB DD statement, which
identifies system and private macro libraries. The assembler sends its output to the physical device described in the **SYSGO** DD statement:

```
XXSYSGO   DD   DSNAME=&&LOADSET,SPACE=(400,(100,20)),
XX             DISP=(OLD,PASS),UNIT=SYSDA,
XX             DCB=(LRECL=80,BLKSIZE=400,RECFM=FB)
```

It defines a temporary data set named &&LOADSET; the object module
produced by the assembler program will be its only member. The secret to
placing an object module on a private library is simple: change this statement.

For example, assume that the program being assembled is called
MYPGM. We have already created a library named MYLIB. The following
JCL would assemble the program and place the object module on the
library:

```
//            EXEC   ASMFC
//ASM.SYSGO   DD     DSNAME=MYLIB(MYPGM),DISP=(OLD,KEEP),
//                   DCB=(RECFM=FB,LRECL=80,BLKSIZE=400)
//ASM.SYSIN   DD     *

     }source program

/*
```

Coding a SYSGO DD statement in the job stream overrides the cataloged procedure. The object module will no longer go to a temporary data set named &&LOADSET; instead it will be stored in MYLIB, under the name MYPGM. Note: Once again, given an existing library, we could skip the DCB parameter. If coded, the logical record length, blocksize, and record format must match the library.

Load Modules

An object module containing unresolved external references cannot be loaded and executed. External references are resolved by the linkage editor.

Figure 13.10 pictures an object module. The main program is MAIN. It references two subroutines, an access method (SEQAM) and a private subroutine (SUBR1). The linkage editor faces the situation pictured in Fig. 13.12. SEQAM resides on a system object module library. SUBR1 is on a private library. The just compiled object module, MAIN, is on another private library (or, perhaps, on a temporary data set).

The linkage editor begins by reading the primary object module, MAIN. The external symbol dictionary is separated from the object code, and the beginning of MAIN is established as the base address or reference point for the load module (Fig. 13.13).

Next, the linkage editor scans the external symbol dictionary. An object module named SEQAM is referenced. The system library is searched, SEQAM is found, the access method is read into main memory, its ESD is

Fig. 13.12   As the linkage editor begins its work, the object modules it must link may be stored on several different libraries.

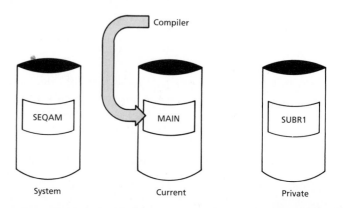

Fig. 13.13   The linkage editor combines object modules to form a load module. The start of the primary object module is the load module's base address.

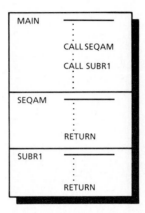

separated from the object code, and the object module is placed just after MAIN (Fig. 13.13).

SEQAM's external symbol dictionary is then scanned. (To simplify this example, we'll assume the access method does not call a lower level subroutine.) Once the reference to SEQAM has been fully resolved, the linkage editor can return to the main program's external symbol dictionary.

MAIN also calls SUBR1. The system library is searched, but SUBR1 is not found. Thus, the private subroutine library is searched; SUBR1 is there. The object module is read into memory, the ESD and the object code are separated, and the code is placed after SEQAM in the load module (Fig. 13.13). Now the external symbol dictionary for SUBR1 is scanned for unresolved external references; once again we'll assume there are none.

Returning to the main program's external symbol dictionary, the linkage editor finds no more unresolved external references. Thus the load module is complete, referring only to locations that are contained within itself. It is ready to be loaded and executed.

Imagine a somewhat more complex program. The primary module is named CONTROL. It calls four subroutines: A, B, C, and D. Routines A, C, and D are relatively simple, performing a computation and returning to CONTROL, but routine B contains subsequent calls to X, Y, and Z. When the linkage editor reads module B and scans its external symbol dictionary, three lower level unresolved external references will be encountered. These references must be resolved before the linkage editor returns to the main program; thus subroutines X, Y, and Z will follow B in the load module (Fig. 13.14).

Fig. 13.14   In a more complex program, the linkage editor may resolve a
                        chain of secondary external references before returning to the
                        primary object module.

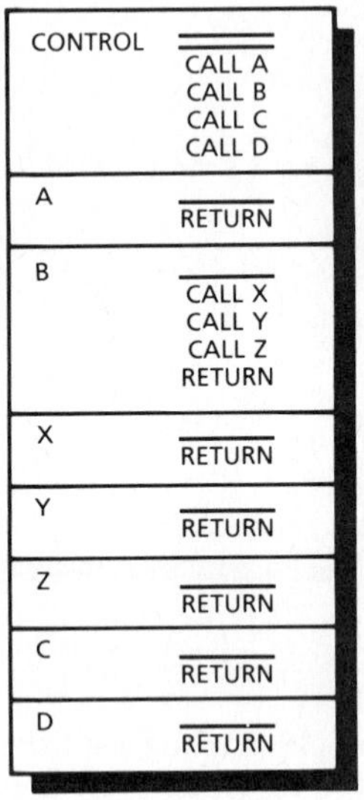

The Linkage Editor (IBM OS/JCL)

The linkage editor is a program. Its input consists of one or more object
modules. It produces a load module. If you have ever programmed an IBM
System/360-370 computer, you have almost certainly used the linkage editor, but you have probably never looked at the JCL that supports it. Figure
13.15 shows an expansion of the cataloged procedure ASMFCL (compile
and link edit). Let's read through the statements in the link edit step.
     The first statement

```
//    EXEC    PGM=IEWL
```

names the linkage editor program. The input data set is SYSLIN. Note the
DSNAME, &&LOADSET. Where have you seen that before? It's the same
name the assembler used to store the object module—look at the SYSGO
DD statement.
     A few lines below SYSLIN is a DD statement with no DDNAME

```
//    DD      DDNAME=SYSIN
```

This is another source of linkage editor input; it is concatenated to SYSLIN.

Fig. 13.15   The ASMFCL cataloged procedure. Statements that begin with //
                        are coded by the programmer. Those that begin with XX are part
                        of the procedure.

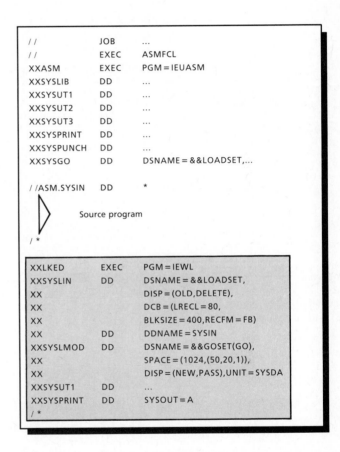

```
//                JOB       ...
//                EXEC      ASMFCL
XXASM             EXEC      PGM = IEUASM
XXSYSLIB          DD        ...
XXSYSUT1          DD        ...
XXSYSUT2          DD        ...
XXSYSUT3          DD        ...
XXSYSPRINT        DD        ...
XXSYSPUNCH        DD        ...
XXSYSGO           DD        DSNAME = &&LOADSET,...

//ASM.SYSIN       DD        *

                  Source program

/*

XXLKED            EXEC      PGM = IEWL
XXSYSLIN          DD        DSNAME = &&LOADSET,
XX                          DISP = (OLD,DELETE),
XX                          DCB = (LRECL = 80,
XX                          BLKSIZE = 400,RECFM = FB)
XX                DD        DDNAME = SYSIN
XXSYSLMOD         DD        DSNAME = &&GOSET(GO),
XX                          SPACE = (1024,(50,20,1)),
XX                          DISP = (NEW,PASS),UNIT = SYSDA
XXSYSUT1          DD        ...
XXSYSPRINT        DD        SYSOUT = A
/*
```

The parameter, DDNAME=SYSIN, is a bit unusual. It postpones the
data definition. Essentially, the DDNAME parameter tells the operating
system to look ahead in the job stream for a DD statement with the specified
DDNAME (in this example, SYSIN). The programmer can code a SYSIN
DD statement to pass object modules and control statements to the linkage
editor; we'll consider an example shortly.

The **SYSLMOD** (for system load module) statement defines the linkage
editor's output data set (the load module). The DSNAME is &&GO-
SET(GO). It defines a temporary partitioned data set on the system direct
access device (SYSDA); this particular load module is given the member
name GO. Note the SPACE parameter. Space is requested in 1024-byte
blocks. The primary request is for 50 blocks, with a secondary request for
20 more; a single 256-byte block is set aside to hold the directory.

The Primary Object Module (IBM OS/JCL)

If the linkage editor is to produce a valid load module, it must start some-where. The primary object module is input through **SYSLIN** (system linkage editor input). Typically, it is the most recently compiled object module; in the compile, link edit, execute sequence, it's the one that started as source code. Figure 13.15 shows the output from the assembler going to SYSGO, where it is stored under data set name &&LOADSET. This DSNAME also appears on the SYSLIN statement as input to the linkage editor. If the object module is stored on a private library, both SYSGO and SYSLIN must be overridden (Fig. 13.16).

Programmers tend to view the compile, link edit, and execute sequence almost as a single operation—compilelinkeditgo. In reality, three distinct

Fig. 13.16   If the primary object module is stored on a private library, both SYSGO (compile or assemble step) and SYSLIN (link edit step) must be overridden.

```
//                EXEC    ASMFCL
XXASM             EXEC    PGM = IEUASM
XXSYSLIB          DD      ...
XXSYSUT1          DD      ...
XXSYSUT2          DD      ...
XXSYSUT3          DD      ...
XXSYSPRINT        DD      ...
XXSYSPUNCH        DD      ...

//ASM.SYSGO       DD      DSNAME = MYLIB(MYPGM),
//                        DISP = (OLD,KEEP),
//                        DCB = (RECFM = FB,LRECL = 80,
//                        BLKSIZE = 400)

//ASM.SYSIN       DD      *

        ▷   Source program

/*

XXLKED            EXEC    PGM = IEWL

//LKED.SYSLIN     DD      DSNAME = MYLIB(MYPGM),
//                        DISP = (OLD,KEEP)
//                DD      DDNAME = SYSIN

XXSYSLMOD         DD      ...
XXSYSUT1          DD      ...
XXSYSPRINT        DD      ...
```

programs must be run. They are usually separated by just a few seconds (or even microseconds). However, it is possible to run the compile on Monday, the link edit on Tuesday, and the execute step on Wednesday (substitute January, February, and March, if you wish). Once a source, object, or load module is written to a nontemporary file, it is captured for later use, and can be accessed at virtually any time.

System Libraries (IBM OS/JCL)

There are several different types of system libraries. One, a true system library, contains such object modules as the standard access methods that are used by almost every program. The operating system knows where to find them.

Other system libraries are language dependent. FORTRAN, for example, supports a number of scientific subroutines. The programmer who wants to use one of these scientific subroutines must clearly specify to the linkage editor where the subroutine library can be found. Thus the FOR-TRAN compile, link edit, and execute procedure normally references one additional DD statement

```
XXSYSLIB  DD  DSNAME=SYS1.FORTLIB,DISP=SHR
```

Other subroutine libraries can be identified by concatenating additional DD statements to SYSLIB. Similar language-dependent functions are supported in COBOL, PL/1, and most other languages.

Note the difference between these two types of system libraries. The first is language independent—almost every program will require one or more of these object modules. System pointers allow the linkage editor to locate a system library; no programmer-generated DD statement is required. The other libraries are language dependent. FORTRAN programs access FORTLIB; COBOL programs request object modules from COBLIB. The programmer (or cataloged procedure) must identify such language-dependent libraries through a SYSLIB DD statement.

Private Libraries (IBM OS/JCL)

Unless the programmer provides a complete description of a private library, the linkage editor will be unable to find it. The cataloged procedure for the link edit step normally contains an unnamed DD statement concatenated to SYSLIN. This statement, in turn, points to DDNAME=SYSIN. The programmer can take advantage of the SYSIN statement to pass private library information to the linkage editor.

For example, assume that a subroutine named SUBR1 resides on a private library named MYLIB. You have just compiled a program that references SUBR1. You can tell the linkage editor to include the subroutine in the load module by passing it a control statement via SYSIN (Fig. 13.17).

Follow the code carefully. Start with the "normal" JCL as it exists in the cataloged procedure, with the SYSLIN DD statement concatenated to an

Fig. 13.17   Control statements are passed to the linkage editor through
                      SYSIN.

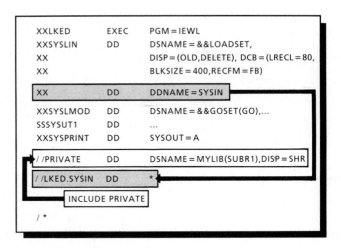

```
XXLKED         EXEC      PGM = IEWL
XXSYSLIN       DD        DSNAME = &&LOADSET,
XX                       DISP = (OLD,DELETE), DCB = (LRECL = 80,
XX                       BLKSIZE = 400,RECFM = FB)

XX             DD        DDNAME = SYSIN

XXSYSLMOD      DD        DSNAME = &&GOSET(GO),...
SSSYSUT1       DD        ...
XXSYSPRINT     DD        SYSOUT = A

//PRIVATE      DD        DSNAME = MYLIB(SUBR1),DISP = SHR

//LKED.SYSIN   DD        *
               INCLUDE PRIVATE

/*
```

unnamed DD statement that points to SYSIN. Following SYSPRINT is a
new statement—the // in the first two positions shows it was coded by the
programmer. This statement, named PRIVATE, describes the private library. Next comes the SYSIN statement (LKED. is a step qualifier). It
precedes the linkage editor control statements. In this example, only one
control statement has been coded:

INCLUDE PRIVATE

It tells the linkage editor to look for a DD statement named PRIVATE for a
detailed description of one or more object modules that are to be included
in the load module.

Go through the process one more time. The SYSIN statement passes a
series of control statements to the linkage editor. An **INCLUDE** statement
identifies one or more DD statements. Each DD statement defines, in turn,
one or more object modules that are to be included in the load module. The
skeleton of another, more complex, example is shown in Fig. 13.18.

This is only one example of how the programmer might use the linkage
editor. There are several ways to identify private object modules, and numerous other commands can be coded. It is not our intent to cover all the
features of this most useful program, however.

Load Modules Libraries (IBM OS/JCL)

A **load module library** is a partitioned data set. Under DOS/VSE, a load
module library is called a core image library.

Load modules are output by the linkage editor. The output is sent to

Fig. 13.18   This example shows how the linkage editor can be given the
names of multiple private libraries, each containing multiple
object modules.

```
//              EXEC     ASMFCL
//ASM.SYSIN     DD       *

       Source program

/*
//LIBRA         DD       DSNAME = ALIBRARY(A,B,C,D),
//                       DISP = SHR
//LIBRX         DD       DSNAME = XLIBRARY(X,Y,Z),
//                       DISP = SHR
//LKED.SYSIN    DD       *
     INCLUDE LIBRA
     INCLUDE LIBRX
/*
```

the partitioned data set defined by

```
XXSYSLMOD  DD  DSNAME=&&GOSET(GO),SPACE=(1024,(50,20,1)),
XX             DISP=(NEW,PASS),UNIT=SYSDA
```

To place a load module on a private library, simply change the SYSLMOD
DD statement (Fig. 13.19).

Fig. 13.19   To place a load module on a private library, change the
SYSLMOD DD statement.

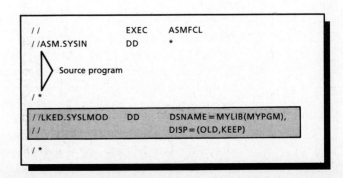

```
//              EXEC     ASMFCL
//ASM.SYSIN     DD       *

       Source program

/*
//LKED.SYSLMOD  DD       DSNAME = MYLIB(MYPGM),
//                       DISP = (OLD,KEEP)
/*
```

Load modules can be loaded and executed by the system in response to an EXEC statement. The system can find load modules that are stored on a system program library. The programmer must identify a private library through a JOBLIB or STEPLIB statement; for example,

```
//          EXEC   PGM=MYPGM
//STEPLIB   DD     DSNAME=MYLIB,DISP=SHR
```

The Loader

The **loader** does everything the linkage editor does, except output a load module. Instead, it builds a load module in main memory, and then simply gives it control. With the linkage editor, the load module is written to disk and then read back in. With the loader, these two I/O operations are dropped, saving considerable time. Because the loader outputs no load module, there is no SYSLMOD DD statement. To access the loader, the programmer codes cataloged procedures such as ASMFCG or COBVCG; the CG stands for compile and go.

Some advanced linkage editor functions (for example, generating overlay structures) are not supported by the loader. Still, for the compile and test activities common to program development, the loader is usually more than adequate, and it does represent a considerable savings in computer time and, hence, in computer cost.

Summary

The chapter began with a brief discussion of the compile, link edit, and execute sequence. We defined source modules, object modules, and load modules, and briefly described the functions of the compiler, interpreter, and linkage editor. Libraries can be maintained at the source, object, or load level.

Assembler macro instructions and COBOL COPY statements refer to a source statement library. The difference between private and system libraries was explored, and an example illustrating the expansion of source code into a source module prior to compilation was developed using COBOL.

On an IBM computer, a library is called a partitioned data set or PDS. The creation of a PDS was illustrated, and a utility program named IEBGENER was used to add members to a source statement library. We then briefly considered the nature of an object module, pointing out that most contain unresolved external references, and thus must be link edited before execution. A member is placed on an object module library by controlling the destination of the compiler output.

Load modules are built from a set of object modules by the linkage editor. The link edit process was discussed in general terms, and then a specific example using the IBM linkage editor was developed. Because a load module is output by the linkage editor, the secret to placing a load module on a library is to control the destination of the linkage editor's output. The chapter ended with a brief discussion of the loader program.

Key Words

directory	load module	partitioned data
external reference	load module	set
external symbol	library	source module
dictionary	loader	source statement
IEBGENER	macro	library
IEFBR14	member	SYSGO
INCLUDE	object module	SYSLIB
library	object module	SYSLIN
linkage editor	library	SYSLMOD

Exercises

1. Distinguish between a source module, an object module, and a load module. Don't simply say that a source module is produced by a programmer, an object module is produced by a compiler, and a load module is produced by a linkage editor; listing the sources doesn't answer the question. How do these modules differ from each other?

2. Briefly explain how a compiler or an assembler incorporates source statement library members into a source module.

3. Explain the difference between a system library and a private library.

4. Describe the structure of a typical library.

5. Explain how a partitioned data set can be created on an IBM System/360-370.

6. How can a programmer add a member to a source statement library?

7. Why does a typical object module contain unresolved external references?

8. What is an external symbol dictionary?

9. Explain how a member can be added to an object module library.

10. What does the linkage editor do?

11. What is a concatenated data set?

12. Explain how the linkage editor follows a chain of unresolved external references as it builds a load module.

13. How is a load module placed on a private library? How is this load module eventually executed?

14. What is the loader program?

The following exercises are intended for readers who have access to an IBM System 360-370 computer. Users of other systems might consider parallel assignments.

15. Submit a program (any program) using a cataloged procedure such as ASMFCLG, COBVCLG, or one you have used in class. Include MSGLEVEL=(1,1) on the EXEC statement. Read and explain each generated job control statement.

16. For this exercise you will need a main program and a subroutine written in any language (or even in two different languages). Use source code from a previous class. If you don't have the source code, write a main program to read two values, call a subroutine that adds them, and write their sum. Don't waste time on the code—this is a library manipulation exercise. Do the following:
    a. Compile the subroutine and store it on a private library.
    b. Independently compile the main program and store it on a private library.
    c. Link edit the two object modules and store the load module on a private library.
    d. Execute the load module.

Operating System Internals

CHAPTER
14

MS-DOS

Evaluating an Operating System

Most people begin seriously studying computers by learning an application programming language. In Part III, you moved a step closer to the hardware by investigating command languages. The hardware itself is directly controlled by its microcode. In between, serving as a hardware/software interface, is the operating system (Fig. 14.1). To the application programmer or user, most of what happens below the command language level is transparent. We are about to drop below that level and turn our attention to operating system internals.

If an operating system is to be a hardware/software interface, it makes sense to design an *efficient* interface. Thus, on most modern computers, the operating system serves as the primary resource manager, responsible for processor time, main memory space, registers, input and output devices, secondary storage space, and data and program libraries. A well-designed operating system attempts to optimize the utilization of all the system resources.

Measures of Effectiveness

That objective seems obvious, but it isn't. Consider an analogy. What is the optimum engine for an automobile? The answer depends on your definition of effective performance. Are you primarily interested in speed? safety? fuel efficiency? space? a comfortable ride? cost? status? or some combination? In other words, what are your measures of effectiveness, and how do you weight them? Tell me what characteristics you consider important. Then we can *begin* to discuss the precise meaning of the word optimum. "Best" is a relative term.

A number of criteria are used to measure a computer system's performance, including:

1. Throughput. Generally, total execution time (for all programs) divided by total elapsed time.

Fig. 14.1　　The operating system acts as a hardware/software interface.

2. Turnaround. The elapsed time between job submission and job completion.
3. Response time. The elapsed time between a request for the computer's attention and the computer's response.
4. Availability.
5. Security.
6. Reliability.
7. Cost.
8. Ease of use.

The perfect operating system would maximize throughput while minimizing both turnaround and response time. The system would be available to any programmer or user on demand, and would be remarkably easy to use. Security would, of course, be absolute, and system reliability would approach 100 percent. All this would be accomplished at very low cost.

System Objectives

Unfortunately, such a perfect operating system is impossible to achieve, because the measures of effectiveness conflict. For example, throughput can be increased by overloading a system, but overloading negatively impacts turnaround and response time. Conversely, turnaround and response time can be helped by underloading a system which, of course, destroys throughput, since an underloaded system is bound to be idle at times.

Does this imply that turnaround and response time are compatible? Not always. Consider a time-sharing system designed to minimize response time. To prevent any single user from monopolizing the processor, programs are limited to brief time slices. Imagine a ten-second program. If that program is limited to one-tenth second of actual run time each second, it would need 100 seconds of elapsed time. Emphasizing response time can hurt turnaround.

System availability and throughput obviously conflict; how can a busy system be available? Security involves various controls and checks, and time spent on security cannot be used for production. Reliability is gained by duplicating key components, and that's expensive; reliability and cost are conflicting objectives.

Recognizing that the criteria conflict, system objectives are often stated as targets; for example, "Maintain a minimum of 75 percent throughput while keeping turnaround under one hour," or "Maintain response time at a maximum of three seconds for at least 95 percent of system requests," or "Keep average response time below two seconds." The ideal operating system for a particular installation is a function of its application mix. For example, a large time-sharing computer concurrently accessed by hundreds of users will probably stress response time, security, and reliability. An equally large business system might be more concerned with generating massive, end-of-period accounting reports in a timely fashion and at reasonable cost; throughput and turnaround thus become crucial. The operating systems for these two machines will be quite different.

When studying an operating system, it is useful to begin with two questions:

1. What hardware is it designed to support?
2. What is the typical (or assumed) application mix?

The answers are essential if you are to understand *why* a particular operating system works as it does.

Microcomputer Operating Systems

The Microcomputer Environment

Let's start with a microcomputer. Although 8- and 32-bit systems are available, the typical micro is a 16-bit word machine. Most contain limited main memory and support a limited number of peripheral devices (often, a keyboard, a screen, a printer, two diskette drives, and, perhaps, a hard disk). Basic systems cost less than $1000; a typical configuration might cost $2000 to $5000.

Many early users were hackers, who enjoyed "fooling around" with the machine. Such people require (and probably desire) very little support. While hackers still exist, today's typical owner wants a microcomputer for a specific purpose such as tracking inventory, playing games, writing papers, or supporting research, and doesn't want the hardware to get in the way. Most programs are small and process a limited amount of data. On a given day, relatively few programs will be run. (In fact, the computer is likely to be unused most of the time.) These are, of course, assumptions, but they are reasonable.

For a machine used perhaps two to three hours a day, throughput is not relevant. Given small programs processing limited data, turnaround is not a problem. Even a slow computer is much faster than any human user, so response time is generally not a factor. Forget availability. Modern microcomputers are so inexpensive that almost anyone who needs one can afford one. Given the limited number of users, security it is not a major concern, either.

What, then, are the microcomputer user's criteria for measuring effectiveness? Basically, there are three—cost, reliability, and ease of use. Cost is the big one. People are drawn to microcomputers because they are inexpensive. Each operating system function increases development cost, and hence selling price. An operating system occupies main memory, and the larger the system, the more memory it needs. Thus microcomputer operating systems generally contain only essential functions.

Reliability and ease of use vie closely for second place. Reliability, unfortunately, is difficult to measure, and tends to be viewed in a negative light: the ABC model 50 is always going down. From an operating system perspective, reliability is largely a function of complexity. Put simply, on a micro it is better to do a few things well than many things badly. Once again, the argument favors simplicity.

Finally, consider ease of use. Must users are uninterested in the subtle nuances of I/O device control or diskette track configurations. As a minimum, they require a simple command language and the ability to store and retrieve data and programs by name. Application programs may provide more sophisticated interfaces, but commands and file names are needed before an application program can even be loaded.

Basic Operating System Functions

Microcomputer operating systems are generally small. The resident operating system, sometimes called the **nucleus**, the **kernel**, or the **supervisor**, typically contains a **command processor**, or **shell**, an **input/output control system**, or **IOCS**, a **file system**, and interrupt handler routines (Fig. 14.2). Another region holds system constants, parameters, and control fields. These modules reside in main memory and provide real-time support to the application programs.

Fig. 14.2   Microcomputer operating systems typically contain a command processor, an input/output control system, and a file system. Other transient operating system modules are stored on disk and read into memory on demand.

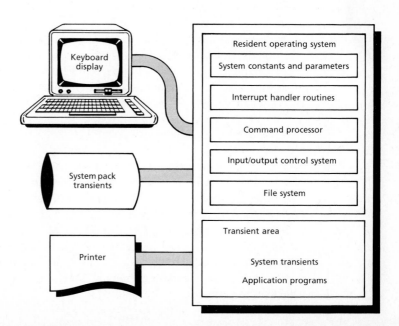

Not all operating system modules must be **resident**. Consider, for example, formatting a disk. The routine that performs this task is needed only when a disk is being formatted. Thus, it is stored on disk and loaded into memory on demand. The free or **transient area** of main memory (Fig. 14.2), containing all the space not allocated to the resident operating system, can hold one of these **transient** modules or an application program.

Where in memory is the operating system found? That depends on the system. The architecture of many computers requires that key control information be stored at specific main memory locations, thus defining the address of at least the system parameters. Other systems assume a standard load address for a primary control program. Figure 14.2 shows the components of an operating system in a general sense, without regard for their placement.

Few microcomputers operate 24 hours a day. Main memory is generally volatile; in other words, it loses its contents when power is removed. Thus the resident operating system is not permanent; it must be reloaded each time the system is restarted. Normally, a copy of the operating system is kept on disk and loaded into memory by a **boot** routine each time the system is activated. The boot is another essential microcomputer operating system module.

MS-DOS Internals

MS-DOS is the world's most commonly used microcomputer operating system. Developed for the IBM Personal Computer by Microsoft Corporation, versions of MS-DOS are available on all IBM and IBM-compatible machines. (The IBM-PC version is called **PC-DOS.**)

The IBM PC is constructed around an Intel 8086 processor. Internally, the PC manipulates a 16-bit word. However, the 8086 communicates with its peripheral devices over an 8-bit bus. Selecting this chip gave IBM 16-bit processing speed while allowing the company to use a number of commercially available 8-bit input and output interfaces; the PC was literally constructed from off-the-shelf components.

The Shell

MS-DOS is command driven. (You studied the command language in Chapter 8.) Users request support by typing commands in response to a system prompt (Fig. 14.3). When the return key is pressed, the shell, called **COMMAND.COM**, interprets the command and calls the appropriate lower level routine or program. COMMAND.COM consists of a command interpreter and a number of resident operating system routines that remain in memory at all times (Fig. 14.3). Other routines are transient and are read into memory on demand. Generally, those routines needed to support an active program are resident.

Fig. 14.3   MS-DOS is a command-driven operating system. To request
support, a user types a command in response to a system prompt.
The operating system then reads and interprets the command
and calls the routine that carries out the command.

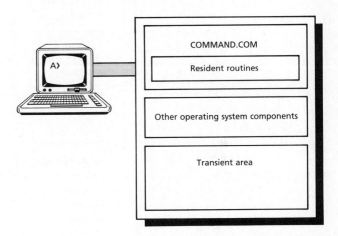

Resident commands		Transient commands	
BREAK	PATH	ASSIGN	LIB
CHDIR	PAUSE	BACKUP	LINK
CLS	PROMPT	CHKDSK	MAP
COPY	REM	COMMAND	MODE
CTTY	REN	COMP	MORE
DATE	RMDIR	CONFIGUR	PART
DIR	SET	DEBUG	PREP
ECHO	SHIFT	DETECT	PRINT
ERASE	TIME	DISKCOMP	RDCPM
EXIT	TYPE	DISKCOPY	RECOVER
FOR	VER	EDLIN	RESTORE
GOTO	VERIFY	FC	SHIP
IF	VOL	FIND	SORT
MKDIR	d:	FORMAT	SYS
			TREE

Accessing Peripherals

The task of accessing peripheral devices is divided between two operating
system modules (Fig. 14.4). **IO.SYS** (called IBMBIO.COM under PC-DOS)
is a hardware-dependent module that issues *physical* data transfer commands. On an IBM PC, this module interacts with a proprietary, basic
input/output system, or BIOS, implemented in read-only memory. This
ROM BIOS distinguishes an IBM PC from compatible computers made by
other manufacturers.

Fig. 14.4   Two modules, IO.SYS and MSDOS.SYS, share responsibility for
                         accessing peripheral devices.

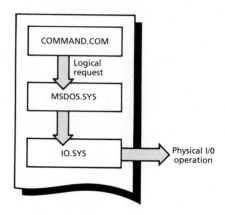

Logical I/O is implemented by a hardware-independent module called
MSDOS.SYS (IBMSYS.COM under PC-DOS). MSDOS.SYS accepts logical
I/O requests from application programs or other operating system modules,
translates them into physical I/O commands, and passes the physical commands to IO.SYS. Note that only IO.SYS, the machine-dependent module,
deals directly with peripheral devices. A version of MS-DOS written for a
COMPAQ computer and one written for a Zenith computer will differ only
in their IO.SYS; other operating system modules will be the same.

Each physical device attached to the computer is described in a special
file called a **device driver** (Fig. 14.5). Character drivers control such devices as the keyboard, the screen, and the printer. Block drivers control disk
and similar block-oriented devices, and transfer data in 512-byte blocks.
The device driver is used by MSDOS.SYS to translate logical I/O requests to
physical form. Certain standard device drivers are built into the operating
system (Fig. 14.5). Additional devices can be defined by adding a description to a special file called CONFIG.SYS.

The File System

MSDOS.SYS converts logical I/O requests to physical form. One of its
responsibilities is directory management. Chapter 8 introduced the MS-
DOS directory structure; if you completed the chapter tutorial, you know
how to create and delete directories with operating system commands. For
example, when a make directory command, such as

MKDIR LETTERS

Fig. 14.5   MSDOS.SYS uses a device driver to translate logical I/O requests
                       to physical form.

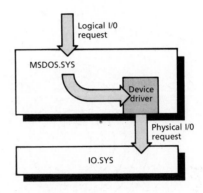

Standard character device drivers	
Name	**Description**
AUX	First serial printer or modem
COM1	Same as AUX
CLOCK$	Real-time clock
COM2	Second serial device (printer or modem)
CON	Console—keyboard/display
LPT2	Second parallel device (usually, printer)
LPT3	Third parallel device
NUL	"Null" device—output discarded
PRN	First parallel printer
LPT1	Same as PRN

is read by COMMAND.COM, the shell calls MSDOS.SYS (Fig. 14.6a),
which, in turn, asks IO.SYS to read the directory (Fig. 14.6b). MSDOS.SYS
then adds the new directory entry (Fig. 14.6c), and asks IO.SYS to write the
modified directory back to disk (Fig. 14.6d). Generally, MSDOS.SYS creates, deletes, and modifies directory entries in response to requests from
COMMAND.COM (or an application routine), and relies on IO.SYS to
perform the actual data transfer operations.

MSDOS.SYS also supports application programs. When a disk file is
first opened, MSDOS.SYS asks IO.SYS to read the directory. It then extracts
the location of an existing file or creates a directory entry for a new one and,
if necessary, asks IO.SYS to rewrite the directory. As the program runs,
logical input and output operations result in a transfer of control to MS-
DOS.SYS. Using the start-of-file address from open, the operating system
computes the physical address of the data, and then passes the address to
IO.SYS. Additionally, MSDOS.SYS blocks and deblocks data.

Fig. 14.6   MSDOS.SYS is responsible for directory management.

a. Commands are read and interpreted by COMMAND.COM. Following a make
directory (MKDIR) command, COMMAND.COM calls MSDOS.SYS.

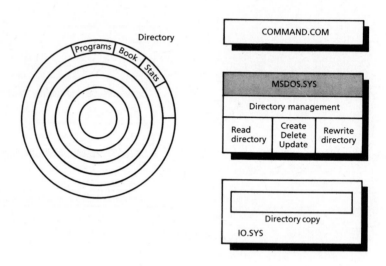

b. MSDOS.SYS then asks IO.SYS to read the directory.

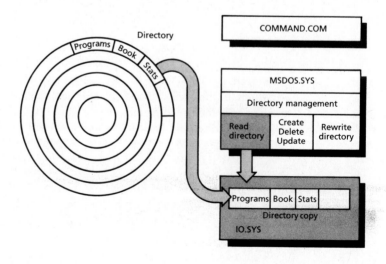

c. Once the directory is in memory, MSDOS.SYS can modify it. In this example, a new directory entry is added.

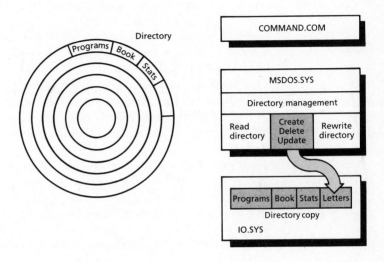

d. Finally, MSDOS.SYS asks IO.SYS to rewrite the directory entry to disk.

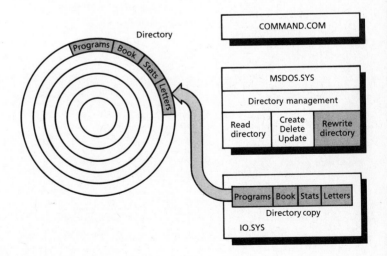

Another MSDOS.SYS responsibility is allocating space on disk. Start with an overview of a disk's format (Fig. 14.7). Track 0, sector 0 (the first sector on the disk) holds the boot routine. Next, in sectors 1 and 2, are two copies of the file allocation table (FAT). The root directory begins with track 0, sector 5. On system disks, the various components of the operating system follow the root directory (Fig. 14.7 shows a system disk); on disks that do not contain a copy of the system, this space (and the rest of the disk) is used for data storage.

Disk space is allocated in **clusters**. On a single-sided disk, each cluster holds 512 bytes (one sector); on a double-sided disk, each cluster holds 1024 bytes (two sectors). The clusters are numbered sequentially starting with zero, and the **file allocation table** contains an entry for each cluster on the disk.

When a file is created, the number of its first cluster is stored in the directory. As data are added to the file, the second cluster is assigned dynamically by recording its number in the first cluster's FAT entry; thus the first cluster points to the second one (Fig. 14.8). As additional data are added, the third cluster's number is recorded in the second cluster's FAT entry, and so on; by following a chain of pointers from the directory through the file allocation table until an end-of-file marker is reached, it is

Fig. 14.7   This diagram shows the format of a typical MS-DOS disk. If the disk does not contain a copy of the operating system, the space set aside for IO.SYS, MSDOS.SYS, and COMMAND.COM is used for data.

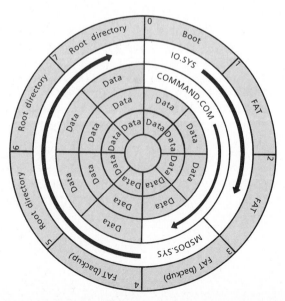

Fig. 14.7

Fig. 14.8   A file's first cluster number is recorded in the disk directory. To locate the clusters that comprise a file, follow the chain of pointers through the file allocation table.

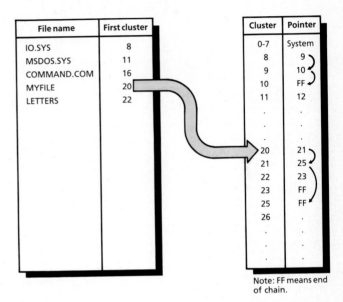

File name	First cluster
IO.SYS	8
MSDOS.SYS	11
COMMAND.COM	16
MYFILE	20
LETTERS	22

Cluster	Pointer
0-7	System
8	9
9	10
10	FF
11	12
.	.
.	.
.	.
20	21
21	25
22	23
23	FF
25	FF
26	.
.	.
.	.

Note: FF means end of chain.

possible to step, cluster by cluster, through a file. Note that the clusters belonging to a file need not be contiguous.

MS-DOS views the data stored in a disk file as a continuous stream of bytes. Logical I/O operations request data by relative byte (rather than by relative record or relative sector). Assuming a double-sided disk, a file's first cluster holds relative bytes 0 through 1023, its second cluster holds relative bytes 1024 through 4095, and so on. As part of its blocking and deblocking functions, MSDOS.SYS calls IO.SYS to perform whatever physical I/O operations are necessary to access the requested string. Logically, data on disk are addressed just like data in main memory.

In addition to managing disk space, MSDOS.SYS also manages main memory space.

Interrupt Processing

The Intel 8086 relies on **interrupts** to establish communication with its peripheral devices. Consequently, processing interrupts is an important MS-DOS function.

The key to interrupt processing is an **interrupt vector table** that occupies the first 1K bytes of main memory (Fig. 14.9). This table holds the

Fig. 14.9   MS-DOS contains modules to process interrupts.

a. When an interrupt occurs, the contents of the instruction pointer register are copied to the stack.

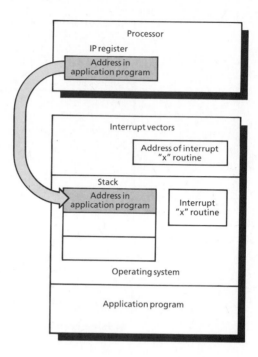

b. Next, the specified interrupt vector is loaded into the instruction pointer.

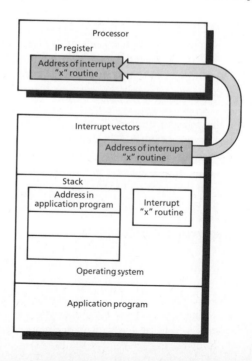

c. With the next machine cycle, the first instruction in the interrupt processing routine is fetched.

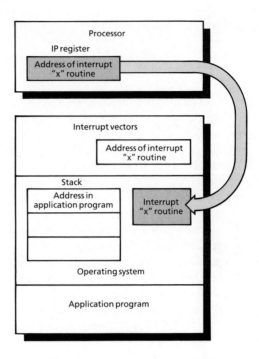

d. Finally, the contents of the stack are loaded back into the instruction pointer register, and the application program resumes processing.

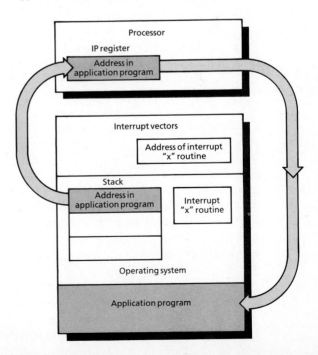

addresses (interrupt vectors) of up to 256 different interrupt processing modules, most of which are found in MSDOS.SYS or IO.SYS. Two special registers are also crucial. The 8086's instruction counter is found in the IP (instruction pointer) register. Another register points to a main memory stack.

The interrupt itself consists of an electronic pulse and the address of an interrupt vector. When an interrupt occurs, hardware immediately copies the contents of the IP register (along with a few other registers) to the stack (Fig. 14.9a), and loads the specified interrupt vector into the IP register (Fig. 14.9b). As the next machine cycle begins, the first instruction in the interrupt processing routine is fetched (Fig. 14.9c). Once the interrupt is processed, the contents of the stack are copied back into the IP register, and the original program resumes processing (Fig. 14.9d).

Interrupts are much more common than you might imagine. For example, each time you press a key on the keyboard, an interrupt is generated. In response, the operating system copies a single character into main memory, and then waits for the next interrupt to herald the arrival of the next character. A few keys, such as return and escape, signal the operating system to take a different action. Interrupts also allow the printer, a disk drive, and other peripherals to communicate with the main processor.

Not all interrupts originate with hardware, however. Although it is legal for an application program to communicate directly with IO.SYS, most rely on MSDOS.SYS to translate their logical I/O requests to physical form. Branching to or calling an operating system module implies a knowledge of MS-DOS internals that few people possess. Thus, by convention, an assembler language programmer who wants to perform I/O loads descriptive information into a few registers and then executes an interrupt instruction referencing vector 33 (21 hex).[1]

Hardware responds to a software-generated interrupt exactly as if the source had been hardware, copying the IP register to the stack and loading the contents of the specified vector into the IP register. The address in vector 33 points to an MSDOS.SYS module that analyzes register contents and determines the requested I/O operation. In compiler languages, the instructions to set registers and interrupt the operating system are generated for you.

Booting MS-DOS

Main memory is volatile; it loses its contents when the computer loses power. Consequently, the operating system must be read into main memory each time the computer is switched on. Under MS-DOS, the boot routine is stored on the first sector of each disk. Flipping the power switch (or simultaneously pressing the control, alt, and delete keys) causes hard-

---

[1] There is nothing special about vector 33. It's just a widely accepted coding standard adopted by Microsoft and used by most software developers.

Fig. 14.10   When you turn on the computer, hardware reads the boot
                   routine from the first sector on the system disk into main
                   memory.

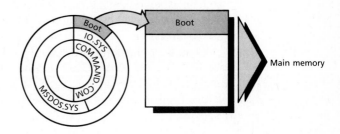

ware to read into memory the first sector from the disk in the system drive
(Fig. 14.10). The boot then reads IO.SYS, which, in turn, initializes key
system tables, reads MSDOS.SYS, and, finally, reads COMMAND.COM
(Fig. 14.11).

The COMMAND.COM modules that immediately follow MSDOS.SYS
are resident. Other COMMAND.COM modules are stored at the high end of
main memory, following the transient area. While technically resident, this
second group of routines can be overlaid, if necessary, by a large application
program. If they are overlaid, they must be restored after the program is
finished.

Fig. 14.11   After the system is booted, the operating system's resident
                   components occupy main memory.

| Interrupt vectors (first 1K) |
| IO.SYS |
| MSDOS.SYS |
| COMMAND.COM (resident) |
| Transient area |
| COMMAND.COM (overlay) |

Running MS-DOS

Once loaded, MS-DOS controls literally everything that happens on the computer. First, COMMAND.COM gets control and, by calling IO.SYS, displays a system prompt on the screen. As the user types a command, each character generates an interrupt. Responding to the interrupt, the operating system reads the character, stores it in main memory, and, again using IO.SYS, displays it.

Eventually, the user presses return. Like any other key, it generates an interrupt. Sensing that this key is different, the operating system transfers control to the COMMAND.COM module that interprets commands. This module, in turn, either displays an error message or takes whatever action is necessary to carry out the command.

For example, imagine the user has typed a resident command. Since the appropriate routine is already in memory, COMMAND.COM simply gives it control. When it finishes carrying out the command, the resident module returns control to COMMAND.COM, which displays a prompt and waits for the next command.

What if the command refers to a transient module, or to an application program? COMMAND.COM simply calls MSDOS.SYS, passing it the module name. MSDOS.SYS, in turn, reads (by calling IO.SYS) the disk directory, searches it, finds the referenced module, and instructs IO.SYS to read it into the transient area. Once the requested module is in memory, control is returned to COMMAND.COM. At this point, with the transient module in memory, there is no real difference between calling it and calling a resident module.

The basic work flow is simple. A prompt is displayed. The user types a command or a program name. The appropriate operating system module or application program gets control. As the program runs, the operating system supports it by processing interrupts. Eventually, it returns control to COMMAND.COM, and the process is repeated, again and again, until the machine is shut down. MS-DOS is command driven.

Summary

The operating system is the computer's resource manager. Several criteria are used to measure a computer's effectiveness, including throughput, turnaround, response time, availability, security, reliability, cost, and ease of use. Unfortunately these criteria conflict. When evaluating the effectiveness of an operating system, it is important to consider the hardware environment and the expected application mix.

Next, we considered the hardware environment and application mix of a microcomputer system, emphasizing three key measures of effectiveness: cost, reliability, and ease of use. Most microcomputer operating systems include a command processor, an input/output control system, and a file system. Because main memory is volatile, a boot routine is needed to load the system.

The MS-DOS command processor is called COMMAND.COM. Physical I/O is controlled by IO.SYS; logical I/O is the responsibility of MSDOS.SYS. The boot occupies the first sector of a disk. Next come two copies of the file allocation table, the root directory, the operating system (on a system disk), and, finally, data storage.

Space on disk is allocated in clusters. The clusters are numbered sequentially, and an entry for each one is recorded in the file allocation table. The number of a file's first cluster is recorded in the directory. The clusters making up a file are linked by a series of pointers through the file allocation table.

The Intel 8086 processor relies on interrupts to control communications between the main processor and its peripherals; thus, interrupt processing is an important MS-DOS function. The first 1K bytes of main memory hold up to 256 interrupt vectors. When an interrupt occurs, the contents of the instruction pointer are copied to the stack, and the contents of the designated interrupt vector are loaded into the instruction pointer. Thus, the interrupt processing routine gets control. After the interrupt is processed, the contents of the stack are loaded back into the interrupt pointer, and the original program resumes processing. Some interrupts originate with hardware; others originate with software.

The MS-DOS boot is stored on the first sector of each disk. When the computer is turned on, hardware reads the boot, which loads the rest of the operating system.

The chapter's last section, "Running MS-DOS," summarizes the operating system's primary features.

Key Words

boot	input/output	MSDOS.SYS
cluster	control system	nucleus
command	interrupt	PC-DOS
processor	interrupt vector	resident
COMMAND.COM	table	shell
device driver	IOCS	supervisor
file allocation	IO.SYS	transient
table	kernel	transient area
file system	MS-DOS	

Exercises

1. Why does it make sense to use the operating system as a resource manager?

2. Briefly define several common measures of computer performance.

3. A computer's measures of performance often conflict. Explain.

4. When evaluating an operating system, it makes sense to consider the hardware environment and the application mix. Why?

5. Briefly describe the hardware environment of a typical microcomputer system.

6. Briefly describe the assumed application mix of a typical microcomputer system. Does this mix seem reasonable to you? Why, or why not? Can you think of any exceptions?

7. What criteria are typically used to measure a microcomputer system's effectiveness? Why?

8. Microcomputer operating systems generally contain a command processor, an input/output control system, and a file system. Why *these* components?

9. Distinguish between an input/output control system and a file system. Relate your answer to the difference between physical and logical I/O.

10. Distinguish between resident and transient modules. Why does it make sense to have some modules transient? Why must other operating system modules be resident?

11. Why is a boot routine necessary?

12. Relate the functions of COMMAND.COM to the general functions of a command processor or shell as described in Chapter 5.

13. The task of accessing physical devices is divided between IO.SYS and MSDOS.SYS. Briefly explain the functions performed by these two modules. Why does it make sense to split these sets of functions?

14. What is a device driver?

15. Relate the functions performed by IO.SYS and MSDOS.SYS to the basic concepts of logical and physical I/O.

16. Sketch the contents of an MS-DOS disk.

17. Briefly explain how the clusters making up a disk file are linked through the file allocation table.

18. What is an interrupt? Explain how MS-DOS processes interrupts.

19. Some interrupts originate with hardware; others, with software. Why?

20. Sketch the contents of main memory immediately after MS-DOS has been booted.

15

Segmentation, Paging, and Virtual Memory

Memory Utilization

Multiprogramming involves loading several programs into memory and allowing them to share the processor. As the number of programs increases, interference eventually overwhelms gains in efficiency, but the limiting factor is usually memory space, not processor time. Generally, adding another program to memory means improving system efficiency and utilization.

As you learned in Chapter 6, fixed-partition memory management wastes space. Dynamic memory management is more efficient, but tends to leave small chunks of unused space spread throughout memory—fragmentation. Often, these fragments can be utilized if programs are broken into independently addressed segments or pages and loaded into noncontiguous memory. With virtual memory, programs are stored on a secondary device, and only active pages or segments are loaded into main memory.

Each technique represents an improvement in memory utilization and, hence, processor utilization. However, moving from simple fixed-partition to virtual memory management does have a price. On a fixed-partition system, a program is loaded into contiguous memory; thus, every location in the program can be addressed relative to a single entry point. With segmentation, paging, and virtual memory, portions of the program may be loaded into widely separated regions of memory. Consequently, a reference address or entry point must be maintained for *each* page or segment, and that adds to the operating system's complexity.

Address Translation

Each memory location in a computer is assigned a unique **absolute address**. Usually, the bytes or words are numbered sequentially, starting with zero. Hardware fetches and stores data by absolute address.

While absolute addresses are essential to hardware, they are inconvenient for software. For one thing, referencing absolute addresses can restrict a program to a fixed load point. That might be acceptable on a single-user system, but on a time-sharing or multiprogramming system, specifying an absolute address can force a program to wait until a particular region of memory is available (and that might *never* happen).

Another problem is instruction size. A typical instruction consists of an operation code and two operands, each of which can be a main memory address. Most 32-bit mainframes use 32-bit absolute addresses. Thus, an instruction referencing two main memory locations would contain two 32-bit address operands, yielding at least a 64-bit instruction. With such lengthy instructions, a tremendous amount of memory would be required to perform even a simple function. Also, transferring a 64-bit instruction over a 32-bit bus requires two fetches. Multiple fetches take time, and that means fewer instructions per second.

Q1

Relative addressing is a common solution. Programs are written as though they begin at address 0, and every location in the program is addressed relative to its entry point. When the program is loaded into memory, the absolute address of its entry point is loaded into a base register. As the program runs and instructions are fetched, the addresses found in the operands will be expressed in relative terms. The processor computes the absolute address of any referenced location by adding its displacement to the base address (Fig. 15.1).

With **base-plus-displacement** addressing, a program can be relocated in memory each time it is loaded. For example, if a program is loaded at absolute address 10000, its 100th byte is absolute address 10100. If, next time the program runs, it is loaded at 20000, its 100th byte will be 20100. In either case, a reference to the base address plus 100 will get the program's 100th byte.

Another advantage is reduced instruction size. For example, relative addresses on an IBM mainframe consist of a 4-bit base register and a 12-bit displacement. On an extended architecture machine, absolute addresses are 31 bits. Relative addresses are only 16-bits; thus the size of each operand is cut in half. On some computers, the base register is fixed, so only the displacement must be coded, yielding even smaller, more compact instructions.

Q2

There is, of course, a cost (nothing is free). While it makes sense for software to record and manipulate relative addresses, *hardware* still requires *absolute* addresses. Thus, before an instruction can be executed, the addresses specified in its operands must be translated, and that takes time. **Address translation** is performed by the instruction control unit (hardware) during I-time, immediately before the instruction is executed.

Fig. 15.1   As a program runs, the absolute address of any referenced main memory location is computed by adding a displacement to the contents of a base register.

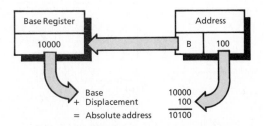

Segmentation

Q3-7

With **segmentation** programs are divided into independently addressed segments and stored in noncontiguous memory (Fig. 15.2). Structured programming stresses independent modules and subroutines, so segmentation requires little additional effort on the programmer's part. Individual segments are smaller than complete programs, and thus better fit into small openings in memory, yielding improved memory utilization. There are additional costs, however. If a program is loaded as a set of independently addressed segments, the operating system must keep track of each segment's entry point. This complicates address translation.

Translating Segment Addresses

Often, the solution is adding a step to the address translation process. Programmers still write the same code, and compilers still generate base-plus-displacement addresses. After fetching an instruction, the instruction control unit still expands each operand address by adding the base register and the displacement. Up to this point, there is no apparent difference between a segmented system and a contiguous program system.

Traditionally, the expanded address was an absolute address. On a segmented system, however, the expanded address consists of two parts: a segment number and a displacement within the segment (Fig. 15.3). To compute the absolute address, hardware extracts the segment number, uses that number to search a **segment table**, finds the segment's entry point

Q3

Fig. 15.2   Segmentation complicates address translation because programs are broken into independent segments and stored in noncontiguous memory.

| Operating system |
| Other programs |
| Program A—Segment #1—20K |
| Other programs |
| Program A—Segment #2—10K |
| Other programs |
| Program A—Segment #3—10K |
| Other programs |

Fig. 15.3   To compute an absolute address using segmentation, break the
address into segment and displacement portions, use the
segment number to find the segment's entry point address in a
segment table, and add the displacement to the entry point
address.

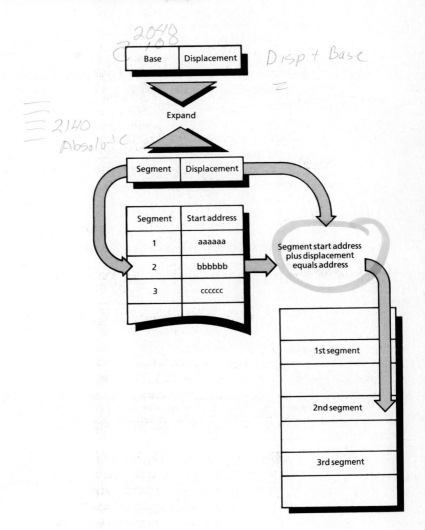

address, and, finally, adds the displacement to it, yielding an absolute
address.

When a program is loaded, the operating system builds a segment table
listing the entry points of each of its segments. This segment table is stored
in the operating system. Later, when the program gets control of the processor, the address of its segment table is loaded into the **segment table**

location register. During program execution, this register and the segment table are used by the processor to translate addresses dynamically.

For example, picture a computer that uses a 16-bit address consisting of a 4-bit segment number and a 12-bit displacement. Follow Fig. 15.4 as we step through the **dynamic address translation** process. The first program in memory is the operating system. It contains resident modules, some tables and pointers, and a region to hold transients. Next come several application programs. Focus on program A. Its segment table, located in the operating system and pointed to by the segment table location register, holds the entry points of the program's three segments (Fig. 15.4a).

Imagine the processor has just fetched an instruction. One operand contains the address shown in Fig. 15.4b. After checking the operation code, the instruction control unit expands this address, adding the contents of the base register and the displacement. Now, the final address translation process begins. Using the high-order 4 bits, the program's segment table (which, remember, is pointed to by the segment table location register) is searched, yielding the segment's entry point address. The last 12 bits are then added to this base address, giving an absolute address in main memory.

Addressing the Operating System

Look back at Fig. 15.4, and note the relative positions of the operating system's segments. Generally, the operating system occupies low memory beginning with address 0. Thus, the operating system's segment table has a

Fig. 15.4   An example of dynamic address translation.

a. The operating system creates a segment table when it loads a program. Each program has its own segment table. When a program gets control, the address of its segment table is loaded into the segment table location register.

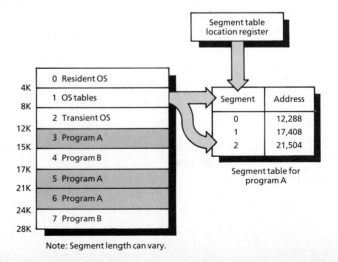

Note: Segment length can vary.

b. As the program runs, the segment table provides a base address for computing absolute addresses.

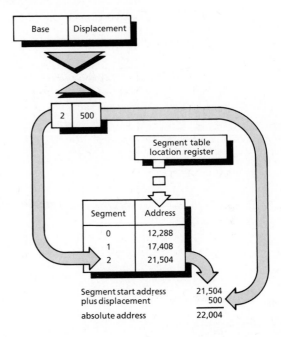

rather unusual property: its segment/displacement and absolute addresses are identical (Fig. 15.5). Except by chance, this happens only in low memory and, since the operating system occupies low memory can be assumed only in the operating system.

Why is this important? The operating system is the one place where machine-dependent programs must be written and absolute addressing must be used. When the operating system is running, once the instruction control unit completes its initial base-plus-displacement computation, no

Fig. 15.5

Because the operating system begins at main memory address 0, its segment/displacement and absolute addresses are identical.

Address Seg.	Disp.	Absolute address	Binary address Seg.	Disp.	Absolute binary address
0	000	0	0000	000000000000	0000000000000000
0	FFF	4095	0000	111111111111	0000111111111111
1	000	4096	0001	000000000000	0001000000000000
1	FFF	8191	0001	111111111111	0001111111111111
2	000	8192	0010	000000000000	0010000000000000
2	FFF	12,287	0010	111111111111	0010111111111111

Fig. 15.6   The operating system manages memory space by maintaining a
                       table of free space. Before loading a program, the operating
                       system searches this table. Note that segment size can vary.

Start address	Length	Status
0K	16K	In Use
16K	8K	Free
24K	16K	In Use
40K	4K	Free
44K	12K	In Use
66K	10K	Free

Note: Status
is usually
represented by
a simple bit flag.

additional address translation is needed. Generally, a special flag that tells
hardware to skip dynamic address translation is turned on when the operating system has control.

Segmentation and Memory Management

To manage main memory, the operating system maintains a table (something like the one pictured in Fig. 15.6) listing regions of memory that are
in use and regions that are free. Before it loads a new program, the operating system searches this table to locate free space. Note that the table has
nothing to do with programs already in memory; it is used to determine
where *new* programs can be loaded.

Segmentation allows efficient program loading simply because segments are smaller than complete programs and will therefore fit into
smaller spaces. It is somewhat programmer oriented in that it allows for
variable-length segments attuned to actual program logic. Note that segment sizes can vary. If, for example, the *maximum* segment size is 64K, a
given segment might hold 1 byte, 64K bytes, or any number in between.

Paging

A program's segments can vary in length. The number of bits in the displacement portion of the address does set an upper limit on segment size,
but the program's logic is the key to segmenting it. Although segmentation

is much more efficient than dynamic memory management, if no segment is small enough to fit into an available fragment of memory, that space will be wasted. Also, because segments can vary in length, memory management involves tracking numerous dynamically changing regions of memory, and that adds complexity.

Under **paging** a program is broken into *fixed-length* pages. Page size is generally small (2K to 4K), and chosen with hardware efficiency in mind. Given small, fixed-length pages, fragmentation is no longer a problem, and memory management is relatively easy to implement.

A program's pages can be loaded into noncontiguous memory (Fig. 15.7). Addresses consist of two parts (Fig. 15.8), a page number in the high-order positions and a displacement in the low-order bits. Addresses are dynamically translated as the program runs. When an instruction is fetched, its base-plus-displacement addresses are expanded by hardware. Then, an absolute address is computed by looking up the page's base address in a program **page table** and adding the displacement. What was called a segment table location register becomes a **page table location register**.

Paging and Memory Management

Memory management is easier under paging simply because all pages are the *same* length, and thus the system never has to check size. The operating system maintains a **page frame table** (Fig. 15.9) holding flags that indicate each page's status (free or in use). For example, to locate a free page, the operating system might search the page frame table for a "0" status bit, assign the first free page to the program, and then change the status bit to a "1."

Note the difference between this page frame table and the program page table described earlier. The page frame table is used by the operating

---

Fig. 15.7   A program's pages can be loaded into noncontiguous memory.

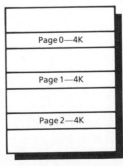

Fig. 15.8   To compute an absolute address under paging, break the address
into page and displacement portions, use the page number to
find the page's entry point address in a page table, and add the
displacement to this entry point address.

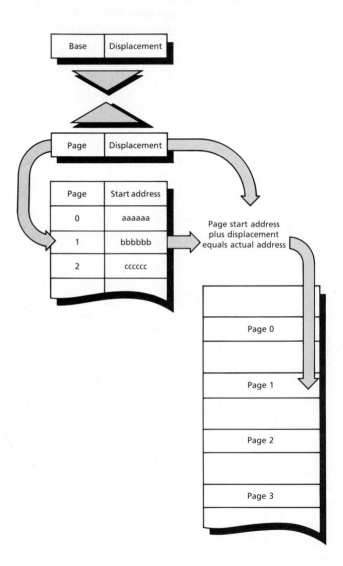

system to allocate main memory space. The program page table supports
dynamic address translation for programs already in main memory.

Some wasted space is inevitable with *any* memory allocation scheme,
and paging is no exception. Programmers do not code in fixed-length increments. Thus, almost every program will have at least one page that is only

Fig. 15.9   A paging operating system maintains a page frame table to track the status of each main memory page.

Page frame number	Program ID	Page number	Status
0	Operating system	1	1
1	Operating system	2	1
2	Operating system	3	1
3	Operating system	4	1
4	Program A	1	1
5	Program B	1	1
6	Program A	2	1
7	Program C	1	1
8			0
9			0
10	Program A	3	1
11	Program C	2	1
. .			0

partially filled. In effect, *any* fixed-length page is bound to be the wrong length.

Segmentation and Paging

When it comes to memory efficiency, segmentation and paging are comparable. Segmentation complements actual program logic. Paging is more hardware oriented, with page sizes geared to a system's memory allocation scheme; consequently, it's a bit easier to manage loading pages. Why not combine segmentation and paging? Programs could then be broken into logical segments, and the segments subdivided into fixed-length pages. Thus, a programmer could plan a segment structure, while the system loads pages.

With **segmentation** *and* **paging**, addresses are divided into a segment number, a page number within that segment, and a displacement within that page (Fig. 15.10). After the instruction control unit expands the relative address, dynamic address translation begins. First, the program's segment table is found (through the segment table location register) and searched for the segment number. This table, in turn, gives the address of the segment's page table. The page table is then searched for the page's base address, which is added to the displacement to get an absolute address.

Fig. 15.10   A segment *and* paging address is divided into three parts: a
                      segment, a page, and a displacement. Thus, dynamic address
                      translation involves two table look-up operations.

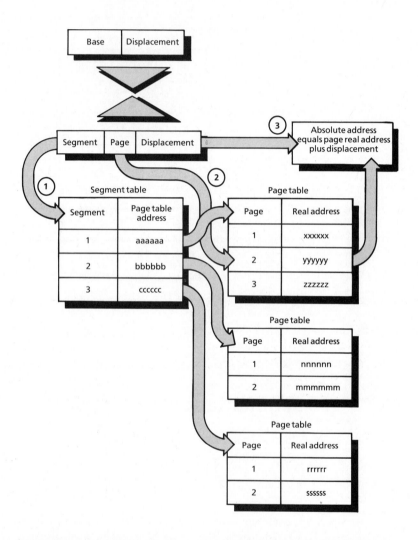

To help minimize overhead, most segmentation and paging systems
boost dynamic address translation through a series of **page address registers**. In a well-designed program, data storage areas are grouped together.
Thus, if a program references an address on a particular page, the chances
are very good that the next instruction will reference the same page. Thus,
as instructions are executed, the base addresses of the last several pages
referenced are stored in the page address registers. As dynamic address
translation begins, these registers are checked, in parallel. If the desired
base address is there, no additional address translation is needed. If it is not

in the page address registers, the segment and page tables are used, and the newly translated address replaces the least currently accessed address on the page address registers.

Consider, for example, a small program consisting of a single page. As the program begins, its first instruction references a data field on that page. Thus, the entry point address is dynamically translated through the tables and stored in a page address register. As additional instructions reference data fields on the same page, the base address is already in the registers, so addresses are quickly translated.

Eventually, the program finishes processing. The computer, however, continues working with other programs, dynamically translating their addresses. Given time, all other entries in the page address registers will be more current than the reference to the original program's page. Thus, its page address will be the next one dropped from the array to make room for a new page address.

Under segmentation and paging, memory is managed much as it is in a pure paging system, with the operating system maintaining a page frame table. Once again, remember that the page frame table is used by the operating system to allocate memory space and has nothing to do with the actual execution of already loaded programs.

Virtual Memory

If a processor can execute only one instruction at a time, why is it necessary for *every* instruction in a program to be in main memory before that program can begin executing? It isn't. We've already considered overlay structures in which only portions of a program are in memory at any given time. Those early overlay structures were precursors of modern **virtual memory** systems.

The word virtual means "not in actual fact." Virtual memory *seems* like real memory, but it isn't. On a traditional system, programs are loaded from a library directly into main memory. On a virtual memory system, programs are loaded from a library into *virtual* memory (Fig. 15.11). Once in virtual memory, selected portions are then paged into real memory for execution.

To the programmer, virtual memory looks just like real memory. Space on disk is broken into fixed-length partitions or variable-length regions, and one program is loaded into each one. Pages or segments are then transferred between virtual and real memory; the programmer has no control over the physical paging process.

Addressing Virtual Memory

Figure 15.12 shows an example of virtual memory. The programs are physically stored on disk. Visualize the disk space as a series of segments and pages. Granted a disk's contents are *really* addressed by track and sector,

Fig. 15.11   On a virtual memory system, programs are loaded into partitions
                      or regions on secondary *virtual* memory, and then paged into *real*
                      memory for execution.

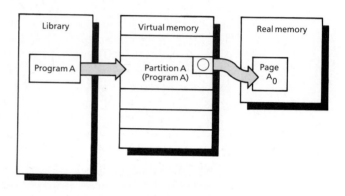

Fig. 15.12   The contents of virtual memory can be assigned segment and
                      page addresses.

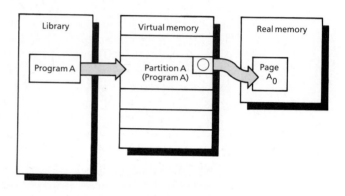

but because both are essentially sequential, it's easy to convert between a track/sector address and a segment/page address.

Now, move inside real memory. The operating system maintains a real page frame table to help it allocate real memory pages (Fig. 15.13). Segment and page tables (Fig. 15.14) describe all the pages associated with any active program, no matter where they may be physically stored.

To read a page from virtual into real memory, the operating system searches the page frame table for a free page. Once it finds one, the page's status is changed to "busy," and the page-in operation begins. Finally, the physical address of the selected page frame is recorded in the segment and page tables.

The instructions that run on a virtual memory system are identical to the instructions that run on a regular system. The operands hold relative (base-plus-displacement) addresses. Thus, immediately after an instruction is fetched, the instruction control unit expands the address by adding the displacement to the contents of a base register. On a regular system, the base register holds the program's load point in real memory. On a virtual system, the base register holds the program's load point in *virtual* memory. Thus, the computed address reflects the page's *virtual* memory location.

Unfortunately, the real processor can't work with virtual addresses. Thus, additional address translation is necessary. Assume segment/page addressing. To convert a virtual address to a real address, hardware,

1. using the high-order bits of the address as a key, accesses the segment table,
2. using the pointer in this table, locates the proper page table,

Fig. 15.13   A virtual memory operating system allocates *real* memory by maintaining a page frame table.

Page	Program	Program segment and page		Status
0	OS	0	0	1
1	OS	0	1	1
2	OS	0	2	1
3	OS	0	3	1
4	OS	0	4	1
5	OS	0	5	1
6	OS	0	6	1
7	A	3	5	1
8	B	2	9	0	← Free page
9	E	1	1	1
10	B	2	1	0
11	D	5	12	1

Fig. 15.14   A virtual memory operating system keeps track of active
programs by maintaining segment and page tables for all
program pages, no matter where they are physically stored.

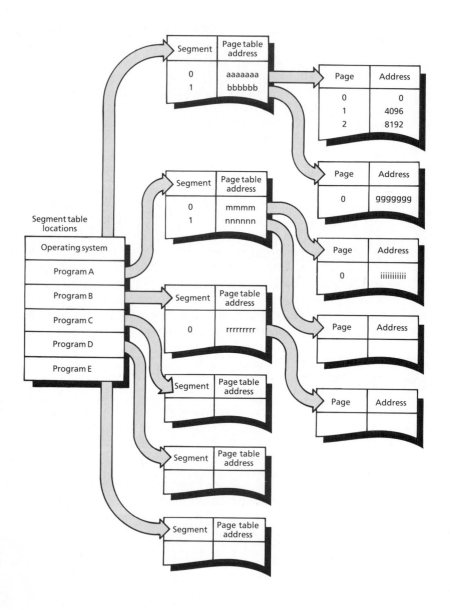

3. using the middle bits as a key, accesses the page table to find the page's base address, and, finally,

4. adds the displacement found in the low-order bits of the virtual address to the base address.

On most systems, the translation process is streamlined through the use of page address registers. (In other words, virtual address translation is just like segment/page/displacement address translation.)

What happens when a virtual address points to a page that is not in real storage? Each page table entry contains a flag called (by IBM, at least) the invalid bit. If it's off (a 0 bit) the page is in real storage; if it's on (a 1 bit) the page is in virtual storage. When hardware encounters a 1 bit at the end of the translation process, a **page fault** is recognized and an interrupt generated, causing a link to the operating system's page-in module. What if a survey of the page frame table shows no real memory available for the new page? Some other page must be paged-out. Which one? While many different schemes have been implemented, most are based on a least currently accessed algorithm.

Bringing pages into memory only when they are referenced is called **demand paging**. An option is to predict the demand for a new page and bring it into memory before it is actually needed—**prepaging**. Many prepaging algorithms assume that segments hold logically related code. Thus, for example, if instructions on page 1 are currently executing, the chances are that instructions on page 2 will be executed next. While far from perfect, such techniques can significantly speed up a program.

Virtual-Equals-Real Area

You may have noticed that the operating system, as pictured in Figs. 15.12 and 15.13, occupies the same locations in both real and virtual memory. Operating system routines perform such tasks as dynamically modifying channel programs and often refer to absolute addresses. Thus, it makes sense to load the operating system in such a way that its virtual, real, and absolute addresses are identical. This is possible only in low memory. Thus, the operating system begins at address 0 both in virtual and real. The region of memory where virtual, real, and absolute addresses match is called the **virtual-equals-real area**. It is used to hold the operating system and other key routines.

Thrashing

When real memory is full, a demand for a new page means that another must be paged-out. If this happens frequently, the system can find itself doing so much paging that little time is left for useful work. This is called **thrashing**, and it can seriously degrade system performance. The solution is to remove a program or two from real memory until the system settles down.

One possible cause is poor program design. For example, a program that branches frequently to widely separated modules or references data fields spread haphazardly throughout memory can be a disaster on a virtual memory system. Top-down or structured programming can help.

Implementing Virtual Memory

In a traditional multiprogramming system, the operating system and several application programs are loaded into main memory. On a virtual memory system, programs are loaded into secondary storage, and then paged into real memory as necessary. Think of virtual memory as a staging area. Visualize it holding the operating system and application programs. Then visualize selected, active pages moving into real memory, and you'll have a good mental picture of how virtual memory systems work.

The only problem with this visual image is that much of the operating system must be stored in real memory. Thus, it appears twice, once in real and once in virtual. Figure 15.15 illustrates a more common approach. It shows three levels of storage—virtual memory, the **external paging device**, and real memory. Virtual memory contains the operating system and all the application programs; it matches the visual image described in the prior paragraph. But it does not physically exist anywhere; it is just a model. Virtual memory's contents are physically stored in real memory and

Fig. 15.15   Virtual memory is an imaginary model holding space for the operating system and several application programs. The operating system and selected pages occupy real memory. Application programs are physically stored on an external paging device.

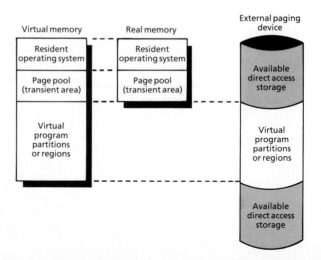

on the external paging device. Real memory is good, old-fashioned main memory, directly addressable by the processor. The paging device is usually disk.

Virtual memory is divided into two components. The first is exactly equal to the amount of real memory on the system, and is physically stored in real. It contains the resident operating system and the transient program area (called the **page pool**). The second component consists of space over and above real memory capacity and is physically stored on the external paging device. It contains the application programs. The operating system is loaded into real memory at initial program load or boot time. Application programs are loaded into partitions or regions on the external paging device. Selected pages are then swapped between the real memory page pool and the external paging device (Fig. 15.16).

For example, picture a system with 1000K (1 megabyte) of real memory. Its virtual memory might hold 4 megabytes—four times as much. Visualize virtual memory's contents. Start with a 250K operating system and a 750K page pool. Those two components alone match the available real memory space. The remaining 3 megabytes represent space over and above real memory's capacity (Fig. 15.17). The first megabyte, containing the operating system and the page pool, is stored in real memory (Fig. 15.18). The second 3 megabytes are stored on the external paging device, and pages are swapped back and forth between it and the page pool.

Traditionally, the operating system's memory management module was concerned with allocating space in main memory. On a virtual system, an

Fig. 15.16   Pages are swapped between the external paging device and the real-memory page pool.

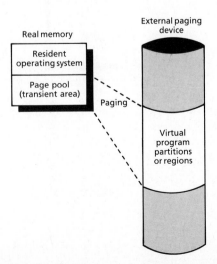

Fig. 15.17   In this example, 4 megabytes of virtual memory will be supported
                       by a computer containing only 1 megabyte of real memory.

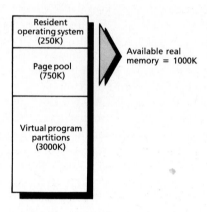

Fig. 15.18   The operating system and the page pool are in real memory. The
                       external paging device holds contents of virtual memory over
                       and above real memory's capacity (the application programs).
                       Selected pages move between the external paging device and the
                       page pool.

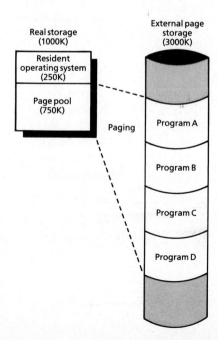

equivalent module allocates space on the external paging device. This space can be divided into fixed-length partitions, variable-length regions, segments, pages, or any other convenient unit. Transferring pages between the external paging device and real memory is a system function and thus is transparent to the programmer. In fact, it is reasonable to view the act of paging much as you view the transfer of an instruction from main memory into the instruction register for execution.

Why Virtual Memory? *Advantage*

At the risk of belaboring a point, virtual memory does not physically exist anywhere. It is simply a logical model of memory contents. Why, then, is virtual memory so important? Basically because having that logical model greatly simplifies the task of keeping track of a relatively complex memory structure.

Start with a programmer's view of a virtual memory system. Imagine a program has just failed. Some pages are almost certainly in real memory, while others are still on the external paging device. A dump showing the actual physical locations of each page would be almost impossible to understand. Instead, with virtual memory as a model, the operating system can reconstruct the program as it would have existed in virtual, and thus present the programmer with a dump showing the pages as though they were stored in contiguous memory (Fig. 15.19).

The key is addressing. Virtual addresses are sequential. So are real addresses. Thus, using the techniques discussed earlier, it is easy to convert between virtual and real addresses. A disk's cylinder, track, and (perhaps) sector addresses are also sequential. Thus, it is easy to convert between virtual and external paging device addresses.

Fig. 15.19   When a program fails, the operating system, using virtual memory as a model, reconstructs a contiguous memory dump.

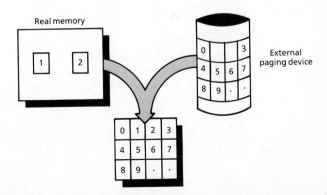

Fig. 15.20   Although virtual memory does not physically exist, it does
represent a useful model of a computer's address space. Real
addresses are easily converted to and from virtual. External page
device addresses are easily converted to and from virtual. Thus,
the virtual address becomes the system's common reference
point.

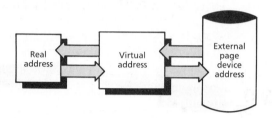

Note that the virtual address appears in both algorithms (Fig. 15.20).
Virtual memory is a model. Given a virtual address, it is easy to find the
equivalent address in real memory, on the external paging device, or both.
Thus, the model becomes the basis for managing both types of physical
memory. Although virtual memory does not *physically* exist, the system
acts as though it is directly manipulating the contents of virtual memory.
To an outside observer, the task of translating virtual addresses is completely transparent.

Summary

Hardware deals with absolute main memory addresses. Software normally
works with relative addresses. Thus, when an instruction is fetched, the
instruction control unit translates its relative addresses to absolute form
before executing it.

Under segmentation, a program is broken into variable-size segments
that can be independently loaded into noncontiguous memory, thus improving memory utilization. Because the segments must be independently
addressed, the address translation process is a bit more complex. Once an
address is expanded, its high-order bits are used to look up a base address
in a segment table. The base address is then added to the displacement to
get an absolute address. Paging is similar except that pages are fixed in
length. A segmentation *and* paging system enjoys many of the best features
of both, with programs broken into logical segments and the segments
subdivided into pages.

On a virtual memory system, programs are loaded, in segment or page
form, on a direct access device, and individual pages are paged-in as

needed. Virtual memory is a logical model that contains everything traditionally stored in main memory, including the operating system and application programs. Real memory holds the operating system and a page pool. Virtual memory space above and beyond the available real memory contains the application program; physically, they are stored on an external paging device, which is divided into partitions or regions. Pages are swapped between real memory and the external paging device.

Virtual memory is a model of memory's contents. Because it is easy to convert between virtual and real addresses or between virtual and external paging device addresses, the system uses virtual addresses, translating them as necessary.

Key Words

absolute address	page fault	segment table
address translation	page frame table	segment table
base-plus-	page pool	location register
displacement	page table	segmentation
demand paging	page table location	segmentation and
dynamic address	register	paging
translation	paging	thrashing
external paging	prepaging	virtual-equals- real
device	real memory	area
page address	relative address	virtual memory
registers		

Exercises

1. Explain the difference between an absolute address and a relative address. Why are both types needed?

2. Normally, the instruction control unit must translate the addresses it finds in an instruction's operands before that instruction can be executed. Why?

3. Explain how a program's segments can be loaded into noncontiguous main memory and independently addressed. How are the segment table and segment table location register involved?

4. Why is segmentation more difficult to implement than fixed-partition memory management?

5. Distinguish between segmentation and paging.

6. Why is a page-oriented memory management system easier to implement than a segment-oriented memory management system?

7. Explain segmentation *and* paging.

8. Explain dynamic address translation. Why are associative array registers or page address registers necessary?

9. How does a virtual memory system work? Distinguish between virtual memory and real memory.

10. What is a page fault? If a virtual memory system finds it necessary to page-out a page to free some space, how is this page selected?

11. Distinguish between demand paging and prepaging.

12. Why is something like a virtual-equals-real feature needed on a virtual memory system?

13. What are the advantages of virtual memory? What are the disadvantages?

14. Virtual memory does not make a computer faster—just more efficient. Explain.

15. Virtual memory does not physically exist. Explain.

16. If virtual memory is a logical model of memory's contents, where are those contents physically stored?

17. Why is it useful to have a logical model of a virtual memory system?

CHAPTER

16

UNIX

The UNIX System

When Thompson and Ritchie developed UNIX, their primary objective was creating a friendly working environment for writing programs. Because program development is an interactive task, response time was an important measure of effectiveness; thus UNIX became a time-sharing system. Simplicity, ease of use, and elegance were key design criteria; hardware efficiency and throughput were not.

A UNIX user communicates with the system through a **shell** (Fig. 16.1). Essentially a command interpreter, the shell is treated much like an application program and is technically not part of the operating system. This is an important UNIX innovation, because it allows a user to replace the standard shell with a custom shell. For example, a professional programmer might consider the rather terse commands associated with the Bourne shell (see Chapter 9) easy to use, while a nontechnical user might find the same commands intimidating. The solution is a custom shell for that nontechnical user, with, perhaps, pictorial icons or a menu replacing traditional commands.

It is even possible to bypass the shell. For example, imagine a user who, day after day, performs a single application such as data entry. Instead of forcing this user to learn shell commands, the appropriate application program can be loaded, and the user allowed to communicate directly with it. Another advantage is security. Since this user is limited to a single application, and is already inside the shell, he or she cannot poke around in other parts of the system by typing shell commands.

Among its resident modules, UNIX contains an input/output control system, a file system, and routines to swap segments, handle interrupts, schedule the processor's time, manage main memory space, and allocate peripheral devices. Additionally, the operating system maintains several tables to track the system's status. Routines that communicate directly with

---

Fig. 16.1   A UNIX user communicates with the operating system through a shell. Hardware-dependent logic is concentrated in the kernel.

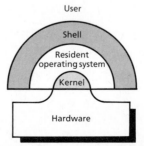

the hardware are concentrated in a relatively small **kernel** (Fig. 16.1). The kernel is hardware dependent and varies significantly from system to system. However, the interface to the kernel is consistent across implementations.

Because most operating systems are written in assembler language, they are limited to a single family of computers. UNIX, on the other hand, was written primarily in a high-level language (C), making it highly portable (only a small portion of the kernel is written in assembler). Today, UNIX is a standard, particularly in the academic world, and is available on a variety of machines. More important, however, is the impact UNIX has had on the design of other operating systems. For example, the current versions of MS-DOS (see Chapter 15) clearly reflect the UNIX influence.

UNIX is a time-sharing system, with program segments swapped in and out of memory as required. To ensure reasonable response time, processor access is limited by time-slicing. Segmentation is the most common addressing scheme, and most UNIX systems implement virtual memory techniques.

Images and Processes

The pseudocomputer concept is another important UNIX innovation. A user's routine is viewed as an **image**, defined by Ritchie and Thompson as an "execution environment" that consists of program and data storage, the contents of general-purpose registers, the status of open files, the current directory, and other key elements. To the user, it *appears* that this image is executed on a private **pseudocomputer** under control of a command-driven operating system. In reality, UNIX is a multiple-user, time-sharing system.

An image consists of three segments (Fig. 16.2). First, starting at virtual address 0, is a program **text segment**, followed by a **data segment**. The image ends with a **stack segment**. Between the data and the stack segments is a free area. As the program runs, the data segment grows toward high

Fig. 16.2   An image consists of a program text segment, a data segment, and a stack segment.

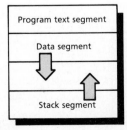

memory (down in Fig. 16.2), and the stack segment grows toward low memory.

The execution of an image is called a **process**. As a process executes, the image's text, data, and stack segments must be in memory. (Note: they need not occupy contiguous memory.) Thus, the image is not *really* executed on a pseudocomputer. Instead, the image and the pseudocomputer serve as virtual models of the user's environment.

The program text segment is reentrant; it can be shared. UNIX, remember, is a multiple-user system. If two or more users access the same program, only one text segment is physically stored in memory. Both users will have their independent images. Both will *imagine* that they, and they alone, have access to their program code. Physically, however, they will share a single text segment (Fig. 16.3).

The data and stack segments, on the other hand, are private; for example, if two users are executing the same code, main memory will hold one text segment, two data segments, and two stack segments. Additionally, each process has its own **system data segment** containing data needed by the operating system when the process is active. This system data segment is not part of the user's image; the user cannot access it. When the user calls the system (for example, to request I/O), the process switches from a user state to a system state, making the system data segment available to UNIX.

Process Creation

A process is created by a system primitive named *fork*. The *fork* routine, part of the operating system, is called by an executing process. In response, UNIX duplicates that process, creating two identical copies. Because both

Fig. 16.3   The text segment is reentrant. Thus, if two or more processes are executing the same code, only a single shared text segment is physically stored in real memory. The data and stack segments, however, are private.

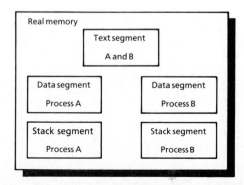

copies contain the system data segment, they share open files and other key data. The operating system distinguishes between the **parent** and the **child** by giving them different return codes. Thus, although the parent and the child are identical, they can check the return code and take different actions.

The parent starts the process by calling *fork*. It's a system call, so a return address is stored in the process's system data area and UNIX gets control. After the duplicate process is created, control returns to the parent, which checks the return code. By convention, the parent gets the process number of the child (a positive integer), while the child gets a return code of 0 (a negative return code indicates an error). Because the return code is positive, the parent normally calls *wait*, and waits for the child to die[1] (Fig. 16.4a).

Eventually, the child begins to execute. Because it is a duplicate of the parent, the return address in its system data area points to the instruction immediately following *fork* (addresses are virtual). Thus, the child begins by checking the return code (Fig. 16.4b). It's 0, so the child calls another system primitive, *exec*. The *exec* routine responds by overlaying the child's text and data segments with the contents of a new file (Fig. 16.4c). Technically, the resulting image is still the same process, but its contents are different. Later, when the child dies, the parent can resume processing (Fig. 16.4d).

Briefly review the process creation sequence, because it's important. The parent calls *fork*. In response, UNIX duplicates the process, and returns control to the parent. Because the return code is a positive integer (the child's process number), the parent calls *wait*, and "goes to sleep" until the child dies.

Eventually, the child gets control. It is a duplicate of the parent. When the parent called *fork*, the address of its next instruction was recorded in the system data area. The child's system data area contains the same (virtual) return address. Thus, when the child gets control, the instruction following fork is executed. Typically, this instruction checks the return code. Because the return code is 0, *exec* is called, and a new program overlays the child. Following *exec*, the first instruction in this new program gets control. Eventually, the new program calls *exit*, and thus the child dies. Consequently, the parent is awakened, and, eventually, gets control again.

Some applications call for parallel parent and child processes. The child is created when the parent calls *fork*. But, instead of calling *wait*, the parent executes regular instructions; thus, both the parent and the child are active. With most operating systems, radically different commands or parameters are used to define parallel and serial processes. UNIX is remarkably consistent; in fact, its consistency is one reason why professional programmers find it so easy to use.

---

[1] Or to finish processing. UNIX terminology can be a bit morbid.

Fig. 16.4   UNIX process creation.

a. The parent calls *fork*. In response, the operating system creates a duplicate
   process (the child), and returns control to the parent. Since the return code is a
   positive integer, the parent drops into a wait state.

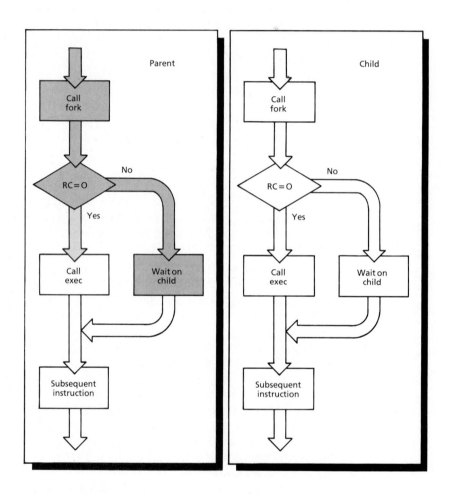

Initialization

When UNIX is booted, a process named **init** is activated. This "original
ancestor" creates one system process for each terminal channel; for example, if the system supports eight concurrent terminals, eight processes are
created. A user logs on to one of these processes. The logon process then
(normally) executes (*exec*) the shell, and thus is overlayed. Later, when the
shell dies (in other words, when the user logs off), *init* creates a new logon
process.

b. The child begins by checking the return code. Because it's 0, the child calls *exec.*

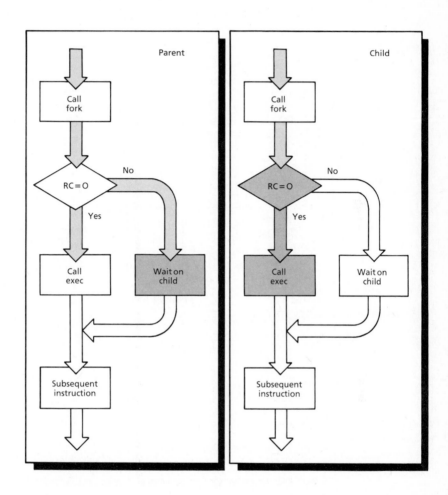

When a user logs on, the logon process scans a table of login names, identifies the user's default shell, and, typically, executes either the Bourne shell or the C shell. Because the shell is treated as a process, it's relatively easy to substitute a custom shell. Another option is no shell. In response to a particular login name, the logon process can start an *application* routine, effectively placing the user inside the shell, and thus restricting that user to commands and responses appropriate to that application routine. The log-on process overlays itself with the user's primary system interface. When that interface dies, *init* spawns another logon process, which waits for another user to log on.

The image described earlier allows a user to visualize a program. Real memory is a bit more complex, however. Imagine a UNIX system support-ing four concurrent users (Fig. 16.5). Three are active; thus, main memory

c. The *exec* routine overlays the child's text and data segments with the contents of a new file.

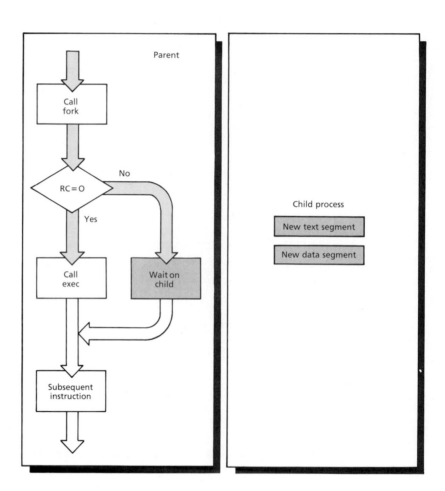

holds three shells. Running under each shell are user processes; note that two or more parallel processes can be associated with a single shell. A fourth potential user has not yet logged on; thus, the logon process is still active.

The user sees the image of *a single process*, and can imagine that process running, all by itself, on a private pseudocomputer. The details associated with time-slicing, swapping, real-memory allocation, and physical device access are buried in UNIX, and thus are transparent to the user.

Process Management

UNIX is a multiple-user operating system, with several concurrent programs occupying main memory. It is inevitable that two or more programs

d. When the child dies, the parent resumes processing. Note that the child process no longer exists.

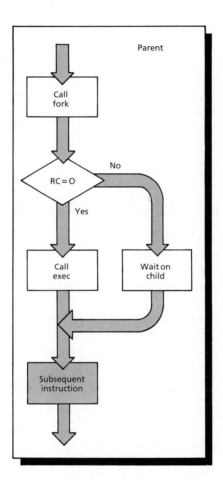

will want the processor at the same time, so the operating system must carefully schedule them. Thus, UNIX contains a dispatcher.

The UNIX dispatcher relies on a **process table** that contains one entry for each process (Fig. 16.6). The entry is allocated when the process is created (*fork*) and freed when the process dies. Each entry contains all the data needed by UNIX when the process is *not* active. Among other things, the process table entry indicates whether the process is ready (awake) or waiting (asleep).

For example, imagine the shell (the parent) has just received a command that requires a new process, and thus has called *fork*. In response, the kernel creates the new process, assigns it a process number (a positive integer), adds a new entry to the process table, and returns control to the shell. The shell then (typically) calls *wait*, and goes to sleep until the newly created child dies.

Fig. 16.5   This diagram shows the possible contents of real memory on a
                       UNIX system supporting four concurrent users.

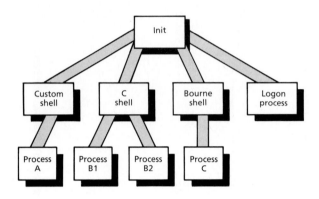

Meanwhile, the child gets control, calls *exec*, and carries out the command. As it finishes processing, it calls *exit* and thus dies. The death of a
process generates an **event** that produces a **signal**. The event is reported to
the operating system's ***event-wait*** routine as a positive integer—the event
number or process number. UNIX responds by searching the process table
and waking (setting to a ready state) every process waiting for that event.

Each user process has a priority. Priorities are recomputed frequently
by dividing execution time by elapsed real time; the smaller the number,
the higher the priority. When an event signal is sensed, the operating
system's *event-wait* routine gets control. First, it awakens all processes
waiting for that event. Then, it searches the process table, selects the highest priority ready process, and gives it control.

Fig. 16.6   UNIX maintains a process table with one entry per process. The
                       dispatcher uses this information to schedule processes.

```
Each entry contains:

    Process number
    Process state (ready, waiting)
    Process priority
    Event number process is waiting on
    Text table address
    Data segment address
    Stack segment address
    System data segment address

One entry per process.
```

Events occupy no memory. They are represented by an electronic signal. When a signal is sensed, *event-wait* scans the process table and awakens all processes waiting for the associated event. Then the system forgets the event ever happened. What if some time passes between the decision to wait and the implementation of the wait state? For example, imagine a process calls *fork*, performs some calculations, and *then* calls *wait*. What if, between *fork* and *wait*, the new process gets control and dies? By the time the parent calls *wait*, the event it plans to wait for has already happened.

Because the child process has already died, it will not appear in the process table. When the UNIX *wait* routine gets control, it checks the process table, and, if the calling routine has no children, returns an error code. A programmer should be prepared for this sequence of events any time parallel processes are activated.

The Shell

The UNIX shell is a customized command line interpreter. As you learned earlier in the chapter, UNIX sees the shell as simply another process, and thus subject to change. The idea of a custom shell was an important UNIX innovation.

When *init* creates a logon process, it opens the standard input, output, and error files; thus the logon process can accept user input from the terminal and display both normal output and error messages. When a user logs on, the shell overlays the logon process's text and data segments, but the system data segment is not affected; thus the shell's standard input, output, and error files are open. Consequently, the user can begin issuing commands without opening these standard files.

In response to a command, the shell sets up an *exec*, calls *fork*, and then waits for the child process to carry out the command. If the command is followed by an ampersand (&), the shell does not wait. Instead, it spawns a new process to carry out the command in parallel, and immediately displays a prompt for the next command.

Incidentally, pipes (see Chapter 9) are implemented in the shell. For example, consider

cat file1 | sort

This *cat* command reads the contents of *file1* and sends them to its standard output device, the console. This *sort* command accepts data from its standard input device, the console, sorts them, and sends the output to its standard output device, the console, again. In response to the pipe operator, the shell closes the standard output device for *cat*, reassigns it to a pipe, closes the standard input device for *sort*, and reassigns it to the same pipe. Thus, *cat* sends its output to *sort*'s standard input device; the pipeline is transparent to the child processes.

Time-slicing and Interrupts

Under UNIX, the operating system schedules processes by responding to event signals. An event occurs when a process dies. If the process is compute-bound, considerable time can pass between events, and that, in turn, can negatively impact response time. To minimize the risk that a single process will monopolize the system's time, time-slicing is imposed.

Programs are generally limited to a single second of processor time. If, during that second, the process voluntarily surrenders control, fine; normal dispatching rules are adequate. If, however, a process exceeds one second, a special event (perhaps, a timer interrupt) is signaled. As a result, *event-wait* is called. After recomputing priorities (thus lowering the offending process's priority), *event-wait* searches the process table and selects the highest priority ready process.

Interrupt handling routines are located in the UNIX kernel. (Because UNIX is supported on a variety of computers, each of which may implement interrupts differently, we won't discuss the hardware details.) When an interrupt occurs, control is transferred to the kernel. Once the interrupt is handled, *event-wait* awakens any processes waiting for the interrupt, and then schedules the next process.

Memory Management

UNIX relies on virtual memory and segmentation techniques to manage main memory space. The user's image is a virtual model of a pseudocomputer. The text, data, and stack segments making up that image are independently loaded into real memory. As necessary, segments (and even complete images) are swapped out to secondary memory to free space for active processes.

Swapping (or Paging)

Let's consider **swapping** in more detail. When a process first enters real memory, the entire image is loaded. As the process grows, new primary memory is allocated, the process is copied to the new space, and the process table is updated. If sufficient main memory is not available, the growing process is allocated space on secondary memory and swapped out. At this point, the process is ready to be swapped back in. Over time, several processes can reside on secondary memory.

The swapping process is part of the kernel (Fig. 16.7), and thus can be activated each time UNIX gets control. It scans the process table, looking for a ready process that has been swapped out. If it finds one, it allocates primary memory and swaps in the process. If insufficient main memory space is available, the swapping routine selects a process to be swapped out, copies the selected process to secondary storage, frees the memory space, and then swaps in the ready process.

Fig. 16.7   The swapping process is part of the kernel. It scans the process table, locates a process ready to be swapped in, allocates main memory, and reads the process. If insufficient primary memory space is available, it looks for a waiting process to swap out.

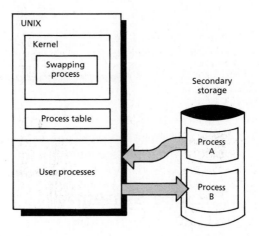

The swap-in decision is based on secondary storage residency time—the longer a process resides on disk, the higher its priority. Generally, processes waiting for slow events are primary swap-out candidates; if there are several such processes, age in primary memory is a secondary criterion. A slight penalty is imposed on large programs. To help minimize thrashing, processes do not become candidates for swapping out until they have achieved at least a minimum age in primary memory.

Early versions of UNIX swapped segments. Newer versions designed to run on page-oriented hardware subdivide segments into pages and swap pages.

Memory Space and Reentrant Code

The fact that text segments contain reentrant code has memory management implications. On the one hand, because a single text segment can be physically shared by several processes, the total amount of space that must be allocated to support all those processes is reduced. On the other hand, if several processes share the same text segment, that segment's space cannot be released until *all* processes using it have died.

To keep track of active text segments, UNIX maintains a **text table** that lists each current text segment, its primary and secondary addresses, and a count of the number of processes sharing it (Fig. 16.8). As a process dies, the count is decremented. Although the space associated with the data,

Fig. 16.8

To keep track of active segments, UNIX maintains a text table. Note that a single text segment can be shared by several processes. Each process table entry points to the text table.

Each text table entry contains:

    The text segment's identification
    The text segment's primary memory address
    Its secondary memory address
    A count of the number of processes using this text segment

stack, and system data segments can immediately be freed, the text segment must remain in memory until its count reaches zero.

The File System

According to its designers, the **file system** is the key to UNIX. It offers compatible device, file, and interprocess I/O; in essence, the user simply sends and receives data. All data are treated as strings of bytes, and no physical structure is imposed by the system. Instead, the user's program overlays its own structure on the data. The result is considerable freedom from any concern for physical I/O.

Block (structured) **devices** (normally, disk) hold files. A hierarchical directory structure (see Chapter 9) maps the entire file system, and allows the operating system to create, retrieve, and update data files by name. The information associated with a directory is itself kept in a file (another important UNIX innovation). We'll discuss disk I/O in some detail later.

Character devices include printers, terminals, and other nonblock peripherals. They operate through a simple queuing process. For example, to output data to a printer, UNIX places bytes, one by one, on the printer's output queue, and the printer's controller subsequently retrieves them, one by one.

Character devices, block devices, and data files are accessed by a common set of system calls (*open, read, write,* and so on); all three are treated as files. Data files are called ordinary files. Files that represent a block or character device are called special files. Once again, consistency makes the operating system easier to use.

Inside the operating system, each physical device is controlled by a **device driver** (Fig. 16.9). All devices attached to the system are listed in a **configuration table** and identified by a major **device number** and a minor device number. When UNIX receives a request to start I/O, it uses the major device number to search the configuration table, finds the address of the appropriate device driver, and then activates the device driver. The

Fig. 16.9   Each physical device is controlled by a device driver. A configuration table lists all the device drivers. When a program requests I/O, UNIX uses the device number to search the configuration table, finds the address of the appropriate device driver, and activates it.

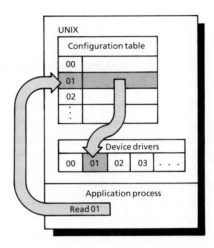

minor device number is passed to the device driver. It might designate a specific disk drive on a multiple drive system, a specific peripheral on a multiplexer channel, or, depending on the device, some other detail. As a system changes, device drivers and configuration table entries can be added or deleted, usually by the system's super user.

Accessing Disk Files

Disk is the standard block device. The disk surface is divided into four regions (Fig. 16.10). The boot block, as the name implies, holds a boot routine. It is followed by a **super block** that identifies the disk, defines the sizes of the disk's regions, and tracks free blocks. The third region holds the **i-list**. Each entry on the i-list is an **i-node**, a 64-byte file definition that lists the disk addresses of blocks associated with a single ordinary file.[2] The i-nodes are numbered sequentially. An i-node's offset from the beginning of the i-list is its **i-number**; the combination of a device number and an i-number defines a specific file. Following the i-list, the remaining space on disk is divided into 512-byte blocks that hold data and/or directories.

---

[2] A special file describes a physical device. A special file's i-node holds the device's major and minor device numbers.

Fig. 16.10   A UNIX disk is divided into four regions.

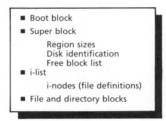

A known i-node (often, i-number 2) points to the root directory. When a user logs on, UNIX reads the root directory, finds the user's home directory, and records the home directory's i-number in the process's system data area. In response to a change directory command, UNIX replaces the recorded i-number with the new directory's i-number.

When a program opens an ordinary file (Fig. 16.11), UNIX uses the working directory's i-number to begin its search for the requested file. Each directory entry consists of a file name and an i-number. Once the file name is found, the associated i-number points to the file's i-node. That i-node, in turn, holds the disk address of the file's first block, and starts a chain of pointers that link all the file's blocks.

UNIX, remember, is a multiple-user system. Thus, at any given time, numerous devices and files will be open, and it is likely that two or more

Fig. 16.11   When a file is opened, the disk directory is read and searched for the file name. Associated with the file name is an i-number that points to a specific i-node. Recorded in that i-node is the file's disk address.

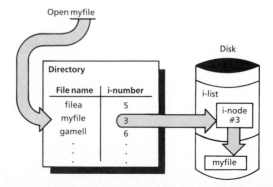

processes will concurrently access the same disk (or even the same file). To avoid conflicts, the operating system maintains a **system file table**, sometimes called the **i-node table** (Fig. 16.12). When the file is opened, its i-node is copied into the system file table.

To the user's process, the open file is identified by a small, nonnegative integer number called a **file descriptor**. Within the process's system data area, the file is listed in a **process file table**. The process file table entry points, in turn, to an i-node in the system file table. Thus, the process is aware only of its own open files. UNIX, on the other hand, can track every open file, no matter what process it might be associated with.

Later, when the user process calls read or write, UNIX uses the *process* file table's pointer to locate the file's i-node in the *system* file table. That i-node, in turn, provides a start-of-file address. Because the file is viewed as a simple string of bytes, individual substrings can be accessed by using relative byte numbers. The UNIX file system assumes responsibility for converting relative byte addresses into physical disk addresses and reading or writing the appropriate block or blocks. The application program makes sense of these data by overlaying its own data structure.

Fig. 16.12   UNIX maintains a system file table of the i-nodes of all open files. Each process maintains a table of its own open files. A process file table entry points to a system file table entry which, in turn, points to the file's location on disk.

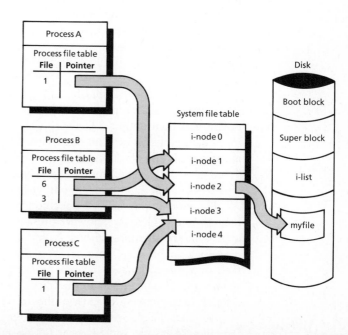

Managing Disk Space

UNIX is also responsible for managing disk space. When a file is created or an existing file grows, the operating system scans the free block list in the super block and allocates space to the file. The free block list is a series of pointers that link unused disk blocks. After allocating space, UNIX updates the pointers.

Note that space is allocated dynamically. When a file is first created, it might be assigned several contiguous blocks. Subsequent requests for space might be filled by allocating blocks located anywhere on the disk's surface, however. In addition to pointing to the start-of-file address, the i-node starts a list of pointers that link a file's blocks.

Buffering

All block I/O takes place through a **buffer pool** located in the operating system (no system buffers are found in the user's image). A read command implies a buffer search. If the requested block is already in memory, no physical input operation is needed. If physical I/O is necessary, the least currently accessed buffer is renamed, and the block is read into it. Additionally, whenever UNIX must physically read a block, it automatically prereads the next one. Consequently, given the nature of most programs, the data are often already in memory when the next read command is issued.

Normally, when UNIX selects the least currently accessed buffer and renames it, the contents of that buffer are lost. To avoid destroying valid output data residing in a buffer, UNIX responds to a write command by marking the appropriate buffer "dirty" (basically, the operating system sets a switch). No physical output occurs at write time, however. Instead, when the buffer is later identified as least currently accessed, its contents are physically copied to disk before the buffer space is reassigned. Delaying the physical data transfer until a buffer is no longer active also tends to reduce physical I/O.

UNIX implements pipes by taking advantage of its buffering scheme. When data are sent to the standard output device, they are first copied to a buffer, and then output. Likewise, when data are read from the standard input device, they flow from the device, into a buffer, and are subsequently made available to the process. With pipes, the standard output is transferred to a buffer and simply held. The next process then gets its input directly from the first process's output buffer.

By reducing physical I/O operations, UNIX dramatically improves system efficiency. There are, however, disadvantages to the dynamic buffering approach. For one thing, although physical I/O may *appear* synchronous, it is really asynchronous (in other words, physical data transfers and logical read or write commands do not necessarily occur in a predictable time sequence). This makes real-time error reporting or user error handling difficult to implement. Because of the delayed write described earlier, valid output data can be lost if UNIX goes down unexpectedly. Finally, the sequence of logical and physical I/O operations can differ, and this can cause serious problems for applications that rely on data sequence.[3] In spite of these problems, however, the UNIX I/O model has been adopted by a number of modern operating systems.

UNIX Internals

One of the best ways to get an overview of an operating system is to follow the pointers that link the system's components. Figure 16.13 summarizes the key UNIX tables. Start with the process table. For each process, it holds

---

[3] UNIX does allow a user to open a file in raw mode. Such files maintain a logical/physical correspondence.

Fig. 16.13   This diagram summarizes key UNIX system tables.

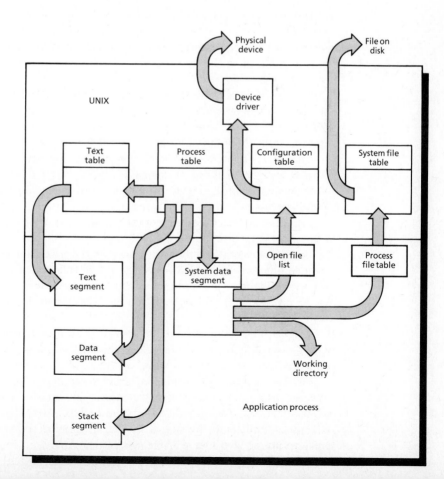

pointers to the process's data segment, stack segment, and system data segment. Additionally, the process table entry points to a text table entry which, in turn, points to the process's text segment. Thus, the process table and the text table link all the process's segments.

Each process has a system data segment. The i-number of the user's working directory is stored here. Physical devices are linked to the process through a list of open files. Each open file reference points to a configuration table entry that, in turn, points to a device driver. The files themselves are identified through pointers (in the process file table) to the system file table. Each system file table entry is an i-node that holds a file's disk address.

At first glance, Fig. 16.13 appears complex, but, compared to other operating systems, its use of tables and pointers to link a system's components is remarkably elegant. Indeed, that's one reason why UNIX is so popular with computer professionals.

Summary

UNIX was created as a pleasant working environment for developing programs. Users communicate with the system through a shell. Process management, scheduling, interrupt handling, and memory management routines, as well as device drivers, are concentrated in a relatively small, memory-resident kernel.

To a user, an executing program image appears to be running on a personal pseudocomputer. The image consists of a text segment, a data segment, and a stack segment. To run, the image must be loaded on a real computer; the execution of an image is called a process.

The shell is treated as a process. When a user logs on, a default shell is assigned, but the shell can be changed.

Processes are created by the *fork* system primitive. The parent requests a child process by calling *fork*. In response, the operating system creates a child process, an exact duplicate of the parent, and enters the new process in the process table.

Because the child and the parent are passed different return codes, they can take different actions. Normally, the parent calls *wait* and goes to sleep until the child dies. The child routine calls *exec*. UNIX responds by overlaying the process with the contents of a new file. When the new image has finished processing, it calls *exit*, and dies. The death of a process creates an event signal. The operating system's *event-wait* routine then awakens those processes waiting for that event, selects the highest priority ready process, and starts it.

UNIX manages main memory space by swapping or paging processes between primary and secondary memory. The process table contains pointers that link the segments making up each process. The text segment is reentrant and might be shared by two or more processes. Thus, text segments are tracked in a separate system text table.

UNIX supports both block and character devices. Files that represent devices are called special files; data files are called ordinary files; both special and ordinary files are accessed by a common set of system calls. Physical I/O operations are controlled by device drivers (one per device). A system's device drivers are listed in a configuration table. An I/O operation references a device number that is used to search the configuration table for the address of the appropriate device driver. A table of open devices is maintained in each process's system data segment.

A UNIX disk is divided into four regions: a boot block, a super block that identifies the disk and links free blocks, an i-list, and a data area. The i-list contains a series of i-nodes, each of which defines the disk address of a file. A given i-node's relative position on the i-list is its i-number; the combination of a device number and an i-number uniquely defines a file. A special file's i-node holds its major and minor device numbers.

A list of open file i-nodes, called the system file table, is maintained by the operating system. Each process's system data segment holds a process file table with a pointer to a system file table entry for each open file. UNIX manages disk space by maintaining a list of free block pointers in the super block. The i-node starts a series of pointers that link a file's blocks; thus the blocks need not be contiguous.

Block I/O takes place through a system buffer pool. When an application process calls read, UNIX searches the buffer pool; if the data are already in memory, no physical input is necessary. If a physical read is necessary, UNIX reads not only the requested block, but the next one as well. If all buffers are full, the least currently accessed buffer is renamed and overlayed. On output, a buffer's contents are not physically transferred following each logical write. Instead, the buffer is marked "dirty." Subsequently, when the buffer becomes the least currently accessed, its contents are physically written before the space is renamed and reused. Because of its dynamic buffering technique, pipes are relatively easy to implement on UNIX. Although this approach efficiently minimizes physical I/O, the fact that logical and physical I/O operations are asynchronous can cause problems.

The chapter ended with a summary of UNIX tables and pointers. Take the time to understand Fig. 16.13.

Key Words

block device	file descriptor	process table
buffer pool	file system	pseudocomputer
character device	*fork*	shell
child	i-list	signal
configuration table	image	stack segment
data segment	*init*	super block
device driver	i-node	swapping
device number	i-node table	system data
event	i-number	segment
event-wait	kernel	system file table
exec	parent	text segment
exit	process	text table
	process file table	*wait*

References

1. American Telephone and Telegraph Company (1978). *The Bell System Technical Journal*, July/August, Vol. 57, No. 6, Part 2. Several articles, including: Ritchie, D.M. and Thompson, K., "The UNIX Time-Sharing System"; Thompson, K., "UNIX Implementation"; Ritchie, D.M., "A Retrospective"; and Bourne, S.R., "The UNIX Shell."
2. Bourne, S.R. (1983). *The UNIX System*. Reading, Massachusetts: Addison-Wesley Publishing Company.
3. Deitel, Harvey M. (1984). *An Introduction to Operating Systems*. Reading, Massachusetts: Addison-Wesley Publishing Company.
4. Foxley, Eric (1985). *UNIX for Super-users*. Reading, Massachusetts: Addison-Wesley Publishing Company.
5. Sobell, Mark G. (1984). *A Practical Guide to the UNIX System*. Menlo Park, California: The Benjamin/Cummings Publishing Company.

Exercises

1. What is the shell? What is the kernel?

2. UNIX is highly portable. What is portability? What makes UNIX so portable? Why is portability important?

3. Briefly explain the pseudocomputer concept. Relate the pseudocomputer concept to the ease-of-use criterion.

4. Describe (or sketch) a UNIX user's program image.

5. Distinguish an image from a process.

6. A user's text segment is reentrant, and thus can be shared. Data and stack segments, on the other hand, are private. What does this mean? Why is it significant?

7. Why is the system data segment necessary? It isn't part of the user's image. Why?

8. Briefly explain how processes are created under UNIX.

9. The *fork* primitive creates two *identical* processes. Yet, those processes can yield very different results. Explain.

10. Briefly explain UNIX dispatching.

11. Distinguish between an event and a process.

12. Briefly explain the UNIX swapping process.

13. Why does UNIX need a text table?

14. Explain how UNIX links a peripheral device and an application process.

15. Sketch the contents of a UNIX disk.

16. Briefly explain how UNIX converts a file name to the file's location on disk. Why is the system file table necessary?

17. All block I/O takes place through a buffer pool. Explain.

18. The UNIX buffering scheme makes pipes easy to implement. Explain.

19. Under UNIX, logical and physical I/O are asynchronous. What does this mean? Why is it significant?

20. Briefly explain how UNIX links the various segments that make up a process. Explain how that process is linked to its physical devices and files.

CHAPTER

17

Operating Principles of the IBM System/370

The Hardware Environment

An operating system functions within a specific hardware environment; the hardware both limits and supports the software. Initially established with the release of System/360 in 1964, IBM's System/370 architecture remains the foundation of the company's latest mainframes. This chapter introduces IBM System/370 principles of operation. Chapters 18, 19, and 20 describe three operating systems designed to work within that environment.

Addressing Memory

The IBM System/370 is a byte-addressed machine. The bytes are numbered sequentially starting with 0 (Fig. 17.1), and grouped to form 16-bit halfwords, 32-bit fullwords, and 64-bit doublewords. The first fullword occupies bytes 0 through 3; the second, bytes 4 through 7; and so on. A fullword's address is simply the address of its first byte—0, 4, 8, . . .; note that fullword addresses are evenly divisible by 4.

In addition to main memory, a programmer also has access to 16 general-purpose registers numbered 0 through 15 (0 through F in hexadecimal). Because 15 is 1111 in binary, 4 bits are enough to identify a register.

Main memory addresses can appear as operands in an instruction. There are problems with absolute addressing (see Chapter 15), so relative addresses are used. Programs are written as though they begin at location zero, and the address of any byte in the program is expressed as a **displacement** from this base. When the program is loaded, its absolute entry point address is stored in a base register. As it executes, the instruction control

Fig. 17.1   An IBM System/370 computer is a byte-addressed machine. The bytes are numbered sequentially, starting with 0. Bytes are grouped to form halfwords, fullwords, and doublewords.

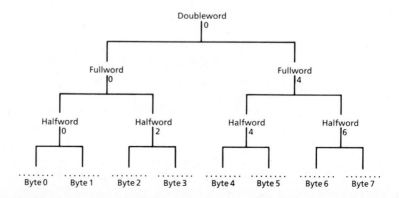

unit converts relative base-plus-displacement addresses to absolute form by adding the displacement to the contents of the base register.

Displacements are 12 bits long. Because the largest possible 12-bit number is equivalent to decimal 4095, programs exceeding 4096 bytes (displacements 0 through 4095) require multiple base registers. To specify a base register (4 bits) and a displacement (12 bits) requires 16 bits or 2 bytes. Thus, a relative base-plus-displacement address occupies 2 bytes.

Translating relative addresses to absolute form is a hardware function performed by the processor. Current versions of the System/370 family (such as the new 3090 "Sierra" series) incorporate additional dynamic address translation hardware to translate segment/page virtual addresses.

The Program Status Word

A computer executes one instruction during each machine cycle. The instruction control unit looks to the instruction counter for the address of its next instruction. An IBM System/370's instruction counter is called the **program status word**, or **PSW**.

The program status word has two different forms (Fig. 17.2). The **basic control (BC) mode** is compatible with the original System/360 architecture, and is used only when the dynamic address translation feature is disabled. The **extended control (EC) mode** implies virtual memory; in other words, adding a base register and a displacement yields a virtual address that must be translated through segment and page tables. Bit 12 is set to 0 for the basic control mode, and 1 for extended control.

Executing Instructions

The program status word (actually, a doubleword) occupies a special system register. Its key function is program control. For example, consider the assembler language program segment shown in Fig. 17.3. It loads binary numbers into registers 3 and 4, adds the numbers, and stores their sum, eventually repeating the instructions. Variables X, Y, and Z are symbolic memory locations (for simplicity, we'll work with the source statements rather than their machine-language equivalents). The numbers to the left in Fig. 17.3 are assumed to be absolute addresses expressed in decimal.

The PSW's last three bytes (Fig. 17.2) contain the address of the instruction to be executed next. As this program segment begins, the instruction address holds the binary equivalent of the decimal number 1000. The processor looks at the PSW, gets the address of the next instruction, and fetches it. Thus, the machine-language equivalent of

```
GO  L  3,X
```

is copied into the instruction register. While the instruction is moving from memory to the processor, the instruction control unit has plenty of time to

Fig. 17.2   The program status word (PSW) has two forms. The BC (basic control) mode PSW is used when the dynamic address translation feature is disabled. Current virtual memory systems use the EC (extended control) mode.

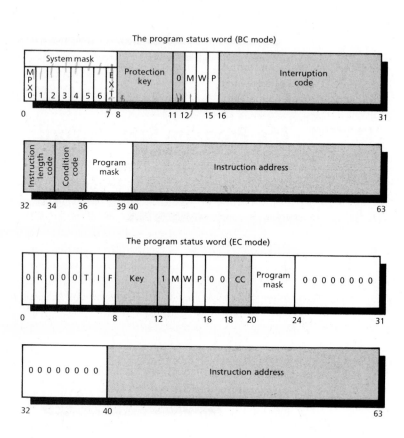

increment the PSW's **instruction address** field by 4 (the length of the load instruction). Thus the PSW points to 1004, the address of the *next* instruction.

The load instruction's first operand references register 3. The second operand, X, is a symbolic main memory address; it will appear as a base register and a displacement. Before the instruction can be executed, this relative address must be converted to absolute. Thus, the instruction control unit adds the base register and the displacement. If PSW bit 12 is 0, the result is the absolute address. If PSW bit 12 is 1, the dynamic address translation feature is activated, and segment and page tables are used to compute an absolute address.

Note carefully the difference between the instruction address in the PSW and the instruction's operand addresses. The PSW holds the absolute

Fig. 17.3   This assembly language program segment is used to illustrate how the PSW's contents control the order in which instructions are executed.

Address	Instruction
1000	GO L 3,X
1004	L 4,Y
1008	AR 3,4
1010	ST 3,Z

Several more instructions

| 1050 | B   GO |

Balance of program

1100	X DS F
1104	Y DS F
1108	Z DS F

Other data storage areas

address of the instruction. The operands, on the other hand, point to the memory locations that are to participate in the operation. The operand addresses are relative (and, perhaps, virtual), and must be translated to absolute form before the instruction can be executed.

Once its operand addresses have been translated, the first instruction is executed; thus, the value stored at location X is copied into register 3. Now, another instruction cycle begins. As before, the processor

1. finds the instruction address in the PSW,
2. fetches the instruction stored at that address,
3. increments the instruction address so it points to the "next" instruction,
4. translates the instruction's operands, and
5. executes the instruction.

Thus the second load is fetched, the instruction address is incremented to 1008, and the contents of memory location Y are copied into register 4.

During the next cycle, the instruction stored at location 1008 is fetched, the instruction address is incremented to 1010, and the contents of registers 3 and 4 are added. Note that the instruction address was incremented by 2 instead of 4 this time. The "AR" instruction is only 2 bytes long.

The PSW points to address 1010. Thus, during the next cycle, the store instruction is fetched and executed, and the instruction address is incremented by 4. Continuing in its single-minded way, the processor executes several other instructions until, finally, the instruction address is 1050. Thus,

B   GO

is fetched. It's an unconditional branch (a GOTO). The single operand, GO, is a relative (base-plus-displacement) address that must be translated to absolute. When the processor executes an unconditional branch, it replaces the contents of the PSW's instruction address with the address specified in the operand—in this case, with 1000. Thus, the next instruction to be fetched is the one labeled GO.

The instruction address is 3 bytes or 24 bits long. The biggest binary number that can be stored in 24 bits is equivalent to 16,777,215; thus, an IBM System/370 computer is limited to 16 megabytes of main memory. Newer extended architecture machines use the last 31 bits of an EC mode PSW to hold the instruction address. With 31 bits, the largest possible address is slightly over 2 billion, yielding up to 2 gigabytes of main memory!

Instruction Length

In the just-completed example (Fig. 17.3), most instructions occupied 4 bytes, but one (the AR) needed only 2. Actually, an IBM System/370 series computer supports three different instruction lengths (Fig. 17.4). Each instruction contains an operation code and two operands. The key to the instruction's length is the number of bytes needed to represent operand addresses. The sixteen general-purpose registers are numbered 0 through 15; thus a register can be uniquely identified by a 4-bit number. Main memory addresses are represented as a base register (4 bits) and a 12-bit displacement, yielding a 16-bit or 2-byte relative address.

Some instructions involve two registers. Combining a 1-byte operation code with two half-byte register numbers yields a 2-byte (halfword) instruction. Other instructions move data between memory and a register. The 1-byte operation code, combined with a half-byte register address, a half-byte index register, and a 2-byte memory address, totals 4 bytes. Storage-to-storage instructions include an operation code, two memory addresses, and, frequently, a 1-byte length field, for a total of 6 bytes.

How does the processor know the instruction's length? The operation code of every 2-byte, register-to-register instruction begins with bit values 00. Instructions referencing a register and a storage location start with 01 or 10; those involving two storage locations all start with 11. The processor can determine an instruction's length by checking its operation code.

Fig. 17.4   An IBM System/370 computer can execute 2-, 4-, and 6-byte instructions. An instruction's length is determined by the number of bits needed to represent its operands.

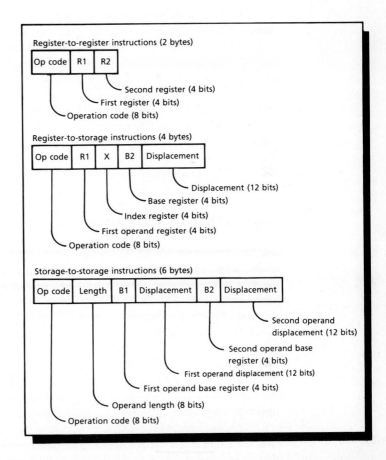

Bits 32 and 33 of a BC mode PSW indicate the length of the instruction currently being executed (Fig. 17.2), and are set when the instruction address is incremented. The program status word points to the "next" instruction, not the current one. Should an error occur, it is possible to use the instruction length code to compute the address of the current instruction. The instruction length code does not appear in an EC mode PSW.

The Condition Code

The key to decision logic on an IBM System/370 computer is a 2-bit condition code in the program status word (bits 34 and 35 in BC mode; bits 18 and 19 in EC mode; see Fig. 17.2). Comparison instructions and certain arithmetic instructions set the condition code. When a conditional branch is executed, the processor checks the condition code and, if its value is correct, replaces the PSW's instruction address with an operand address.

Memory Protection

On a multiprogramming system, it is possible for one program to destroy the contents of memory belonging to another. Thus, most systems include a memory protection feature. On an IBM System/370 computer, each active program is assigned a 4-bit **protection key**. The operating system uses 0000; the first program in memory gets 0001, and so on; each program has a different key. Memory is allocated in 2048-byte (2K) blocks. A program's protection key is associated with each block of memory space assigned to it. Later, during program execution, the protection key is stored in PSW bits 8 through 12 (Fig. 17.2, both modes). Access to any 2K block whose protection key does not match the one in the PSW is a protection exception, and can cause program termination.

Controlling Physical I/O

One of the most important elements of a computer's architecture is its link to peripheral devices. External devices are attached to an IBM System/370 computer through channels. A channel is a special-purpose computer. Because it has its own, independent processor, it can function in parallel with the main processor, and thus free the computer to do other work.

Like any computer, a channel executes instructions. Its function is to transfer a certain number of bytes from a peripheral device into main memory (or vice versa). Thus, it must be given a byte count and a main memory address. The channel program and key control data are stored in the computer's main memory and passed to the channel when the I/O operation begins.

A channel program consists of one or more **channel command words** (Fig. 17.5). Each **CCW** contains a command code that specifies the operation to be performed (read, write, seek), a data address, a byte count, and several flags. For example, near the bottom of Fig. 17.5 is a channel program that tells an IBM 3211 printer to skip one line and then write a line of data. Programmers can write their own channel programs, but they rarely do. Instead, the channel program is typically part of an access method.

If the channel program is stored in the computer's main memory, how does the channel find it? Just before the main processor sends the channel a start I/O command, the operating system places the address of the first CCW in the **channel address word** (Fig. 17.6). The **CAW** is always found at main memory address 72. Thus, when the channel's processor receives a start I/O command, it copies the channel address word into its own instruction counter (Fig. 17.7). Then the channel fetches and executes its first channel command (CCW).

The channel passes status information to the computer through the

Fig. 17.5   A channel program consists of one or more channel command
words (CCWs). The sample channel program tells an IBM 3211
printer to skip one line and then print a line of data.

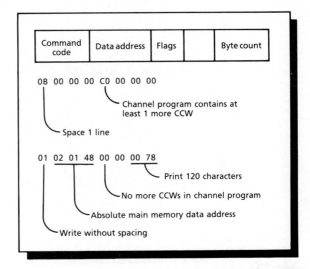

channel status word (Fig. 17.8) (main memory address 64). The **CSW**
contains the channel program address, a data address, a byte count, and
several flags that indicate the I/O operation's status. The program's protection key is found in both the channel address word and the channel status
word. Because it's in the CAW, the channel can recognize protection excep-

Fig. 17.6   The address of the first channel command word in the channel
program is passed to the channel through the channel address
word (CAW).

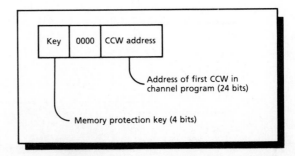

Fig. 17.7   The main processor sends the channel's processor a start I/O
command. The channel responds by copying the channel address
word from main memory (address 72) into its own instruction
counter. Then it fetches its first channel command word.

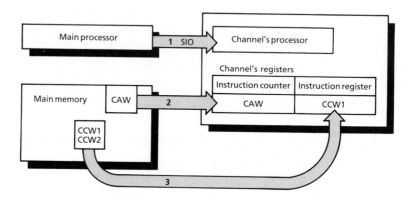

tions. Following completion of the I/O operation, the operating system uses
the protection key in the CSW to identify the program waiting for I/O.

Most channel programs are found in access methods. The linkage editor creates a load module by grafting access methods and other subroutines
onto the main object module. The main program requests a logical I/O
operation by calling the access method (Fig. 17.9a). Using parameters
passed to it by the calling routine (for example, a data address and a logical
record length), the access method completes the channel program and
transfers control to the operating system.

The operating system stores the address of the channel program's first
CCW in the channel address word (main memory address 72), and executes a start I/O instruction (Fig. 17.9b). The channel responds by copying
the channel address word and then fetching the first CCW (Fig. 17.9c). At
this point, the channel has assumed full responsibility for the I/O operation,
and the main computer can process instructions in some other program.

Fig. 17.8   The channel passes status information to the main computer
through the channel status word (CSW).

Key		Command address	Status	Byte count

Fig. 17.9   Controlling I/O on an IBM System/370 computer.

a. The application program calls the access method, which completes the channel
    program and transfers control to the operating system.

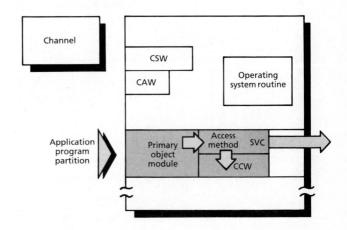

b. The operating system gets control, stores the address of the channel program in
    the channel address word, and executes a start I/O instruction.

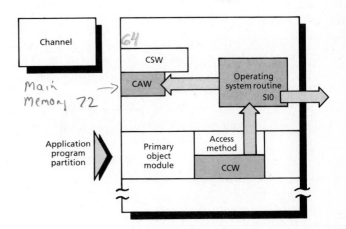

c. The channel copies the contents of the channel address word and then fetches its first channel command word.

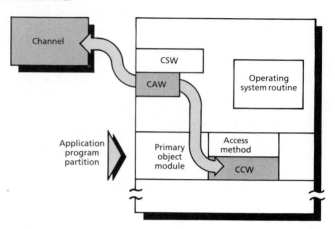

d. When the I/O operation is complete, the channel signals the main processor.

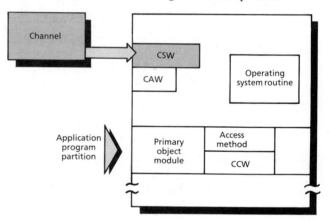

e. After checking the channel status word, the operating system returns control to the application program.

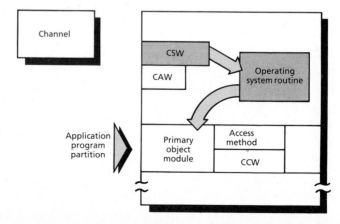

The channel and the computer are asynchronous; in other words, they function independently. Consequently, the main processor has no way of knowing when the channel has completed its work unless the channel tells it. Thus, when the I/O operation is finished, the channel signals the main processor and reports its status to the operating system through the channel status word (Fig. 17.9d). Assuming the CSW indicates successful completion, the operating system can return control to the application program (Fig. 17.9e).

Privileged Instructions

On a computer running multiple concurrent programs, it is essential that all input and output operations be funneled through a single operating system module. To prevent cheating, the instructions that communicate directly with a channel are **privileged**; in other words, they can be executed only by an operating system routine. PSW bit 15 (both modes) holds the problem state bit. This bit is set to 0 when the operating system is running. Before executing a privileged instruction, the processor checks this bit. If it's not 0, a privileged instruction exception is recognized, and the application program is usually terminated. Thus, to start an I/O operation, the programmer must first transfer control to the operating system.

Interrupts

Because the operating system and an application program have different protection keys, it is illegal to branch to or call an operating system module. The only way for an application program to transfer control to the operating system is by issuing an **interrupt**. Of course, application programs are not the only source of interrupts; they can originate in hardware or software.

An IBM System/370 computer responds to an interrupt signal by switching PSWs. Three fields are involved: the **current PSW**, an **old PSW**, and a **new PSW**. The current PSW is the special register that holds the address of the next instruction. The old PSW is located in main memory. The new PSW, also found in main memory, holds the address of an interrupt handling routine in the operating system.

When an interrupt occurs, hardware stores the current program status word in the old PSW field and then loads the new PSW into the current PSW register (Fig 17.10). As the processor begins its next cycle, it fetches the instruction whose address is in the program status word. Because of the interrupt, the current PSW points to the operating system's interrupt handling routine. Note that the old PSW holds the address of the next instruction in the original application program. Thus, after the interrupt has been processed, the application program can be resumed.

Sometimes an example helps. Imagine a program loaded at memory location 50000. The operating system's interrupt handling routine starts at

Fig. 17.10   An IBM System/370 responds to an interrupt by switching PSWs. First, the current PSW is stored in the old PSW field. Then, the new PSW is loaded into the current PSW register.

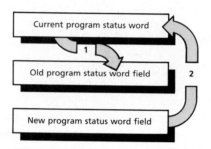

address 1000. The new PSW has protection key 0000 and points to instruction address 1000 (Fig. 17.11a). The contents of the old PSW are unknown. The current PSW points to memory location 50500 (an address in the application program). The program's protection key is 0010.

When an interrupt occurs, hardware stores the current PSW in the old PSW (Fig. 17.11b). A fraction of a nanosecond later, the new PSW is copied into the current PSW (Fig. 17.11c). This completes the interrupt.

Interrupt processing begins with the next machine cycle. The address in the current PSW is 1000. Thus, the processor fetches the first instruction in the interrupt handling routine (Fig. 17.11d). Since the operating system is in control, privileged instructions are legal. Eventually, the old PSW is

Fig. 17.11   An example of PSW switching.

a. The current PSW points to an instruction in the application program.

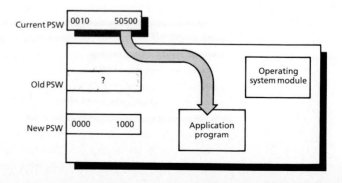

b. When an interrupt occurs, the current PSW is stored in the old PSW field.

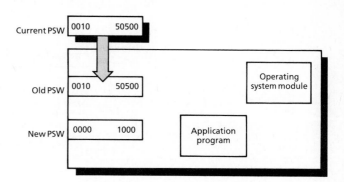

c. Then, the new PSW is loaded into current PSW register.

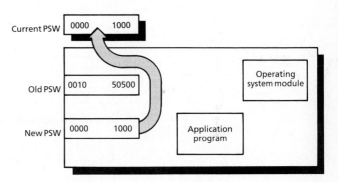

d. Because the new PSW now points to an operating system routine, the first instruction in the interrupt handler is fetched.

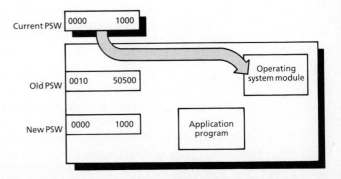

e. Eventually, the old PSW's contents are loaded back into the current PSW, and the application program resumes processing.

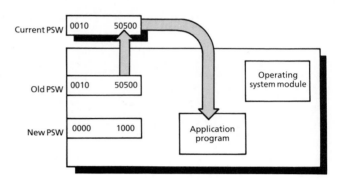

loaded back into the current PSW, and the application program resumes processing (Fig. 17.11e).

Interrupt Types

IBM System/370 computers recognize six different interrupt types. Sources include application programs, peripheral devices, the operator's console, the computer's self-checking error circuitry, and other processors.

External interrupts come from the operator's console, another processor, or the timer. When an external interrupt is sensed, hardware stores the current program status word at memory address 24 (the old external PSW), and then loads the contents of the doubleword beginning at address 88 (the new external PSW) into the current PSW register (Fig. 17.12). If the interrupt arrives while the processor is executing an instruction, it is ignored until the instruction is completed; in other words, external interrupts are recognized between instructions.

In BC mode, PSW bits 16 through 31 contain an **interruption code** (Fig. 17.2). By checking these 16 bits, the external interrupt handler routine can determine the exact cause of the interrupt. Under EC mode, the interruption code is stored in a special register.

A supervisor call or **SVC interrupt** starts when a program executes an SVC instruction, such as

SVC 17

The operand requests a particular supervisor module. In response to an SVC instruction, the processor generates an interrupt. Hardware reacts by storing the current program status word at memory address 32 (the old SVC PSW), loading the doubleword beginning at address 96 (the new SVC

Fig. 17.12 When an external interrupt occurs, hardware stores the current
PSW at memory address 24, and then loads the contents of
address 88 into the current PSW.

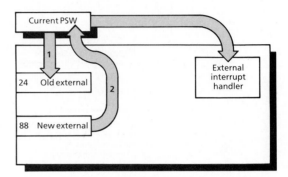

PSW) into the current PSW, and copying the operand field (the 17 in the
instruction illustrated) into the interruption code (Fig. 17.13).

An SVC interrupt is generated by a valid instruction. A **program interrupt** results from an illegal or invalid instruction. The processor recognizes
errors as they occur and generates the interrupt. In response, hardware
stores the current PSW into the old program PSW field (address 40), loads
the new program PSW (address 104) into the current PSW, and stores the
interruption code (Fig. 17.14).

Fig. 17.13 When an SVC interrupt occurs, hardware stores the current PSW
in the old SVC field, and then loads the new SVC into the current
PSW.

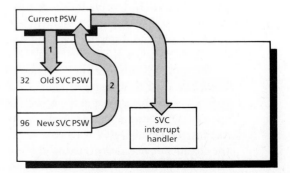

Fig. 17.14   When a program interrupt occurs, hardware stores the current
PSW in the old program PSW field, and then loads the new
program PSW into the current PSW. Listed below the diagram
are the valid program interrupt codes.

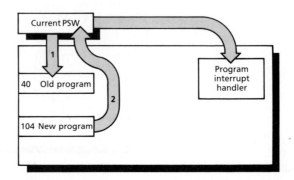

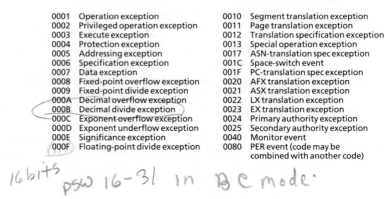

0001	Operation exception	0010	Segment translation exception
0002	Privileged operation exception	0011	Page translation exception
0003	Execute exception	0012	Translation specification exception
0004	Protection exception	0013	Special operation exception
0005	Addressing exception	0017	ASN-translation spec exception
0006	Specification exception	001C	Space-switch event
0007	Data exception	001F	PC-translation spec exception
0008	Fixed-point overflow exception	0020	AFX translation exception
0009	Fixed-point divide exception	0021	ASX translation exception
000A	Decimal overflow exception	0022	LX translation exception
000B	Decimal divide exception	0023	EX translation exception
000C	Exponent overflow exception	0024	Primary authority exception
000D	Exponent underflow exception	0025	Secondary authority exception
000E	Significance exception	0040	Monitor event
000F	Floating-point divide exception	0080	PER event (code may be combined with another code)

16 bits   psw 16-31 in BC mode·

A **machine check interrupt** occurs when the computer's self-checking
circuitry detects a hardware failure. If an instruction is executing, it is
terminated—no sense performing computations or logical operations on a
computer known to be malfunctioning. Hardware responds to a machine
check interrupt by storing the current PSW in the old machine check PSW
(address 48), loading the new machine check PSW (address 112) into the
current PSW, and dumping the contents of key control fields into the next
few hundred bytes of memory (Fig. 17.15).

Because the channels and the main processor work independently, the
channel must signal the processor when an I/O operation is completed by
sending it an input/output or **I/O interrupt** (Fig. 17.16). Hardware responds by storing the current PSW in the old I/O PSW (address 56),
loading the new I/O PSW (address 120) into the current PSW, and storing
the channel/device address of the unit causing the interrupt in the interruption code. If the processor is executing an instruction when an I/O interrupt
occurs, the instruction is completed before the interrupt is recognized.

Fig. 17.15   When a machine check interrupt occurs, hardware stores the current PSW in the old machine check PSW field, and then loads the new machine check PSW into the current PSW.

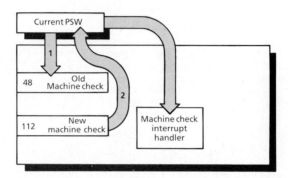

A **restart interrupt** allows an operator or another processor to start a program. This interrupt type was not available on the original IBM System/360 computers; it was added after the basic architecture was established. The new restart PSW is found at memory location 0; the old restart PSW is at memory location 8.

Permanent Storage Assignments

The old and new PSWs, the channel status word, and the channel address word are stored in fixed memory locations (Fig. 17.17); in other words, these key fields are found at the same addresses on every IBM System/370

Fig. 17.16   When an I/O interrupt occurs, hardware stores the current PSW in the old I/O PSW field, and then loads the new I/O PSW into the current PSW.

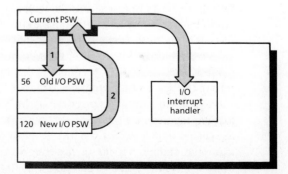

Fig. 17.17   The old and new PSWs, the channel address word, the channel
status word, and other key control fields are stored at fixed main
memory locations.

Address			
Decimal	Hexadecimal	Length	Purpose
0	0	Doubleword	Restart new PSW
8	8	Doubleword	Restart old PSW
16	10	Doubleword	Unused
24	18	Doubleword	External old PSW
32	20	Doubleword	Supervisor call old PSW
40	28	Doubleword	Program old PSW
48	30	Doubleword	Machine check old PSW
56	38	Doubleword	Input/output old PSW
65	40	Doubleword	Channel status word
72	48	Word	Channel address word
76	4C	Word	Unused
80	50	Word	Timer
84	54	Word	Unused
88	58	Doubleword	External new PSW
96	60	Doubleword	Supervisor call new PSW
104	68	Doubleword	Program new PSW
112	70	Doubleword	Machine check new PSW
120	78	Doubleword	Input/output new PSW

computer. Along with the computer's control registers, they represent the
primary interface between hardware and software.

Masking Interrupts

A typical mainframe computer supports several channels. The channels
operate independently. Thus, it is possible that two or more I/O interrupts
might be generated by different channels in a very brief time span, perhaps
even simultaneously. Consider what might happen if two I/O interrupts
were to occur within a few nanoseconds.

An application program is executing. In response to the first I/O interrupt, hardware copies the current program status word to the old I/O PSW,
and loads the new I/O PSW into the current PSW (Fig. 17.18a). Within a
single machine cycle, a second interrupt arrives. Clearly, the first interrupt
is still being processed, but that makes no difference to hardware, which, in
its automatic way, drops the current PSW into the old I/O PSW and loads
the new I/O PSW (Fig. 17.18b). As a result, the link back to the application
program is destroyed. Consequently, the operating system will be unable to
restart the application program, and that is unacceptable.

The solution is **masking** interrupts. The first 8 bits of the BC mode
program status word hold a **system mask** (Fig. 17.19). The first bit is
associated with channel 0. If it's 1 the processor can accept an interrupt
from the channel; if it's 0, the interrupt is ignored. (The channel will

Fig. 17.18   Two or more interrupts occurring in a brief time span can destroy the trail back to the original program.

a. When the first interrupt occurs, the link back to the application program is stored in the old PSW.

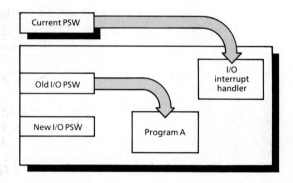

b. The second interrupt overlays the link and thus destroys it.

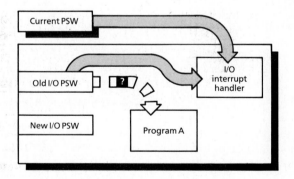

continue to send the interrupt signal, again and again, until the processor acknowledges it.) Bits 1 through 5 control channels 1 through 5; again, a 1-bit permits an interrupt from the associated channel, and a 0-bit means the processor will ignore interrupts from that channel. Bit 6 controls channels 6 through 255. In an EC mode PSW, a single bit (bit 6) serves to mask I/O interrupts from *all* channels.

Normally, the system mask or the I/O interrupt bit is set to 1, so I/O

Fig. 17.19

Several program status word bits are used to mask interrupts. If the appropriate bit is on (1), the interrupt can be recognized. If the bit is off, the interrupt is ignored.

The program status word (EC mode)

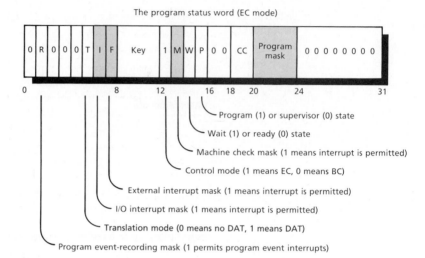

Program (1) or supervisor (0) state

Wait (1) or ready (0) state

Machine check mask (1 means interrupt is permitted)

Control mode (1 means EC, 0 means BC)

External interrupt mask (1 means interrupt is permitted)

I/O interrupt mask (1 means interrupt is permitted)

Translation mode (0 means no DAT, 1 means DAT)

Program event-recording mask (1 permits program event interrupts)

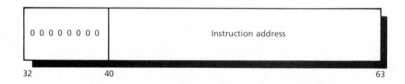

The program status word (BC mode)

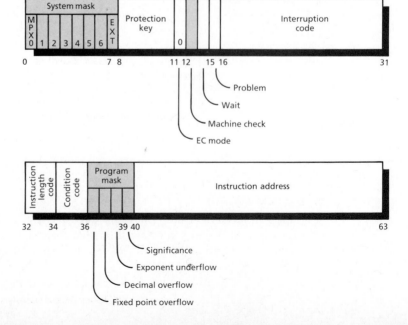

Problem

Wait

Machine check

EC mode

Significance

Exponent underflow

Decimal overflow

Fixed point overflow

interrupts can be accepted. In the new I/O PSW, however, these key mask bits are set to 0 (Fig. 17.20). Thus, once an I/O interrupt is accepted, subsequent I/O interrupts are ignored until the operating system changes the PSW.

Bit 7 masks external interrupts in both PSW modes. Like I/O interrupts, external interrupts are generated asynchronously, and thus can occur, unexpectedly, at any time. Picture an I/O interrupt, followed closely by an external interrupt, followed closely by another I/O interrupt. That sequence could destroy the original program's PSW in the old I/O PSW field. The same thing could happen with an external, I/O, external sequence. Thus, both I/O and external interrupts are masked when either type is processed.

Machine checks can be masked by turning off PSW bit 13 (both modes). Once a hardware failure is detected, the error checking circuitry sends an interrupt signal and continues to send signals until the problem is fixed or the machine is shut down. Thus, if machine check interrupts were not masked, hardware, responding to an unending series of interrupt signals, would simply load the new machine-check PSW over and over again, and the system would be unable to respond to the interrupt.

Closely spaced SVC and program interrupts are not a problem. Both are generated by program instructions, and since the processor can execute only one instruction at a time, simultaneous SVC and program interrupts are impossible. An SVC transfers control to the operating system, which has no need to issue a subsequent SVC. (Why call the supervisor when you're already there?) A program interrupt also transfers control to the operating system, which is assumed to be bug free. (In fact, operating system bugs usually lead to a system crash.)

Following a program interrupt, normal system action is to terminate the offending program and generate a dump. At times, a programmer may choose to override the standard procedure, trapping and handling such potential problems as overflows or underflows in a program subroutine. Bits 36 through 39 (BC mode) or bits 20 through 23 (EC mode) allow the programmer to suppress fixed-point overflows, decimal overflows, exponent underflows, and significance exceptions.

Fig. 17.20   In the new I/O PSW, the I/O interrupt mask bits are set to 0. Thus, when the new I/O PSW is loaded, all subsequent I/O interrupts are masked while the first one is processed.

New I/O PSW	Mask 0000 0000	Key 0000		I/O interrupt handler address

Interrupt Priority

"If it can possibly happen, it will." Engineers and programmers recognize
the essential truth behind that old cliché. Given time, it is almost inevitable
that every possible type of interrupt will hit the processor at the same
instant. Which one goes first? A well-designed system anticipates such
problems and has procedures for dealing with them.

On an IBM System/370 computer, machine checks are serviced first—
no sense trying to do anything else on a malfunctioning machine. Once the
machine check is out of the way, here's what happens (Fig. 17.21):

1. The program (or SVC) interrupt is accepted, dropping the application program's PSW into the old program PSW.
2. The external interrupt is accepted, dropping the current PSW
   (which by now points to the program interrupt handling routine)
   into the old external PSW.
3. The I/O interrupt is accepted, dropping the external interrupt's program status word into the old I/O PSW.

Fig. 17.21   When simultaneous interrupts occur, hardware accepts the
program (or SVC) interrupt first, then the external interrupt,
and, finally, the I/O interrupt. Because of their relative positions
on the old PSW queue, they are processed in reverse order.

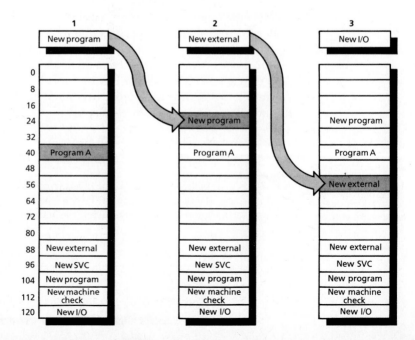

Note that the current PSW points to the I/O interrupt handler. Additional I/O or external interrupts will be ignored because they are masked. Additional SVC or program interrupts can't possibly happen until another instruction is executed. Thus, the I/O interrupt handler begins processing. When it finishes, the old I/O PSW is made current; thus the external interrupt handler takes over. Finally, the program interrupt handler gets control.

Program States

The computer, at any given time, is either executing an application program or a supervisor routine; in other words, it is either in the **problem state** or the **supervisory state**. PSW bit 15 (both modes, Fig. 17.19) indicates the computer's state—1 means problem and 0 means supervisory. Privileged instructions can be executed only in supervisory state. Protection exceptions are ignored when the system is in supervisory state.

Additionally, a given program is either ready to resume processing or waiting for the completion of some event such as an I/O operation; in other words, it's either in a **ready state** or a **wait state**. A 0 in PSW bit 14 means ready; 1 means wait. As you'll see in subsequent chapters, this bit is crucial on a multiprogramming system.

Two other EC mode bits deserve mention. Bit 1 is associated with program event recording (a new System/370 facility we won't cover in detail). Bit 5 controls dynamic address translation. If it's set to 0, addresses are not dynamically translated (which makes sense for operating system routines in the virtual-equals-real area). If bit 5 is set to 1, addresses are dynamically translated through the segment and page tables.

An Example

Perhaps the best way to pull together all these concepts is through an example. Start with a single program in main memory (Fig. 17.22a). The program needs data, and thus executes an SVC. The result is an SVC interrupt (Fig. 17.22b), which transfers control to the SVC interrupt handler (Fig. 17.22c). Note that the old SVC PSW points to the application program.

The SVC interrupt handler starts the physical I/O operation (Fig. 17.22d) by

1. storing the address of the first channel command word in the channel address word, and
2. executing a start I/O instruction, thus signaling the channel.

Before returning control to the initial program, the operating system repeatedly checks the channel status word (CSW) until the channel reports either

Fig. 17.22   An example

a. Main memory holds a single application program.

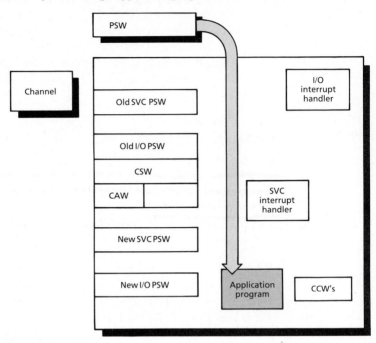

b. The program issues an SVC.

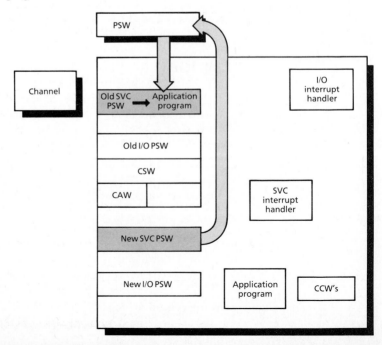

c. The SVC interrupt handler routine gets control.

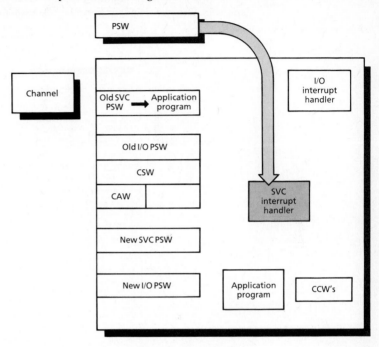

d. The interrupt handler routine starts the physical I/O operation by storing the channel program address in the channel address word and executing a start I/O instruction.

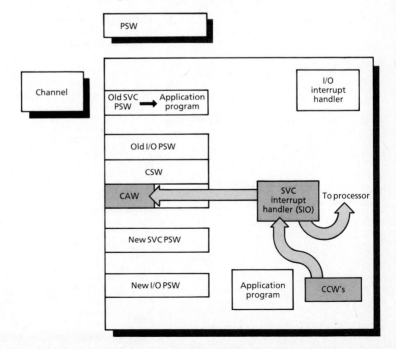

e. The SVC interrupt handler routine then checks the channel
status word until the channel reports the I/O operation's
status.

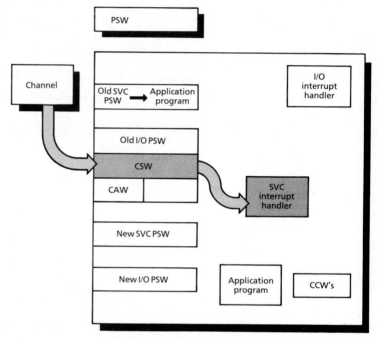

f. The original PSW is loaded, thus dropping the computer into
a wait state.

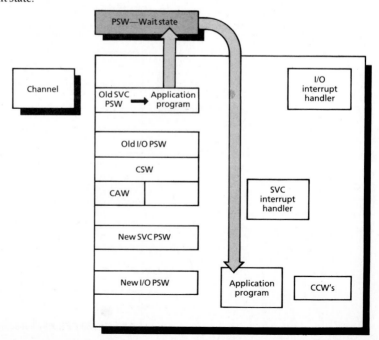

g. Following an I/O interrupt, the I/O interrupt handler routine gets control.

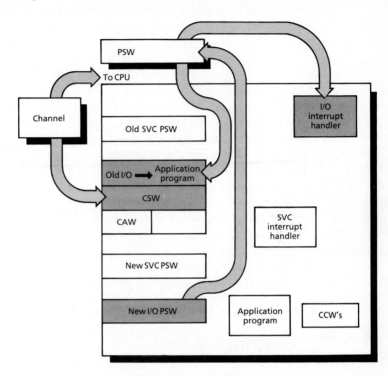

h. Eventually, the application program resumes processing.

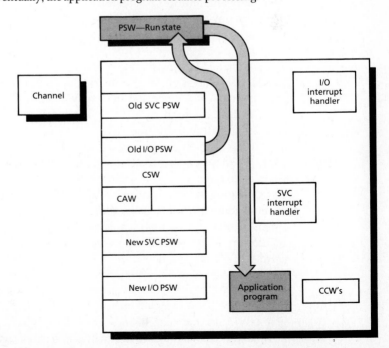

a successful or unsuccessful start (Fig. 17.22e). Assuming success, the channel is now responsible for the I/O operation. Thus, the interrupt handler places the application program in a wait state by turning on bit 14.

Next, the operating system tries to start another program. Since there is only one application program in memory, its old PSW is loaded (Fig. 17.22f). Because PSW bit 14 is set to 1, the computer is in a wait state, so the processor does nothing for a while.

Eventually, the channel completes the input operation and sends an I/O interrupt. Consequently, the current PSW is copied to the old I/O PSW, and the new I/O PSW is loaded (Fig. 17.22g). The current PSW's bit 14 is now 0, so the processor can execute instructions. The first instruction in the I/O interrupt handler routine is fetched. The channel status word is checked, and the application program's PSW is set to a ready state. Eventually, the application program resumes processing (Fig. 17.22h).

With multiprogramming, of course, the problem is a bit more complex. If a program drops into a wait state, the operating system will attempt to start a different one, and the new program is likely to generate its own interrupts. Because there is only one old PSW for each interrupt type, the original program's PSW must be saved if a return trail is to be preserved. We'll consider this problem in the next two chapters.

Summary

IBM System/370 computers are byte addressed. The bytes are grouped to form halfwords, fullwords, and doublewords. Memory addresses appearing in instruction operands are expressed in relative, base-plus-displacement form, and must be translated to absolute form before the instruction can be executed.

A System/370's instruction counter is called the program status word. It holds the address of the next instruction to be executed. Two forms—the basic control (BC) mode and the extended control (EC) mode—are used. The instruction length code (BC mode only), condition code, and protection key are all found in the PSW.

An application program starts an I/O operation by calling an access method. The access method completes a channel program (one or more channel command words), and transfers control to the operating system. The operating system, in turn, stores the address of the first CCW in the channel address word (CAW), and issues a privileged start I/O instruction. When the I/O operation is completed, the channel notifies the processor by sending an interrupt and reporting its status through the channel status word (CSW).

An IBM System/370 computer responds to an interrupt by storing the current PSW in the old PSW field, and loading the new PSW into the current PSW. Six types of interrupts are supported—external, I/O, program, SVC, machine check, and restart. Each type has its own old and new PSW fields. To avoid losing the trail back to the original program, I/O and external interrupts are masked. Machine-check interrupts and selected program interrupts can be masked, too. Given simultaneous interrupts, the program (or SVC) interrupt is accepted first, then the external interrupt, and, finally, the I/O interrupt. They are processed in reverse order.

Other PSW bits identify a program's state, activate the dynamic address translation feature, and control program event recording.

The chapter ended with an example. If you haven't already done so, take the time to read and understand that example.

Key Words

base	displacement	privileged
basic control mode	extended control	instruction
PSW	mode PSW	problem state
CAW	external interrupt	program interrupt
CCW	instruction address	program status
channel address	instruction length	word
word	code	protection key
channel command	interrupt	PSW
word	interruption code	ready state
channel program	I/O interrupt	restart interrupt
channel status	machine check	supervisory state
word	interrupt	SVC interrupt
condition code	masking	system mask
current PSW	new PSW	wait state
CSW	old PSW	

Exercises

1. The IBM System/370 is a byte-addressed machine. Explain.

2. Distinguish between an absolute address and a relative address. Briefly explain the structure of both address types on an IBM System/370 computer.

3. Explain how the PSW determines the order in which instructions are executed.

4. How can an IBM System/370 computer determine the length of its instructions? What distinguishes 2-byte, 4-byte, and 6-byte instructions?

5. Explain how I/O is controlled on an IBM System/370. What functions are performed by
   a. the access method?
   b. the channel program?
   c. the channel command word?
   d. the channel address word?
   e. the operating system?
   f. the channel status word?

6. What is a privileged instruction? Why are such instructions important?

7. What is an interrupt? How is the interrupt concept implemented on an IBM System/370?

8. Name the types of interrupts recognized on an IBM System/370. Describe the source of each.

9. What are permanent storage assignments? Why are they necessary on an IBM System/370?

10. Why must certain types of interrupts be masked at certain times? How are they masked?

11. Explain the IBM System/370's interrupt priority.

12. Distinguish between the BC mode and the EC mode. When is each used? How do the PSWs differ?

13. Assume an IBM System/370 is running under basic control mode. The contents of certain fixed locations in main memory are:

Address	Contents in Hexadecimal
0	FF040000D001C000 ←
8	0000000000000720
16	0000000000000000
24	00550082C0026400
32	FF550008C0031424
40	FF55000BC003F340 ←
48	00550000C004A000
56	00550003C00422FA
64	0000000000000000
72	0000000000000000
80	0000000000000000
88	000400000001A000
96	FF040000D0017000
104	FF040000D0013000 ←
112	0000000000011000
120	000400000015000

The current PSW holds:

FF04000B00013000

Sketch a map of main memory showing the location of each interrupt handling routine. What kind of interrupt has just happened? What is the address of the "bad" instruction? Can an I/O interrupt happen now? How do you know? Can a privileged instruction be executed? How can you tell the computer is in basic control (BC) mode?

Current PSW

Old   PSW

New   PSW

C003F 340 Hex
      — 2 Hex
─────────────────
C003F 33 E Hex

C H A P T E R
18

IBM DOS/VSE

The DOS/VSE Environment

IBM's **DOS/VSE**, or disk operating system/virtual storage extended, is a batch-oriented operating system that includes modules to handle interrupts, coordinate job-to-job transition, communicate with channels, manage I/O operations, maintain libraries, compile and link edit programs, and supervise multiprogramming. All these functions are performed within an IBM System/370 environment; thus, the operating system must deal with the PSW, interrupt handling, and channel communication concepts built into this computer series. First released in the mid-1960s as DOS, it was considered IBM's most dependable System/360 small business operating system. Recently, IBM announced that DOS/VSE would no longer be developed or improved. In spite of this deemphasis, organizations continue to use DOS/VSE because it works, and converting to another operating system would be too costly. DOS/VSE has several years of useful life remaining.

Virtual Memory Contents

DOS/VSE is a virtual memory operating system. Generally, the amount of virtual memory exceeds the available real memory by a factor of three or four; for example, 1 megabyte of real memory might support 4 megabytes of virtual. Virtual memory is divided into two components (Fig. 18.1). The first part, beginning with address 0, exactly equals the available real mem-

Fig. 18.1   Virtual memory space is divided into a real address area and a virtual address area.

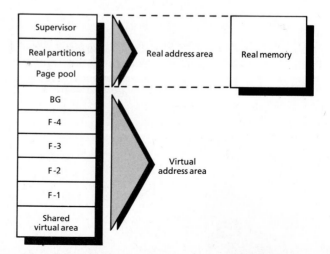

ory, and is called the **real address area**. Virtual space over and above available real memory is called the **virtual address area**.

The resident operating system, called the **supervisor**, occupies the low-address region of the real address area. Following the supervisor come several **real partitions**, one (potentially) for each application program partition. Certain types of applications (for example, data communication routines) require that key modules not be paged but remain in real memory; such modules are stored in a real partition. The remainder of the real address area contains the **page pool**.

The virtual address area is divided into from one to five application program **partitions**. The low-priority **background** partition comes first, followed by up to four **foreground** partitions (Fig. 18.1). Following the application program partitions is a **shared virtual area** that holds routines designed to be shared by all partitions (for example, a data base manager).

The contents of the real address area occupy real memory (Fig. 18.2). The partitions in the virtual address area reside on an external paging device, usually disk. Pages are swapped between the external paging device and the real memory page pool. Because paging is a hardware function, it is transparent to software. Thus, it is reasonable to pretend that programs and

Fig. 18.2   The contents of the real address area are stored in real memory. The partitions in the virtual address area are stored on an external paging device (usually, disk). Pages are swapped between the external paging device and the real page pool.

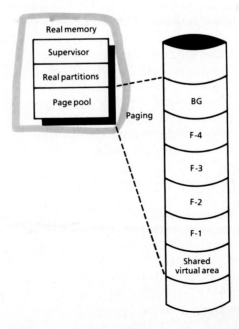

the operating system really reside in virtual memory. Focusing on the virtual memory model makes the operating system much easier to visualize.

SYSGEN and IPL

An operating system does not simply spring into being; it must come from somewhere. For DOS/VSE, the source is a procedure called system generation (SYSGEN).

IBM maintains a complete master copy of the operating system. When a customer decides to purchase or lease a computer, the customer's data processing environment is reviewed and necessary operating system functions are identified. Key modules are concentrated in the supervisor, while infrequently used routines are assigned transient status. Tables are created to support the specific I/O devices and the partition configuration chosen by the customer, and this made-to-order operating system is copied to a system residence device, usually a disk pack. The SYSRES pack then becomes the source of the operating system on the customer's computer.

As long as the operating system, even a disk operating system, remains on disk, it does little or no good. If the operating system is to perform useful work, it must be copied into main memory. The process of copying the resident operating system into real memory is called initial program load (IPL). Generally, small computers are booted, and mainframes are IPLed.

Memory Management

When main memory contains several independent programs, space must be carefully managed to avoid conflicts. At the virtual memory level, DOS/VSE is a fixed-length partition operating system. At system generation time, virtual memory is divided into from one to five application program partitions. The operator, at IPL time, can change the standard configuration, but once the system starts running, virtual memory allocation is fixed and constant.

Memory protection is related to memory allocation. Each partition is assigned a unique protection key. Any attempt to execute an instruction that would destroy the contents of any storage location in another partition generates a protection interrupt. Usually, the offending program is terminated.

Note that application program partitions are defined in virtual memory. How is real memory managed? On an IBM System/370 computer, virtual addresses are broken into segment, page, and displacement portions and are dynamically translated by hardware. Consequently, to support dynamic address translation, DOS/VSE maintains program segment and page tables. Additionally, the operating system relies on a page frame table to keep track of available real memory space. However, the tasks associated with swapping pages are transparent to system users. Thus, it is reasonable to focus on the virtual memory model.

Loading Application Programs

Data processing applications often call for executing a series of related programs; for example, payroll might involve data entry and verification, a sort, the payroll program, and a check printing routine. Under DOS/VSE, such applications form a **job**. The computer, however, does not concurrently load and execute all the programs making up a job; instead, it loads one **task** at a time. A task is a single program or routine. A job is a set of related tasks.

Following IPL, the system is ready to accept application programs. On early versions of DOS, the computer operator directly controlled loading tasks by communicating with the single program initiation (SPI) routine, but SPI is no longer supported. Instead, job control language statements are prepared by the programmer and submitted through the job stream.

Each job begins with a JOB statement and ends with a /& statement. EXEC statements identify individual job steps. Generally, several jobs are submitted, back to back, and processed in sequence, one after another. JOB and /& statements serve to separate jobs; within a job, the EXEC statements serve to identify individual job steps or tasks. Because the control statements can be converted to electronic form, job-to-job and step-to-step transition can be handled by an operating system module; thus, little or no operator intervention is required.

The Job Control Program

Job steps or tasks are loaded by a **job control program**. When a transition point (such as end-of-job step) is reached, the supervisor loads the job control program into the newly freed partition. (Note that this routine is *not* part of the resident operating system). The job control program then reads job control statements, makes device assignments, prepares the partition for the application routine, performs other housekeeping functions, and in response to an EXEC statement, asks the resident supervisor to load the requested program.

For example, consider the sequence of events outlined in Fig. 18.3. A program in the background partition has just reached successful completion and executed a RETURN (Fig. 18.3a). Thus, the supervisor gets control and loads the job control program from the SYSRES pack into the background partition (Fig. 18.3b). The job control program, in turn, reads job control statements for the next job step and performs any requested services. Normally, the job step ends with an EXEC statement. In response, the job control program gives control back to the resident supervisor, which loads the requested program from a library into the background partition (Fig. 18.3c).

Figure 18.3 illustrates how a program is loaded into virtual memory. What *really* happens? First, the supervisor attempts to load all the new task's pages into real memory. However, except for the first few programs

Fig. 18.3   An example of program loading.

a. An application routine in the background partition returns control to the supervisor.

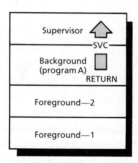

b. The supervisor loads the job control program into the background partition.

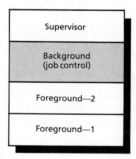

c. The application program then overlays the job control program.

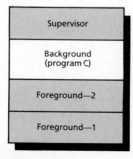

following IPL, there simply will not be enough room in real memory. Thus the incoming application program will immediately be paged-out to the external page device. In effect, the program is copied, page by page, through real memory and onto the external paging device. From there, pages are swapped into the real page pool as needed.

Spooling and Queuing

Under DOS/VSE, a separate job stream is maintained for each partition. When a partition becomes free, the job control program is loaded into the partition and reads the partition's job stream. Jobs are processed in sequential order—first come, first served. Within a job, the individual job steps are loaded and executed in sequential order.

On smaller computers, job control statements are prepared on punched cards or diskettes, or typed through a terminal. Often, the job stream is spooled to disk before being read by the job control program. A single job stream containing jobs for all partitions might be read by the spooler and, based on a job class, queued to the appropriate partition's job stream. Thus, the job control program reads high-speed disk rather slow character devices. POWER/VS is a popular spooling routine designed to run under DOS/VSE. The spooler normally occupies the high-priority foreground-1 partition.

Multiprogramming and Physical I/O

DOS/VSE is a multiprogramming operating system. The key to multiprogramming is the speed disparity between a computer and its I/O devices. Rather than forcing a high-speed processor to wait for a (relatively) slow I/O device, the processor switches its attention to another program. By executing several programs concurrently, both throughput and turnaround are improved.

If a multiprogramming operating system is to utilize otherwise wasted I/O time, it must take action at the beginning and end of each physical I/O operation. Under DOS/VSE, physical I/O is implemented through a **physical I/O control system (PIOCS)**.

To use PIOCS, the programmer first writes a channel program (see Chapter 17). Next, a **CCB** macro creates a **command control block** containing such information as the symbolic name of the actual I/O device, the address of the first CCW in the channel program, and various flags. Both the CCB and the channel program are stored in the program partition (Fig. 18.4a).

To request an I/O operation, the programmer codes an **execute channel program (EXCP)** macro (Fig. 18.4b). The EXCP references the command control block (which, remember, points to the channel program), and generates a supervisor call interrupt. Once it gets control, the supervisor stores the address of the channel program in the channel address word,

Fig. 18.4 The physical input/output control system.

a. The programmer codes a channel program and a command control block (CCB).

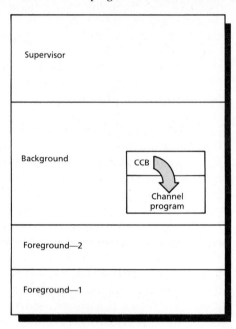

b. The programmer requests an I/O operation by coding an EXCP macro. The resulting supervisor call interrupt transfers control to the superviser, which stores the channel program address in the channel address word and executes a start I/O instruction.

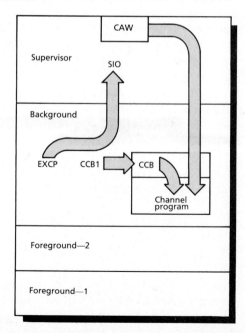

c. Unable to continue until the I/O operation is completed, the program asks the supervisor to put it into a wait state.

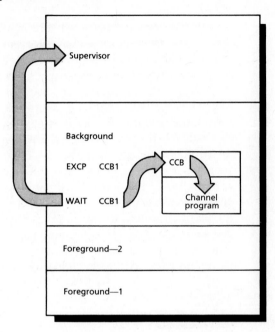

d. The supervisor responds by saving the program's most current PSW, changing the wait state bit (14) to 1, and giving control to another task.

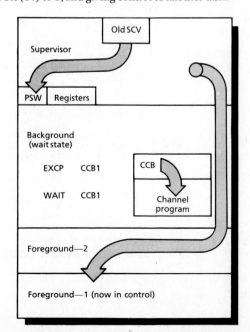

and executes a start I/O command. Thus, the channel assumes responsibility for the I/O operation. The supervisor then returns control to the application program.

In most cases, the program is unable to continue until the requested I/O operation is completed and thus issues a **WAIT** (Fig. 18.4c). The WAIT macro generates another supervisor call. In response, the operating system drops the program into a wait state, saves the old SVC PSW (which points to the application program), and starts another task (Fig. 18.4d). Eventually, when the I/O operation is completed, the program's PSW is reset to a ready state, and the task becomes eligible to regain control.

Where is the old PSW saved? Each partition has a **control block** (Fig. 18.5). Following *any* interrupt, the PSW associated with the interrupted program is copied from the old PSW field and stored in the partition's control block. The control blocks are linked by pointers. This linked list of control blocks is the key to DOS/VSE dispatching. The dispatcher searches the partition control blocks in priority order, starting with F-1, then F-2, and so on down to the background partition, checking the PSW stored in each one for a ready task. As soon as it finds one, the supervisor loads the partition's PSW, thus giving the program control.

Fig. 18.5

Each partition has a control block. The most current PSW associated with the task in that partition is stored in the control block. The dispatcher searches the control blocks in priority order, and gives control to the first ready program it finds.

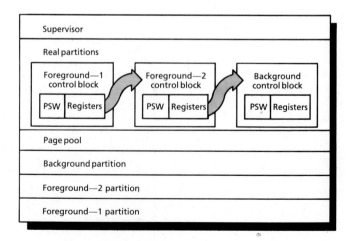

The Logical I/O Control System

Few application programmers are willing (or even able) to write their own channel programs. Thus, few DOS/VSE programmers use PIOCS. Instead, they rely on the **logical (I/O) control system (LIOCS)**.

For each file accessed by a program, the programmer codes a **DTF (define the file)** macro. The DTF generates a table that specifies the file's logical record length, block size, record format, and other descriptive information needed by the access method. (In effect, the DTF defines the access method.) As it builds a load module, the linkage editor grafts a copy of the appropriate access method onto the program object module. Once the resulting load module (or phase) is loaded and begins running, the programmer's GET and PUT or READ and WRITE macros reference the DTF table and call the access method (Fig. 18.6).

The access method contains a channel program. A second key component is the PIOCS logic (CCB, EXCP, and WAIT) needed to support physical I/O—LIOCS uses PIOCS. Finally, the access method contains instructions to support blocking, deblocking, and buffering.

Fig. 18.6

A programmer codes a DTF to define each file. Logical I/O instructions generate calls to the access method which, in addition to a channel program and blocking/deblocking logic, includes the necessary PIOCS commands.

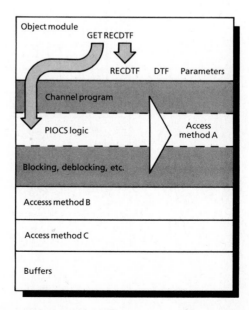

Allocating Peripheral Devices

DOS/VSE uses three key tables to control I/O device allocation. The **physical unit block**, or **PUB**, table lists the peripheral devices attached to the system (Fig. 18.7). Each device has a single, 8-byte PUB table entry; the first byte identifies the channel number, the second identifies the device number, the other six hold various pointers and flags. This table, stored in the supervisor partition, is created at system generation time and maintained in channel sequence.

Programmers rarely refer to physical I/O devices. Instead, they use symbolic names. The symbolic names are listed in a **logical unit block**, or LUB, table—there is one LUB table for each partition. LUB table entries are

Fig. 18.7

Each physical device attached to a DOS/VSE system is listed in the PUB table.

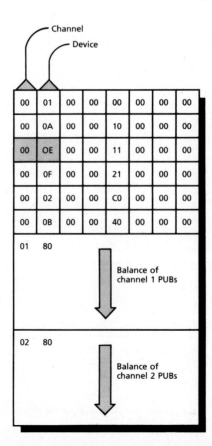

Fig. 18.8   Each partition has its own LUB table that provides logical names
for the physical devices. The logical names are always listed in a
fixed sequence.

SYSRDR	Input unit for job control statements
SYSIPT	Input unit for application programs
SYSIN	(Optional) System input device for spooling
SYSPCH	Punched card output unit
SYSLST	Printer output unit
SYSOUT	(Optional) System output device for spooling
SYSLOG	Operator messages output unit
SYSLNK	Disk extent for linkage editor input
SYSRES	System residence device (or extent)
SYSVIS	Disk extent for virtual storage support
SYSCAT	Disk extent for VSAM master catalog
SYSCLB	Private core image library
SYSRLB	Private relocatable (object module) library
SYSSLB	Private source statement library
SYSREC	Disk extent for error logging
SYS000-	Other units. Exact meaning is
SYSmax	installation dependent

stored in a fixed sequence (Fig. 18.8). Each entry is 2 bytes long and points
to a PUB table entry.

The best way to visualize the relationship between the PUB and LUB
tables is through an example (Fig. 18.9). Assume a program in the background partition has just issued an SVC requesting input data from logical
device SYSIPT. To find the physical device, the supervisor looks at the
background partition's LUB table. SYSIPT is always the second entry in any
LUB table (Fig. 18.9a). The first byte of this entry identifies PUB table entry
03 as the one containing information on the physical device assigned to
SYSIPT—it's channel 0, device 14 (00 0E in hex, Fig. 18.9b).

A start I/O (SIO) instruction's operands specify the channel and device
address of the physical unit. Under DOS/VSE, the PUB table is the source of
this information (Fig. 18.9c). Assuming the channel is free, the channel/
device address is moved into an SIO instruction, the instruction is executed, and the channel takes over.

What if the channel is busy? Rather than keep the system waiting, an
I/O operation that cannot be started because of a channel-busy condition is
placed on a **channel queue** for later processing. Following any I/O interrupt, the supervisor checks the channel queue for pending requests before
resuming normal processing. Individual channel queue entries are 4 bytes
long. Each one contains the address of a command control block (CCB) and
a pointer to the next channel queue entry (Fig. 18.10).

Fig. 18.9   Each LUB table entry points to a PUB table entry, and thus links the logical name to a physical device.

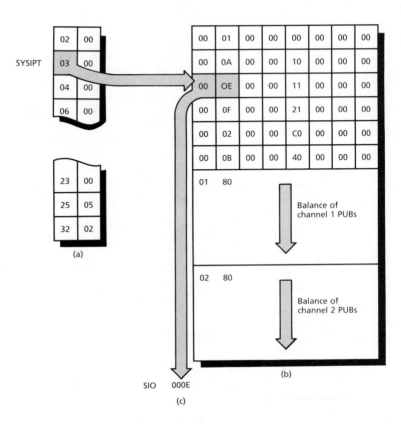

The meaning of a logical device name can vary from partition to partition. For example, assume the standard system input device is a terminal, and that the foreground-1, foreground-2, and background partitions all require terminal input. Each partition has its own LUB table. In F-1, SYSIPT might be assigned to PUB entry 1 and thus, indirectly, to channel 00

Fig. 18.10   The channel queue holds pending I/O requests. Each channel queue entry holds the address of a command control block and a pointer to the next channel queue entry.

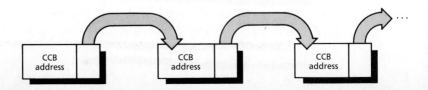

Fig. 18.11   Because each partition has its own LUB table, the same logical name can refer to different physical devices in different partitions.

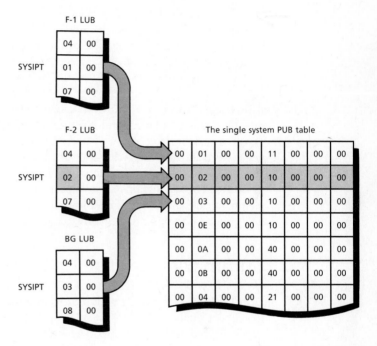

device 01 (Fig. 18.11), while in F-2, SYSIPT is linked to PUB entry 2 and channel 00 device 02. Meanwhile, in the background LUB, SYSIPT points to PUB 3 and thus to channel 00 device 03.

Spooling is implemented in much the same way. If, for example, the spooling routine resides in the F-1 partition, this partition's SYSRDR and SYSIPT refer, respectively, to an actual card reader and an actual terminal. In all other partition LUB tables, SYSRDR and SYSIPT refer to the disk files created by the spooling program. Under DOS/VSE, another logical input device, SYSIN, can be designated as a system input device that contains both control statements and data. On output, SYSOUT can be designated as the spooled system output device.

Libraries

DOS/VSE supports three levels of program libraries. A **source statement library** holds assembler or compiler source code in modules called **books**. For example, macros are stored on a source statement library. When a macro is referenced in a programmer's source code, the associated book is added to the module and then compiled or assembled. Another option is to store data structures and add them to the source module by coding COPY statements. The system source statement library resides on SYSRES; private source statement libraries are also supported and can reside on almost any secondary storage device.

A **relocatable library** holds object modules. Access methods reside on the system relocatable library (which is found on SYSRES), and subroutines can be found on system and private relocatable libraries. Private relocatable libraries can reside on any secondary storage device.

A load module, the output of the linkage editor, is a complete, machine-level, ready-to-execute program. Load modules are maintained on a **core image library**. An EXEC statement references a core image library member (called a **phase**), and tells the supervisor to load and execute the phase. The system core image library is found on the system residence device. Private core image libraries are also supported.

DOS/VSE includes programs to maintain, service, and copy library members. These programs allow a programmer to add, delete, or rename members, maintain library directories, list or punch library members, create new private libraries, and reorganize a library.

Summary

DOS/VSE is a fixed-partition multiprogramming operating system designed to support small to medium-size IBM System/370 computers. Virtual memory is divided into two regions. The real address area contains the supervisor, optional real partitions, and the page pool; its total size equals the available real memory. The virtual address area holds space in excess of real memory capacity and is divided into a background partition, from one to four foreground partitions, and a shared virtual area. The real address area is physically stored in real memory; the virtual address area is stored on an external page device, usually disk. A customer's version of the operating system is created during SYSGEN. The operating system is copied into primary memory during IPL.

A task is a single program or routine; a job is a set of related tasks. Tasks are loaded into memory under control of the job control program. When a partition becomes free, the supervisor loads the transient job control program, which reads job stream commands and identifies the next program to be loaded. Often, the job stream is spooled or queued.

The key to controlling multiprogramming is I/O. Under DOS/VSE, a programmer can code physical input/output control system (PIOCS) macros. The CCB macro creates a command control block that points to a channel program. The command control block is referenced by an execute channel program (EXCP) macro, which generates an SVC interrupt that tells the supervisor to start the I/O operation. A third PIOCS macro, WAIT, generates another SVC; in response, the supervisor drops the program into a wait state and transfers control to another task.

Few programmers code PIOCS macros. Instead, most rely on logical input/output control system (LIOCS) macros, such as DTF, GET, PUT,

READ, and WRITE. Under LIOCS, physical I/O is performed by an access method which contains the channel program, necessary PIOCS logic, and blocking/deblocking routines.

I/O device allocation is controlled through system tables. The physical unit block, or PUB, table holds one entry for each I/O device attached to the system. The logical unit block, or LUB, table relates symbolic device assignments to the physical devices listed in the PUB table. If a channel is busy at the time an input or output operation is requested, the request is kept pending by placing it on a channel queue; later, when an I/O interrupt occurs, the supervisor checks for pending I/O requests before starting the next program.

When an interrupt occurs, the PSW associated with the interrupted program is copied from an old PSW field into a partition control block. The supervisor determines internal priority by searching the partition control blocks in fixed sequence, from foreground-1 to background. Each partition has its own job stream. When the partition becomes free, the job control program loads the next program in that partition's job stream.

DOS/VSE supports system and private source statement, relocatable, and core image libraries.

Key Words

background	job	PUB
book	job control	real address area
CCB	program	real partition
channel queue	LIOCS	relocatable
command control	logical I/O	library
block	control system	shared virtual area
control block	logical unit block	source statement
core image library	LUB	library
define the file	page pool	supervisor
DOS/VSE	partition	SYSGEN
DTF	phase	SYSRES
EXCP	physical I/O	task
execute channel	control system	virtual address
program	physical unit	area
foreground	block	WAIT
IPL	PIOCS	

Exercises

1. Distinguish between the real address area and the virtual address area.

2. Sketch a map of virtual memory under DOS/VSE. Assume four application program partitions.

3. How are the contents of virtual memory physically stored under DOS/VSE?

4. Briefly describe memory management under DOS/VSE.

5. Distinguish between a job and a task.

6. Explain how application programs are loaded from a core image library under DOS/VSE. The job control program is transient. What does this mean?

7. Explain how PIOCS supports multiprogramming under DOS/VSE.

8. Explain the difference between PIOCS and LIOCS. Which one does an application programmer use? Why? When LIOCS is used, where is the PIOCS logic normally found?

9. Briefly describe processor management under DOS/VSE. In other words, explain how the supervisor selects the next program to be given control.

10. Explain how I/O device access is controlled under DOS/VSE. Why is there one LUB table for each partition? Why is there a single PUB table for the entire system?

11. Briefly explain how the external priority decision is made under DOS/VSE. In other words, explain how the supervisor selects the next program to be loaded into memory.

12. Distinguish source statement, relocatable, and core image libraries.

CHAPTER 19

IBM System/370 OS/VS1 and OS/VS2

OS/VS1 and OS/VS2

IBM's System/360 computer family was announced in 1964. Initially, it supported three operating systems—DOS, OS/MFT, and OS/MVT. The current version of DOS is called DOS/VSE (see Chapter 18). OS/MFT (multiprogramming with a fixed number of tasks) incorporated fixed-partition memory management, and has evolved into **OS/VS1**. OS/MVT (multiprogramming with a variable number of tasks) utilized dynamic memory management. It became **OS/VS2**, and, eventually, MVS. This chapter discusses OS/VS1 and OS/VS2 internals.

Virtual Memory Contents

OS/VS1 and OS/VS2 are virtual storage operating systems. Virtual memory is divided into a **real address area** and a **virtual address area** (Fig. 19.1). The resident supervisor begins with real address area byte 0. Next comes space for key system control blocks—we'll discuss them later. The rest of the real address area is called the **virtual-equals-real** (or **V=R**) area; the line separating the real and virtual address areas is called the V=R line. If necessary, application routines can be loaded into the V=R area. The remaining V=R space forms the page pool.

The virtual address area ends with a pagable supervisor that holds transient supervisor modules. Under VS1, the remaining virtual address area is divided into as many as fifteen fixed-length application program

Fig. 19.1   Under OS/VS1 and OS/VS2, virtual memory is divided into a real address area and a virtual address area.

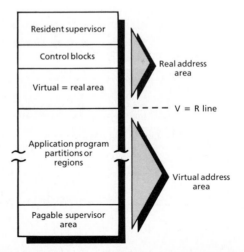

partitions. Partition sizes are set at SYSGEN time and can be changed by the operator at IPL time, but once the system begins running, the partition configuration is fixed. Under VS2, this remaining virtual address area is treated as a pool of free space to be dynamically allocated at run time to as many as fifteen variable-length application program **regions**.

The real address area occupies the available real storage (Fig. 19.2), while the virtual address area is stored on an external paging device. Paging takes place between the external paging device and that portion of the V=R area not allocated to real partitions (the page pool).

Managing Virtual Memory

Internally, OS/VS1 and OS/VS2 are similar. In fact, the major difference between these two operating systems is the way they manage virtual memory space. Under OS/VS1, programs are loaded into fixed partitions, and the only way to change the partition configuration is to re-IPL the system. Under OS/VS2, the operating system maintains a table of free space and dynamically allocates application program regions at run time.

Fig. 19.2

The contents of the real address area are stored in real memory. The virtual address area is stored on an external paging device. Under VS1, most of the virtual address area is divided into fixed-length partitions. Under VS2, variable-length regions are allocated from a pool of free space.

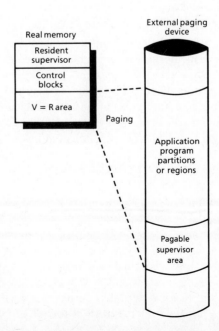

Of course, virtual memory is just a model. In reality, application routines move, page by page, between real memory and an external paging device. However, paging is a hardware function and thus is transparent to the user. Consequently, it is reasonable to analyze OS/VS1 and OS/VS2 by focusing on the contents of virtual memory.

This chapter discusses both operating systems. In most cases, there is little difference in the way they work. Since the phrase "partition or region" would become tedious, the chapter generally refers to partitions only.

Job and Task Management

Jobs and Tasks

To a programmer, a test run is a single job that generates a listing and a set of results. To the computer, this job involves three distinct steps or tasks: compile, link edit, and execute. A task is a single program or routine that has been loaded on the computer and is ready to run. (Before it is loaded, the routine is called a job step.) A job consists of one or more related tasks or job steps.

Within the operating system, the routines that dispatch, queue, schedule, load, initiate, and terminate jobs or tasks make up job management. Note that job management is concerned with job-to-job and task-to-task transitions. Once a program or routine has been loaded, task management supports it as it runs, basically handling interrupts.

The Master Scheduler

The master scheduler (Fig. 19.3), a key job management routine, is the OS/VS1 and OS/VS2 dispatcher. With several application tasks sharing main memory, it is inevitable that two or more will want the processor at the same time. The master scheduler resolves this conflict by following a scheduling algorithm (we'll investigate the algorithm later). The operator can communicate with the master scheduler, and thus override standard system action, perhaps improving the priority of a "hot" routine, or canceling a task locked in an endless loop.

The Job Entry Subsystem

The job entry subsystem (JES), a second job management routine, reads the job stream and assigns jobs to class queues (Fig. 19.4). First, JES scans job control language statements for accuracy and, if errors are encountered, cancels the job before it even enters the system. Assuming valid JCL, cataloged procedures are added to the job stream. A series of tables listing programs by class and, within class, by priority is created and maintained. Additionally, output data are spooled to secondary storage and later printed or punched under control of the job entry subsystem (Fig. 19.5).

Fig. 19.3

Following any interrupt, the master scheduler determines which task gets control of the processor next. The operator can override standard system action by communicating with the master scheduler.

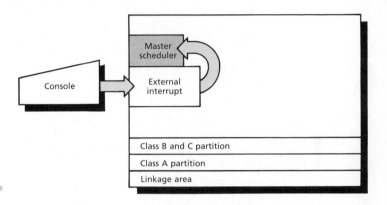

Fig. 19.4

The job entry subsystem (JES) reads the job stream and copies jobs to queues based on their class.

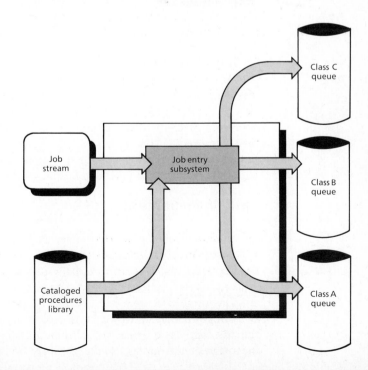

Fig. 19.5   The job entry subsystem also acts as an output spooler.

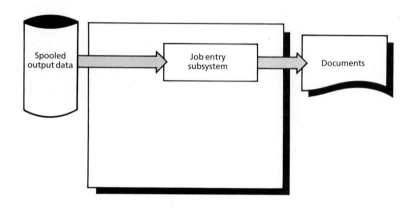

The Initiator/Terminator

Under OS/VS1, there is one **initiator/terminator** for each partition; under OS/VS2, the rule is one per region. Like the DOS/VSE job control program, the initiator/terminator is a transient module that occupies the partition only when needed. As a partition becomes available, the initiator/terminator reads the next job step from a class queue and loads it into memory (Fig. 19.6). The terminator takes control when the task ends. Because the initiator/terminator starts and ends tasks (two obvious transition points), it, too, is part of job management.

At SYSGEN or IPL time, a specific job class (or classes) is associated with each partition or region. The partition's initiator/terminator considers only the designated job class queue or queues. Note that the job entry subsystem works with the complete job, reading all the job stream statements and enqueueing them, while the initiator/terminator concentrates on individual tasks, reading one at a time from its job class queue, loading it, and, following task completion, cleaning up the partition.

Task Management

Task management supports a program as it runs. A task management interrupt handler routine gets control following an interrupt. After the interrupt has been processed, control normally passes to job management's master scheduler, which selects the next task to be executed.

On an IBM System/370 computer, interrupts are implemented by switching program status words; the old PSW field provides a link back to the task that was executing at the time the interrupt occurred. Following the interrupt, the master scheduler will not necessarily return control to the

Fig. 19.6   Each partition or region has an initiator/terminator. The
initiator/terminator is loaded into the application program
partition, and subsequently loads an application routine from a
class queue. After the task has finished, the terminator routine
prepares the partition for the next task.

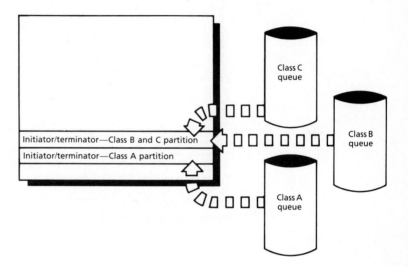

Initiator/terminator—Class B and C partition

Initiator/terminator—Class A partition

Class C queue

Class B queue

Class A queue

original task. Thus, the contents of the old PSW must be stored; otherwise, if another program gains control, the link back to the initial program might be destroyed by a subsequent interrupt of the same type. Task management is responsible for saving the old PSW.

Control Blocks

Job management, task management, and application program routines are linked through a series of **control blocks**. The **communication vector table**, or **CVT** (Fig. 19.7), holds system constants and pointers to most of the key control blocks.[1] Each partition or region has its own **task control block**, or **TCB** (Fig. 19.8). The communication vector table points to the first TCB, which points to the second TCB, which points to the third, and so on, forming a TCB queue.

The contents of a given partition or region are described by a series of **request blocks** spun off the task control block (Fig. 19.9). The existence of

---

[1] The CVT's address is stored at absolute address 16. Thus, the operating system can always find the CVT.

Fig. 19.7   The communication vector table holds the addresses of key
                  system control blocks.

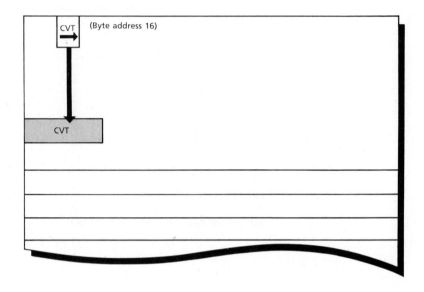

Fig. 19.8   The contents of a partition or region are defined in a task control
                  block. The TCBs (one per partition or region) are linked by
                  pointers.

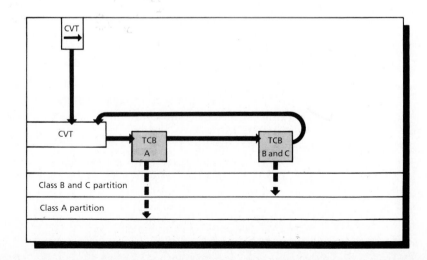

Fig. 19.9

Additional details about the contents of a partition or region are specified in a request block queue linked to the task control block.

Know

Q10

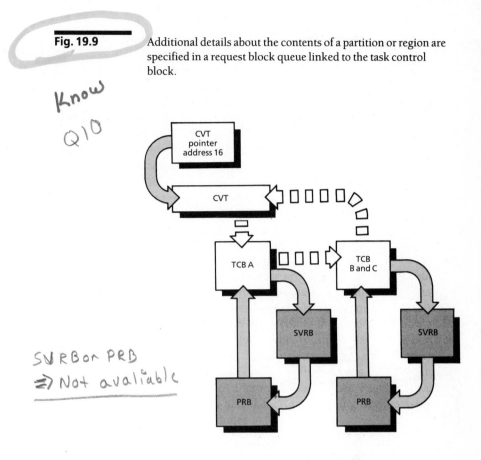

SVRB or PRB
⇒ Not avaliable

an active task is indicated by a **program request block**, or **PRB**. If a supervisor call interrupt is being processed in support of the partition, this fact is indicated by a **supervisor request block**, or **SVRB**. Request blocks identify active modules executing in (or in support of) a partition; if the request block queue is empty, so is the partition. The terminator wipes out these request blocks following task completion.

Dispatching

The master scheduler gets control of the processor after any interrupt. It selects the next task by following the task control block queue. The communication vector table points to the high-priority partition's task control block. If the task in this first partition is ready to go, the master scheduler looks no further. If the task in the first partition is waiting, however, the master scheduler looks to the second partition's task control block. One by one, it follows the pointers from TCB to TCB, starting the first ready task it finds. Thus, on a system with fifteen active partitions or regions, the task at

CVT

the end of the TCB queue can get control only if the fourteen higher priority tasks are all in a wait state.

Let's use an example to illustrate OS/VS1 and OS/VS2 dispatching. The computer, we'll assume, holds two partitions, one for class A jobs and the other for class B and class C jobs (Fig. 19.10). As we begin, both partitions are empty (no request blocks) and a number of programs have already been spooled to the job class queues. The master scheduler has control. To simplify the logical flow, we'll diagram the contents of virtual memory. Don't forget, however, that virtual memory is just a model of the physical system.

The master scheduler's job is to start a task. Thus, it searches the TCB queue (Fig. 19.10). The communication vector table points to the first task control block, which has no active request blocks. Because this first partition is empty, the master scheduler creates a program request block, loads the initiator/terminator, and gives it control (Fig. 19.11).

The initiator/terminator reads the first task from the class A queue and loads it into the partition. (For simplicity, we'll ignore the time delay inherent in reading a program.) After executing several instructions, the

Fig. 19.10   The master scheduler is in control. By following the task control block queue, it has discovered that partition A is empty, and thus loads the initiator/terminator.

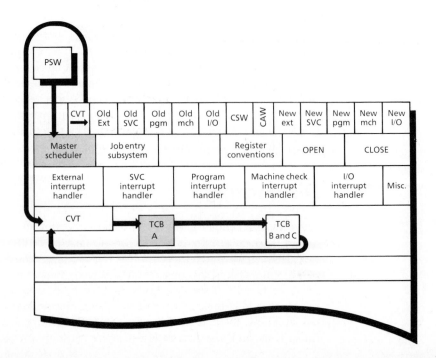

Fig. 19.11   The initiator/terminator loads a task from the class A queue. The
program request block shows that the partition is active.

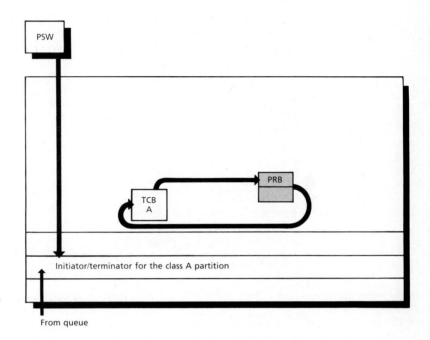

Initiator/terminator for the class A partition

From queue

application routine finds itself in need of data, so it issues a supervisor call
(Fig. 19.12). The resulting SVC interrupt transfers control to the SVC
interrupt handler routine (Fig. 19.13).

The interrupt handler stores the old SVC PSW in the class A partition's
program request block and attaches a supervisor request block to the queue
(Fig. 19.13). After storing the channel program address in the channel
address word, the interrupt handler executes a start I/O instruction, and
then waits until the channel reports its status through the channel status
word. Finally, the wait state bit in the original program's PSW (it's stored in
the program request block) is set to 1 (wait state), and the master scheduler
is called.

Once again, the master scheduler searches the TCB queue. The communication vector table points to the class A partition's task control block.
The partition is active (there are request blocks), but the PSW field in the
program request block indicates a wait state (Fig. 19.14). Since the first
partition's task is waiting, the master scheduler follows the pointer to the
second task control block. Because there are no request blocks attached to
this second TCB, the master scheduler knows the partition is empty. Thus,
the initiator/terminator is loaded into the partition (Fig. 19.15), and it loads
a task from the class B queue (Fig. 19.16).

Fig. 19.12

Once the application task is loaded, it's only a matter of time before it needs input data.

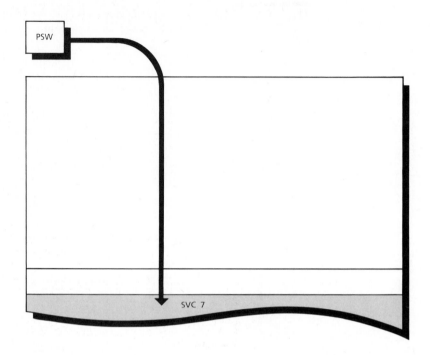

Fig. 19.13

Following the SVC interrupt, the interrupt handler routine gets control, saves the application routine's most current PSW, stores the channel program address in the channel address word, and starts the I/O operation.

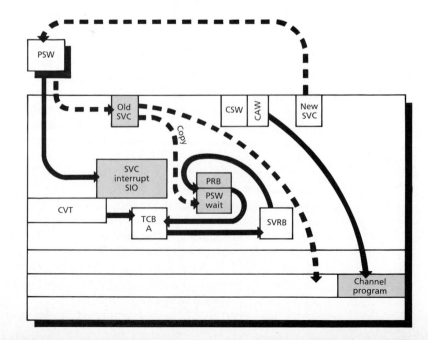

Fig. 19.14   The master scheduler gets control and determines that the
program in the class A partition is in a wait state.

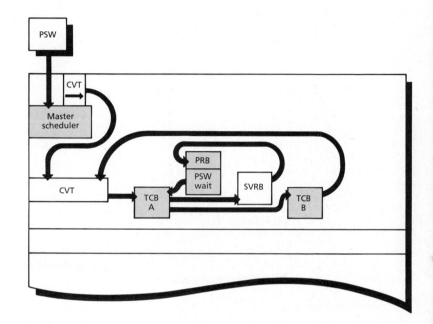

Fig. 19.15   The master scheduler continues following the TCB queue.
Discovering that no program occupies the class B partition, the
master scheduler creates a program request block and loads the
initiator/terminator.

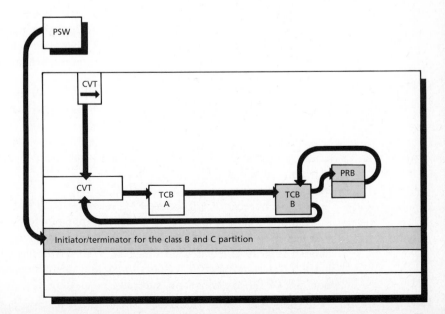

Fig. 19.16   A second application program begins processing.

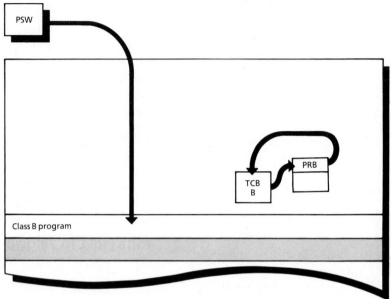

Suddenly, an I/O interrupt occurs. After PSWs are switched, the I/O interrupt handler, a task management routine, takes over (Fig. 19.17). The old I/O PSW field, don't forget, still points to the class B program, and this program is in a ready state; even so, the old PSW is copied to the program request block. The interrupt handler checks the protection key in the channel status word, and thus identifies the partition that requested the I/O operation. By following the CVT/TCB/PRB chain, the interrupt handler locates the partition's most current program status word and resets its wait state bit to a ready state (Fig. 19.18).

Once again, the master scheduler is called and begins searching the task control block queue. The first TCB is associated with the class A program. Because it's ready, its PSW is loaded, and the class A program resumes processing (Fig. 19.18), even though that the class B task is also ready. Note that a supervisor call routine is still actively supporting this partition—you can tell by the presence of an SVRB on the request block queue. This particular I/O operation involved the system input device, and there are a number of unprocessed logical records left in the buffer.

Soon, the class A program is ready to output data to the printer. Thus, it issues an SVC interrupt. As a result, control passes to the SVC interrupt handler (Fig. 19.19), which stores the old SVC PSW in the program request block, creates another SVRB, starts the output operation, sets the application task's PSW to a wait state, and calls the master scheduler (Fig. 19.20).

Fig. 19.17   Following an I/O interrupt, the I/O interrupt handler gets control, saves the class B program's most current PSW, and deals with the interrupt.

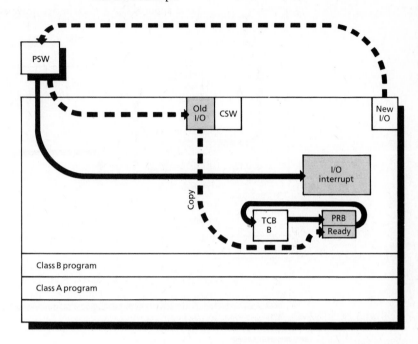

Fig. 19.18   After handling the interrupt, the I/O interrupt routine calls the master scheduler. Following the task control block queue, the master scheduler finds that the class A task is now ready. Thus, the class A routine's PSW is loaded.

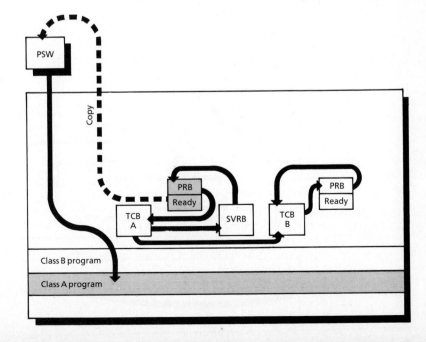

Fig. 19.19 Eventually, another supervisor call returns control to task management.

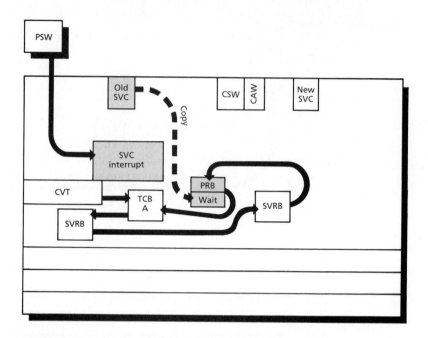

Fig. 19.20 Once again, the master scheduler gets control. The first ready task on the TCB queue is the class B program, so its PSW is loaded.

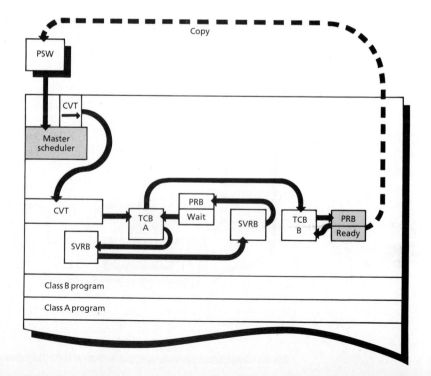

The master scheduler, once again, searches the TCB queue. The program in the first partition is in a wait state, so it moves to the class B partition. The class B task is in a ready state, so its most current PSW is loaded, and the class B program resumes processing (Fig. 19.21).

Eventually, the class B task issues an SVC requesting input data. Thus, the SVC interrupt handler takes over, saves the old SVC PSW, creates an SVRB, starts the input operation, sets the class B task's PSW to a wait state (Fig. 19.22), and calls the master scheduler (Fig. 19.23).

This time, as it searches the TCB queue, the master scheduler discovers that the programs in both partitions are in a wait state. Because no application task is ready to go, control is passed to the job entry subsystem (Fig. 19.24), which requests an input operation and calls the master scheduler (Fig. 19.25).

Once again, all active tasks are waiting, so control is passed to the job entry subsystem (Fig. 19.26), which starts an output operation and calls the master scheduler (Fig. 19.27). The application tasks are still waiting, and the job entry subsystem has both input and output operations pending. Thus, the system settles into a hard wait (Fig. 19.28).

Eventually, an I/O interrupt occurs (Fig. 19.29). The interrupt, we'll assume, is for the class A program, so its PSW is set to a ready state. Because the output data had a blocking factor of one, the supervisor is completely finished with this I/O operation; thus the associated SVRB is removed from the request block queue, and the master scheduler is called. Because the

Fig. 19.21   Thus, the class B task gets control.

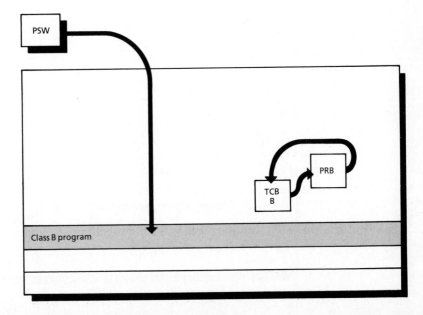

Fig. 19.22 Eventually, the class B task needs data, so it executes an SVC, and the SVC interrupt handler routine gets control!.

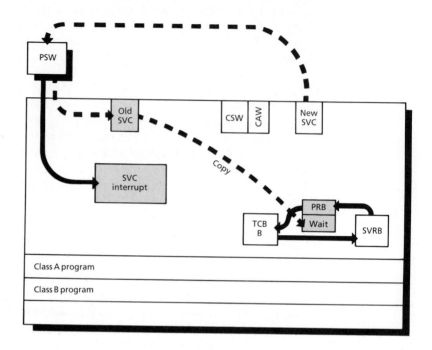

Fig. 19.23 The SVC interrupt handler calls the master scheduler. This time, both application routines are in a wait state.

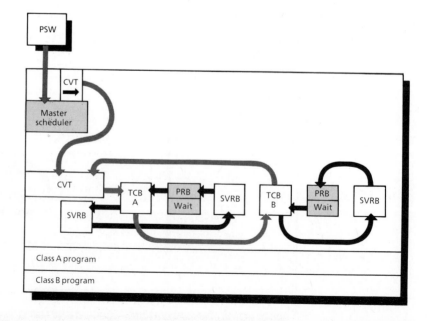

Fig. 19.24 Thus, the job entry subsystem gets control and starts an I/O operation to spool in one record.

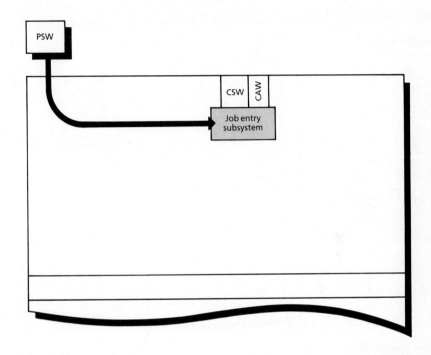

Fig. 19.25 Once again the master scheduler gets control. Both application tasks are still in a wait state.

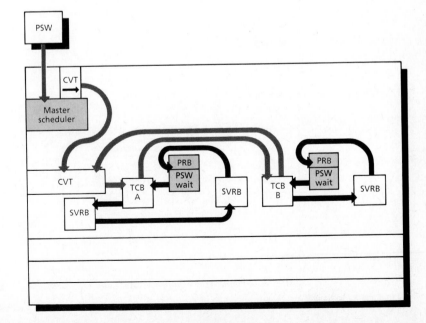

Fig. 19.26

The job entry subsystem is still waiting for the input operation to be completed, so it writes a record from the spooled output data set to the printer.

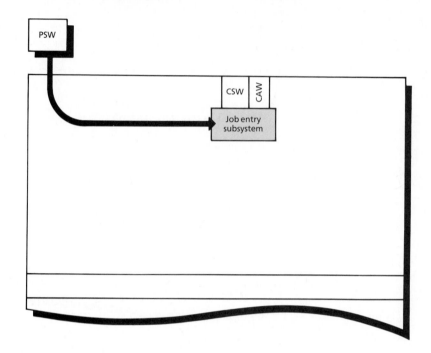

Fig. 19.27

This time, the master scheduler finds both application tasks in a wait state and the job entry subsystem waiting on two I/O operations.

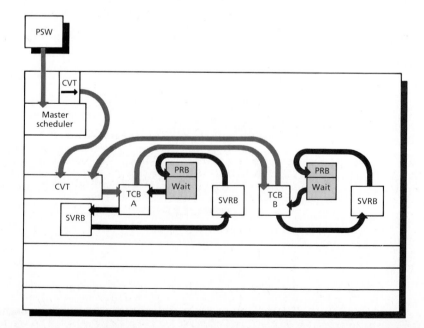

Fig. 19.28

Thus, the entire system waits.

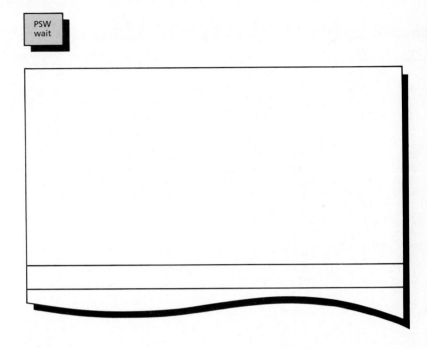

Fig. 19.29

Eventually, one of the pending I/O operations is completed, and the channel sends an I/O interrupt. Because the new I/O PSW is in a ready state, the system begins executing instructions. After handling the interrupt, the task management routine sets the class A's PSW back to a ready state.

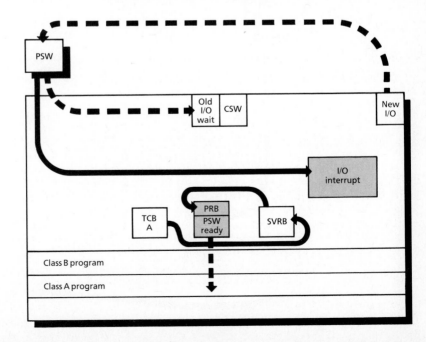

class A task's PSW is ready, it is loaded, and the class A program resumes processing (Fig. 19.30).

Unfortunately, two instructions into the program is a zero divide, which generates a program interrupt (Fig. 19.31). As a result, the program interrupt handler gets control, prepares a dump, and calls the partition's terminator. The terminator (Fig. 19.32) erases the links to the partition's request blocks and calls the master scheduler.

Once again, the master scheduler searches the TCB queue. Because there are no requests blocks, the first partition must be empty (Fig. 19.33). Thus, the initiator/terminator is loaded into the class A partition, and the system moves on to its next task.

Note how predictable the dispatching process is. Following any interrupt, the master scheduler gets control. It finds the address of the first task control block in the communication vector table. Pointers link the TCBs in a fixed sequence. The master scheduler follows the chain of TCB pointers, assigning control of the processor to the first ready task it finds.

Fig. 19.30   The master scheduler finds a ready state PSW and loads it. Thus, the class A task resumes processing.

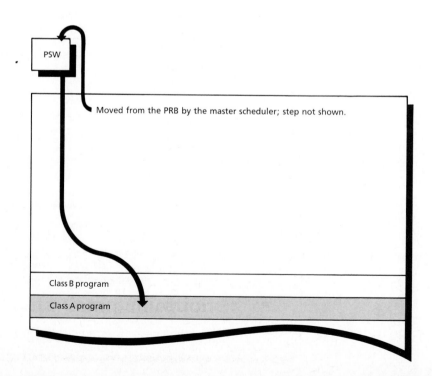

Fig. 19.31   The class A routine executes a zero divide. The resulting program interrupt gives control to the program interrupt handling routine.

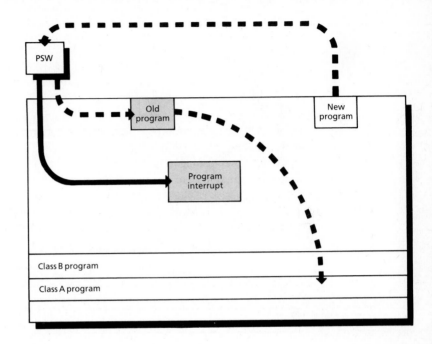

Fig. 19.32   The terminator prepares the partition from the next program by erasing the link to active request blocks.

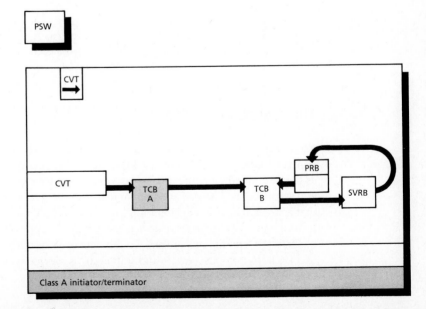

Fig. 19.33   The master scheduler notes that the class A partition is empty.
                      Thus, the initiator/terminator is loaded, and the process con-
                      tinues.

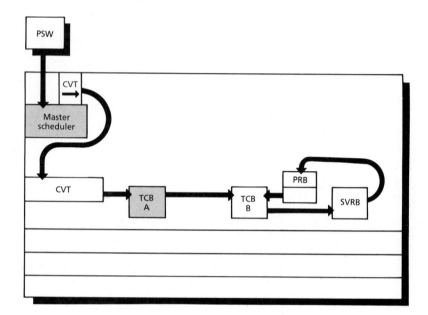

Allocating Peripheral Devices

On a single-user system, an active program has access to all input and
output devices. On a multiprogramming system, however, conflicts are
inevitable and must be resolved by the operating system. To implement I/O
device controls, OS/VS1 and OS/VS2 build and maintain a series of control
blocks and pointers.

The Unit Control Block

Each peripheral device attached to a computer is listed in at least one **unit
control block**, or **UCB** (Fig. 19.34). The UCB contains such information
as the peripheral's channel/device address, its device type, and several sense
and status fields. Each UCB points to the next one, forming a table or queue
that is created at system generation time. If a DD statement's UNIT parameter (Chapter 12) specifies a device that does not appear in a unit control
block, a JCL error is recognized. To the operating system, devices not listed
in a UCB do not exist; each valid unit address, device type, or group name
must have its own UCB.

Fig. 19.34   Each peripheral device attached to the system is listed in a unit control block (UCB). The UCBs are linked to form a queue by a series of pointers.

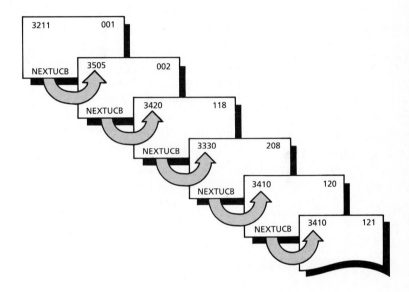

Should a job step require exclusive access to a device, a UCB flag informs other initiator/terminators that additional tasks requesting this device should not be loaded. Other flags mark the device busy, thus helping the operating system to avoid illegal concurrent access by two or more tasks.

The Task Input/Output Table

The **task input/output table**, or **TIOT** (Fig. 19.35), is created by job management just before a task is loaded. The TIOT lists all the DDNAMEs from the step's DD statements. Pointers allow the system to find the other DD parameters and to link each DDNAME to a unit control block.

The DCB and the DEB

The **data control block (DCB)** is a series of constants that describe such things as the access method, the logical record length, the block size, the record format, the DDNAME of the associated JCL statement, and other data characteristics. There is one data control block for each device accessed by the task. The **data extent block (DEB)** is an extension of the data

Fig. 19.35   The task input/output table (TIOT) lists information from the task's DD statements and ties each DDNAME to a unit control block entry.

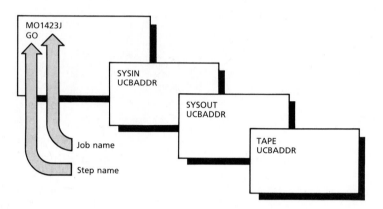

control block. The DCB lies entirely within the programmer's own region and thus is subject to programmer modification. The DEB is not accessible to the programmer.

Open

Logically, a program calls open when it is ready to begin requesting input or output on a particular device. Open generates an SVC interrupt, which transfers control to a task management routine. A key function of the open logic is completing the data control block. Not all data control block parameters must be coded within the program DCB. Some can be coded in the DD statement's DCB parameter (see Chapter 12); others are found on the data set label. The open routine merges DCB parameters from all three sources.

   When the open routine is executed (Fig. 19.36), any parameters coded as zero in the program data control block (uncoded fields are zero fields) are filled from the DCB parameter of the associated DD statement. The DDNAME, remember, must be coded in the program DCB; thus the open routine can find the right DD statement by checking the task input/output table. After inserting parameters from the DD statement, the open routine reads and checks the data set label. At this time, any remaining zero-value DCB fields are filled from label information. (Open *creates* a label for a *new* data set.)

Linking I/O Control Blocks

Actual physical I/O operations are controlled by a channel. The channel gets its instructions from a channel program—one or more CCWs. Chan-

Fig. 19.36   The open logic completes the program data control block
by merging DD parameters from the DD statement and
then merging values from the data set label.

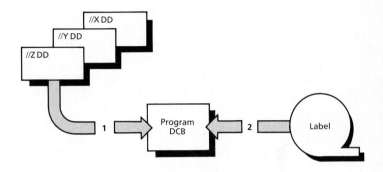

nel programs are found either in the operating system or in the access
method and thus cannot normally be modified by the programmer.

The data extent block is an extension of the data control block that lies
outside the application program partition. It provides a link between the
DCB and the unit control block (Fig. 19.37). The DCB and the channel
program are linked by an **input/output block**, or **IOB**. As a result of these
links, the supervisor is able to find the physical device and its channel
program given only the DCB address.

Fig. 19.37   The data control block is found in the user's partition. Other
control blocks outside the partition create a complete link
between the program, the physical device, and the channel
program.

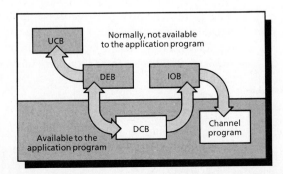

Data Management

Data management consists of routines to access and manage files and libraries. To simplify access to key libraries, pointers to their directories are stored in the communication vector table. For example, SYS1.LINKLIB contains routines used by the linkage editor, and SYS1.SVCLIB holds SVC and other transient operating system routines. Because the operating system can find their directories through the CVT, these critical libraries can be accessed quickly.

The system input and output devices are a part of data management. These two data sets provide an excellent example of the difficulty involved in separating functions into neat, clean categories. Data are placed on the system input device by the job entry subsystem, a job management routine, and moved from the device into memory under the control of task management. Yet, the system input device is part of data management. Direct communication between operating system routines is the rule rather than the exception.

System Generation

System generation is the process of creating an installation's operating system. A key is specifying which modules should be included in the resident supervisor. One possible answer is all of them; after all, it takes time to read a transient module into main memory. Unfortunately, operating system routines take up space, and that space is not available for application programs. The other extreme is to keep most of the operating system on disk. Unfortunately, a great deal of time can be wasted while modules are loaded, and that's inefficient.

Somewhere between these two extremes is the best solution. On a large computer running a variety of small programs, the ideal might be close to the all-in-real alternative. A scientific machine running lengthy, compute-bound programs might lean toward a minimum-nucleus operating system. Most systems lie somewhere between these two extremes. OS/VS1 and OS/VS2 were designed to be general-purpose operating systems, capable of supporting all types of applications.

Modularity is the key to flexibility. Certain routines (the master scheduler and interrupt handlers, for example) and key control blocks must be resident. Other modules can be made resident or transient at the user's option during system generation. In effect, both OS/VS1 and OS/VS2 can be somewhat customized to fit a particular user's needs.

Limits

Multiprogramming exists because of the speed disparity between the computer and its I/O devices. By placing several tasks in storage at the same time and allowing the processor to switch its attention from task to task, much otherwise wasted time can be utilized. The operating system handles the inevitable conflicts.

As the number of programs in memory increases, the amount of system wait time decreases; generally, additional concurrent programs mean greater processor utilization. Eventually, interference between programs becomes so great that it offsets the advantages, but this theoretical limit is rarely reached because IBM System/370 architecture imposes several more practical limits on multiprogramming.

For example, because addresses are only 3 bytes or 24 bits long, an IBM System/370 computer can have no more than 16 megabytes of main memory. When the IBM System/360 was developed in the mid-1960s, 16 megabytes was simply unimaginable—a 512K machine was considered big. Today, 16 megabytes is a limiting factor.[2] Real memory capacity restricts the amount of virtual memory that can be supported. Generally, total virtual memory space is no more than three or four times the real memory capacity; in other words, a computer with 1 megabyte of real memory can support between 3 and 4 megabytes of virtual.

Why not increase the virtual-to-real ratio? Why not support 5 megabytes of virtual on a 1 megabyte real computer? (After all, it's only virtual memory.) More virtual space would mean more virtual partitions. More partitions would mean more application programs concurrently sharing the processor, and, hence, more throughput.

Unfortunately, as the virtual-to-real ratio increases, a smaller percentage of active pages will reside in real memory. Consequently, the probability that a nonresident page will be referenced increases. As a result, paging increases, and thrashing becomes a problem; in effect, the system spends so much time paging in and paging out that it literally has no time for useful work. The amount of real memory limits the amount of virtual memory.

Finally, each partition must have its own protection key. The PSW contains a 4-bit protection key field. There are only sixteen different combinations of 4 bits, (0000) through (1111). The operating system uses (0000), leaving keys for only fifteen application program partitions. There are techniques for running more than fifteen concurrent application routines on an IBM System/370 computer, however. We'll consider some in Chapter 20.

Summary

This chapter introduced OS/VS1 and OS/VS2, two operating systems designed to run in a virtual environment on an IBM System/370 computer. Virtual memory is divided into a real address area containing the resident supervisor and the page pool, and a virtual address area containing the application program partitions or regions and a supervisor transient area.

---

[2] IBM recently announced several extended architecture computers with a 31-bit address, yielding a memory capacity of over 2 billion bytes!

The line dividing the real address area from the virtual address area is called the virtual-equals-real (V=R) line; the real partitions plus the page pool make up what is called the virtual-equals-real area.

A task is a routine loaded on the computer and ready to run. A job is a set of related tasks. (Before it is loaded, a task is called a job step.) Job management is concerned with job-to-job and task-to-task transitions. Task management supports the tasks as they run.

Job management includes the master scheduler, the job entry subsystem (JES), and a transient routine called the initiator/terminator. The master scheduler dispatches tasks, identifies empty or available partitions, loads the initiator/terminator in an empty partition, and communicates with the operator. The initiator/terminator loads tasks from a library, reading and interpreting the job control language statements from the job stream as a guide. The job entry subsystem enqueues jobs and spools both input and output data. Task management is composed of interrupt handler routines.

System constants and pointers to key control areas are recorded in the communication vector table. The contents of a given partition are defined (in general terms) by a task control block. The specific functions active in a given partition are described by a chain of request blocks spun off the task control block. TCBs are linked in a fixed order, with the CVT pointing to the first TCB, the first TCB pointing to the second, and so on. Internal priority is determined by the master scheduler as it follows this chain. IBM's dispatching scheme was illustrated by an example showing a second or two of computer time.

The unit control block queue contains at least one entry for each physical device on the system. The task input/output table holds information taken from a job step's DD statements and describes the task's I/O device requirements. The data extent block and the input/output block link the channel program, the data control block, and the unit control block. The OPEN macro establishes this linkage.

Data management was briefly discussed. A customized version of OS/VS1 or OS/VS2 can be created at system generation time. The amount of available real memory limits virtual memory size, which, in turn, limits the number of application program partitions. An IBM System/370 computer is limited to roughly 16 million bytes of memory. The 4-bit memory protection key limits a system to 16 concurrent programs (including the operating system).

Key Words

communication vector table	job management job step	task task control block
control block	master scheduler	task input/output table
CVT	OS/VS1	task management
data control block	OS/VS2	TCB
data extent block	partition	TIOT
DCB	PRB	UCB
DEB	program request block	unit control block
initiator/terminator	real address area	virtual address area
input/output block	region	virtual-equals-real area
IOB	request block	
JES	supervisor request block	V=R area
job	SVRB	
job entry subsystem		

Exercises

F19.1

1. Under OS/VS1, what are the contents of the real address area of virtual memory? of the virtual address area?

2. What might be found in the area assigned to the pagable supervisor?

3. What distinguishes OS/VS1 from OS/VS2?   *Transint Modules*

4. Distinguish between a job, a job step, and a task.   *400*

5. Distinguish between job management and task management.   *400*

6. What are the functions of job management?   *400*

7. What are the functions of task management?   *400*

8. What does the job entry subsystem (JES) do? Describe the relationship, if any, between JES and the master scheduler.   *400*

9. The initiator/terminator is a transient module. Why? What does this mean?   *402*

10. How does the master scheduler discover if a partition is free or busy? Mention all the tables, control blocks, and pointers involved in this process.

11. The master scheduler supports operator/system communication. How? (Hint: refer back to Chapter 17, and review the external interrupt.)

12. Add a third partition (for class D jobs) to the example system developed in the text. Explain how this third partition might change the flow of control through the system.

13. Describe the series of control blocks involved in linking an application program's DCB to a unit control block and a channel program. What is the function of each of these control blocks?

14. How are DD statement DCB subparameters and label information merged with the program DCB?

15. OS/VS1 is designed to be a general-purpose operating system. What does this mean?

16. A key objective of a multiprogramming operating system is maximizing the number of different programs occupying memory. With more programs sharing the processor, greater throughput can be gained. Briefly describe some of the factors that limit the number of programs that can run under OS/VS1 or OS/VS2.

Current Topics

Virtual Machines

Operating System Development

Early first-generation computers did not have operating systems. Primarily scientific machines, they were dedicated to a single user who wrote and tested programs at the console. As a result, response time was excellent, but, given the cost of the equipment, the single-user mode of operation was economically unsound.

The first operating systems supported efficient, serial-batch job-to-job transition. Typically, responsibility for running these early systems was assigned to a professional operator. Instead of working at the console, programmers prepared job decks on punched cards, submitted them to the operator, and returned a few hours later to pick up the results. Most multi-programming operation systems were designed with such batch processing in mind.

The objective of batch processing is machine efficiency; ideally, there is always at least one job waiting for the computer, so the computer is never idle. Unfortunately, a batch system is not an efficient program development environment. Imagine writing a program on coding sheets, waiting a day or two for the punched cards to come back from the keypunching center, visually checking them, submitting the deck for compilation, waiting several hours (sometimes, a day or more) for the results, correcting a few cards, resubmitting the deck, waiting a few more hours, and so on. Programming requires concentration. With brief bursts of activity separated by lengthy wait times, it's difficult to write a good program on a batch system.

Time-sharing was an alternative. On a time-sharing system, programs are developed interactively, which is far more efficient. Unfortunately, most early time-sharing systems restricted a programmer's access to system resources, and many supported only a few languages such as BASIC and APL, making it difficult adequately to write and test a large program. Consequently, most business applications continued to be developed in a batch environment.

Modern personal computers have brought us full circle. Once again, it is possible to dedicate a complete machine, and all its resources, to a single programmer. However, although personal computers are at least as powerful as a typical first-generation machine, the definition of computing power has changed. Today's mainframes contain millions of bytes of main storage, execute millions of instructions per second, and support scores of secondary storage devices. Personal computers are simply not powerful enough to support testing and debugging mainframe applications.

The ideal program development environment combines the interactive nature of a personal computer with the power of a mainframe. The programmer has access to a full set of peripherals, megabytes of main memory, mainframe computing speed, and a mainframe's full, rich instruction set. Such environments can be supported on a modern virtual machine system.

The Virtual Machine Concept

Start with a full-featured mainframe. Share its resources among several concurrent users. If those users occupy partitions, regions, or work spaces, you have a traditional multiprogramming or time-sharing system. Take the idea a step further. Instead of simply allocating each application routine some memory and running it directly under the operating system, simulate several imaginary computers on that real computer (Fig. 20.1). Assign each **virtual machine** its own virtual operating system and its own virtual peripherals. Traditionally, *application routines* are multiprogrammed. The virtual machine concept calls for multiprogramming *operating systems*.

Each virtual machine has its own virtual operating system, its own virtual memory, and its own virtual peripherals. Because all the virtual machines run on the same real computer, their access to facilities is limited only by the facilities of the real machine. Thus, each virtual machine has access to megabytes of storage and scores of peripherals, and can execute millions of instructions per second. Because they share a single real computer, program development can take place on one virtual machine in interactive mode, while production applications run on another virtual machine under a traditional multiprogramming operating system.

To the user, the virtual machine is *the* computer; the details associated with the real machine are **transparent**, hidden by the facilities of the real operating system. Thus, much as a time-sharing user can ignore other concurrent users and imagine that he or she directly controls the computer, a virtual machine user can ignore other virtual machines.

A UNIX user (Chapter 16) can visualize an image running on a per-

Fig. 20.1   The virtual machine concept implies multiprogramming at the operating system level. Each virtual machine has its own virtual operating system and its own virtual peripherals.

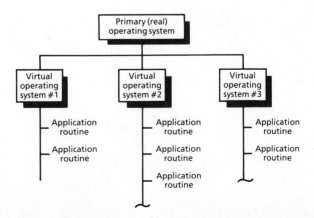

sonal pseudocomputer. Details, such as the number of users sharing a text segment, dispatching, swapping, and peripheral device linkage, can be ignored because the operating system makes them transparent. The UNIX pseudocomputer is a virtual machine. This concept is one reason why professional programmers consider UNIX such a friendly program development environment.

IBM has implemented the virtual machine concept under **VM/SP** (virtual machine/system product). Chapters 17 through 19 discussed IBM principles of operation and two operating systems designed to work in this environment. Let's consider VM/SP in some detail, building on the base established in the last three chapters.

VM/SP

In the early 1960s, the computer industry switched from discrete transistors to integrated circuits. As a result, second-generation computers quickly became obsolete. For example, IBM's System/360, announced in 1964, the company's 1400 line.

The change was not entirely positive, however. Third-generation technology was radically different, supporting advanced operating systems and enhanced instruction sets. Thus, most second-generation programs were rendered obsolete. The manager of a second-generation computing center was faced with three almost equally unacceptable choices: keep the old, obsolete, inefficient hardware; emulate a second-generation computer on a third-generation machine, thus losing many of the advantages of the new hardware; or rewrite existing programs.

Several new operating systems were developed to support the IBM System/360 and its successors (Fig. 20.2). Initially, DOS proved quite popular, but IBM's mainstream operating system was OS. OS/MFT and OS/MVT were released in the 1960s. By the mid-1970s, they had evolved, respectively, to VS1 and VS2; eventually, VS2 became MVS. While signifi-

Fig. 20.2   Since IBM's System/360 was announced, several new operating systems have evolved to support it and its successors.

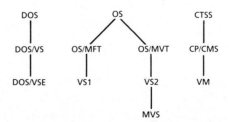

cant improvements were made in DOS, IBM has consistently urged its users to migrate toward its OS products.

Many DOS users have been reluctant to change, however. Programs written under DOS and OS are different, particularly when they communicate with an external device. Consequently, converting a DOS program to an equivalent OS program, even in the same source language, means, at a minimum, changing all the input and output routines. A typical business data processing shop might have hundreds of such programs, and converting them is a significant expense. Although IBM dominates the mainframe marketplace, there are competitors who would be more than happy to pick up dissatisfied DOS users; not even IBM can dictate such a change. Thus, the company has continued to support DOS.

System/360 architecture imposes some limitations on a computer's capacity. Because absolute addresses are only 24 bits long, main memory is limited to 16 megabytes. Because only 4 bits are available for the protection key, only fifteen concurrent application routines can share the processor with the operating system.

In 1964, these limits were irrelevant; a large computer had perhaps 512K of main memory, and running five or six applications concurrently was considered impressive. Today, however, a modern mainframe is capable of supporting more main memory and more concurrent applications than anyone dreamed possible in 1964. These new, more powerful machines require new, more powerful operating systems. However, the aggregate investment in software is thousands of times what it was in the 1960s, and it is unrealistic to assume that potential customers will willingly convert all those programs just to gain speed or computing power. If a new computer is to sell, it must maintain compatibility with applications written under the old operating systems.

If all IBM applications had been written under OS, upgrading to a new, more powerful operating system would be relatively easy, but DOS has proved surprisingly popular. Consequently, IBM faced a problem. Clearly, a new operating system was needed. Maintaining compatibility with two essentially incompatible operating systems, DOS and OS, was considered essential. VM has emerged as a solution.

Under IBM's VM, the **real computer's** resources are managed by a high-level operating system called the **control program**, or **CP** (Fig. 20.3). Normally, application routines run under the operating system. With VM, operating systems are managed by the control program, and application routines run under those **virtual operating systems**.

The result is considerable leverage. For example, on a normal VS1 system, up to fifteen application routines share main memory with the operating system. With VM, up to fifteen concurrent virtual operating systems can each manage up to fifteen application routines, yielding 225 potential concurrent programs! It is also possible to run a virtual control program under a real control program (Fig. 20.4). Imagine fifteen copies of CP, each of which manages fifteen virtual operating systems. That's 225

Fig. 20.3   Under VM, the real computer is managed by a control program. Other virtual operating systems run under CP, managing their own application routines.

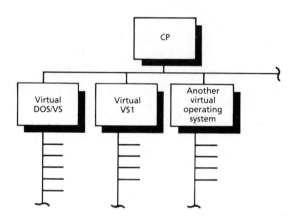

operating systems. Now, picture each of them managing fifteen application routines. That's leverage!

Each virtual operating system manages a virtual machine and controls its own virtual memory and virtual peripheral devices. A virtual machine is functionally equivalent to a real machine. The control program simulates a

Fig. 20.4   It is even possible to run another control program under CP.

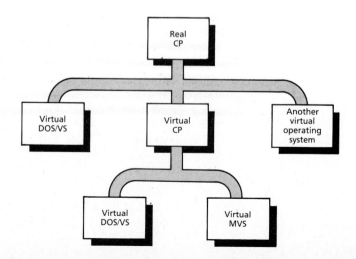

real computer on each virtual machine; consequently, the virtual operating systems can function without change. Any DOS- or OS-based operating system can run under VM.

For example, consider the problem faced by a DOS shop that has outgrown its system. A faster computer, with more main memory, capable of supporting more concurrent application routines is needed, but hundreds of DOS programs exist, and revising all of them is clearly out of the question. With VM, the programs need not be revised. Instead, two virtual copies of DOS/VSE can be loaded. Each one can support up to five concurrent application routines, thus doubling the system's capacity. Additionally, those routines can run on a larger, faster, more powerful computer.

VM's Structure

Under VM, the real computer's resources are managed by the control program (Fig. 20.5). As with any current IBM mainframe, memory starts with several fixed locations—old PSWs, new PSWs, the channel address word, the channel status word, and so on. Next comes the resident portion of CP; it holds key tables and control blocks plus routines that dispatch virtual machines, manage real memory, control paging, handle interrupts, and so on. Some CP modules are pagable; space for them comes next. Finally, the remaining real memory is divided into real page frames. Pages are swapped between the real page frames and the external paging devices associated with one or more virtual machines.

Visualize each virtual machine as though it were a complete computer in its own right. Its virtual memory begins with a set of virtual fixed memory locations; in other words, each virtual operating system has its own old and new PSWs, its own channel command word, and its own channel status word. Following the fixed locations comes the virtual oper-

Fig. 20.5   The basic structure of a VM system.

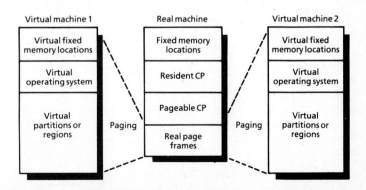

ating system itself. Remaining virtual memory holds virtual program partitions or regions.

On every operating system you've studied to this point, key modules and control fields were stored in fixed main memory locations. Since virtual operating systems are subject to paging (Fig. 20.5), a virtual operating system's modules will *not* occupy the expected, real, absolute addresses. Instead, a virtual operating system runs under the control program in much the same way an application routine runs under a traditional operating system.

For example, consider the fixed memory locations. The real computer has a set of fixed locations that start at *real* address 0. Each virtual machine has its own set of fixed locations that start at its *virtual* address 0. When an interrupt is sensed, which PSWs are switched? The real ones. Interrupts are sensed by hardware, and, as far as hardware is concerned, there is only one real computer. Once PSWs have been switched, the control program's interrupt handler routine is activated. If necessary, CP can then switch (through software) the appropriate virtual machine's PSWs, thus *simulating* the interrupt at the virtual machine level.

The real control program does not concern itself with the application routines. Each virtual operating system is responsible for managing its own processor time, virtual memory space, and virtual peripheral devices. CP communicates with the hardware, simulates the results for the virtual machines, protects the virtual machines from each other, and allows the virtual operating systems to handle the details.

Figure 20.6 lists operating systems that can control a virtual machine. Note that VM can run under VM. RSCS, the remote spooling and communication system, supports remote processing; we'll consider network operating systems in Chapter 21. CMS, the conversational monitor system, is an interactive, single-user operating system that supports program development. It's a key part of VM, and thus deserves a more detailed description.

CMS

Traditional operating systems are not very good for program development. Multiprogramming implies batch processing. Time-sharing systems are interactive, but most limit the programmer to a small subset of a mainframe's

---

Fig. 20.6   All these operating systems can run under VM.

DOS	OS/PCP	PS44	MVS/TSO
DOS/VS	OS/MFT	RSCS	VM
DOS/VSE	OS/MVT		CMS
	OS/VS1		
	OS/VS2		
	MVS		
	OS-ASP		

Fig. 20.7

CMS is an interactive, single-user operating system that controls a virtual machine under VM. It supports an interactive program development environment.

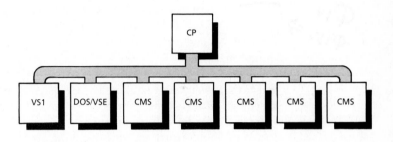

resources. An ideal program development environment would combine the interactive nature of a personal computer and the resources of a large mainframe. Running as a virtual operating system under CP, CMS does exactly that (Fig. 20.7).

CMS, the **Conversational Monitor System**, simulates a personal computer. The user's terminal acts as a console. Each user has his or her own CMS virtual machine, complete with virtual memory, virtual batch devices (a reader, a printer, and a punch), and virtual disk space. Because it runs under CP, a CMS virtual machine's facilities are limited only by the mainframe's facilities. Each user has access to a variety of compilers, a linkage editor, utility routines, and a spooler. Additionally, users can assign work to the CMS batch facility, and thus run two or more independent tasks in parallel. CMS supports a powerful, interactive program development environment.

The Control Program (CP)

Processor Management

The control program uses a time-slicing algorithm to manage the real processor's time. A virtual machine is given control of the processor for a fixed amount of time. When the time slice expires, CP passes control to another virtual machine. Interactive virtual machines (for example, CMS users) are assigned frequent but brief time slices. Noninteractive virtual machines (for example, a DOS/VSE system running accounting applications) are assigned fewer but longer time slices. Each virtual operating system manages its own time, shifting from application routine to application routine by responding to interrupts or by implementing a secondary time-slicing algorithm. Thus, each virtual operating system "thinks" it controls access to the processor.

Memory Management

VM can be implemented only on computers that support dynamic address translation. Memory space is managed using segmentation and paging techniques, with 64K-byte segments divided into 4K pages. A demand paging algorithm controls swapping between real memory and one or more external paging devices. The control program maintains a separate set of page frame tables and a separate set of paging and segmentation tables for each virtual machine.

Paging can be initiated by the control program or by one of the virtual operating systems. If it's initiated by CP, paging is transparent to the virtual machine. As far as the control program is concerned, a paging request coming from a virtual operating system is an I/O operation.

With both virtual and real operating systems initiating paging, a VM system can appear confusing. Sometimes, a simple visualization helps. Imagine a page of data stored on disk. Mentally transfer the page into a virtual machine's virtual memory (Fig. 20.8). Next, move it to the *real* machine's virtual memory. Finally, transfer the page to real memory. Note

Fig. 20.8   Visualize a page of data moving, step by step, from an external device into real memory.

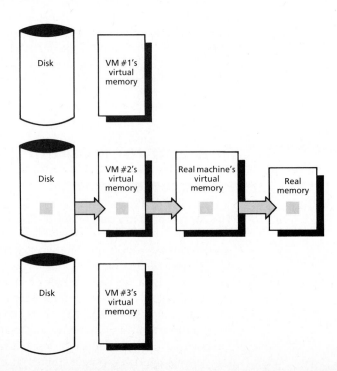

that a single computer's real memory supports a much larger "real" virtual memory, which, in turn, supports several "virtual" virtual memories. That's the source of VM's leverage.

Of course, no computer actually performs all these data transfer operations (that would be terribly inefficient). Instead, pages are swapped between an external paging device and the real page frames, and an algorithm is used to translate virtual addresses to real. For example, imagine starting with a relative address in a virtual machine's virtual memory. Adding the base register and the displacement yields an absolute virtual address. Passing that virtual address through the virtual machine's segmentation and paging tables yields an absolute address in the real machine's virtual memory. Finally, passing that address through the control program's segmentation and paging tables yields a real absolute address. Various mathematical techniques and page address registers can help streamline these computations.

Managing Peripheral Devices

Each virtual machine has a set of **virtual peripheral devices**. All *real* peripherals, however, are controlled by the control program, CP. Some devices are nonsharable. For example, the user's terminal is treated as a console dedicated to a specific virtual machine, and thus becomes the source of that machine's operator commands. Other nonsharable devices, such as a reader, a printer, and a punch (a source of machine-readable output), are simulated through spooling. Magnetic tapes are generally dedicated to a single virtual machine upon request.

One future possibility is running a personal computer as a virtual machine (perhaps with MS-DOS or UNIX as the virtual operating system). On such a system, the personal computer's keyboard, display, printer, diskette drives, and hard disk would be private, dedicated devices; in effect, CP would ignore them. Pages would be swapped between the personal computer's main memory and the mainframe's real memory. The personal computer would be able to function as a dedicated, stand-alone machine or as a virtual machine with access to the storage capacity and computing power of a large mainframe. We'll return to this concept in Chapter 21.

Sharable devices, such as disk, are supported through the **minidisk** concept. When a user logs onto CP, the main control program generates the appropriate virtual machine. For each disk file requested, CP allocates several tracks or cylinders to the virtual machine. To the control program, these disk extents are files; the virtual machine, however, sees them as dedicated, independent "mini" disk packs.

Under CMS selected minidisks can be shared by several users. For example, in a university system, the instructor and each student might have a private minidisk. An additional minidisk is shared by the instructor and the students. The instructor has read/write access; the students have read-only access; the shared minidisk serves to pass assignments and common code (for example, data structures) to the students.

Fig. 20.9

CP maintains a system directory that holds one entry for each virtual machine. When a user logs on to CP, the system directory entry is used to generate a virtual machine environment.

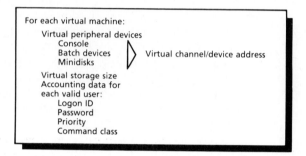

Principles of Operation

Q 17

The control program maintains a **system directory** with one entry for each virtual machine (Fig. 20.9). The entry completely describes the virtual machine environment, and includes such data as a list of virtual peripherals, the virtual storage size, valid logon IDs and passwords, accounting data, user priorities, and each user's command class. Valid command classes are listed in Fig. 20.10; they limit the commands a given user is authorized to issue.

A user logs onto the control program. CP then checks its system directory, verifies the user number and password, and generates the virtual machine environment. Given control, the user can then IPL the appropriate operating system and begin working.

When an interrupt is sensed, control is passed to an interrupt handling

Q 18

Fig. 20.10

A user's command class indicates the commands he or she is permitted to issue.

Class	User
A	Primary system operator
B	System resource operator
C	System programmer
D	Spooling operator
E	Systems analyst
F	Service representative
G	General user
H	Reserved for IBM use

routine in the control program. Interrupts, remember, are sensed by hardware, which switches PSWs stored in fixed memory locations. Since only CP controls real memory, it follows that the addresses of CP's interrupt handling routines are stored in the real new PSW fields. Consequently, a CP routine gets control following any interrupt.

Normally, the control program passes the interrupt to the virtual operating system by copying the appropriate old PSW's contents into the virtual machine's old PSW field, and then loading the virtual machine's new PSW. Other relevant fields, such as the channel status word or channel address word, are also copied if necessary. When the virtual operating system's interrupt handler gets control, its fixed memory locations contain exactly what they would have held had its virtual machine sensed the interrupt. Thus, as far as the virtual machine is concerned, the control program's manipulations are transparent.

Privileged instructions, such as SIO, are used to start or control *physical* I/O operations. Because a virtual machine has no physical peripherals (only virtual, imaginary peripherals), it cannot be allowed to directly control physical I/O. Consequently, the control program traps privileged instructions and performs the requested physical I/O operations itself. It then simulates the results and returns control to the appropriate virtual machine.

Virtual operating systems run under CP in the control program's *problem* state. (Normally, an operating system runs in supervisory state.) Privileged instructions are illegal in problem state; they generate program interrupts. All interrupts, remember, result in a transfer of control to a CP interrupt handler routine. If the interrupt cause code indicates anything but a privileged instruction, CP passes the interrupt to the virtual machine's operating system. Otherwise, it reads the privileged instruction and performs the operation.

Each virtual device assigned to a virtual machine has its own virtual channel/device address. For each virtual machine, the control program maintains a list of virtual devices and their real channel/device equivalents. The virtual peripheral device address can be any valid channel/device address; it need not match the real device address. When an I/O operation is requested, the control program extracts the virtual channel/device address, finds the associated real channel/device address in the table, substitutes it, and performs the operation. Results are then reported back to the virtual operating system using the virtual address.

Does this mean that application programs on a virtual machine can issue their own privileged instructions? No. Each virtual operating system has its own problem state bit. When it issues a privileged instruction, a program interrupt is generated because the virtual operating system runs in the *real* operating system's problem state. The control program checks the *virtual* machine's problem state bit. If it's 0 (supervisor state), the virtual operating system must have issued the privileged instruction, and that's legal. If, however, the problem state bit is 1, an application routine issued the privileged instruction, and that's illegal. Thus, the interrupt is passed back to the virtual operating system for handling.

A New Standard

The virtual machine concept solves a number of problems. It supports a program development environment that combines access to the full power of a mainframe with the response of a personal computer. It provides an efficient means of increasing the number of levels of multiprogramming while protecting customers' software investments. Compatibility with existing operating systems is a real key, because it allows a customer to move up to more powerful hardware without changing operating environments.

VM is particularly valuable for testing. For example, with VM, it is possible to test an operating system without dedicating a computer to the task (and thus postponing other work). When application routines are modified, the old and new versions can be tested in parallel. Another, related opportunity is running parallel production and development systems.

There are, of course, some disadvantages. Time-dependent code is illegal on a virtual machine, and channel command words can no longer be dynamically modified simply because the virtual operating system no longer controls real peripherals. However, time-dependent code and dynamically modified CCWs are no longer considered acceptable programming practice; these restrictions generally apply only to older programs. More relevant is the fact that VM adds one more level of overhead and thus introduces potential inefficiencies. On a small machine, these inefficiencies could be fatal, but VM is intended for large, fast mainframes.

Traditional operating systems insulate application routines from the hardware. VM's real potential is derived from the fact that the control program insulates the user's *entire operating environment* from the hardware. Consequently, future hardware changes can be implemented without affecting the existing customer base. As long as the control program acts as an interface between the user's operating system and the hardware, even radical changes in architecture will remain transparent. Look for VM to continue as an important operating system for the next several years.

Also, expect more user operating systems to move under the VM umbrella. UNIX (more accurately, IBM's version of UNIX) is a likely candidate. So is PC-DOS (or MS-DOS); the idea of using personal computers as intelligent workstations in a program development network is an intriguing one. VM is remarkably flexible.

Summary

Traditional multiprogramming operating systems emphasize batch processing, and thus are not effective for program development. Time-sharing supports interactive program development, but most time-sharing systems limit the programmer to a small subset of the computer's facilities. An ideal program development environment would offer interactive access to the full power of a mainframe. The virtual machine concept is a solution.

On a virtual machine system, a mainframe's resources are managed by a real operating system that simulates one or more virtual machines. Each virtual machine is the functional equivalent of a real computer, with its own virtual memory, virtual operating system, and virtual peripheral devices; in effect, the real operating system multiprograms at the operating system level. UNIX pseudocomputers (Chapter 16) are one example. This chapter focused on IBM's VM/SP.

Moving from the second to the third generation was a conversion nightmare; because the new machines were so different, most programs had to be rewritten, and this was expensive. Today, the investment in software is thousands of times what it was in the 1960s, and new technology that does not maintain compatibility with existing software is probably doomed to failure. Again, the virtual machine concept offers a solution.

Under VM, a single control program (CP) manages the real computer's resources. Individual virtual machines run under CP. Because CP simulates a real computer for each virtual machine, a variety of virtual operating systems can be supported, including both DOS and OS derivatives. Multi-programming at the operating system level gives VM tremendous leverage, and allows a computer to support an impressive number of concurrent application routines. One key VM operating system, CMS, simulates a personal computer, and thus supports an efficient program development environment.

The control program relies on time-slicing to manage the real processor's time. A virtual machine is assigned a slice of time. The virtual operating system manages that time. When a time slice expires, CP assigns the processor to a different virtual machine. Generally, interactive virtual machines are given frequent, brief time slices, and noninteractive virtual machines get less frequent but longer time slices.

Segmentation and paging techniques are used to manage memory space. Paging initiated by CP is transparent to a virtual machine; CP treats paging requests initiated by a virtual operating system as I/O operations. The control program maintains page frame tables, paging tables, and segmentation tables for each virtual machine. It is possible to visualize a page moving from an external device, to a virtual machine's virtual storage, to the real machine's virtual storage, and finally into real memory.

CP manages all real peripheral devices. Each virtual machine has a set of virtual peripherals. Most nonsharable devices are simulated by spooling. A few, such as the console or a tape drive, are dedicated to a virtual machine. Disk is sharable. When CP generates a virtual machine environment, it assigns disk space to the virtual machine. To CP, each minidisk is a file; to the virtual machine, a minidisk resembles a dedicated drive.

CP maintains a system directory that holds one entry for each virtual machine. A user logs onto CP, which generates the virtual machine environment. The user can then IPL the appropriate operating system and start working.

Interrupts are sensed by hardware, which responds by switching PSWs. Because CP controls real memory, its new PSWs are stored in the real computer's fixed locations; thus, following any interrupt, a control program interrupt handler routine is activated. Normally, CP software switches PSWs, thus simulating the interrupt to the virtual machine; the virtual operating system then handles the interrupt.

Virtual operating systems run in CP's problem state. Thus, when a virtual operating system issues a privileged instruction, a program interrupt is recognized. If the virtual machine was in supervisory mode when the privileged instruction was issued, CP performs the requested operation and simulates the results for the virtual machine. If the virtual machine was in problem mode, the interrupt is passed to the virtual operating system and treated as a program exception.

VM supports an effective program development environment. It allows users to move up to more powerful hardware while protecting their existing software investments. Although it adds another level of overhead, its impact is generally positive. At least for the near future, VM appears likely to be IBM's mainframe operating system standard.

Key Words

CMS	real computer	virtual
control program	system directory	peripheral
conversational	transparent	devices
monitor system	virtual machine	VM/SP
CP	virtual operating	
minidisk	system	

Exercises

1. Briefly describe the ideal program development environment. Why are batch processing systems, time-sharing systems, and personal computers less than ideal?

2. Distinguish between virtual and real.

433 3. Briefly explain the virtual machine concept.

436 4. Real machine details are transparent to the virtual machine. Explain what this means.

5. The fact that two different operating system families, DOS and OS, support applications on IBM mainframes created a serious conversion problem for the company. Explain. How does VM help solve the problem? VM Runs Both

6. System/360 architecture imposes several limitations on a computer's capacity. Describe at least two. Why weren't these restrictions recognized in 1964?   *24 bit address = 16 Meg*

7. The virtual machine concept generates considerable leverage, significantly increasing the potential number of concurrent application routines. How?   *with 15 × 15 system can run insted of 15*

8. Sketch the components of a virtual machine.

9. Sketch the contents of real memory on a computer running under VM.

10. On the real machine and each virtual machine, the contents of certain fixed memory locations are considered important. Each set of fixed memory locations begins at address 0. How is this possible? Hardware deals with only one set. Which one? Why?

11. The real control program simulates interrupts for the virtual machine. Explain.   *Because of time slices*

12. What is CMS? Why is CMS considered an important component of IBM's VM/SP?   *438* *4*

13. Briefly explain how the control program manages the real processor's time.   *Demand Paging*

14. Explain how memory is managed under VM.   *SEG & PAGINGs* *440*

15. Briefly explain paging under VM.   *440*

16. Distinguish between a real peripheral and a virtual peripheral. How does VM handle nonsharable devices? Explain the minidisk concept.

17. Explain how the control program keeps track of its various virtual machine environments.   *SPOOL Queue* *442*

18. Explain how interrupts are handled under VM.   *442*

19. Explain how the control program traps privileged instructions. Why is this necessary?

20. Why is the virtual machine concept so useful?   *444*

Networks and Distributed Systems

Why Distributed Systems?

On most early data processing systems all the hardware was located in a single room. Unfortunately, however, the data were often generated and the results utilized throughout the organization. Initially, couriers (and even the post office) served as data collection and distribution services, but they were simply too slow. Thus, data communication became an early data processing concern.

Traditional time-sharing systems were among the first to link user terminals to a central computer by telephone lines or other communication media. With numerous users concurrently sharing a single mainframe, time-sharing supports relatively low-cost, interactive data entry, scientific problem solving, program development, and central data base access, and has proved particularly valuable in educational settings. However, most time-sharing systems limit a user's access to the computer's facilities, and for large-scale data processing applications, the cost of maintaining a line while a clerk types numerous input transactions is prohibitive.

Remote job entry (RJE) is a common solution for applications requiring transmission of a great deal of data. Instead of individual terminals, an RJE station equipped with a card reader and a line printer is placed at the remote site. Source data are keypunched, read as a batch, and transmitted to the central computer. (Today, key-to-disk or key-to-tape units often replace the keypunch.) Later, results are returned to the remote site and printed. Because a link is established only when data are actually being transferred, remote job entry saves communication costs.

Modern networks consist of two or more *computers* linked by communication lines. With networking, key resources (such as expensive peripherals or a central data base) can be shared. On some jobs, independent tasks can be processed, in parallel, on two or more computers, thus speeding up processing. When necessary, tasks can be shifted between processors, thus helping the system balance its workload. The redundancy offered by the network's various computers improves system reliability—if one machine goes down, another can take its place. Finally, networks support electronic mail, electronic bulletin boards, and similar communication services.

Recently, the declining cost of microcomputers has prompted many organizations to replace their terminals with intelligent workstations. A microcomputer has considerable stand-alone computing power, but can't quite match a mainframe. Linking microcomputers to a mainframe via a network gives the user both personal computer convenience and access to mainframe facilities. Often, intelligent workstations run as virtual machines under a modern virtual machine operating system.

Data Communication

Clearly, there are many reasons for communicating data. Unfortunately, several things happen to electronic signals when they move through a wire or some other medium. First, much as a bicycle coasts to a stop on a level

Fig. 21.1   A signal tends to lose intensity or die down due to the resistence of the medium. Eventually, noise overwhelms the signal, and the data are lost.

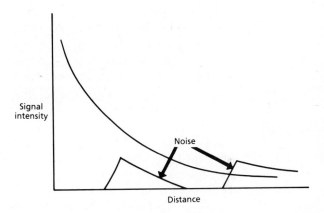

surface, the signal tends to lose intensity or die down as distance increases (Fig. 21.1). At the same time, it picks up interference, called noise. If you've ever listened to a distant station on a car radio, you've experienced both phenomena. As you drive away from the source, the signal weakens and the static increases, until, eventually, the noise overwhelms the signal.

Signal degradation and noise combine to limit the distance over which data can be transmitted. Special shielded cables help to minimize noise, but **local** data transmission between two devices linked by a wire is limited to little more than a mile or two. When the separation is such that data cannot be directly transmitted between two devices, they are considered **remote**. Communication between remote devices is possible only if the signal is boosted (to increase its strength), or filtered (to decrease noise), or both.

The distinction between local and remote is not simply defined by linear distance. For example, if a terminal is linked to a computer by telephone lines, that terminal is considered remote, even if it is physically located in the same room as the computer. The key is the path the data actually follow, not the shortest potential distance.

Analog and Digital

Some signals are easier to boost and filter than others. One of the simplest techniques is to transmit a carrier signal, such as the sine wave pictured in Fig. 21.2. Data are represented by changing the carrier signal's amplitude or frequency. Most noise will appear nonstandard and can thus be filtered. Various amplification techniques can be used to boost the signal.

A sine wave represents data in analog form. We use analogs every day. The height of a column of mercury in a thermometer isn't the temperature,

Fig. 21.2   Data can be transmitted in the context of a carrier signal such as
                    this sine wave. Values are represented by selectively varying the
                    carrier signal.

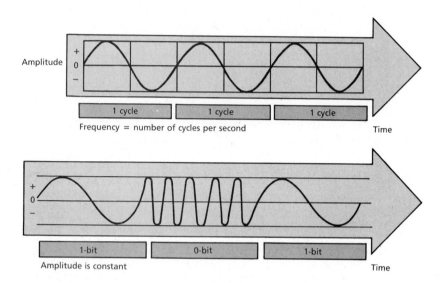

but it represents the temperature. The position of a needle on your automobile's control panel isn't speed, but it represents speed. A continuous wave passing over a communication medium isn't the actual data, but it is analogous to the data.

Inside a computer, data are stored in digital form as discrete pulses of current, 0s and 1s. Analog and digital data are different; thus, computers and analog communication lines are electronically incompatible. When data move from a computer (or a terminal) to a communication line, they must be changed from digital to analog form, a process called modulation. When they move from the line to a computer, they must be converted back (demodulation). This conversion is performed by a data set or modem (*modulator/demodulator*) placed at each end of the line (Fig. 21.3).

When the telephone was first invented, the technology to transmit and receive digital signals did not exist, so most early communication facilities were analog. Because of the capital investment in telephone lines and switching hardware, many local telephone systems continue to use analog technology. However, long-distance lines and other modern media are primarily digital. With a digital line, data can be transmitted as discrete pulses, and modems are not necessary.

Communication Media

Perhaps the best known communication medium is the telephone system. A standard, voice-grade line can support both voice and data communication, transmitting roughly 2400 bits per second (2400 baud). Special hardware

Fig. 21.3   A data set or modem placed at each end of a communication line
converts data from digital to analog form and back again.

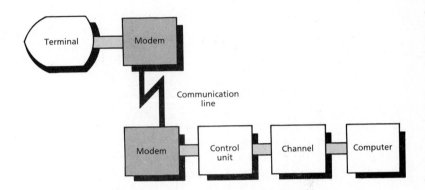

can be used to transmit at 4800, 7200, or 9600 baud, and wide-band
channels with speeds ranging from 19,200 to over 1 million baud can be
leased. The telephone network is a public utility. Most people pay a set
monthly fee, and an additional charge for each long-distance call. Leasing a
private line is an alternative to dial-up service.

Not everyone uses the telephone system, however. Microwave is one
option. Unfortunately, microwaves are restricted to a line of sight—they
won't pass through solid matter. Because the earth curves, long-distance
microwave transmission requires expensive relay stations or satellites (Fig.
21.4). Because a satellite has an unrestricted line of sight to a significant
part of the earth's surface, microwaves can be transmitted between widely
separated points. By linking two or more satellites, worldwide communications are possible.

Fiber optics represents an interesting alternative to traditional copper
wires, with laser pulses moving over fine glass fibers. The laser pulses don't
degrade as quickly as electronic signals, and noise is greatly reduced. Also,
the glass fibers have considerably more data transmission capacity than an
equivalent cross section of copper wire.

Fig. 21.4   Microwave data transmission is limited to a line of sight.
Long-distance microwave transmission requires relay stations or
satellites.

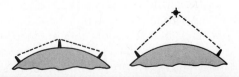

A great deal of data communication takes place within an organization. Rather than paying the telephone company or some other vendor for the use of public facilities, many firms have created their own local area networks. Although the geographic area covered by such networks is limited, they can save a great deal of money.

Trying to distinguish all these media can be confusing. This book is about operating systems, not telecommunications; thus, we'll use the general term **line** to mean any data communication medium.

Switching

In the simplest form of data communication, a permanent line links points A and B. More realistically, particularly when a public network is used, there are several optional paths between any two points. The act of establishing a link is called switching. On circuit switching systems, a fixed connection is made for the life of a task; for example, a physical link might be maintained from the time a user logs on until he or she issues an explicit termination command such as logoff. With message switching, a link is established for each discrete transmission. For example, on a time-sharing system, a new link might be assigned for each transaction.

Packet switching is a good choice for high-volume data communication. Start with a message. Break it into small units called packets. Flowing over the packet switching medium is a continuous stream of such packets. A network computer monitors the line and, when an opening is sensed, inserts a packet into the message stream. Eventually, all the packets making up a single message are flowing over the line (although they are probably not contiguous). Eventually, another computer extracts the packets, reassembles the message, and sends it on its way.

Circuit switching is relatively inefficient, because the line's potential for transmitting data is wasted between transactions. Message switching does a better job of utilizing the line's capacity, but the dynamic nature of this technique requires more sophisticated equipment. Packet switching is efficient, but relies on special computers to monitor and manage the line.

Protocols

At a minimum, data communication involves a medium and two devices. One problem is the speed disparity between these components. For example, consider a terminal linked to a mainframe by a telephone line. The terminal (at least for input) is limited to typing speed—a few characters per second. A typical telephone line can transmit at 2400 baud; assuming 8-bit characters, that's 300 characters per second. A mainframe can process millions of characters per second. The data communication system must adjust for the relative speeds of its components.

A second problem arises from the asynchronous operation of the components; in other words, they are independent, and each one is controlled by its own internal clock. With bits moving at high rates of speed, even minor timing discrepancies can mean lost data. Since they do not share a common clock, independent devices must be synchronized before they can begin communicating.

Additional timing problems are caused by the communication lines themselves. Although electronic communication seems instantaneous, it isn't; data take a measurable amount of time to move from point A to point B, and the time varies with distance. Consequently, if one message is transmitted directly between New York and Boston, and a second goes by way of Los Angeles, transmission times will differ. This complicates synchronization.

As if this isn't enough, the computers and related hardware manufactured by different companies are often incompatible. For example, some use the ASCII code, others EBCDIC to represent characters. Parity rules and word sizes can vary, and different machines use different internal representations for numeric data.

As a result of these (and other) differences, data communication involves more than simply connecting components. Establishing a link means following a precise **protocol**. Often, the first step is exchanging a predefined set of signals (handshaking) that allow the components to identify each other and synchronize their signals. Some protocols also define buffering rules, and most specify a message format.

Several standards have been developed. The International Standards Organization (ISO) has an Open System Interconnection (OSI) standard that specifies seven levels ranging from the user interface to the line interface. The Consultative Committee for International Telephony and Telegraphy (CCITT) recommendation X.25 specifies a user interface that has been included in several broader standards. Many organizations have established their own protocols, including IBM (SNA, or system network architecture) and Digital Equipment Corporation (DNA, or digital network architecture).

Communicating with a Single Mainframe

On a time-sharing system, users at terminals (both local and remote) communicate with a single mainframe. Remote job entry involves a batch terminal linked to a central computer. On such systems, the mainframe's processor is the only intelligent component. (A network of intelligent workstations running as virtual machines under a mainframe operating system is a special case; we'll ignore it for the moment.)

Occasionally, the entire mainframe is dedicated to data communication. More often, time-sharing runs in a single partition or region (Fig. 21.5), with a **data communication monitor** managing the partition and serving as an interface to the communication media, polling terminals and performing necessary protocol functions (Fig. 21.6).

Partition management involves controlling a user's access to processor time, memory space, and peripheral devices. (In effect, the data communication monitor serves as a virtual operating system in its own partition.)

Fig. 21.5   On many time-sharing and remote job entry systems, a data
                          communication monitor manages a partition and serves as an
                          interface to the communication lines.

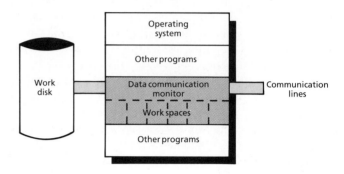

Generally, each user is assigned a limited amount of disk space. When the
user logs on, the data communication monitor checks his or her user
number and password, assigns a workspace, and loads relevant code from
disk. Between transactions, the monitor rolls the workspace out to disk,
and reloads it when the next transaction arrives.

Normally, the processor's time is managed through time-slicing. The
data communication monitor maintains a queue of ready tasks. The processor is assigned to a particular user task for a single time slice. Eventually,
the task either requests the monitor's support or exceeds its time allotment,
and control is given to the next user task on the queue.

Generally, a user is restricted to his or her own terminal and disk space;
the data communication monitor maintains a table of assigned devices. On
many systems, results can be spooled for eventual printer output.

In addition to managing the partition, the data communication moni-

Fig. 21.6   A data communication monitor polls terminals, performs
                          protocol functions, and manages a partition.

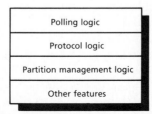

tor serves as a link to the communication medium. Often, the monitor establishes communication with an individual terminal through **polling**. Picture a user typing a transaction. As characters are typed, they enter a buffer. Eventually, the user indicates the end of the message by pressing the enter or return key.

Meanwhile, the data communication monitor goes through a list of terminals, one by one, sending polling signals. If, when a terminal receives a polling signal, the user has already pressed enter, the terminal returns an acknowledgment, and a link is established. If, however, the user is still typing or thinking, no acknowledgment is returned. Thus, the data communication monitor polls its next terminal.

Establishing a link with a terminal means following a protocol. Although protocol management seems relatively trivial, it does require some intelligence. Often, protocol logic is part of the data communication monitor.

Polling and protocol management are I/O operations, and a processor is at its least efficient when performing I/O. Thus, the responsibility for polling terminals and executing protocol logic is often assigned to a front-end device or transmission control unit (Fig. 21.7). Generally, the front-

Fig. 21.7   Responsibility for polling terminals and executing protocol logic is often assigned to a front-end device.

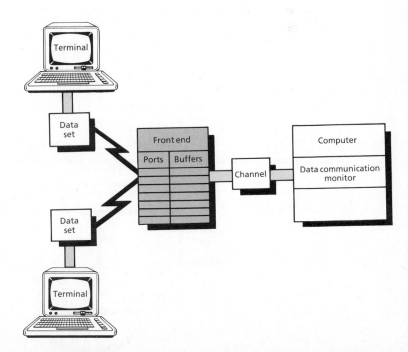

end device consists of a series of ports (complete with necessary modem circuitry) and associated buffers. Each communication line is linked to a port. As characters are typed, they flow across the line and into the buffer. Pressing enter or return marks the end of a message.

Note that the data communication monitor still polls users, but, instead of polling their terminals, it polls their buffers in the front-end device. Thus, the mainframe is not affected by communication time delays; it always communicates at computer speed.

Polling and protocol management require some intelligence. Thus, the front-end must contain at least a rudimentary processor and the software (or firmware) necessary to control it. In effect, the logic for these two functions can be implemented in data communication monitor routines, in a front-end program, or as part of the front-end device's hardware. It is not at all unusual for well-tested, highly repetitive operating system or system software functions to migrate to hardware.

Networks

On a single-computer system, the processor is the only source of intelligence. A **network** consists of two or more computers linked by communication lines. Because they contain more than one intelligent component, networks are inherently more complex than single-computer systems.

Fig. 21.8   A computer network covers a large geographic area, and thus involves remote data communication. Generally, special communication processors control access to the network.

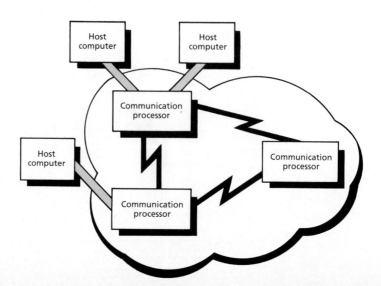

Fig. 21.9   Local area networks (LANs) link computers over local communication lines.

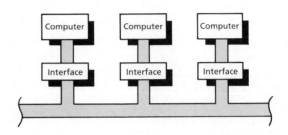

Computer networks (Fig. 21.8) cover a large geographic area and, thus, involve remote data communication. The individual "end-user" computers are called **hosts**. Generally, special communication processors control access to the network and link the host computers to the system.

Local area networks, or **LANs** (Fig. 21.9), rely on local data communication, and thus are limited to a single site. Because they are not limited by public data communication services, they can achieve high transmission rates and lower error rates.

Some local area networks use **collision detection** technology. Picture a network component ready to transmit a message. Before doing so, it listens (electronically) to make sure the line is not in use. Assuming the line is free, the component transmits its message. It then listens (for an interval of time) for a collision (in other words, for noise generated when its message interferes with another). If a collision is detected, the component waits a random interval of time before retransmitting.

Token passing is a second option. An electronic signal called a token is passed continuously, from component to component, around the network. A given component is authorized to transmit a message only when it holds the token. In a somewhat similar approach, several **message slots** move continuously around the network. When a component has a message to transmit, it waits for an empty slot.

Collision detection is most efficient on a lightly used network, because, with relatively few messages, the risk of a collision is slight. As the network's load increases, however, more and more messages will require retransmission, and performance quickly degrades. With token passing or message slot transmission, the risk of a collision (and, thus, the need to retransmit) is eliminated.

Network Configurations

In some networks, the host computers are linked to form a hierarchy (Fig. 21.10). For example, many supermarket chains have installed computer-controlled checkout systems. Individual checkout stations are controlled by

Fig. 21.10   In some networks, the host computers are linked to form a
                        hierarchy.

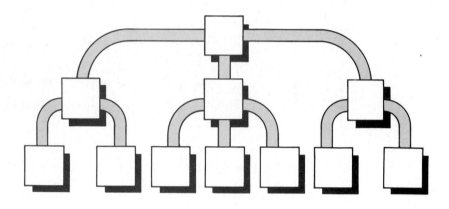

microcomputers that are tied into the store's minicomputer. These minis, in
turn, are linked to regional computers, and the regional machines are tied
to a central corporate system. Data collection takes place at the bottom of
the hierarchy; data analysis takes place at the top.

An option is a **star network** (Fig. 21.11), with each host linked to a
central "star" machine. Occasionally, such networks function like single-
computer systems, with the star communicating with its satellite computers
on its own schedule. Often, the star houses the system's data base.

Fig. 21.11   In a star network, all the host computers communicate through a
                        central "star" computer that often houses the organization's
                        central data base.

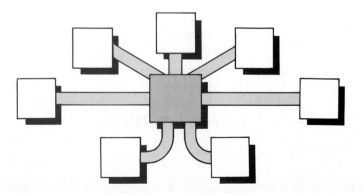

Fig. 21.12   In a ring network, the host computers are linked to form a ring.

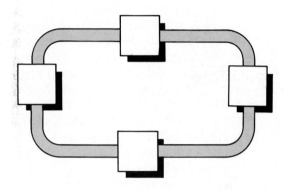

In a **ring network**, the host computers are linked to form a ring (Fig. 21.12). Messages can be passed, from computer to computer, around the ring. Such configurations support excellent backup, allow all the hosts to share data and programs, and make possible load sharing.

Many local area networks use a **multiple-access bus** configuration (Fig. 21.13). A single bus serves to link the hosts and various peripheral devices. Multiple-access bus networks have been developed using collision detection, token passing, and message slot technologies.

Fig. 21.13   On a multiple-access bus network, host computers are plugged into a common bus. Typically, such configurations are limited to local area networks.

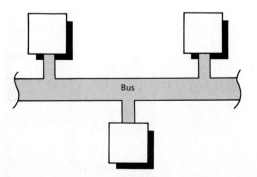

Network Operating Systems

Because networks are relatively complex, special **network operating systems** have been developed to control access to them. Typically, each host computer has its own, nonnetwork operating system, and an **agent process** (analogous to a data communication monitor) provides a link to the network (Fig. 21.14). Note that the individual host operating systems can be mutually incompatible; the agent process provides a common interface.

A single operating system assigned to all network hosts is called a **distributed operating system**. Obviously, compatibility problems are minimized when a common operating system is used. Distributed operating systems are most common on a local area network belonging to a single firm. A workstation configuration, with personal computers running as virtual machines under a mainframe's control program, falls somewhere between the network and distributed approaches.

Dealing with a host operating system, the network itself, and, perhaps, incompatible operating systems on other hosts is a complex task. A good network operating system makes the network and the various host operating systems transparent. Often, it implements uniform accounting procedures, thus sparing the user the need to establish an account on each host.

Fig. 21.14   On a typical network, each host computer has its own, non-network operating system. The network operating system, implemented through a series of agent processes (one per host), controls access to the network.

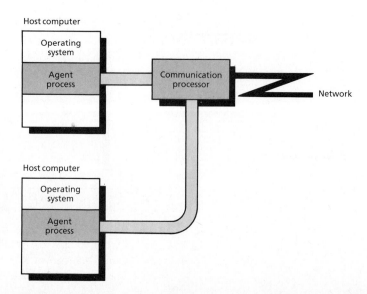

Ideally, the network operating system provides on-line documentation in a consistent format.

One advantage of a network is that resources can be shared. If, however, a user must know exactly where each resource is physically located, that advantage is largely negated. The network operating system makes all resources, even those attached to remote hosts, appear local.

The network operating system also controls the transfer of complete files or selected data elements between hosts (**data migration**). Shared files might be located on a central computer, or each host might have both sharable and private files. To further complicate matters, different computers often store data in different formats. The network operating system performs necessary data transformations.

On some systems, tasks are transferred between hosts (**computation migration**). In effect, instead of moving data, a host performs computations on its own data and transfers the results. Computation migration allows a network operating system to balance its processing load. Assigning parallel tasks to independent mainframes helps speed up computation. Occasionally, a particular task will call for a preferred hardware or software configuration; with computation migration, such tasks can be assigned to the most appropriate host computer. Finally, the ability to assign a task to an alternate processor can improve the network's reliability and provide effective backup.

At a more mundane level, the network operating system supports communication between the system and its users and between individual users (electronic mail). Finally, it is the obvious place to implement security procedures, screening users, restricting access to authorized personnel, and, perhaps, encrypting data to make them more difficult to intercept.

The Future of Networks

Numerous public and private networks are in common use today. Unfortunately, although many standards have been proposed, none has really taken command. Still, the marriage of computer and telecommunication technologies is an established fact and a technological revolution in the making. If you are currently studying a computer-related discipline, you may have already had an opportunity to communicate over a network. If not, once you become a computer professional, you will.

Summary

Data communication is necessary because the data are often generated, processed, and the results utilized in different places. A network consists of two or more computers linked by communication lines. Modern networks support resource sharing (hardware, software, and data) and effective communication (electronic mail), help speed up processing, support load balancing, and improve a system's reliability and backup.

Signal degradation and noise combine to limit the distance over which data can be transmitted. Local data communication is typically limited to a few miles. Remote data communication requires that the signal be boosted, filtered, or both. Early data communication facilities relied on analog techniques. Most modern facilities rely on digital technology.

Several common data communication media were briefly described. With circuit switching, a line is defined when a user first requests it, and maintained until a termination command is issued. With message switching, a link is established for a single transaction; subsequent transactions may follow the same or different paths. Packet switching is a good choice for high-volume data communication. A message is broken into discrete packets. The packets are then placed, one by one, into a continuous stream; at the other end of the line, a computer extracts the packets and reassembles individual messages.

The processing speeds of components linked to a communication network can vary. Generally, these components function asynchronously, and their internal data formats can differ. Consequently, a protocol is needed to establish communication. Numerous standards have been developed.

Time-sharing and remote job entry applications generally involve a single mainframe. On some systems, a data communication monitor runs under the mainframe's operating system, managing its partition, polling terminals, and executing protocol logic. Responsibility for polling and protocols can be transferred to a front-end device.

A computer network involves remote communication between two or more host computers. Often, communication processors serve as links to the network. A local area network supports local communication. Collision detection, token passing, and message slot transmission techniques are options for controlling access to the network. Several network configurations, including hierarchical, star, ring, and multiple-access bus, were described.

A distributed operating system is a single, common operating system used by all the host computers on a network. With a network operating system, each host has its own nonnetwork operating system, with an agent process (typically) serving as a network interface.

A network operating system makes the network and the various host operating systems transparent to a user. Most support data migration, allowing hosts to share data and performing necessary data transformations. Computation migration allows the network operating system to balance the work load and speed up processing by executing tasks in parallel. Additionally, the ability to move tasks from processor to processor improves system reliability and backup. Finally, the network operating system supports necessary security features.

Key Words

agent process	host	network operating
collision detection	LAN	system
computation	line	partition
migration	local	management
computer network	local area network	polling
data	message slot	protocol
communication	multiple-access	remote
monitor	bus	ring network
data migration	network	star network
distributed		token passing
operating system		

Exercises

1. Why is data communication necessary?

2. What is a network? List several advantages associated with networks.

3. Signal degradation and noise combine to limit the distance over which data can be transmitted. Why?

4. Distinguish between local and remote data communication.

5. Distinguish between analog and digital data. How does this difference affect data communication?

6. Briefly describe several alternative data communication media.

7. Distinguish circuit switching, message switching, and packet switching.

8. What is a protocol? Why are protocols necessary?

9. Why are data communication standards so important?

10. What functions are performed by a data communication monitor? Briefly explain each function.

11. Often, a front-end device serves as a computer's interface to a communication line. Why? What functions does the front-end device perform?

12. Distinguish between computer networks and local area networks.

13. What is a host? What is a communication processor?

14. Distinguish collision detection, token passing, and message slot transmission.

15. Distinguish hierarchical, star, ring, and multiple-access bus networks.

16. Distinguish distributed operating systems and network operating systems. What is an agent process?

17. What functions are performed by a network operating system?

18. What is data migration? What is computation migration?

CHAPTER
22

Data Base Systems

The Evolution of System Software

Data communication software (see Chapter 21) has an interesting history. Routines to use communication lines first appeared as access methods. Because the need for data communication was limited, replicating key logic in each application routine made sense but as demand grew, the access method approach became inefficient, and shared data communication monitors were developed. Today, teleprocessing is common, and network operating systems have evolved.

That pattern is not unusual. Initially, a programmer who needed a service wrote a subroutine. Other programmers, impressed by the routine's utility, asked for a copy, so the subroutine was placed on a system library. Eventually, the routine became so popular that it was assigned to an on-line partition or region and concurrently shared by several application programs. Finally, the logic migrated into the operating system.

Most users, and many application programmers, regard their operating system as almost magical—a gift from some higher authority. This is simply not the case. Operating systems were written by programmers, using the same instructions that are available to any application programmer. Studying the evolution of a particular system software routine can help to strip away some of the mystery associated with operating systems. Data base software, the subject of this chapter, is just beginning to migrate into mainframe operating systems, and thus is an excellent example.

Traditional Data Management

Payroll was, for many firms, one of the first computer applications. As an organization grows, the cost of processing payroll grows with it; by automating this highly repetitive task and doing it on a computer, these costs can be brought under control. Because the alternative to computerization might be several full-time clerks, the payroll application is easy to cost justify. Add the advantages of speed and accuracy, and it is simply impossible for any organization with a significant number of employees to justify processing payroll any other way.

Other, similar applications—accounts payable, accounts receivable, general ledger, inventory—are equally easy to cost justify on their own merits. The basic argument in each case is cost reduction: It's cheaper to do the job on a computer than by hand. These bread-and-butter applications formed the foundation of the modern computer industry.

Custom Files

Cost justification makes sense, particularly in a business environment. Unfortunately, with each application standing on its own, efficiency tends to be defined at the application level. The ideal program thus becomes one that minimizes processor time and main memory space. Because computers are at their least efficient when performing I/O, one of the best ways to achieve program-level optimization is to custom-design the data files to fit the application. Thus, a typical organization has a set of payroll files, an independent set of accounts receivable files, and yet another set of files for each major application. The independence of these files, the lack of integration of all these data, can create problems.

Data Redundancy

Perhaps the most obvious problem is **data redundancy**. With so many independent files, it is almost certain that the same data will appear again and again. For example, consider the files maintained by your school. Information about *you* probably appears in several different places. For billing purposes, the bursar's file contains your name and address. These same data elements also appear in the registrar's file, your major department's file, several social groups' files, housing files, library files, alumni files, automobile registration files, and, probably, many more.

What happens if you change your address or your name? The correction will be made on some of the files, perhaps even most of the files, but it almost certainly will not be made on all the files. Thus, the computer will hold two or more different versions of the same data element. With different versions of the truth, **data integrity** is subject to question.

Clearly, if two different values are listed for the same person's address, one of them must be wrong. Why can't the school simply correct the error? Remember that, because the applications are considered independent, the files are independent. Consequently, correcting each file requires independent action. When does the bursar need your name and address? Probably just before the beginning of the term, when bills are mailed. When does the registrar need your name and address? At the end of the term, when grades are mailed. Billing and grade distribution are independent applications with different timing requirements. The bursar and the registrar will update their files at different times. Thus, at any given time, they might legitimately have different values for a given student's name and address.

How important is your name and address to the bursar? If you don't receive your bill, you won't pay it. The bursar considers your name and address very important, and will make a serious effort to see that they are correct. How important are the same data elements to the registrar? If you don't get your grade report, you will be mildly inconvenienced, but a telephone call or a visit to the administration building will usually solve the problem. It's not that the registrar doesn't care, but the penalty for bad data is not as great as it is for the bursar, and, thus, it is not reasonable to expect the registrar to assign the same priority to updating the file.

Your department probably has your name and address on file, too. How often does a department try to contact students at home? Only occasionally. Most departments update their student files during slack periods when the secretary has nothing else to do. If you have moved, your department probably still has your old address. The accuracy of a particular data element depends on the importance the file's owner attaches to it.

When selected data values are clearly wrong, the integrity of the entire file is subject to question. For example, most schools use the number of majors in each discipline as a basis for distributing resources such as teaching positions. When a student changes majors, the new department updates its records as soon as the necessary papers are signed, but the registrar's file may not be corrected until the end of the term. Consequently, the department's and the registrar's counts won't match. Given different versions of the truth, the tendency is to trust neither.

Such problems are not, of course, limited to universities. Whenever files are custom fit to applications, data redundancy is almost inevitable. Given redundant data, different values of the same data element will be found on the computer. With different versions of the truth, how can anyone trust the data?

Data Ownership

Users tend to define data integrity strictly in terms of their own applications. The bursar's office will take steps to ensure the accuracy of financial data. The registrar will carefully verify academic data. Each user group is concerned with the integrity of the data it considers important.

Each time a data element is accessed, its value can be changed. By denying access to untrained individuals, the risk of incorrect data being accidentally introduced is minimized. Thus, given the opportunity, most users will choose to restrict access to key data. As a result, only the bursar's office is allowed to access the bursar's files, and only the registrar's office can use the registrar's files.

Security is another concern. Along with names, addresses, and telephone numbers, the bursar's files contain highly confidential data that simply cannot be shared. If only authorized personnel are allowed to access the files, confidentiality can be preserved. The result, however, is that access to data is denied to all but a handful of people.

Who owns the data? The answer is not always clear. Operations controls the hardware on which the data are stored, and thus has a claim. Without software to create, maintain, and manipulate the data, there would be no files, so systems and programming might claim ownership. The user, on the other hand, is responsible for data integrity, and thus has a right to define conditions for accessing them. All three groups can claim ownership.

To access a given file, it is often necessary to first get permission from operations, programming, and a user group. The result is red tape and bureaucracy. The bursar may have the most accurate list of student names and addresses, but because the bursar's file holds other confidential data, no other group is allowed to access these records. Custom files tend to limit **data accessibility**.

Data Dependency

Programs designed to access custom files are, almost by definition, **data dependent**. Consider, for example, a sequential master file update program. A master file and a transactions file are sorted into sequence. The program then reads transactions, matches them with master file records, and generates a new master file.

Much of the program's logic is concerned with input and output—first-record processing, last-record processing, matching records, sequence errors, and so on. To the user, who simply wants results in the form of valid paychecks or bills, I/O is irrelevant. In addition to solving the user's problem, the programmer is concerned with efficiently controlling data movement between the processor and two or more peripherals. If the data's structure or organization changes, the program will not work. Clearly, it is data dependent.

Often, data dependency is more subtle. For example, imagine a program that ages accounts receivable, applying no carrying charge to bills less than 30 days old, adding 5 percent to bills between 30 and 60 days old, and flagging as overdue bills over 60 days in arrears. Clearly, the program's logic will include a comparison to the current date. To save space, the year is often stored as a two-digit number (87 instead of 1987). What happens on January 1, 2000? The current date will include year 00. Does 87 mean 13 years in the past, or 87 years in the future? Beginning on January 1, 2000, the program simply will not work!

Why not change the date field to hold a four-digit year? Changing the length of the date field means changing the logical record length. Changing the logical record length means changing every program that accesses the file (even those that don't use the date). Clearly, all these programs are data dependent.

Whenever a data file is customized to meet the needs of a particular program, that program becomes data dependent. Any change in the data structure requires a change in the program. As a result, management is faced with three equally unacceptable choices: (1) patch the existing programs, (2) rewrite those programs, or (3) risk falling behind the competition. Simple maintenance is almost impossible.

Actually, all a programmer really wants are values for a set of data elements, and the physical details associated with retrieving them are irrelevant. (In fact, a surprising number of programmers don't understand the details, and simply follow a pattern, by rote.) Although the precise cost of data dependency is difficult to quantify, it is substantial.

The Central Data Base Approach

Instead of creating independent files for each application, why not combine all the data to form an integrated **data base**? Clearly, a single data base would reduce the problems associated with data redundancy and data integrity. Centralized data implies centralized control, and that clarifies ownership. With all programs sharing data, access can be managed by a "super access method" called a **data base management system** (Fig. 22.1). Future changes in the data's physical structure would affect only the data base management system, making application routines independent of their physical data. Let's investigate the central data base concept.

Data Integrity

A data base contains a single value for each data element. On custom files, redundant data are replicated in two or more places, but with a data base, only one copy is stored. Clearly, a central data base almost eliminates data redundancy. For example, imagine that student names and addresses are stored on a data base. If your name or address changes, the data are corrected once, on the data base. Subsequently, every program has access to the correct version.

With custom files, data are generally edited or verified at a *record* level, with the responsible department carefully scrutinizing critical fields. All too often, however, secondary fields are checked haphazardly, if at all. With a data base, data can be verified at the *element* level; thus, responsibility for each data element can be assigned to the department or individual most concerned about its accuracy. Reducing data redundancy and clearly defining responsibility for the accuracy of each data element both help to dramatically improve data integrity.

With custom files, the existence of a single confidential data element is often cited as sufficient reason to deny access to the entire file. With a data base, a data base management system sits between the application routines and the data, and all access is routed through this common module. Typi-

Fig. 22.1   If an organization's data are collected in a central data base, all application routines can access the data through a common data base management system.

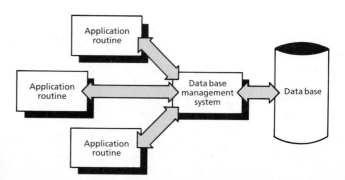

cally, security is implemented at the data element level. Thus, a given application routine can be denied access to unauthorized data without affecting its access to other data. Consequently, data accessability is improved without risking data integrity.

Data as a Resource

The central data base approach clearly defines data ownership. With all data stored in a central data base, the data become an organizational resource, not the property of any single department. In today's increasingly complex world, information may well be the organization's most valuable resource.

Traditionally, the organizational structure of Management Information Systems, or MIS, resembles Fig. 22.2. The Operations Department runs the computer, maintains equipment, and enters the data. The Systems and Programming Department plans, implements, and maintains software. Who is responsible for the data? *Physical* responsibility rests with the department that controls the hardware on which the data are stored—Operations. *Logical* responsibility rests with the group that writes the programs that create and maintain the data—Systems and Programming. Often, the user, who is not even represented on the organizational chart, is responsible for data integrity. Thus, responsibility is split among three groups.

With a data base, centralized control becomes possible. Many organizations have added a new function to their MIS group, the **data base administrator** (Fig. 22.3). Operations is still responsible for hardware, and Systems and Programming still controls software, but the responsibility for data is now clearly and unambiguously defined.

Lying between application software and the data base is a data base management system. It implements the organization's rules for accessing the data. The data base administrator maintains the data base management system, ensuring that it accurately reflects the rules, as defined by company policy.

Fig. 22.2   Management Information Systems traditionally includes two departments: Operations, and Systems and Programming.

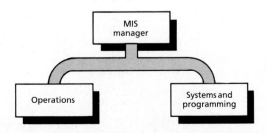

Fig. 22.3   With a data base, a data base administrator is often assigned
                     responsibility for the data.

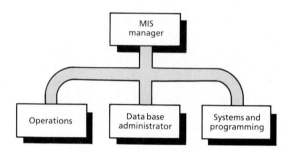

Data-independent Software

The problems associated with poor data integrity and unclear data ownership are well known to application programmers, but data dependency is
more subtle. The programmer accessing custom files is often concerned
both with the user's application and with data access, rarely seeing them as
independent problems. Instead, data manipulation and the user's application are so tightly linked that they become a single problem in the programmer's mind and in the code. Thus, a relatively minor change in the data
structure can mean a major program revision.

For example, if a change in the tax laws renders the payroll system
obsolete, programming sees a need for a new system development project.
Management, on the other hand, sees considerable money being spent to
allow the organization to continue doing what it already was doing—
generating valid paychecks. Management considers such projects maintenance and sees the need to redesign and recode significant parts of the
payroll system as highly inefficient. The argument that an apparently simple change in the data structure can render program logic obsolete does not
impress nontechnical management. All too often, computer professionals
are too close to the data dependency problem to see it.

When accessing a traditional file, a programmer requests logical I/O by
calling an access method (Fig. 22.4). The access method converts the logical I/O request to physical form and passes it to the operating system, which
issues the necessary physical I/O commands. Except for extracting logical
records from a physical block, the access method does not manipulate the
data. Thus, the programmer's logical data structure must match a physical
data structure; in other words, the programmer must know the exact physical format of the data before he or she can access them. This is why a
change in the data's physical structure means a change in the program.

Now, place a data base management system between the application
program and the access method (Fig. 22.5). Although the data base man-

Fig. 22.4   When accessing a traditional file, a programmer requests logical
I/O by calling an access method.

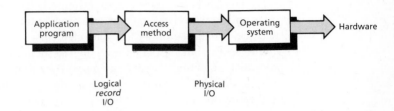

agement system still uses traditional access methods to read and write
physical records, the application routine is insulated from this physical
interface. Thus, the application program can request true logical I/O at a
data element level.

For example, imagine an application program needs an employee's
name and address. It asks the data base management system for a new set of
values for these two data elements. The data base manager accepts the
program's logical request, performs whatever physical I/O operations are
necessary to get the two values, extracts the name and address from whatever physical records or blocks it reads, and passes only the requested
values back to the original program. As far as the application routine is
concerned, it requested and got values for two data elements. The physical
operations needed to find them are transparent. The application program is
data independent.

Consider carefully the difference between true logical I/O and traditional logical I/O. When a program reads a traditional record from a traditional file, that record must physically exist. It might be part of a larger

Fig. 22.5   The data base management system insulates the application
routine from the physical data, and thus supports true logical I/O
at a data element level.

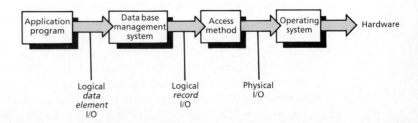

block, or it might span two or more physical records, but every byte, every element in the data structure, must physically exist in the prescribed order. Using the traditional approach, the programmer must accept the entire logical record, as it is physically stored, or accept none of it.

A data base management system supports true logical I/O. If a program needs only certain data elements, the programmer can create a logical data structure containing only those data elements. The data base management system accepts the programmer's logical requests, issues the necessary physical I/O commands, and assembles the requested data elements. It is possible that the logical data structure might match a physical data structure. More often, however, the requested logical data structure does not exist until the data base management system assembles it. Thus, the programmer can ignore the physical data structure.

What if the physical data structure changes? Since application programs are not concerned with the physical data, they are not affected. Rather than modifying hundreds of application routines, the new physical data structure can be implemented by modifying only the data base management system. Thus, the application routines are data independent.

Advantages and Disadvantages

A data base improves data integrity by reducing data redundancy and improving verification and security. Because the data base permits centralized control, it clarifies data ownership. The data base management system insulates the application routine from the physical data, thus promoting data independence. These are compelling arguments for implementing a data base.

No improvement is without cost, however. One problem is efficiency. With a data base management system between the application routine and the access method, I/O operations involve one more level of overhead. There is little question that a well-written program accessing traditional custom files will run faster than an equivalent program accessing a data base.

Unfortunately, efficiency is defined primarily in hardware terms. In addition to execution time and memory, the total cost of any program includes development, coding, testing, and maintenance. A data base helps to reduce each of these costs by promoting data independence. Another concern is the relationships between the data processed by several application routines. With a data base, all applications can share a single copy of a given data element; with traditional custom files, that data element might be stored, redundantly, many times. From an organizational viewpoint, the efficiency argument loses much of its appeal.

There is, however, one legitimate objection to using a data base—cost. Commercial data base management systems are relatively expensive, and the cost of developing the data base can be prohibitive. A typical organization might have hundreds of custom data files, all of which must, in some way, be merged. Additionally, every program that previously accessed a custom file must be rewritten.

These costs are concrete, representing dollars that must be spent now. The benefits—data integrity, clear data ownership, and data independence—are less concrete, accruing only in the future. Management is asked to spend a great deal in the short run for a somewhat questionable long-run payoff. Not surprisingly, many organizations have decided not to change.

Unfortunately, postponing the decision only makes the problem worse. While the cost of upgrading to a data base may seem prohibitive, the cost of *not* upgrading may be even more so. The future computer professional will almost certainly deal with data bases.

Implementing a Data Base

The key to implementing a data base is the data base management system. It allows a programmer to request specific data elements or logical data structures without regard for the physical data structure. In effect, the data base management system creates a custom data structure at the time the data are requested.

Obviously, the data must still be stored on a physical device, and physical records, blocks, or sectors must still move between primary and secondary storage. Most data base management systems rely on the traditional access methods for physical I/O (Fig. 22.6). Given a request for selected data elements, the data base management system identifies the physical record or records containing the data, issues the necessary physical I/O commands, extracts the requested data, and then returns them to the application routine.

Fig. 22.6   A data base management system relies on traditional access methods to read and write physical data.

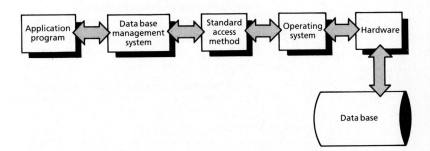

Data Base Organization

The data base consists of one or more (usually, more) related files. Pointers are sometimes used to link a master record to related secondary data (Fig. 22.7). Other data base systems maintain a set of detailed indexes that show where key data elements are stored.

Some data base systems impose a **hierarchical** structure on the data. For example, a university might use a hierarchical data base to store student data (Fig. 22.8), with a student master record pointing to that student's financial, academic, housing, and activity records. These secondary records could, in turn, point to lower level records. Records nearer the top of the hierarchy are called parents. Each parent can have one or more children. The academic record in Fig. 22.8 is a child of the student record. It is also a parent in its own right, with two children.

Generally, while a parent can have many children, a child can have only one parent. This limits the flexibility of a hierarchical data base. On a **network data base**, a child can have many parents (Fig. 22.9). On a hierarchical data base, the data search always starts at the top and works down, through the hierarchy. With a network data base, it is possible to start almost anywhere and move in any direction.

Fig. 22.7   On many data base management systems, pointers link a master record to related secondary records.

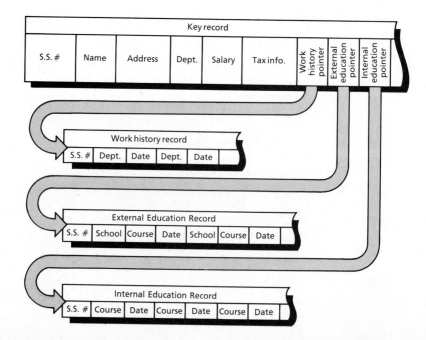

Fig. 22.8   In a hierarchical data base, a parent record can have one or more
children. The data base is typically searched from top to bottom.

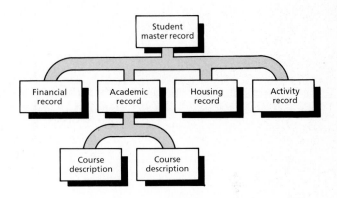

Many current data base systems are **relational**. Instead of relying on
physical pointers or indexes, a relational data base defines the logical relationships between data elements, and uses these relationships as primary
and secondary keys. Often, the data are visualized in tabular form, with a
user selecting a subset or requesting that data from two or more tables be
connected or joined based on some combination of keys. The relational
approach offers significant advantages over hierarchical and network data-
bases, and is rapidly becoming the standard.

Fig. 22.9   In a network data base, a child can have many parents. Thus, a
data search can start almost anywhere and move in almost any
direction.

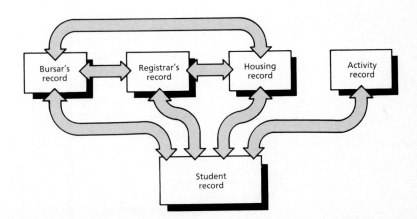

Fig. 22.10   Early data base management systems were little more than
                        sophisticated access methods.

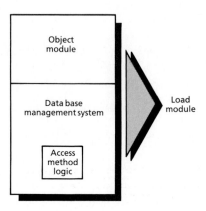

The Data Base Management System

The first data base management systems were little more than sophisticated
access methods (Fig. 22.10). They were physically part of a load module
and supported a single application routine in a single partition. Today, most
data base management systems occupy their own partitions and are shared
by several application routines (Fig. 22.11). Thus, all data base access, from

Fig. 22.11   Most data base management systems occupy an independent
                        partition and deal concurrently with several application routines.

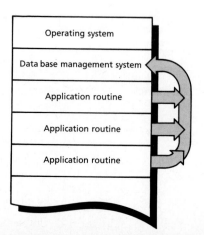

all partitions, must pass through a common routine. The result is centralized control.

Because the data base management system occupies its own partition, the operating system sees it as just another application routine. Thus, any independent software vendor can write and market its own data base management system, and many have. To the computer manufacturer, commercial data base management systems represent lost revenue. Consequently, it is almost inevitable that at least portions of data base software will be tightly linked to the operating system. Independent data base processors, in the form of a dedicated back-end machine, a co-processor in a multiprocessing configuration, or an independent network host, are another possibility.

Software Migration

Like data communication software, data base management systems have evolved from application routines to shared system software, and are now poised to move into the operating system. Indeed, most functions we associate with a modern operating system followed much the same route. There is no great mystery concerning the *functions* performed by even the most sophisticated modern operating systems. They appear complex because they integrate so many logical functions.

An operating system is the application programmer's primary interface with the computer, serving as a hardware/software interface and managing the system's resources. If you understand operating systems, you have a good idea of what a computer can do. Additionally, because they implement so many interrelated tasks, operating systems are among the most complex programs ever written. Consequently, studying an operating system can give an analyst or a programmer insight into the design of any large program. A reasonable understanding of operating systems is valuable to any computer professional.

Summary

Early computer applications were cost justified and developed independently. Often, files were custom designed to fit each application. This led to a variety of problems, including data redundancy, questionable data integrity, unclear data ownership, and data-dependent software.

A data base helps to solve all these problems. By minimizing data redundancy and assigning responsibility for the accuracy of a given data element to the functional group most affected by that element, data integrity can be improved. The fact that the data base is centralized allows centralized ownership and control, often under a data base administrator. The data base management system insulates the application routine from the physical data, so the programmer can focus on true logical, data element I/O. This leads to data-independent software.

There are, of course, disadvantages. Technical people sometimes attack the efficiency of data base I/O, but their concern is with hardware efficiency. Data base management software is expensive, and the cost of creating the data base and modifying existing programs to access it can be prohibitive.

A data base management system allows a programmer to specify I/O at a logical, data element level. The data base management system accepts the programmer's logical requests, performs necessary physical I/O operations, extracts the relevant data elements, and passes them back to the application routine. Thus, the physical structure of the data is transparent to the programmer.

Some data base management systems use pointers to link physical records, perhaps on different physical files. Others rely on indexes. Hierarchical data bases define the relationships between data elements as a hierarchy, with parent structures pointing to child structures. Generally, a parent can have many children, but a child can have only one parent. This limits a hierarchical data base to a one-way (top to bottom) data search. Network data bases maintain multiple links, and a child can have more than one parent. Consequently, a data search can start at any point and move in any direction. Many modern data bases are relational, with the relationships between data elements defined logically, rather than by pointers or indexes.

Initially, data base management systems started as sophisticated access methods functioning in a single partition. Today, most occupy their own partition, where they are shared by numerous application routines. In the future, data base software may be tightly linked to the operating system.

An operating system serves as an interface to the entire computer system, managing all the machine's resources. Thus, studying operating systems provides an overview of all a computer's functions. Additionally, an operating system is an excellent model for any large-scale program.

Key Words

data accessibility	data base	data redundancy
data base	management	hierarchical data
data base	system	base
administrator	data dependency	network data base
	data integrity	relational data
		base

Exercises

1. Why does treating each application independently lead to custom data files?

2. What is data redundancy? How does data redundancy affect data integrity?

3. With files customized to the application, who owns the data? Why? How does this affect data accessability?

4. Programs that access custom files tend to be data dependent. Why? Why is data dependency a problem?

5. How does a data base help to minimize data dependency?

6. How does a data base help to define data ownership? What is a data base administrator?

7. How does a data base help to improve data accessability?

8. How does a data base promote data-independent programs? Why is data independence so important?

9. Technical people sometimes argue that data base access is inefficient. Why? Why does management tend to dismiss this argument?

10. What anti-data base arguments are taken seriously by management? Why?

11. Explain how a data base management system converts logical, data-element I/O requests to physical I/O commands.

12. Explain how pointers and indexes are used to link the elements in a data base.

13. Distinguish between a hierarchical data base and a network data base. Intuitively, which organization seems more flexible? Which one seems easiest to implement?

14. Briefly, what distinguishes a relational data base from a network or hierarchical data base?

15. Where is the data base management system located; in other words, where in memory is it physically stored?

Appendixes

APPENDIX

A

Number Systems, Data Types, and Codes

Number Systems

A decimal number consists of a series of digits—0, 1, 2, 3, 4, 5, 6, 7, 8, 9—written in precise relative positions. The positions are important; 23 and 32 are different numbers in spite of the fact that they contain the same two digits. The value of a given number is found by multiplying each digit by its place or positional value and adding the products. For example, 3582 represents:

```
  3 times 1000 = 3000
 +5 times  100 =  500
 +8 times   10 =   80
 +2 times    1 =    2
                 3582
```

Generally, any number's value is the sum of the products of its digit and place values.

Take a close look at the decimal place values 1, 10, 100, 1000, 10000, and so on. The pattern is obvious. Rather than writing all those zeros, we can use scientific notation, for example, writing 10000 as 10^4. Because any number raised to the zero power is (by definition) 1, we can write the decimal place values as the base (10) raised to a series of integer powers:

$$\ldots 10^8 \; 10^7 \; 10^6 \; 10^5 \; 10^4 \; 10^3 \; 10^2 \; 10^1 \; 10^0$$

A few general rules can be derived from this discussion of decimal numbers. First is the idea of place or positional value represented by the base (10) raised to a series of integer powers. The second is the use of the digit zero (0) to represent "nothing" in a given position. (How else could we distinguish 3 from 30?) Third, a total of ten digits (0 through 9) is needed to write decimal values. Finally, only values less than the base (in this case, 10) can be written with a single digit.

Binary Numbers

There is nothing to restrict the application of these rules to a base-10 number system. If the positional values are powers of 2, we have the framework of a binary or base-2 number system:

$$... \ 2^8 \ 2^7 \ 2^6 \ 2^5 \ 2^4 \ 2^3 \ 2^2 \ 2^1 \ 2^0$$

As in any number system, the digit zero (0) is needed to represent nothing in a given position. Additionally, the binary number system needs only one other digit, 1. Given these digit and place values, we can find the value of any number by multiplying each digit by its place value and adding these products. For example, the binary number 1100011 is:

```
  1 times 2⁶ = 1 times 64 = 64
 +1 times 2⁵ = 1 times 32 = 32
 +0 times 2⁴ = 0 times 16 =  0
 +0 times 2³ = 0 times  8 =  0
 +0 times 2² = 0 times  4 =  0
 +1 times 2¹ = 1 times  2 =  2
 +1 times 2⁰ = 1 times  1 =  1
                            ──
                            99
```

The decimal number 2 is 10 in binary; the decimal number 4 is 100. Decimal 5 is 101 (1 four, 0 twos, and 1 one).

Octal and Hexadecimal

Other number systems, notably octal (base 8) and hexadecimal (base 16) are commonly used with computers. The octal number system uses powers of 8 to represent positional values and the digit values 0, 1, 2, 3, 4, 5, 6, and 7. The hexadecimal number system uses powers of 16 and the digits 0, 1, 2, 3, 4, 5, 6, 7, 8, 9, A, B, C, D, E, and F. The hexadecimal number FF is:

```
 15 times 16¹ = 240
+15 times 16⁰ =  15
                ───
                255
```

There are no computers that work directly with octal or hex values; a computer is a binary machine. These two number systems are used simply because it is easy to convert between them and binary. Each octal digit is exactly equivalent to three binary digits (Fig. A.1); each hexadecimal digit is exactly equivalent to four binary digits (Fig. A.2). Thus, octal and hex can be used as shorthands for displaying binary values (Fig. A.3).

Fig. A.1   Each octal digit is exactly equivalent to three binary digits.

Octal	Binary	Octal	Binary
0	000	4	100
1	001	5	101
2	010	6	110
3	011	7	111

Fig. A.2   Each hexadecimal digit is exactly equivalent to four binary digits.

Hex	Binary	Hex	Binary
0	0000	8	1000
1	0001	9	1001
2	0010	A	1010
3	0011	B	1011
4	0100	C	1100
5	0101	D	1101
6	0110	E	1110
7	0111	F	1111

Fig. A.3   Because it is so easy to convert between octal or hexadecimal and binary, octal and hexadecimal are convenient shorthands for representing binary data.

Binary		
110010101011	000101001000	101100001111
011001100001	100000100011	011101010100
000100000010	011111110000	000010000101
100100100100	100001011111	100000011001

Octal	Hexademical		
6253 0510 5417	CAB	148	B0F
3141 4043 3524	661	823	754
0402 3760 0205	102	7F0	085
4444 4137 4031	924	85F	819

Data Types

Numeric Data

Because binary numbers are so well suited to electronic devices, computers are at their most efficient when working with pure binary. A typical computer is designed around a basic unit of binary data called a word (usually, 8, 16, or 32 bits). Normally, the high-order bit is set aside to hold a sign (0 for +, 1 for −); the remaining bits are data bits. There is no provision for a decimal point; decimal point alignment is the programmer's responsibility. For example, the biggest binary value that can be stored on a 32-bit word computer is

01111111111111111111111111111111

which is 2,147,483,647 in decimal, while the limit on a 16-bit machine is

0111111111111111

or 32,767 in decimal.

Binary integers are fine for many applications, but at times, very large, very small, and fractional numbers are needed. With scientific notation, numbers are written as a decimal fraction followed by a power of 10; for example, the speed of light, 186,000 miles per second, is written as 0.186×10^6. Many computers can store and manipulate binary approximations of scientific numbers called real or floating-point numbers.

Certain applications, particularly business applications, demand precisely rounded decimal numbers. While any data type will do for whole numbers or integers, floating-point and binary numbers provide at best a close approximation to decimal fractions. Thus, many computers support a form of decimal data. Generally, computers are at their least efficient when processing decimal data.

String Data

Computers are not limited to storing and manipulating numbers, however; many applications call for such data as names, addresses, and product descriptions. These string values are typically stored as sets of individual characters, with each character represented by a code. Most modern computers use either ASCII or EBCDIC (Fig. A.4). On many computers, a single coded character occupies 1 byte; thus, the name "Lopez" would be stored in 5 consecutive bytes.

It is important to note that strings and numbers are different. For example, if you type the digit 1 followed by the digit 2, each character will be stored as a 1-byte string in main memory. On a computer that uses the ASCII code, these two characters would appear as:

00110001 00110010

Fig. A.4   Most modern computers use an 8-bit code such as EBCDIC or
ASCII to represent characters.

Character	EBCDIC Binary	Hex	ASCII-8 Binary	Hex
A	1100 0001	C1	0100 0001	41
B	1100 0010	C2	0100 0010	42
C	1100 0011	C3	0100 0011	43
D	1100 0100	C4	0100 0100	44
E	1100 0101	C5	0100 0101	45
F	1100 0110	C6	0100 0110	46
G	1100 0111	C7	0100 0111	47
H	1100 1000	C8	0100 1000	48
I	1100 1001	C9	0100 1001	49
J	1101 0001	D1	0100 1010	4A
K	1101 0010	D2	0100 1011	4B
L	1101 0011	D3	0100 1100	4C
M	1101 0100	D4	0100 1101	4D
N	1101 0101	D5	0100 1110	4E
O	1101 0110	D6	0100 1111	4F
P	1101 0111	D7	0101 0000	50
Q	1101 1000	D8	0101 0001	51
R	1101 1001	D9	0101 0010	52
S	1110 0010	E2	0101 0011	53
T	1110 0011	E3	0101 0100	54
U	1110 0100	E4	0101 0101	55
V	1110 0101	E5	0101 0110	56
W	1110 0110	E6	0101 0111	57
X	1110 0111	E7	0101 1000	58
Y	1110 1000	E8	0101 1001	59
Z	1110 1001	E9	0101 1010	5A
0	1111 0000	F0	0011 0000	30
1	1111 0001	F1	0011 0001	31
2	1111 0010	F2	0011 0010	32
3	1111 0011	F3	0011 0011	33
4	1111 0100	F4	0011 0100	34
5	1111 0101	F5	0011 0101	35
6	1111 0110	F6	0011 0110	36
7	1111 0111	F7	0011 0111	37
8	1111 1000	F8	0011 1000	38
9	1111 1001	F9	0011 1001	39

This is not the number 12. On a 16-bit computer, a pure binary 12 is stored
as

0000000000001100

(Try using the "digit-times-place-value" rule.)

Since numbers and strings are different, in most programming languages you must distinguish strings from numbers. The positional value of each digit in a number is significant. As you move from byte to byte, the positional values of the individual bits have no meaning in a string. (The order of the bits is significant, but arbitrary.)

Data normally enter a computer through an input device in string form. Most computers have special instructions to convert strings to numbers. Arithmetic operations are performed on the numbers, and the results are converted back to string form before they are sent to an output device. Most programming languages perform these data type conversions for you; assembler languages are an exception.

A P P E N D I X

B

Summary of MS-DOS (PC-DOS) Commands

References

The following material is based on two primary sources:

1. Microsoft and IBM Corporation. *Disk Operating System, Version 2.10.*
2. Microsoft and Zenith Data Systems. *MS-DOS, Version 2.*

It represents a brief summary of selected commands and filters. For additional detail, see the primary sources.

General

* Format of a command:

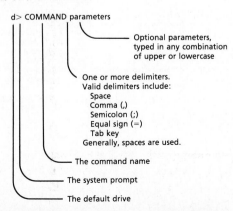

```
d> COMMAND parameters
```

Optional parameters, typed in any combination of upper or lowercase

One or more delimiters.
Valid delimiters include:
  Space
  Comma (,)
  Semicolon (;)
  Equal sign (=)
  Tab key
Generally, spaces are used.

The command name

The system prompt

The default drive

* Rules for defining a file name:

filename.extension

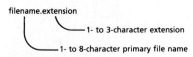

——— 1- to 3-character extension

——— 1- to 8-character primary file name

* Legal characters

A-Z	a-z	0-9	$	&	#	%
'	(	)	-	@	^	
{	}	~	'	!	-	

* Illegal characters

?	.	,	;	:	=	*
/	\	+	"	<	>	

* Lowercase letters converted to upper case
* Primary file name padded with spaces to 8 characters
* Extension padded with spaces to 3 characters
* Wild card characters

 ? Any single character
 * Any group of 1-8 characters

* Rules for defining path names:

\directory \directory ... \filename

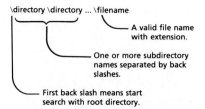

——— A valid file name
with extension.

——— One or more subdirectory
names separated by back
slashes.

——— First back slash means start
search with root directory.

* To define a subdirectory name, use the rules for
defining a file name without an extension.

* Maximum path name length is 64 characters.

* If path name does not start with a back slash,
search begins with current working directory.

* Reserved device names:

CON	PRN	LPT1	AUX	COM1
LPT2	LPT3	COM2	NUL	CLOCK$

* Conventional file name extensions:

ASM	assembler source	EXE	executable file
BAK	backup file	FOR	FORTRAN source
BAS	BASIC source	LIB	library source
BAT	batch file	LST	ASCII list file
BIN	binary file	MAP	ASCII load module
COB	COBOL source	OBJ	object module
COM	command file	OVR	overlay file
DAT	ASCII data file	REF	cross-reference
DIF	difference file	TMP	temporary link
DOC	ASCII document	$$$	temporary work
DVD	device driver		

* Redirection parameters:

Parameter	Meaning	Example
<	Change source to a specified file or device	<MYFILE.DAT
>	Change destination to a specified file or device	>PRN
>>	Change destination, usually to an existing file, and append new output to it	>>HOLD.DAT
|	Pipe standard output to another command or to a filter	DIR | MORE

Commands

* CHDIR changes the current working directory.

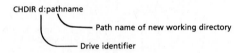

CHDIR d:pathname

———— Path name of new working directory

———— Drive identifier

* . designates the current working directory.

* .. is the parent of the current working directory.

* CHDIR with no parameters displays name of current working directory.

* CHKDSK checks a disk's directory and reports on its contents.

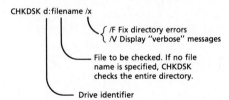

CHKDSK d:filename /x

{ /F Fix directory errors
{ /V Display "verbose" messages

———— File to be checked. If no file name is specified, CHKDSK checks the entire directory.

———— Drive identifier

* CLS clears the screen.

CLS (No parameters)

* COMP compares two files.

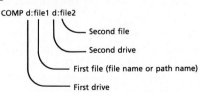

COMP d:file1 d:file2

———— Second file

———— Second drive

———— First file (file name or path name)

———— First drive

COMP is often used after COPY to verify results.

* COPY copies one or more files from a source to a destination.

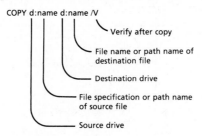

COPY d:name d:name /V

— Verify after copy

— File name or path name of destination file

— Destination drive

— File specification or path name of source file

— Source drive

* If no destination file name is given, the source file name is used. In this case, the drives must be different.

* The source and destination must differ in some way (file name, drive, and/or directory).

* DATE checks and/or sets the system date.

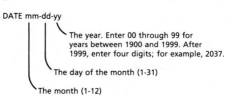

DATE

or

DATE mm-dd-yy

— The year. Enter 00 through 99 for years between 1900 and 1999. After 1999, enter four digits; for example, 2037.

— The day of the month (1-31)

— The month (1-12)

* DIR displays a directory's contents.

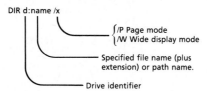

DIR d:name /x

∫ /P Page mode
\ /W Wide display mode

— Specified file name (plus extension) or path name.

— Drive identifier

* Default drive selection.

B: Selects drive B

A: Selects drive A

* DISKCOMP compares the contents of two complete disks.

DISKCOMP d: d:

— Second drive

— First drive

Note: A /V option on a DISKCOPY command implies DISKCOMP.

* DISKCOPY copies the contents of one disk to another.

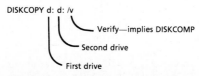

DISKCOPY d: d: /v

— Verify—implies DISKCOMP

— Second drive

— First drive

* ECHO controls the display of batch file commands and displays comments on the screen.

ECHO { ON   Commands displayed
       OFF   Commands not displayed
       message Message displayed

* ERASE (or DEL) erases a file or files.

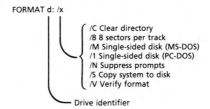

ERASE d: name

— A file name or path name

— Drive identifier

* FORMAT formats a disk.

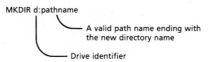

FORMAT d: /x

/C Clear directory
/8 8 sectors per track
/M Single-sided disk (MS-DOS)
/1 Single-sided disk (PC-DOS)
/N Suppress prompts
/S Copy system to disk
/V Verify format

— Drive identifier

* GRAPHICS (PC-DOS only) supports the output of graphic displays to a graphics printer.

GRAPHICS   (No parameters)

Note: Load GRAPHICS before loading application routine.

* MKDIR creates a new directory.

MKDIR d:pathname

— A valid path name ending with
  the new directory name

— Drive identifier

* PRINT sends selected files to the printer in the background.

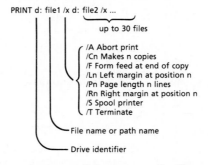

PRINT d: file1 /x d: file2 /x ...

up to 30 files

/A Abort print
/Cn Makes n copies
/F Form feed at end of copy
/Ln Left margin at position n
/Pn Page length n lines
/Rn Right margin at position n
/S Spool printer
/T Terminate

— File name or path name

— Drive identifier

* RECOVER salvages useful portions of a file or files on a disk containing bad sectors.

RECOVER d: file

— File name or path name

— Drive identifier

Note: If no file is specified, all files stored on the specified or default disk are recovered.

* RENAME (or REN) renames an existing file.

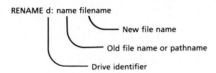

RENAME d: name filename

— New file name

— Old file name or pathname

— Drive identifier

* RMDIR (or RD) removes the specified directory.

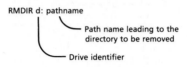

RMDIR d: pathname

— Path name leading to the directory to be removed

— Drive identifier

Note: The directory to be removed must be empty.

* TIME checks and/or sets the system time.

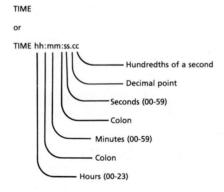

TIME

or

TIME hh:mm:ss.cc

— Hundredths of a second

— Decimal point

— Seconds (00-59)

— Colon

— Minutes (00-59)

— Colon

— Hours (00-23)

* TREE displays the directory paths on the specified disk.

TREE d: /F

— List files in each directory

— Drive identifier

* TYPE displays the selected file's contents on the screen.

TYPE d: name

— File name or path name

— Drive identifier

* VER displays the MS-DOS version number.

VER (No parameters)

━━━━━ **Filters**

* CIPHER encrypts and decrypts files for security.

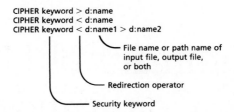

CIPHER keyword > d:name
CIPHER keyword < d:name
CIPHER keyword < d:name1 > d:name2
— File name or path name of
   input file, output file,
   or both
— Redirection operator
— Security keyword

Note: Read the detailed documentation carefully before using CIPHER.

* FIND searches the specified file or files for a string, and displays all lines containing that string.

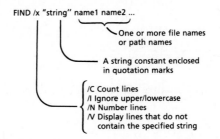

FIND /x "string" name1 name2 ...
— One or more file names
   or path names
— A string constant enclosed
   in quotation marks
/C Count lines
/I Ignore upper/lowercase
/N Number lines
/V Display lines that do not
   contain the specified string

* MORE reads text from the standard input device and displays it one screen at a time.

MORE

usually,

command | MORE
— The pipe operator
— Command whose output is piped to MORE

* SORT sorts data into ascending order.

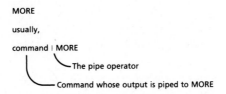

SORT /x
/R Reverse sort, or descending order
/+n Sort field starts at position n

APPENDIX
C

Summary of UNIX Commands

References

The material in this appendix is based primarily on the following three references:

1. Bourne, S.R. (1983). *The UNIX System*. Reading, Massachusetts: Addison-Wesley Publishing Company.
2. Brown, P.J. (1984). *Starting with UNIX*. Reading, Massachusetts: Addison-Wesley Publishing Company.
3. Sobell, Mark G. (1984). *A Practical Guide to the UNIX System*. Menlo Park, California: The Benjamin Cummings Publishing Company.

It represents a brief summary of selected UNIX commands and utilities. For additional details, see the references or your UNIX system manual.

General

* Format of a command

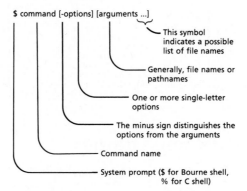

```
$ command [-options] [arguments ...]
```

This symbol indicates a possible list of file names

Generally, file names or pathnames

One or more single-letter options

The minus sign distinguishes the options from the arguments

Command name

System prompt ($ for Bourne shell, % for C shell)

* Fields are separated by one or more spaces.
* Fields enclosed in brackets [..] are optional.

* Rules for defining a file name:

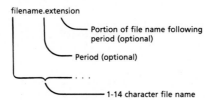

```
filename.extension
```

Portion of file name following period (optional)

Period (optional)

1-14 character file name

* Any character you can type is legal.

* Suggested characters include A-Z, a-z, 0-9, comma (,), and underscore (_).

* UNIX distinguishes between upper and lowercase.

* If you include a period in the file name, the characters following the period form the extension.

* The period and the extension count against the 14-character limit.

* You can code more than one period.

* Rules for defining path names:

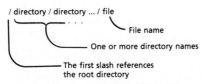

```
/ directory / directory ... / file
```

File name

One or more directory names

The first slash references the root directory

* A directory is a type of file; thus the rules for defining a directory name are the same as the rules for defining a file name.

* If the path name starts with a directory name instead of a slash, UNIX starts searching with the working directory.

* Redirection parameters:

Operator	Meaning	Example
<	Change source to a specified file or device	<myfile
>	Change destination to a specified file or device	>tempfile
>>	Change destination, usually to an existing file, and append new output to it	>>master.pay
		Pipe	cat file1	sort

Commands and Utilities

* *cat* displays the contents of a file or files.

cat [file ...]
    └── One or more file names

* *cd* changes the working directory.

cd [directory]
    └── New working directory. If no directory is coded, the home directory is assumed.

* *chmod* changes a file's access permissions.

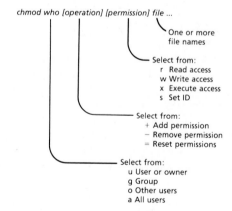

chmod who [operation] [permission] file ...
    ╲ One or more file names
    └── Select from:
        r Read access
        w Write access
        x Execute access
        s Set ID
    └── Select from:
        + Add permission
        − Remove permission
        = Reset permissions
    └── Select from:
        u User or owner
        g Group
        o Other users
        a All users

* *cp* copies a file or files.

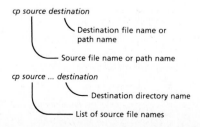

cp source destination
    ╲ Destination file name or path name
    └── Source file name or path name

cp source ... destination
    └── Destination directory name
    └── List of source file names

* *csh* activates the C shell.

csh

    No options or parameters

* *date* displays the system date and time.

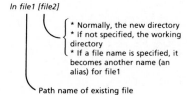

date

    No options

* *ln* creates a link.

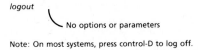

ln file1 [file2]

    * Normally, the new directory
    * If not specified, the working directory
    * If a file name is specified, it becomes another name (an alias) for file1

Path name of existing file

* *logout* logs a user off the system.

logout

    No options or parameters

Note: On most systems, press control-D to log off.

* *lpr* sends the contents of a file to the printer.

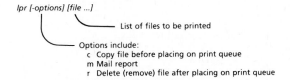

lpr [-options] [file ...]

    List of files to be printed

Options include:
  c Copy file before placing on print queue
  m Mail report
  r Delete (remove) file after placing on print queue

* *ls* lists the contents of a directory or directories.

ls [-options] [directory ...]

    List of directories

Options include:
  a All entries, including invisible files
  d Directory names only
  g Group identification
  l Long form
  r Reverse alphabetical order
  s Show size of each file
  t List files in time order (most recently modified files first)
  u Show time last accessed

* *mail* allows a user to send or receive electronic mail.

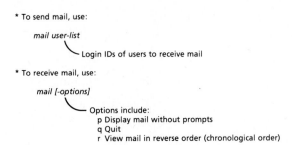

* To send mail, use:

  mail user-list

     Login IDs of users to receive mail

* To receive mail, use:

  mail [-options]

     Options include:
     p Display mail without prompts
     q Quit
     r View mail in reverse order (chronological order)

* *man* displays the UNIX manual page for the indicated command.

man name

   Command or utility name

* *mkdir* creates one or more directories.

mkdir directory ...

   One or more directory names

* *more* displays a file one screen at a time.

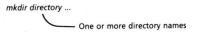

more file ...

   List of files to be displayed

* *mv* moves or renames a file.

mv file file

   New file name or path name
   Old file name or path name

mv file ... directory

   New directory
   List of files to be moved

* *passwd* changes a user's password.

$ *passwd*

   No options

* *pr* prepares standard input or a file for printing.

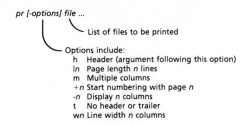

pr [-options] file ...

    List of files to be printed

Options include:
h Header (argument following this option)
ln Page length *n* lines
m Multiple columns
+n Start numbering with page *n*
-n Display *n* columns
t   No header or trailer
wn Line width *n* columns

* *ps* displays the status of a process.

ps [options]

    Select from:
-a All processes (any terminal)
-l Long form

If no options are coded, displays status of all processes controlled by user's terminal.

* *pwd* displays the user's current working directory.

pwd

    No options

* *rm* deletes a file by removing a link.

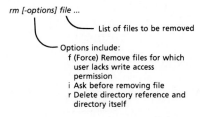

rm [-options] file ...

    List of files to be removed

Options include:
f (Force) Remove files for which
  user lacks write access
  permission
i Ask before removing file
r Delete directory reference and
  directory itself

* *rmdir* deletes one or more directories.

rmdir directory ...

    Pathnames of one or more empty directories

* *sh* activates the Bourne shell.

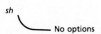

sh

    No options

* *sort* sorts the contents of a file.

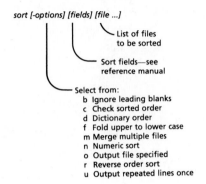

sort [-options] [fields] [file ...]

List of files
to be sorted

Sort fields—see
reference manual

Select from:
b Ignore leading blanks
c Check sorted order
d Dictionary order
f Fold upper to lower case
m Merge multiple files
n Numeric sort
o Output file specified
r Reverse order sort
u Output repeated lines once

* *spell* checks a file for spelling errors.

spell [options] file ...

One or more file names

Select from:
-v Display words not found
-b British spellings

* vi activates the visual editor.

vi file

Name of file to be created or modified

* *who* displays the names of users currently logged on the system.

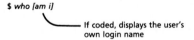

$ who [am i]

If coded, displays the user's
own login name

* *write* sends real-time a message to another user.

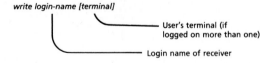

write login-name [terminal]

User's terminal (if
logged on more than one)

Login name of receiver

APPENDIX

D

Summary of DOS Job Control Statements

The primary reference for this appendix is IBM Publication #GC33-5376, *DOS/VSE System Control Statements*. Portions of several of the generalized job control statements are taken directly from this publication. The excerpts are reprinted by permission from International Business Machines Corporation.

Statements

ASSGN assigns a logical I/O unit to a physical device.

// ASSGN SYSxxx, address $\left[\left(\begin{matrix} ,X'cuu' \\ ,UA \\ ,IGN \\ \{,SYSyyy\} \\ ,device\text{-}class \\ ,device\text{-}type \end{matrix}\right)\right]$

where

> **SYSxxx** is the symbolic unit name:
> **address** is the physical device address expressed as
> X'cuu' where c = channel and uu = device, or
> UA which indicates that unit is unassigned, or
> IGN which indicates that the device is to be ignored (i.e., disabled), or
> SYSyyy, which assigns SYSxxx to the same device as SYSyyy, or
> device-class, for example DISK or READER, or
> device-type, for example 3330 or 2501.

A number of optional operands can be coded as well.

CLOSE closes a logical unit.

// CLOSE SYSxx $\begin{bmatrix} \begin{Bmatrix} ,X'cuu'[,X'ss'] \\ ,UA \\ ,IGN \\ ,ALT \\ ,SYSyyy \end{Bmatrix} \end{bmatrix}$

where parameters have the same meaning as in ASSGN.
DATE places a date in the communication region.

//   DATE   mm/dd/yy

or

//   DATE   dd/mm/yy

EXEC indicates end of control information for a job step and identifies the core-image library program (phase) which is to be loaded and executed.

//   EXEC   [programname].GO

or

//   EXEC   PROC = procname

where

> **programname** is the name of the program to be loaded and executed. If blank, the load module just produced by the linkage editor is assumed, **GO** indicates that the output of a compiler is to be link edited and executed, and
> **procname** is the name of a cataloged procedure.

EXTENT defines an area or extent of a direct access file.

//   EXTENT   [symbolic-unit],
                              [serial-number], [type],
                              [sequence-number],
                              [relative-track],
                              [number-of-tracks],
                              [split-cylinder-track],

where

> **symbolic unit** is the SYSxxx form symbolic = unit name of the desired volume. (If omitted, the unit from the last EXTENT is used. If this is the first or only EXTENT, the unit from the DTF is used.)

serial number is the volume's serial number. (If omitted, the serial number from the last EXTENT is used. If this is the first or only EXTENT and no serial number is coded, the serial number is not checked.)

type is 1 for a data area, 2 for an overflow area, 4 for an index area, and 8 for a split-cylinder data area;

sequence number is the relative location of this extent within a multi-extent file;

relative track is relative track address of the track where the data extent (indexed sequential file) is to begin;

number of tracks indicates the number of tracks to be assigned to this file;

split-cylinder track indicates the upper track number for split-cylinder sequential files.

JOB indicates start of a job.

//   JOB   jobname [accounting information]

where

jobname is the 1-8 alphanumeric character name of the job;
accounting information is optional with the installation. (If specified, separate from the jobname by a blank.)

LBLTYP defines the amount of main storage to be reserved at link edit time or at execution time for label processing.

//   LBLTYP $\begin{Bmatrix} \text{TAPE[(nn)]} \\ \text{NSD (nn)} \end{Bmatrix}$

where

TAPE(nn) is used to indicate that only tape labels and no nonsequential DASD file labels are to be processed;
NSD(nn) indicates that nonsequential disk file labels are to be processed. (This also allows for other types as well. The nn indicates the largest number of extents to be processed for a single file.)

OPTION specifies job control options.

//   OPTION   option1[,option2....]

where

typical options include: LOG or NOLOG, DUMP or NODUMP, LINK or NOLINK, DECK or NODECK, LIST or NOLIST, LISTX or NO-

LISTX, SYM or NOSYM, XREF or NOXREF, ERRS or NOERRS, CA-
TAL, STDLABEL, USRLABEL, PARSTD, 48C, 60C (60-character set),
and SYSPARM.

RESET resets certain I/O assignments to the standard assignment, within
the partition.

$$
// \quad \text{RESET} \quad \left\{ \begin{array}{l} \text{SYS} \\ \text{PROG} \\ \text{ALL} \\ \text{SYSxxx} \end{array} \right\}
$$

where

> **SYS** resets all system logical units;
> **PROG** resets programmer logical units;
> **ALL** resets all logical units;
> **SYSxxx** resets the specified unit.

RSTRT allows programmer to restart a checkpointed program.

//   RSTRT   SYSxxx.nnnn[.filename]

where

> **SYSxxx** is the symbolic name of the device on which checkpoint re-
> cords are stored;
> **nnnn** identifies the checkpoint record to be used for restarting;
> **filename** is the symbolic name of a disk file used for checkpoint (disk
> volumes hold multiple files).

UPSI allows the programmer to set program switches in the communications region:

//   UPSI nnnnnnnn

where

> **nnnnnnnn** represents the desired settings of the eight program switch
> bits—a 0 sets the associated switch to 0, a 1 sets the switch to a 1, and
> an X leaves the switch setting unchanged.

The symbol /* is an end-of-data file marker.
The symbol /& is an end-of-job marker.

Linkage
Editor Control
Statements

PHASE assigns a phase name and gives main storage load address for the phase.

INCLUDE indicates that an object module is to be included. If the operands field is blank, the module is on SYSIPT; i.e., it's in object deck form.

ENTRY provides for an optional phase entry point.

ACTION specifies linkage-editor options.

APPENDIX

E

Summary of Job Control Language for the IBM System/360 and System/370 Operating System

References

The primary references for this appendix are:

1. Hannula, R. (1977). *System 360/370 Job Control Language and the Access Methods*. Reading, Massachusetts: Addison-Wesley Publishing Company.
2. IBM Publication GC28-0618. *OS/VS JCL Reference*.
3. IBM Publication GX28-1300. *MVS JCL*.
4. Trombetta, M. and Finkelstein, S.C. (1984). *OS JCL and Utilities*. Reading, Massachusetts: Addison-Wesley Publishing Company.

The format for describing JCL statements in Figs. F.1, F.2, and F.3 is based on the IBM reference material and is used with the permission of the International Business Machines Corporation.

General JCL Rules

JCL Statement Format

//name operation operands comments

> Fields are separated by one or more blanks.
> Operands are separated by commas.
> Each operand consists of one or more parameters separated by commas.
> Positional parameters derive their meaning from their relative positions.
> Keyword parameters derive their meaning from a key word, and thus can be coded in any order.
> A single JOB statement can be followed by one or more EXEC statements.
> Each EXEC statement can be followed by one or more DD statements.

A jobname, stepname, or DDname may consist of from one to eight alphanumeric characters, the first of which must be alphabetic or one of the national characters (#, @, or $).

Continuing a JCL Statement

1. Break after any comma, and include the comma on the original line.
2. Code "/" in the first two columns of the continuation line.
3. Resume the coding of parameters anywhere between positions four and sixteen of the continuation line.

Rules for using parentheses: When the first subparameter is the only one coded, parentheses are not needed. When more than one subparameter or a positional subparameter other than the first one is coded, parentheses are needed.

The JOB Statement

Function: Job separation. Secondary functions allow the programmer to pass accounting information and other parameters to the system. (See Fig. E.1.)

Parameters:
>   **accounting information**: An installation-dependent positional parameter, normally containing an account number followed by other accounting information. It's operational but can, at the installation's request, be made a required parameter.
>   **programmer's name**: Positional parameter consisting of a 1- to 20-character name composed of letters, numbers, and a period. If the field

Fig. E.1   The JOB statement.

//Name	Operation	Operand	P/K
//jobname	JOB	[([acct'] [,acctg information])] [programmer's name] MSGLEVEL = ([0] [,0] / [1] [,1] / [2]) [COND = ((condition),...)] [RD = request] RESTART = ((* / stepname / stepname.procstep) [,checkid]) [PRTY = nn] [MSGCLASS = x] [TYPRUN = HOLD] [TIME = (minutes,seconds,)] [CLASS = jobclass) [REGION = ((nnnnnK / value$_0$K) [,value$_1$K])] [ROLL = (x,y)]	P P K K K K K K K K K K K

Legend:

P   Position parameter.

K   Keyword parameter.

⟨|⟩ Choose one.

[ ] Optional; if more than one line is enclosed, choose one or none.

contains any other characters (a blank, for example) it must be enclosed in a set of apostrophes.

MSGLEVEL=(jcl, allocations): Specifies the printing of job control statements and device allocation messages. The two positional subparameters are interpreted as follows.

JCL	Meaning
0	Print JOB statement only.
1	Print all JCL including that generated by cataloged procedures.
2	Print only JCL in job stream.

Allocations	Meaning
0	Print messages only if job abnormally terminates.
1	Print all messages.

COND=(condition....): Normally coded on an EXEC statement. It allows a programmer to specify conditions for bypassing a job step. If coded on a JOB statement, the JOB COND is logically added to the EXEC COND(s).

RD=request: Allows for automatic restart and suppression of checkpoints.

RESTART=stepname: Requests step restart.

PRTY=nn: Priority within job class—low is zero; high is 13 or 15, depending on the version of JES (the job entry subsystem) used.

MSGCLASS=x: Allows the programmer to specify the device to which job scheduler messages are to be spooled.

TYPRUN=HOLD: Holds the job in the input queue until the operator issues a RELEASE command.

TYPRUN=SCAN: Checks JCL for syntax errors, but does not execute job.

TIME=(minutes, seconds): Normally coded on an EXEC statement. If coded on the JOB statement, sets a time limit for the entire job.

CLASS=jobclass: Specifies the job's class. The job class is normally specified as a single letter, and indicates the job's external priority.

REGION=nnnnnK: Another parameter that is more commonly coded on an EXEC statement. If coded on the JOB statement, the parameter sets an upper limit on the amount of main storage space allocated to any job step; thus, you must allow enough space for the biggest step.

The EXEC Statement

Function: Identifies the specific program (directly or through a cataloged procedure) to be executed. (See Fig. E.2.)

Parameters:

PGM=program name, or PROC=procedure *name,* or just plain **procedure** *name.* The first positional parameter. It fulfills the primary function of the EXEC statement. If no keyword is coded, PROC is assumed.

COND=(condition1,condition2,...): Allows the programmer to specify conditions for bypassing the job step.

PARM=value: Allows the programmer to pass parameters to a program.

ACCT=(accounting information): A rarely used parameter that allows the programmer to provide jobstep accounting information. Accounting information is usually passed through the JOB statement.

RD=request: As on the JOB statement, allows for automatic restart and suppression of checkpoints.

DPRTY=(value1,value2): The dispatching priority determines which of the several programs concurrently resident in memory gets first access to the processor in the event of conflicts.

TIME=(minutes,seconds): Sets a time limit for the job step.

REGION=nnnnnK: Sets a limit on the amount of storage available to the jobstep.

Fig. E.2   The EXEC statement.

//Name	Operation	Operand	P/K
//[stepname]	EXEC	PGM = program name PGM = *.stepname.ddname PGM = *.stepname,procstepname.ddname [PROC =] procedure name	P
		COND = ({ (condition) / EVEN / ONLY } [,(condition),...])]	
		COND.procstep = ({ (condition) / EVEN / ONLY } [,(condition),...])	
		PARM = value PARM.procstepname = value	K
		ACCT = (acctg information) ACCT.procstepname = (acctg info)	K
		RD = request RD.procstepname = request	K
		DPRTY = (value 1, value 2) DPRTY.procstepname = (value 1, value 2)]	K
		TIME = (minutes,seconds) TIME.procstepname = (min,sec)	K
		REGION = ({ nnnnnK / $value_0$K } [,$value_1$K])] REGION.procstepname = ({ nnnnnK / $value_0$K } [,$value_1$K])	

Legend:

P   Position parameter.

K   Keyword parameter.

⟨|⟩   Choose one.

[ ]   Optional; if more than one line is enclosed, choose one or none.

The DD statement

Function: Specifies details—physical location, logical configuration—of data sets. (See Fig. E.3.)

Parameters: *DSNAME* or *DSN* Identifies a data set by name.

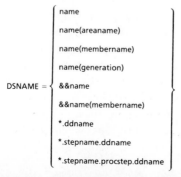

DSNAME = {
name
name(areaname)
name(membername)
name(generation)
&&name
&&name(membername)
*.ddname
*.stepname.ddname
*.stepname.procstep.ddname
}

Fig. E.3   The DD statement. Except for *, DATA, and DUMMY, all
parameters are keyword.

//Name	Operation	Operand	P/K

//⌈ ddname ⌉
 ⌊ procstepname.
      ddname ⌋
	DD	⌈ DSNAME = identification ⌉
		⌊ DSN = identification ⌋
		[UNIT = (unit information)]
		⌈ VOLUME = (volume information) ⌉
		⌊ VOL = (volume information) ⌋
		⌈ DCB = (attributes)
		       ⌠dsname
		DCB = (⟨ *.stepname.ddname ⟩ [,attributes]) ⌉
		       ⌡*.stepname.procstep.ddname
		[LABEL = (label information)]
		DISP = ([status] [,disposition])
		SYSOUT = x
		SYSOUT = (x ⌈ ,progname ⌉ [,form #])
		              ⌊ , ⌋
		[SPACE = (direct access space)]
			K
			
			K
			K
			
			K
			
			K
			K
			K
			
			K

		⟨ * DATA ⟩ [,DCB = ([BLKSIZE = block] [,BUFNO = number])]	P
		DUMMY,...	P
		DDNAME = ddname	K

Legend:

P   Positional parameter

K   Keyword parameter

⟨|⟩   Choose one.

[ ]   Optional; if more than one line is enclosed, choose one or none.

UNIT: Requests a particular type of physical I/O device:

$$
UNIT = \left(\begin{bmatrix} address \\ type \\ group \end{bmatrix} \begin{bmatrix} ,P \\ ,n \end{bmatrix} \; [,DEFER] \; [,SEP=(\text{list of ddnames})] \; \right)
$$

Units can be requested by actual channel/device address (address), by IBM
model number (2400 is a particular model of tape drive—this is the "type"
option), or by a general group name as defined by the installation. The
second positional subparameter allows the programmer to specify parallel
mounting of all the volumes in a multivolume file by indicating the actual
number of volumes; if the number of volumes is specified in the VOL
parameter, the programmer simply codes "P." The DEFER subparameter,
the third positional subparameter, postpones a volume mount message
until the actual OPEN macro is executed. The SEP subparameter is a keyword subparameter that indicates data sets listed as part of the subparameter are to be placed on physically separate devices—if, for example, a
program were to access both input and output disk data sets, the SEP

subparameter could cause these data sets to be maintained on separate disk volumes, thus minimizing head movement.

The second form of the UNIT parameter:

UNIT=AFF=ddname

allows the data set to be mounted on the same physical device used by a previous data set (referenced by DDNAME) in the job.

VOLUME or VOL: Allows for the specification of volumes; i.e., specific tape volumes or disk volumes.

$$\text{VOLUME}=(\text{[PRIVATE]} \begin{bmatrix} ,\text{RETAIN} \\ , \end{bmatrix} \begin{bmatrix} ,\text{VOLSEQ\#} \\ , \end{bmatrix} \begin{bmatrix} ,\text{volcount} \\ , \end{bmatrix} [,] \begin{bmatrix} \text{SER}=(\text{list of serial numbers}) \\ \text{REF}=\text{dsname} \\ \text{REF}=*.\text{ddname} \\ \text{REF}=*.\text{stepname.ddname} \\ \text{REF}=*.\text{stepname.procstep.ddname} \end{bmatrix})$$

The primary option is the SER or REF subparameter that allows the programmer to specify either a specific volume or a group of volumes directly, by serial number, or indirectly by referring back to a prior job step. The PRIVATE subparameter means that no other output data set may be allocated to this volume without a specific volume request.

RETAIN keeps the volume mounted between job steps. The third positional subparameter allows the programmer to indicate that processing is to begin with a volume other than the first one on a multivolume file. The fourth positional subparameter allows the programmer to specify the number of volumes in a multivolume file.

DCB: Specifies details about actual data format.

LABEL: Specifies the label type and the relative file number on a multifile tape volume.

$$\text{LABEL}=(\text{[data set seq\#]} \begin{bmatrix} ,\text{SL} \\ ,\text{SUL} \\ ,\text{NSL} \\ ,\text{NL} \\ ,\text{BLP} \end{bmatrix} \begin{bmatrix} ,\text{PASSWORD} \\ ,\text{NOPWREAD} \end{bmatrix} \begin{bmatrix} ,\text{IN} \\ ,\text{OUT} \end{bmatrix} [,] \begin{bmatrix} \text{EXPDT}=\text{yyddd} \\ \text{RETPD}=\text{nnnn} \end{bmatrix})$$

The first subparameter, which is positional, indicates the relative file number on a multifile volume; if omitted, relative file # 1 is assumed. The second positional subparameter identifies the label type. PASSWORD indicates that a password must be entered before any access to the data set is permitted. NOPWREAD requires a password for write operations only. Specifying

"IN" or "OUT" as the third positional subparameter allows the programmer to override a program specification of INOUT access in the OPEN macro for BSAM files; it's of primary importance to FORTRAN programmers. The final subparameter allows for the specification of an expiration date or retention period.

DISP: Specifies the status and disposition of a data set. The first positional subparameter indicates the status of the data set at the beginning of the job step. The second subparameter indicates what is to be done with the data set at the conclusion of the job step, while the third subparameter indicates the disposition in the event of abnormal jobstep termination.

$$DISP = (\begin{bmatrix} SHR \\ NEW \\ OLD \\ MOD \end{bmatrix} \begin{bmatrix} ,DELETE \\ ,KEEP \\ ,PASS \\ ,CATLG \\ ,UNCATLG \end{bmatrix} \begin{bmatrix} ,UNCATLG \\ ,CATLG \\ ,DELETE \\ ,KEEP \end{bmatrix})$$

SYSOUT: Specifies the use of a standard system output device.

SYSOUT=(class ,program-name ,form-name)

The class is usually A for the printer and B for the punch, although an installation can define its own output classes. Use the program name sub-parameter to identify a program (other than the job entry subsystem) that is to write the data; use the form name subparameter to identify the output form you want used.

SPACE: Specifies the amount of direct access space to be allocated to a data set.

$$SPACE = (\begin{Bmatrix} TRK \\ CYL \\ blocksize \end{Bmatrix} ,(quantity \begin{bmatrix} ,increment \\ , \end{bmatrix} \begin{bmatrix} ,directory \\ ,index \end{bmatrix}) \begin{bmatrix} ,RLSE \end{bmatrix} \begin{bmatrix} ,CONTIG \\ ,MXIG \\ ,ALX \\ , \end{bmatrix} [,ROUND])$$

The programmer can request tracks (TRK), cylinders (CYL), or blocks of a given size. Following specification of the type of space required, the programmer requests an amount of space, asking first, through a series of positional subparameters, for a primary allocation, next, for a secondary allocation in the event that the primary allocation proves to be insufficient, and finally for directory or index space. View the entire "quantity" request as a single positional subparameter, with the quantity, increment, and index sub-subparameters being enclosed in a set of parentheses.

The RLSE subparameter allows the programmer to return all unused space to the system at the conclusion of the job step. CONTIG allows the programmer to request contiguous space, MXIG allows for the allocation of the largest contiguous free area on the volume (as long as it's larger than the request), and ALX provides the five largest contiguous free areas on the volume (again, with a "larger than the request" restriction). ROUND causes space allocated by blocks to be aligned on cylinder boundaries.

DUMMY: Causes the I/O operations specified on the DD statement to be bypassed.

* or DATA: The asterisk or (*) character in the operands portion of the DD statement indicates that data follow in the job stream; this parameter is often used to indicate that punched card data are to be read through the system input device.

DATA implies the same thing, but allows for the inclusion of cards with // punched in the first two columns.

DDNAME: Postpones definition of data set parameters until a subsequent DD statement with the specified DDNAME is encountered.

Special DD statements

The JOBLIB statement

//JOBLIB DD DSN=library-name,DISP=SHR

Allows programs in a private library to be loaded and executed. The JOBLIB statement follows the JOB statement and makes the library available to all subsequent job steps; the JOBLIB, SYSCHK, and JOBCAT statements are the only DD statements that can legally precede the first EXEC statement.

The STEPLIB statement

//STEPLIB DD DSN=library-name,DISP=SHR

like the JOBLIB statement, allows programs in a private library to be loaded and executed. The STEPLIB statement follows the EXEC statement and is effective for a single job step only.

The SYSUDUMP statement

//SYSUDUMP DD SYSOUT=class

Provides an abnormal termination dump of the load module.

The SYSCHK statement

//SYSCHK DD DISP=OLD,DSN=dataset-name

Describes a checkpoint data set. Follows the JOB statement and the JOBLIB statement if present.

G L O S S A R Y

This glossary contains brief definitions intended to convey a sense of the meanings of selected key words. For more precise definitions see:

The American National Dictionary for Information Processing, American National Standards Institute, 1430 Broadway, New York, New York 10018.

The ISO Vocabulary of Data Processing, published by The International Standards Organization.

Absolute address. An address assigned to each memory location in a computer. Generally, an address relative to the very first location in memory.

Access method. A software routine that translates a progammer's logical request for input or output into the physical commands required by the external device.

Address. A location in memory. Often, the bytes or words that make up memory are numbered sequentially; the byte's (or word's) number is its address.

Address translation. The translation from relative form to an absolute address by the instruction control unit.

Agent process. A process on a host computer that represents the link to a computer network.

Architecture. *See* Computer architecture.

Arithmetic and logic unit. The part of a computer's processor that executes instructions.

Assembler language. A programming language in which one mnemonic source statement is coded for each machine-level instruction.

Asynchronous. Independent. Contrast with *synchronous*.

Background. A low-priority fixed-length partition.

Backup. Extra hardware, software, or data intended to keep a computer system running in the event that one or more components fail.

Backward reference. A reference that tells the operating system to look at a previous JCL statement.

Base address. Generally, the absolute address of a program's or module's entry point.

Base-plus-displacement. An addressing system in which a program is addressed relative to its entry point.

Basic control (BC) mode PSW. On an IBM System/370 computer, a form of PSW used when the dynamic address translation feature is disabled.

Batch file. A set of MS-DOS commands, stored as a file, that can be referenced by name. When referenced, the commands are executed in sequence.

Bit. A binary digit.

Block device. A UNIX device (normally disk) that holds files.

Blocking. Storing several logical records in one physical record.

Book. Under DOS/VSE, a source statement library number.

Boot. A routine, read into main memory when the computer is activated, that reads the rest of the operating system into memory. *See also* Initial program load.

Bourne shell. The standard UNIX shell.

Buffer. Temporary storage used to compensate for the different speeds of adjacent devices.

Buffer pool. A set of buffers in main memory. Under UNIX, all block I/O takes place through the buffer pool.

Bus. A set of parallel wires used to transmit data, commands, or power.

Byte. Eight bits. On many computer systems, the smallest addressable unit of main memory.

C shell. A UNIX shell related to the C programming language.

Cataloged procedure. A set of precoded JCL statements inserted into the job stream by the operating system.

CAW. *See* Channel address word.

CCB. *See* Command control block.

CCW. *See* Channel command word.

Central processing unit. *See* Processor.

Channel. A device used to attach input, output, and secondary storage devices to a large computer system. The channel contains its own processor, and thus can free the main processor from responsibility for controlling I/O operations.

Channel address word (CAW). On an IBM System/370 computer, a word lcoated at main memory address 72 that specifies the address where a channel program begins.

Channel command word (CCW). A single instruction in an IBM System/370 channel program.

Channel program. One or more CCWs that control a sequence of channel operations. More generally, a set of primitive commands that control an I/O operation.

Channel queue. The queue for I/O operations during a channel-busy condition.

Channel status word (CSW). On an IBM System/370 computer, a doubleword at main memory address 64 through which a channel communicates its status to the main processor.

Character device. Under UNIX, such non-block devices as printers and terminals.

Checkpoint. A point, generally taken at regular intervals, at which a program's intermediate results are dumped to secondary storage to minimize the risk of work loss.

Child. In UNIX, the second copy of a process. In a data base, a record that is linked, in some way, to a higher level record. *Contrast with* Parent.

Clock. The processor component that generates the regular electronic pulses that drive a computer.

Close. The instruction that signals the operating system when a program is finished accessing a file or peripheral device.

Cluster. Under MS-DOS, the unit used in allocating disk space.

CMS. *See* Conversation monitor system.

Collision detection. A data transmission technique in which a terminal or host computer transmits a message and listens for a collision with another message. If such a collision is detected, the message is retransmitted after a random interval.

Command. (1) A control signal that tells a hardware component to perform a specific function; for example, a fetch command. (2) A request from a programmer, an operator, or a user to an operating system asking that a specific function be performed; for example, a request to load a program.

Command control block (CCB). Under DOS/VSE, a PIOCS block that points to a channel program.

Command driven. An operating system whose main control module is the command processor.

Command language. A language for communicating with an operating system.

Command processor. An operating system module that reads, interprets, and carries out commands.

COMMAND.COM. The MS-DOS comand processor, or shell.

Communication vector table (CVT). Under IBM's OS/VS1/VS2, a table that holds system constants and pointers to most of the key control blocks.

Compiler. A support program that reads a source module, translates the source statements to machine language, and outputs a complete binary object module.

Computation migration. The transfer of tasks between hosts in a computer network.

Computer architecture. The physical structure of a computer; in particular, the way in which a computer's components are linked together.

Computer network. A network in which several computers are linked by communication lines over a large geographic area.

Computer program. A series of instructions that guides a computer through some process.

Condition code. A two-bit code in an IBM System/370 computer that reflects a decision logic.

Configuration table. A table used in UNIX to list all peripheral devices attached to the system.

Contiguous. Adjacent to.

Control block. The block that holds control information for an active program.

Control program (CP). Under IBM's VM/SP, the operating system that manages the real computer.

Control unit, instruction. *See* Instruction control unit.

Control unit, I/O. An electronic device that links an I/O device to a channel.

Conversational monitor system (CMS). Under IBM's VM/SP, a virtual operating system that simulates a personal computer, thus combining the interactive nature of a PC and the resources of a large mainframe.

Core image library. *See* Load module library.

CP. *See* Control program.

CPU. Acronym for central processing unit. *See* Processor.

CSW. *See* Channel status word.

Current PSW. On an IBM System/370, a special register that holds the address of the next instruction to be executed.

CVT. *See* Communication vector table.

Data accessibility. The availability of data to the user.

Data base. A collection of related data. Generally, an integrated, centralized collection of an organization's data.

Data base administrator. The person in an MIS group with unambiguous responsibility for data. Generally, the person responsible for installing and maintaining the data base management system.

Data base management system. Software that controls access to a data base.

Data communication monitor. A module used to manage the partition and serve as an interface to the communication media in a time-sharing system.

Data control block (DCB). Under IBM's OS, a series of constants and addresses that describe the characteristics of the physical and logical records.

Data dependency. A condition that occurs when a program's logic is excessively dependent on its physical data structure. Data-dependent programs are difficult to maintain.

Data element. A single, meaningful unit of data.

Data extent block (DEB). Under IBM's OS, an extension of the DCB that is not accessible to the programmer.

Data integrity. The reliability of data. Loosely, data accuracy.

Data management. Storing data in such a way that they can be retrieved when needed.

Data migration. The transfer of files and selected data elements between hosts in a computer network.

Data redundancy. The same data recorded in several different files.

Data segment. In UNIX, a private segment that follows the text segment and holds the program's data.

Data set. A term coined by IBM to encompass both traditional files and libraries.

Data structure. An organized set of data. Examples include a list, an array, and a file.

DCB. *See* Data control block.

DD statement. An IBM OS/JCL statement that defines a peripheral device.

Deadlock. A consequence of poor resource management that occurs when two programs each control a resource needed by the other and neither is willing to give in.

DEB. *See* Data extent block.

Default. The value assumed by a system when the programmer fails to code a particular parameter.

Default drive. The drive that the operating system assumes will hold programs, routines, and data files.

Define the file (DTF). A DOS/VSE macro that sets key data parameters and specifies an access method.

Delimiter. A flag used to separate data items or fields.

Demand paging. The process of bringing pages into memory as they are referenced.

Device driver. A file that describes the access rules for a particular physical device.

Device number. Under UNIX, a number that uniquely defines an external device.

Directory. The list of files stored on a disk. *See also* Root directory; Subdirectory; Working directory.

Disk. A flat, platelike surface on which data can be stored magnetically.

Diskette. A thin, flexible magnetic disk often used on small computer systems.

Dispatcher. An operating system routine used to manage processor time.

Displacement. A number of memory locations away from a base address. A location relative to a base address.

Distributed operating system. A single operating system assigned to all hosts in a computer network.

DOS/VSE. An IBM batch-oriented, multiprogramming operating system popular on small mainframes.

DTF. *See* Define the file.

Dynamic address translation. The process of changing relative segment and/or page addresses to absolute addresses during execution of an instruction.

Dynamic memory management. Allocation of memory space to application programs as the space is needed.

ESD.   *See* External symbol dictionary.

E-time or Execution time.   The time during which an instruction is executed by the arithmetic and logic unit.

Event.   In UNIX, the event signal generated by the death of a process.

Event-wait.   A routine that causes UNIX to search the process table and wake every process waiting for that event.

EXCP.   *See* Execute channel program.

EXEC.   A UNIX primitive that overlays a process with new text and data segments.

EXEC statement.   Under DOS/VSE and OS/JCL, a statement used to identify a program (or cataloged procedure) to be executed.

Execute channel program (EXCP).   Under DOS/VSE, a PIOCS macro that generates the instructions needed to execute a channel program.

EXIT.   A UNIX system primitive that signals a process's completion.

Extended control (EC) mode PSW.   On an IBM System/370 computer, a form of PSW that implies virtual memory.

Extension.   Part of a file name. Often used to assign the file name to a particular category. Generally, follows a period.

External interrupt.   On an IBM System/370 computer, an interrupt that comes from the operator's console, another processor, or the timer.

External paging device.   A storage device used to hold application programs on a virtual memory system.

External reference.   A reference by an object module to logic that is not part of that object module.

External symbol dictionary (ESD).   A table of unresolved external references placed by the compiler at the beginning of the object module.

File.   A collection of related records.

File allocation table.   Under MS-DOS, a table, stored on disk, containing an entry for each cluster on the disk.

File descriptor.   Under UNIX, a small, non-negative integer used to identify an open file to a user's process.

File name.   The name used to identify a file.

File system.   An operating system routine that manages directories and allocates disk space. The routine that allows programmers and users to access data and programs by name.

Filter.   A routine that accepts input from the standard input device, modifies the data in some way, and sends the results to the standard output device.

Fixed-partition memory management.   A memory management technique in which the available memory space is divided into several fixed-length partitions, and one program is loaded into each partition.

Floppy disk.   *See* Diskette.

Foreground.   A high-priority fixed-length partition.

fork.   A UNIX primitive that creates a new process.

Fragmentation.   Chunks of unused space spread throughout memory as a result of dynamic memory management.

Hard disk.   A rigid disk. *Contrast with* floppy disk, or diskette. Generally, a hard disk spins constantly; consequently, data access is much faster than with diskette. Also, hard disk has a greater data storage capacity.

Hierarchical data base.   A hierarchically structured data base.

Home directory.   The file selected by UNIX as the working directory when a user logs on.

Host.   An individual end-user computer in a computer network.

i-list.   A region on a UNIX disk that holds the i-nodes.

Image.   In UNIX, an execution environment that consists of program and data storage, the contents of general-purpose registers, the status of open files, the current directory, and other key elements.

INCLUDE statement.   Under DOS and OS/JCL, a statement used to specify external references to the linkage editor.

init.   When UNIX is booted, the "original ancestor" that creates one system process for each terminal channel.

Initial program load (IPL).   The process of copying the resident operating system into real memory.

Initiator/terminator.   Under IBM's OS/VS1/VS2, a transient module that starts and ends tasks.

i-node.   An entry on the i-list in UNIX.

i-node table.   A UNIX table listing the i-nodes of all open files.

Input/output block (IOB).   Under OS/VS1/VS2, a block that links the DCB to the channel program.

Input/output control system (IOCS).   The operating system module that assumes responsibility for communicating directly with input, output, and secondary storage devices.

Instruction.   One step in a program. Each instruction tells the computer to perform one of its basic functions.

Instruction address.   On an IBM System/370

computer, the PSW field that holds the address of the next instruction to be executed.

Instruction control unit. The part of a computer's processor that decides which instruction will be executed next.

Instruction length code. On an IBM System/370 computer, a BC mode field that indicates the length of the current instruction.

Interface. On a small computer, an electronic component, often a board, that links an external device to a computer. More generally, an electronic component that links two different devices.

Interpreter. A support program that reads a single source statement, translates that statement to machine language, executes those machine-level instructions, and then moves on to the next source statement.

Interrupt. An electronic signal that causes a computer to stop what it is doing and transfer control to the operating system in such a way that the task being performed at the time of the interrupt can later be resumed.

Interrupt driven. An operating system whose main control module is an interrupt handler routine.

Interrupt handler. An operating system routine that responds to an interrupt.

Interrupt vector table. A table that holds the addresses (interrupt vectors) of several interrupt handler routines.

Interruption code. On an IBM System/370 computer, a code showing the cause of an interrupt.

i-number. Under UNIX, an i-node's offset from the beginning of the i-list.

Invisible file. On UNIX, a file whose name is not displayed when a directory is listed.

I/O control unit. See Control unit, I/O.

I/O interrupt. On an IBM System/370 computer, an interrupt that occurs when the channel signals the processor that an I/O operation is completed.

IOB. See Input/output block.

IOCS. See Control unit, I/O.

IO.SYS. Under MS-DOS, a hardware-dependent module that issues physical data transfer commands. The MS-DOS input/output control system.

IPL. See Initial program load.

I-time, or Instruction time. The time during which the next instruction is fetched from main memory and interpreted by the processor's instruction control unit.

JCL. See Job control language.

JES. See Job entry subsystem.

Job. A set of related tasks.

Job control language (JCL). A batch-oriented language used to identify jobs, identify the program or programs to be executed, define peripheral device requirements, and pass other information to the operating system.

Job control program. Under DOS/VSE, a routine that loads job steps or tasks.

Job entry subsystem (JES). Under OS/VS1/VS2, a job management routine that reads the job stream and assigns jobs to class queues.

Job management. The OS/VS1/VS2 routines that dispatch, enqueue, schedule, initiate, and terminate jobs or tasks.

Job name. The name chosen by the programmer to identify a job.

JOB statement. Under DOS or OS/JCL, a statement used to separate and identify jobs.

Job step. A single program in a job.

Job stream. A series of jobs submitted, in batch mode, to the operating system. Generally, the job stream holds control statements, source code, and data.

Kernel. Under UNIX, the portion of the operating system that is hardware dependent.

Keyword parameter. A parameter that derives its meaning from its name, not its position.

LAN. See Local area network.

Library. A collection of related files or programs.

Line. A data communication medium.

Linkage editor. A system program that combines object modules to form a load module and outputs the load module to a library.

LIOCS. See Logical I/O control system.

Load module. A complete machine-level program in a form ready to be loaded into main memory and executed.

Load module library. A library that holds ready to execute load modules.

Loader. A system program that combines object modules to form a load module, and then loads the program into main memory. Similar to a linkage editor, except that a loader does not output the load module to a library.

Local. Data transmission between two devices without boosting or filtering the signals. Generally limited to a mile or two.

Local area network (LAN). A computer network that relies on local data transmission.

Logical I/O. Input or output operations performed without regard for the physical structure of the data. Under traditional data management, a request for a logical record.

Logical I/O control system (LIOCS). Input

or output operations performed without regard for the physical structure of the data. Under traditional data management, a request for a logical record.

Logical unit block (LUB). Under DOS/USE, a table that lists the symbolic names of physical I/O devices. Each table entry points to a PUB table entry.

Login name. Name used to begin a session in UNIX.

LUB. *See* Logical unit block.

Machine check interrupt. On an IBM System/370 computer, the interrupt that occurs when a computer's self-checking circuitry detects a hardware failure.

Machine cycle. The basic operating cycle of a processor during which a single instruction is fetched, interpreted, and executed.

Machine language. Binary instructions that can be stored in main memory, fetched, and executed by a computer.

Macro. A set of precoded source statements added to a source module by an assembler in response to a source reference.

Main memory. Memory that can be directly accessed by the processor.

Main processor. On a multiprocessing computer, the primary processor. Sometimes used as a synonym for processor.

Masking. A method used to determine whether to acknowledge an interrupt.

Master scheduler. The OS/VS1/VS2 dispatcher.

Member. Under IBM's OS, a module or data file on a partitioned data set.

Message slot transmission. Controlling access to a network by continuously transmitting several message slots. A terminal or host computer can transmit data only through an open slot.

Minidisk. A portion of a sharable device, such as disk, in a virtual machine environment. A virtual disk.

MS-DOS. A popular microcomputer operating system.

MSDOS.SYS. Under MS-DOS, a hardware-independent module that implements logical I/O. The MS-DOS file system.

Multiple-access bus. A network configuration in which computers are linked to a common bus. Generally limited to local area networks.

Multiple-bus architecture. A computer architecture in which more than one bus line is used to link components.

Multiprogramming. One processor concurrently executing several programs.

Network. Two or more computers linked by communication lines.

Network data base. A data base organized as a network. Generally, a parent can have many children, and a child can have many parents.

Network operating system. An operating system for a computer network.

New PSW. On an IBM System/370 computer, a field located in main memory that holds the address of an interrupt handling routine in the operating system.

Noncontiguous. Separated. For example, a program's pages can be stored in widely separated regions of memory.

Nonprocedural language. A programming language in which the programmer describes the logical structure of a problem instead of writing a procedure to solve it. Also called a fourth-generation language or a declarative language.

Nucleus. Another name for the resident operating system.

Object module. A machine-level translation of a programmer's source code.

Object module library. A library of object modules. Sometimes called a relocatable library or a linkage library.

Old PSW. On an IBM System/370 computer, a field located in main memory that holds the PSW associated with the program that was executing at the time an interrupt occurred.

Open. To prepare a file for processing. For example, opening a file on disk involves checking the index to find the file's track/sector address.

Operand. The portion of an instruction that specifies the registers and memory locations that are to participate in the operation.

Operating system. A collection of program modules that control the operation of the computer. A typical operating system allocates resources, schedules programs, controls access to input and output devices, and manages data.

Operation code. The portion of an instruction that specifies the operation to be performed.

OS/VS1. An IBM virtual storage operating system that relies on fixed-partition memory management to manage virtual memory space.

OS/VS2. An IBM virtual storage operating system that relies on dynamic memory management to manage virtual memory space.

Overlay. Storing a program module in the main memory space previously allocated to another, no longer needed module of the same program.

Page. A fixed-length independently addressed portion of a program that can be loaded into noncontiguous memory.

Page address register. A set of registers that hold the base addresses of the most recently accessed pages. Typically, these registers are searched in parallel with dynamic address translation.

Page fault. An interrupt generated when a virtual address references a page that is not in real storage.

Page frame table. A table that holds flags indicating each real memory page's status (i.e., free or in use). Used by the operating system to allocate main memory space.

Page pool. The region of real memory used to hold active application program pages on a virtual memory system.

Page table. A program listing the base addresses of all pages in a program.

Page table location register. A register that holds the address of the current program's page table.

Paging. (1) The process of dividing a program into fixed-length pages. (2) The process of swapping pages between the real page pool and the external paging device.

Parameter. A single operand on a job control language statement.

Parent. In UNIX, the first copy of a process created in response to the *fork* routine. In a data base, a record that is linked, in some way, to one or more lower level records. *Contrast with* child.

Partition. A portion of memory used to hold one program on a fixed-portion memory management system.

Partition management. Management of multiple users' access to processor time, memory space, and peripheral devices in a single partition of a multiprogramming system.

Partitioned data set. A library on an IBM mainframe running under OS.

Password. A unique string of characters that identifies a user.

Pathname. The name used to find a file referenced through more than one subdirectory.

PC-DOS. A version of MS-DOS used on IBM personal computers.

PDS. *See* Partitioned data set.

Phase. Under DOS/VSE, a core image library member.

Physical I/O. The act of transferring a physical block of data to or from a peripheral device. For example, on diskette, each physical I/O operation might transfer one sector; on a printer, each physical I/O operation might transfer one line.

Physical I/O control system (PIOCS). Under DOS/USE, a series of macros that allow a programmer to request physical I/O operations.

Physical unit block (PUB). A table that lists the peripheral devices attached to a DOS/USE system.

PIOCS. *See* Physical I/O control system.

Pipe. An operator that causes one utilty's standard output to be used as the standard input to another utility.

Pointer. An address stored in memory that provides a link to a related field, file, record, control block, etc.

Poll driven. An operating system whose main control module is a polling routine.

Polling. Asking a series of terminals, or checking a series of buffers, one by one, to see if they have data to transmit. A technique for determining who gets to transmit data next.

Positional parameter. A parameter whose meaning is determined by its position in the operands field.

PRB. *See* Program request block.

Prepaging. The process of predicting the demand for a new page and bringing it into memory before it is actually needed.

Primitive command. A machine-level hardware command, such as a fetch or a seek.

Privileged instruction. An instruction that can be executed only by an operating system routine.

Problem state. A state in which a computer is executing an application program.

Process. Under UNIX, the execution of an image.

Process file table. Under UNIX, a table listing a process's open files.

Process table. Under UNIX, a table used by the dispatcher, containing one entry for each process.

Processor, or Central processing unit. The component of a computer that selects and executes instructions. The processor contains a clock, an instruction control unit, an arithmetic and logic unit, and registers.

Program. *See* Computer program.

Program interrupt. On an IBM System/370 computer, an interrupt that results from an illegal or invalid instruction.

Program name. A name that identifies a load module stored in a library.

Program request block (PRB). Under OS/VS1/VS2, a request block that indicates the existence of an active task.

Program status word (PSW). The IBM System/370 instruction counter.

Prompt. A brief message printed or displayed by a program or by the operating system asking the user to provide input.

Protection key. On an IBM System/370 computer, a 4-bit key, stored in the PSW, that is used by hardware to prevent one program from destroying memory belonging to another.

Protocol. A set of rules for establishing communication between two devices.

Pseudocomputer. In UNIX, an imaginary machine on which the user perceives an image to be executing.

PSW. *See* Program status word.

PUB. *See* Physical unit block.

Queuing. Placing application programs on a waiting line (or queue) for eventual loading into main memory.

Ready state. A state in which a program is ready to resume processing.

Real computer. The physical computer in a virtual machine environment.

Real address area. Virtual space equal to available real memory.

Real memory. Actual, physical main memory space.

Real partition. A partition in the real address area that can be used to hold all or part of an application program.

Redirection. An operator used to override or change the standard input or output device.

Reentrant. A program attribute that allows the same copy of a program to be used by two or more programmers. Generally, a reentrant program does not modify itself.

Region. A portion of memory (real or virtual) allocated dynamically to an application program.

Register. Temporary storage used to hold data, instructions, or control information in the processor. Often, the current instruction, the data being manipulated by that instruction, and key control information are stored in registers.

Relational data base. A data base whose organization is based on the logical relationship between data elements.

Relative address. An address relative to a reference point.

Relative record number. The location of a record relative to the beginning of a file. Given the actual track and sector of the first record in the file, it is possible to compute the address of any other record given its relative record number.

Relocatable libarary. Under DOS/USE, a library that holds object modules.

Remote. Distant data transmission in which the signal has been boosted and filtered.

Request block. Under OS/VS1/VS2, a control block that describes the detailed contents of a given partition or region.

Resident. An operating system module that directly supports an application program as it runs and thus must remain in main memory.

Resource management. An operating system responsibility on many large, multiprogramming computer systems. Often includes managing processor time, main memory space, and access to secondary storage devices.

Response time. Time elapsed between entering a transaction and seeing the first character of the system's response appear on the screen.

Restart interrupt. On an IBM System/370 computer, an interrupt that allows an operator or another processor to start a program.

Ring network. A computer network configuration in which the host computers are linked to form a ring.

Roll-in/roll-out. A memory management technique used on time-shared systems in which programs are rolled out to secondary storage between transactions and then rolled back into main memory when a transaction arrives.

Root directory. The directory created when a disk is formatted.

Scheduler. An operating system module used to determine which program will be loaded into main memory when space becomes available.

Secondary storage. Nonvolatile memory such as disk or magnetic tape used for the long-term storage of program instructions and data. Generally, the data and instructions currently being processed by a computer are stored in main memory; all other data and instructions are stored in secondary storage.

Segment. A variable-length, independently addressed portion of a program that can be loaded into noncontiguous memory.

Segment table. A table stored in the operating system listing the entry points of each of a program's segments.

Segment table location register. A register

that holds the address of the current program's segment table.

Segmentation. The process of dividing programs into independently addressed segments.

Segmentation and paging. The process of dividing programs into logical segments and subdividing those segments into fixed-length pages.

Setup. Tasks performed to prepare a computer to run a program.

Shared virtual area. An area of virtual memory that holds pagable routines designed to be shared by all partitions.

Shell. (1) A way to visualize the command processor's relationship to the operating system. (2) In UNIX, a command interpreter treated like an application program, allowing replacement of the standard shell with a custom shell.

Shell script. A UNIX batch file.

Signal. An electronic pulse that can be sensed by the operating system. For example, the death of a UNIX process generates a signal.

Single-bus architecture. A computer architecture in which all internal components are linked by a single bus line.

Source code. Program instructions written in a source language such as BASIC, COBOL, FORTRAN, or Pascal.

Source module. A set of program statements written in a source language.

Source statement library. A program library that holds assembler or compiler source modules.

Speed disparity. The speed difference between a computer and its peripheral devices.

Spooling. On input, transferring data to secondary storage and holding them for eventual processing. On output, transferring data to secondary storage for eventual output to an output device. A technique used to make batch processing applications more efficient.

Stack segment. A private segment at the end of a UNIX image that holds control information.

Star network. A computer network configuration in which each host is linked to a central "star" machine.

Step name. The name of the job step being executed.

Subdirectory. Under UNIX and MS-DOS, a file that holds directory entries. A subdirectory is listed in the root directory or in a higher level subdirectory.

Subparameter. On a JCL statement, a field that provides detailed specifications for a parameter; for example, the label type in an OS/JCL DD statement LABEL parameter.

Super block. The region on a UNIX disk that identifies the disk, defines the sizes of its regions, and tracks free blocks.

Supervisor. Another name for the resident operating system.

Supervisor request block (SVRB). Under OS/VS1/VS2, a request block that indicates a supervisor call interrupt is being processed in support of the partition.

Supervisory state. The state in which a computer is executing a supervisor routine.

SVC interrupt. On an IBM System/370 computer, an interrupt that occurs in response to an SVC instruction.

SVRB. *See* Supervisor request block.

Swapping. Moving processes or pages between main memory and an external paging device.

Symbolic name. Under DOS/VSE, a logical name used to identify an I/O device.

Synchronous. Control of timing by equally spaced clock signals or pulses.

SYSGEN (system generation). The act of creating a custom version of an operating system.

SYSRES. A device, usually a disk pack, that is the source of the operating system on a customer's computer.

System data segment. A segment of a UNIX process that contains data accessed by the operating system when the process is active. The system data segment is part of the process, but not the user's image.

System directory. A directory maintained by the VM/SP control program with one entry for each virtual machine.

System file table. A table maintained by UNIX that lists the i-nodes of all open files.

System input. The default input device.

System mask. On an IBM System/370 computer, a mask that determines whether I/O and external interrupts will be acknowledged.

System output. The default output device.

Task. A single program or routine in main memory.

Task control block (TCB). Under OS/VS1/VS2, a control block that defines the status of a single partition or region.

Task input/output table (TIOT). Under OS/VS1/VS2, a table listing all the DDNAMES from the job step's DD statements with pointers to other information defined in each DD statement.

Task management. Under OS/VS1/VS2, the

routines that manage a program as it runs, generally handling interrupts.

TCB. *See* Task control block.

Text segment. In a UNIX image or process, the segment that holds executable code. Generally, the text segment is reentrant.

Text table. A UNIX table that keeps track of active text segments by listing each current text segment, its primary and secondary addresses, and a count of the number of processes sharing it.

Thrashing. A situation that occurs when paging on a virtual memory system is so frequent that little time is left for useful work.

Throughput. Run time divided by elapsed time.

Time-sharing. A series of techniques that allows multiple users, each controlling an independent terminal, to share a single computer. Roll-in/roll-out is a common memory management technique. Time-slicing is a common processor management technique. Access to terminals is often controlled by polling.

Time-slicing. A processor management technique in which an application program is given a discrete "slice" of time in which to complete its work. If the work is not completed during a single time slice, the program loses control of the processor and must return to the end of the queue to await another turn.

TIOT. *See* Task input/output table.

Token passing. A network access technique in which an electronic signal called a token is transmitted continuously from host to host or terminal to terminal. A given host or terminal can transmit a message only when it holds the token.

Transient. An operating system module that resides on disk and is read into main memory only when needed.

Transient area. The area in main memory where application programs are loaded.

Transparent. Hidden; for example, details associated with the real computer that are hidden by the operating system in a virtual machine environment are said to be transparent.

Turnaround. The time between job submission and job completion.

UCB. *See* Unit control block.

Unit control block (UCB). Under OS/VS1/VS2, a list of the peripheral devices attached to a computer.

UNIX. A popular multiprogramming operating system developed by AT&T.

Utilities. Routines such as assemblers, compilers, linkage editors, loaders, line editors, sort routines, debugging features, library management routines, and so on.

V=R area. *See* Virtual-equals-real area.

Virtual address area. Virtual space over and above the available real memory.

Virtual-equals-real area. The region of memory where virtual, real, and absolute addresses match.

Virtual machine. A functional simulation of a computer and its associated devices, including an operating system.

Virtual memory. A memory management technique in which only active portions of a program are actually loaded into main memory.

Virtual operating system. The operating system in a virtual machine environment that controls application programs.

Virtual peripheral device. Peripheral devices in a virtual machine environment that are simulated by the real operating system.

VM/SP. Acronym for virtual machine system product, an IBM operating system that supports virtual machines.

WAIT. A macro used to drop a program into a wait state while an I/O operation is executing.

wait. A UNIX primitive that puts a process to sleep.

Wait state. The state in which a program is waiting for the completion of some event such as an I/O operation.

Wild card. A character used to generalize parameters. Especially useful for making backup copies of selected files or an entire disk.

Word. The basic storage unit around which a computer system is designed. On all but the smallest microcomputers, a word consists of two or more bytes.

Working directory. The directory currently being used.

D

E

F